THE ROADS TO CONGRESS 1998

EDITED BY

ROBERT DEWHIRST
Northwest Missouri State University

SUNIL AHUJA
Seton Hall University

 **Wadsworth**
Thomson Learning™

Australia • Canada • Denmark • Japan • Mexico • New Zealand • Philippines
Puerto Rico • Singapore • South Africa • Spain • United Kingdom • United States

Publisher: Clark Baxter
Senior Development Editor:
    Sharon Adams Poore
Assistant Editor: Cherie Hackelberg
Editorial Assistant: Melissa Gleason
Marketing Manager: Jay Hu
Print Buyer: Barbara Britton

Permissions Editor: Robert Kauser
Production, Composition, & Illustration:
    Summerlight Creative, Eugene, OR
Copy Editor: Rachel Schick Siegel
Cover Designer: Bill Stanton
Cover Image: ©1999 PhotoDisc, Inc.
Printer/Binder: Webcom Ltd.

For permission to use material from
this text, contact us by

web: www.thomsonrights.com
fax: 1-800-730-2215
phone: 1-800-730-2214

**Library of Congress
Cataloging-in-Publication Data**

Dewhirst, Robert E.
    The roads to Congress 1998 / Robert
E. Dewhirst, Sunil Ahuja
        p.   cm.
    Includes bibliographical references
(p.   ) and index.
    ISBN 0-8304-1529-7 (alk. paper)
    1. United States. Congress--Elections,
1998. 2. United States--Politics and
government--1993-   I. Ahuja, Sunil.
II. Title.
JK 1968 1998
324.97309029--dc21
                    99-38108

Wadsworth/Thomson Learning
10 Davis Drive
Belmont, CA 94002-3098
USA
www.wadsworth.com

International Headquarters
Thomson Learning
290 Harbor Drive, 2nd Floor
Stamford, CT 06902-7477
USA

UK/Europe/Middle East
Thomson Learning
Berkshire House
168-173 High Holborn
London WC1V 7AA
United Kingdom

Asia
Thomson Learning
60 Albert Street #15-01
Albert Complex
Singapore 189969

Canada
Nelson/Thomson Learning
1120 Birchmount Road
Scarborough, Ontario M1K 5G4
Canada

To Our Students

Contents

Editors and Contributors

Sunil Ahuja is Assistant Professor of Political Science at Seton Hall University. His teaching and research focus on American political institutions and political behavior. He has published in such journals as the *American Politics Quarterly* and *Political Research Quarterly*. He is contributor to and coeditor of *Government at Work* (1998). He is coeditor of the *Legislative Studies Quarterly*.

Robert Dewhirst is Professor of Political Science at Northwest Missouri State University. His teaching and research focus on American politics. His writings include *Rites of Passage: Congress Makes Laws* (1997). He is contributor to and coeditor of *Government at Work* (1998). He also has published articles on Congress, elections, policy making, and legislative politics in Missouri.

Rickert Althaus is Professor of Political Science at Southeast Missouri State University, where he teaches public policy and public administration. Much of his scholarship has dealt with domestic and international agricultural issues and has included both legislative formulation and administrative implementation of policy. His work can be found in a variety of professional journals and textbooks.

Harold F. Bass, Jr., is the Moody Professor of Pre-Law Studies and Chair of the Department of Political Science at Ouachita Baptist University. His major research interest is political party leadership. He has authored articles for professional journals, including *Presidential Studies Quarterly* and *American Review of Politics,* and contributed chapters to numerous edited collections, including *Presidents and Their Parties, Guide to the Presidency,* and *Leadership and the Bush Presidency.*

Jocelyn Benson is a 1999 Marshall Scholar at Oxford University and a graduate of Wellesley College. She has written and conducted research for the Southern Poverty Law Center and the Massachusetts State Senate and has campaigned for U.S. Senator John Kerry (D-MA), President Bill Clinton and Vice President Al Gore, and former U.S. Senator Harris Wofford (D-PA).

Peter J. Bergerson is Professor and Chair of the Department of Political Science at Southeast Missouri State University. His teaching and research focus on public policy and public administration. He has published books on ethics and public policy and on the theory, research, and practice of public policy.

Matthew Braunstein is a senior aide and speechwriter for Representative Patrick J. Kennedy (D-RI). A Master of Arts candidate in American government at Georgetown University, Braunstein graduated cum laude from Wesleyan University for his work on minor-party presidential elections.

Stephen Brooks is Associate Director of the Ray C. Bliss Institute of Applied Politics and Associate Professor of Political Science at the University of Akron. He teaches courses on political communication, public policy, and public administration. He has published on elections and policy making. His most recent work has focused on the role of communication techniques in local elections.

Michelle Brophy-Baermann is Assistant Professor of Political Science at the University of Wisconsin, Stevens Point. She teaches a variety of courses in the field of American politics. Her current focus is on integrating technology in the political science classroom. She has published in the *Social Science Quarterly.*

Ling Cao is a Ph.D. candidate in the Department of Economics, Claremont Graduate University.

Chris Fastnow is Assistant Professor of Political Science at Wellesley College and Visiting Assistant Professor at the University of Michigan. She teaches courses on American politics, Congress, religion and American politics, research methods, and statistics. She has written on party leadership in the U.S. House, religion in Congress, interest groups, elections, and state legislatures.

Ronald Keith Gaddie is Associate Professor of Political Science at the University of Oklahoma. His areas of interest include American electoral politics, Southern politics, and the role of money in legislative politics. He has published numerous articles, chapters in edited volumes, and several books, including *The Economic Realities of Political Reform, David Duke and the Politics of Race in the South, The Almanac of Oklahoma Politics 1997–1998,* and *Regulating Wetlands Protection.*

Marcia L. Godwin is a doctoral candidate in the Department of Politics and Policy at Claremont Graduate University. She has more than ten years of experience working in county and municipal government. She is the coauthor of a chapter, "Gun Control Politics in California," in *The Changing Politics of Gun Control.*

Robert K. Goidel is Associate Professor of Political Science at Indiana State University. His research, which generally focuses on congressional elections, has been published in such journals as the *American Journal of Political Science, Journal of Politics, American Politics Quarterly, Political Research Quarterly,* and *Legislative Studies Quarterly.*

Dena Levy is Assistant Professor of Political Science at SUNY Brockport. She teaches courses on American politics, Congress, the presidency, public opinion, and statistics. Her research focuses on Congress and her current projects include the impact of women and minorities on legislative outcomes, the election of women to Congress, and the effect of previous experience on the transition to and legislative activities in the Senate.

Joseph R. Marbach is Assistant Professor of Political Science and Co-Director of the Institute for Service Learning at Seton Hall University. He is also Assistant Director for International Programming at Temple University's Center for the Study of Federalism. His areas of expertise include federalism and intergovernmental relations, state and local government, and New Jersey politics. He is the author of numerous articles and chapters in edited books.

James L. McDowell is Professor of Political Science at Indiana State University. He specializes in Indiana politics and state and local government. He has published in both academic journals and popular periodicals on various aspects of state administrative, political, and policy-making processes.

Steven Puro is Professor of Political Science and Public Policy at St. Louis University. He has written numerous articles on the American legal system. During the last two decades, he has analyzed and written about Missouri national and state politics. He is a former president of the Missouri Political Science Association.

Jean Reith Schroedel is Associate Professor of Political Science at Claremont Graduate University. Her primary research and teaching interests are gender politics, the presidency, and congressional politics. She has written numerous articles and several books, including *Alone in a Crowd; Congress, the President, and Policymaking;* and *Beyond Conception: Is the Fetus a Person?*

Brian Smentkowski is Assistant Professor of Political Science at Southeast Missouri State University. His teaching and research examine the relationship between law and politics, as well as political parties and electoral behavior. In addition to works published in *Law and Policy* and the *Encyclopedia of Third Parties in America,* he is the principal author and section editor for *Civil, Human, and Economic Rights Interest Groups,* forthcoming by M. E. Sharpe.

Sue Thomas is Associate Professor of Government and Director of Women's Studies at Georgetown University. Her research specialty is the study of women officeholders. Her recent works include *How Women Legislate* (1994), *The Year of the Woman: Myths and Realities* (1994), and *Women and Elective Office: Past, Present, and Future* (1998). She is currently working on a project entitled "Legislative Careers: The Personal and the Political."

Charles Tien is Assistant Professor of Political Science at Hunter College, CUNY. His research interests include minorities and women in Congress, presidential elections, and political methodology. He has published in *American Politics Quarterly* and *International Journal of Forecasting.*

Kenneth Warren is Professor of Political Science and Public Policy at St. Louis University. He has written *Administrative Law in the American Political System.* His current research includes analysis of Representative William Clay's political career.

Preface

Across the country, candidates run for political offices in every election and struggle to win those contests. Undoubtedly, for some the combat is less grueling than for others. But, for all candidates, seeking an elective office means going through the hoops to win in a primary and then in the general election.

This book is designed to lead the readers to see the candidates as individuals struggling to win elections. In so doing, we address a number of questions. How do these candidates deal with the whole medley of issues confronting their campaigns? What kinds of decisions do they make and how do they do so? What is the role of parties, issues, and candidates in congressional races? What about campaign strategies and consultants? What of the money and the media? At the end of the day, based upon a variety of selected races from across the nation, our aim in this book is to provide the readers with a detailed understanding of contemporary campaigns and elections in congressional contests at the individual level.

This is a unique approach, heretofore lacking in books on campaigns and elections. In the last decade, a number of books have regularly provided analyses of contemporary campaigns and elections. However, these works have used aggregate data to make national generalizations. They have examined campaigns and elections from a broad, national perspective. We think that our focus at the individual level not only will supplement our understanding of contemporary congressional elections but also will show a previously unseen side of these contests. We hope the readers will learn a good deal about how candidates run campaigns and win or lose those contests. Our focus is strictly on Congress. In this book, we draw upon races for the House and Senate contested in 1998.

We would like to thank all the authors who have contributed to this project. We are also grateful to our colleagues in our departments and in the profession who see merit in our approach and have supported the development of this volume. Moreover, Ahuja would like to express his gratitude to the Department of Political Science and the dean of the College of Arts and Sciences at Seton Hall University for release time from teaching to do this book. Finally, many thanks to Nelson-Hall Publishers and Wadsworth Publishing for accepting this project and for shepherding it to its completion.

Sunil Ahuja
Robert Dewhirst

1

★

The Congressional
Elections of 1998

Sunil Ahuja
Robert Dewhirst

The 1998 congressional elections were contested amid a backdrop of perhaps the most intensely partisan period in the twentieth century. The year began with scandal and allegations blowing strongly against President Bill Clinton and the White House. These ill winds brought with them a great deal of uncertainty for incumbent members of Congress seeking reelection. While it has been a long-established norm among congressional incumbents to "run scared," the added unknown factor of calculating how allegations against President Clinton might affect constituents' opinions led wary candidates in both parties initially to mute comments about the president's troubles in favor of focusing on local concerns. Yet, secretly, Republicans were hoping the allegations would somehow help them, while Democrats were hoping for "damage control" that would limit the party's troubles to the presidency.

As the year wore on, both parties seemed to anticipate that the House of Representatives would be much more of an electoral battleground than the Senate. In the House both parties had ample cause for concern. While Democrats were worrying about a possible backlash from President Clinton's troubles, Republicans were concerned about hanging on to their narrow 228–206 margin in the House. Hence, a net loss of as few as 11 Republican seats would put the Democrats in control when the 106th Congress convened in January 1999. Meanwhile, over in the Senate, the Republicans enjoyed not only a 55–45 advantage overall but also a 16–18 advantage in the number of incumbent seats they would have to defend in 1998. Ironically, with just one-third of the Senate's seats up for reelection in every national election in each even-numbered year, the break in the six-year terms compelled the minority Democrats to have to defend a majority of the 34 contested seats in 1998.

In the individual contests throughout the country, both Republicans and Democrats seemed to vacillate between having to address allegations leveled against President Clinton and preferring to talk about local concerns. During the first half of the year, Republicans seemed to feel as though they could reap political rewards from the Clinton problems and appeared eager to take full advantage of the situation. Democrats were understandably nervous. The second half of the year, however, seemed to reverse the fortunes for both parties. The key element in all this was public opinion. Polls consistently revealed that while the public despised Clinton's affair with Monica Lewinsky, a former White House intern, it was willing to set that aside as a matter of private behavior and not an issue of public concern. More significantly, Democrats were also aided by a healthy economy, which contributed to rather high approval ratings for the president. Republicans, puzzled by the public's refusal to throw stones at the president and the Democrats, decided to move full steam ahead, pressing charges of Clinton's ethical and sexual improprieties and arguing for his impeachment on grounds of principle. As far as the 1998 elections were concerned, pundits felt much would depend on voter turnout.

Both parties entered the fall elections in early November amid this backdrop. How would the Democrats and the Republicans fare at the polls? Would Bill Clinton and the Dow Jones be the issues? Or would voters turn mostly to local affairs in judging candidates as they have done so commonly in the past? What would be the impact of voter turnout? Speculations abounded on both sides about these questions, although no one knew for sure. But, as they say, that's why they hold the elections.

In this book, we answer these questions based upon a selected set of races from across the nation. Our purpose, however, is to go much beyond that. Our aim in this book is to provide the readers with a detailed understanding of contemporary campaigns and elections in congressional contests. What is the role of parties, issues, or candidates in campaigns? What about campaign strategies and consultants? What is the role of money? What of the media? In the subsequent chapters, we present analyses of a variety of individual races from across the nation fought by both Republicans and Democrats during this election cycle. They are designed to serve as detailed examples of how contemporary American campaigns are conducted and elections are won. The book features case studies of one election contest per chapter.

The purpose of each chapter is to explain why the victorious candidate won. Our focus is to examine individual candidates as they struggle to win a particular contest. How do these individuals deal with the whole medley of issues confronting their campaigns? What kinds of decisions do they make and how do they do so? Our explicit purpose is not to expound any new theories of congressional elections. Neither do we wish to focus on offering campaign strategies to candidates. Nor do we intend to follow a particular perspective in this volume. Rather, our purpose is to describe and analyze what happened to individuals in particular races and why. This, we hope, will give the readers a solid understanding of how contemporary congressional campaigns are fought and won or lost at the individual level.

Each chapter examines a number of factors concerning each race. These items include, but are not limited to, campaign strategies and themes, issues, financing, media relations, polling efforts, interest group and media endorsements, and voter turnout. These factors are considered with reference to both the primary and the general elections of candidates. As a way of background and setting for the readers, each chapter provides information on the nature of the constituencies, including such things as their party balance, voting history, electoral trends, and key demographic variables (employment rates, population trends, etc.).

This is a unique approach, heretofore lacking in books on campaigns and elections. In the past decade, a number of works have regularly provided analyses of contemporary campaigns and elections.[1] However, these studies have examined national elections in general. They have featured individual chapters focusing on some overall nationwide themes or trends, such as the overall outcomes of congressional campaigns and elections, the presidential primaries, the presidential general election, third-party efforts, women candidates and voters, black candidates and voters, or the role played by public opinion polls. In sum, these works have concentrated on collapsing a lot of aggregate data to make national generalizations. They cover campaigns and elections from a broad, national perspective.

In this volume, our aim is to provide readers with a wide array of in-depth qualitative examinations of individual contests. It is designed to lead the readers to see the candidates as individuals struggling to win a particular election. Before turning to those specific contests, we set the stage for midterm congressional elections in general and the 1998 elections in particular. We then describe and justify the races selected for this book and note the authors of each chapter. Chapters 2 through 13 cover the individual contests. At the end, in chapter 14, we conclude by discussing the continuity and change in the 1998 congressional elections.

THE MIDTERM CONGRESSIONAL ELECTIONS

In American national politics, "midterm" elections occur every four years, in the even-numbered years between presidential elections. In these midterm elections, all of the 435 seats in the House of Representatives, where members hold two-year terms, and one-third of the seats in the Senate, where members hold six-year terms, are contested. In the 1998 cycle, 228 of the House seats were held by Republicans and 206 by Democrats. In the Senate, 34 seats were up, with 16 of those held by Republicans and 18 by Democrats.

The Republicans in 1998

The Republicans enjoyed several advantages in 1998. Some of those advantages followed established patterns and were generally anticipated by both sides, while other benefits were unique to the political context of the year.

First, turnout has averaged about 15 percent lower for midterm elections than in those years when the presidency is contested.[2] Low turnout elections generally tend to help Republican candidates, as their supporters most commonly range from the middle to higher ends of the socioeconomic status, factors that result in a higher likelihood of voting.

Second, the 1998 contests came at the end of the sixth year of a Democratic presidency. Here, the political history was particularly troubling for the House Democrats. Since 1862, the president's party, regardless of whether it was Democrat or Republican, lost House seats in every midterm election but one. Likewise, over in the Senate, the president's party also traditionally lost seats, although not as many and not as often.[3] Such losses coming at the end of the sixth year of a presidency have been dubbed the "six-year itch." Historically, in a number of the midterm elections, such as those of 1894, 1946, 1958, 1966, 1974, and 1994, the president's party has suffered dramatic losses, which have ignited major policy shifts.

Third, the Republicans, as is their usual circumstance, enjoyed a large fundraising advantage in 1998. With their traditionally strong ties to business and corporate interests long established, Republicans added to this by being the majority party in Congress, thus enabling them to leverage their majority status into an even greater fundraising advantage over the Democrats. During the 1997–1998 election cycle, Republicans raised a total of $260 million compared to the Democrats' $165 million. The National Republican Congressional Committee (NRCC) spent the legal maximum amount in at least 90 House contests during the 1998 elections; the Democratic Congressional Campaign Committee (DCCC) hoped to do the same in about 35 to 45 House contests.[4] In many instances, Republican fundraising advantages significantly outweighed what the Democrats could muster.

Meanwhile, other advantages enjoyed by Republicans in 1998 were unique to the year. For one thing, the Democratic president was under siege in the White House throughout the year as he continually fought allegations of legal and ethical improprieties from independent counsel Kenneth Starr. In January 1998, Starr revealed that President Clinton had had an affair with a one-time White House intern Monica Lewinsky, accusations that the president denied until August 1998, when he admitted having an "improper" relationship with the former intern. Outraged by this conduct and his continuous denials, Republicans simultaneously called for his resignation or impeachment and removal and saw this as an opportunity to hurt the Democrats at the polls.

Second, a healthy economy has always helped incumbents electorally. Since there were more congressional Republican incumbents than Democratic incumbents, this would work well for the Republicans. The Dow Jones Industrials Average and other economic indicators either set records during 1998 or were extremely strong throughout the year. Moreover, public confidence in the economy and the overall condition of the country were also quite high. Of the 1,505 adults, among them 715 likely voters, polled by the *Washington Post–ABC News* in late September 1998, 85 percent of the general public and 90 percent of likely voters registered the economy as good.[5] In the same poll, Congress as an institution and members of Congress as individuals also received high marks. Congress enjoyed a 52 percent approval rating and individual members of the House a "breathtaking" 70 percent.[6]

Despite these benefits, the picture was not completely rosy for the Republicans, partly due to their own doing. In spite of growing public opposition to the impeachment of President Clinton, Republicans decided to move ahead with the issue. On October 8, 1998, the House of Representatives voted to begin a formal impeachment inquiry against the president. This move came in the face of the majority of the general public as well as likely voters opposing Clinton's impeachment and removal from office. Between September 28 and October 10, based upon two polls taken before and after the House vote, public support for both Congress and the Republicans eroded considerably. However, approval of Democratic candidates inched upward during this period. Approval of Congress dropped from 52 percent to 45 percent and of one's representative from 70 percent to 62 percent. Likewise, the public disapproved of the Republicans (62 percent) more than the Democrats (49 percent) in the handling of the impeachment issue. Also, in the latter poll, trust of congressional Republicans dipped to an all-time low (34 percent) since the party's takeover of Congress in 1994.[7]

Meanwhile, in both these and other polls, the president's job performance continued to receive high marks. Indeed, after the House vote to begin the impeachment inquiry, the president became even more popular. Clinton's approval ratings jumped from 63 percent to 67 percent. About half (48 percent) recorded a "strong" approval of Clinton's performance. The president made some gains even among Republicans.[8]

The Democrats in 1998

The aforementioned factors did not bode well for the Democrats in 1998. Obviously, the advantages noted above for the Republicans would work against the Democrats. Lower voter turnout, the "six-year itch" phenomenon, and low fundraising numbers would likely translate into a loss of a number of Democratic seats.

Nevertheless, a number of factors seemed to benefit the Democrats. First, Democratic incumbents, just like Republican incumbents, would be aided by a strong economy. Positive economic numbers tend to help all incumbents, regardless of party. Indeed, as noted earlier, not only were the economic numbers robust, the public also tended to register a high degree of satisfaction with *all* incumbents and the general direction of the country.

Second, on the campaign trail, Democratic candidates were in a position to blame the Republican majority for a variety of issues, ranging from a lack of legislative activity in Congress throughout the year to an obsession with impeaching the president. But many Democratic consultants were advising their candidates to stay away from the scandal and instead stress issues in their campaigns.[9] As several chapters will attest, an individual's campaign strategy, however, would depend upon that individual's constituency. Candidates from liberal districts would be better off accusing the Republicans of launching a partisan investigation of the president, since that would turn out the base voters on election day. Candidates from moderate districts would profit by emphasizing the issues rather than the Republican efforts to impeach and remove the president or the morality of Clinton's conduct.[10]

Finally, a popular president would help the Democrats, although that was a double-edged sword. Ordinarily speaking, a president with high approval ratings benefits the congressional candidates of his party. But, in this instance, that may not have been so. Many Democrats did not want to be seen as too closely associated with the president, for fear that defending him would not sit well with some of their constituents. Indeed, on a personal level, many Democrats expressed a great deal of discomfort and even outrage at the president's behavior. Yet, many also did not want to openly condemn him, for fear that to do so of a popular president of their party could undermine their political base.[11]

For both Democrats and Republicans, much would depend on who ultimately voted on election day. As a general rule, turnout tends to be low in midterm elections. In this particular election, it appeared that the results would really depend upon which party was better able to mobilize its base. Many observers agreed that it was no longer about the moderates. If the Republican party could play up the immorality of the president's acts, it could energize its base and hurt the Democrats. If the Democratic party could portray the president's investigation as a partisan witch-hunt, it could motivate its base and hurt the Republicans.[12] The key, therefore, to success would be who was "madder" on election day. For as one pollster noted, "mad people vote."[13]

IN THIS BOOK

Part I of this book will provide analyses of six campaigns and elections for the House of Representatives while Part II will examine six contests for the Senate. Both parts are divided into three pairs of contests: "safe" seats, "open" seats, and "contested" seats. Safe seats were defined as those where the incumbents won with at least 55 percent of the two-party vote in the previous election. Incumbents in these constituencies were considered established and were widely expected to win reelection by a wide margin. Open seats were those where there was no incumbent in the race. Contested seats were where incumbents were expected to face tough reelection struggles. Incumbents in these constituencies were considered "unsafe."

The Races

The specific election contests considered in this book were selected based upon a variety of criteria. In general, their selection was based upon both their importance and their interest to political observers well before the election. In addition, every attempt was made to pick contests that would be representative of both nationwide contests and constituencies in a whole variety of ways, including demographically, racially, regionally, and so forth. The specific races chosen are shown in the table of contents and presented individually in chapters 2 through 13.

As can be seen in this selection, for the House, the two safe incumbents chosen were Representatives Christopher Smith (R-NJ) and Bill Clay (D-MO). Smith, a Republican, is from a mid-sized eastern state and represents a constituency that is largely suburban. His voting record is moderately conservative and he is approaching the leadership ranks within his party in the House. Clay is a liberal, black Democrat from St. Louis, a midwestern urban area.

For the open seats in the House, we chose the contests for the seats being vacated by the retiring Scott Klug (R-WI) and Lee Hamilton (D-IN). While both these representatives hailed from midwestern states, there were notable differences between the two. One was from a moderate Republican constituency, the other from a moderate Democratic one. The former was a junior member of the House, the latter a senior member. Klug's seat, being vacated by a junior Republican from a politically moderate constituency, was expected to bring about noteworthy candidates and a real debate of issues to the race. Hamilton was an established Democrat in the House and a former chair of the House Foreign Affairs Committee. It was expected that his seat would also spark a great deal of interest among his constituents and his potential successors, particularly since his constituents would be losing the political leverage of a leading House member.

For the two contested seats in the House, we selected the reelections of Representatives Loretta Sanchez (D-CA) and Jo Ann Emerson (R-MO). These two representatives were chosen because they held hotly contested seats, and each race shared notable similarities with the campaign two years before. In her first election since taking the seat in 1996, Sanchez defeated a veteran conservative House incumbent, Robert Dornan, and was facing a rematch against him in 1998. Her narrow victory in 1996 and her rematch against the feisty Dornan made this race particularly interesting. Sanchez is a Mexican-American female from a western state. Emerson is the widow of the late Bill Emerson (R-MO), who died while in office in June 1996. Under the most unusual circumstances, Jo Ann Emerson won her husband's seat in 1996 and was seeking reelection in 1998. She is from a conservative Democratic district in southeast Missouri, which has been increasingly voting Republican.

In the Senate, two safe incumbent seats examined here are those held by Senators Don Nickles (R-OK) and Barbara Mikulski (D-MD). The former is a conservative Republican from a rural state with a southern tradition. The latter is a liberal Democrat from a moderately urban state in the east. Aside from these differences, both these senators held extremely safe seats, indeed faced no noticeable opposition, and have been well-established members of the Senate.

For the open seats in the Senate, we chose the slots being vacated by the retiring Dale Bumpers (D-AR) and John Glenn (D-OH). While there were some similarities between these two incumbents, the states they represented are vastly different. The Bumpers seat was attractive because it is President Clinton's home state and it would give us a Senate contest in the south. It is also a lightly populated rural state. The Glenn seat was attractive because it would give us a Senate race in a heavily populated, urban, midwestern state—one that often has been considered a political "bellwether" for the rest of the nation.

Finally, for the two contested seats in the Senate, we decided to examine the reelection races of Senators Alfonse D'Amato (R-NY) and Barbara Boxer (D-CA). There are a number of obvious reasons for the selection of these two contests. D'Amato is a conservative Republican from an urban state in the east. Boxer is a liberal Democrat from an urban state in the west. The fact that they are ideologically opposite personalities and hail from each end of the nation does not mean that their reelections would have nothing in common. The pair represents two of the most populous and wealthy states in the country. It was widely expected that these two contests would be extremely partisan, viciously negative, and among the most expensive Senate contests in the country's history. As a result, these races were thought to be of a great deal of interest to students of politics.

These contests also present a good mix of race and gender. There are a number of men and women as candidates in these races. These candidates also span racial boundaries. These races therefore covered the nation and are representative of contests and constituencies in 1998.

The Chapters

The safe seat contests for the House of Representatives are considered in the first pair of chapters. Joseph Marbach chronicles Christopher Smith's reelection bid in New Jersey, and Steven Puro and Kenneth Warren look at Bill Clay's campaign in north St. Louis. Both of these contests reveal the ease with which these incumbents won their reelections. Smith's nearly 20 years in the House and Clay's 30 years have allowed them to cultivate their constituencies and, as a result, these incumbents enjoy strong approval ratings from their voters.

The second pair of chapters examines the open seat contests for the House, left open due to the retirements of Scott Klug and Lee Hamilton. Michelle Brophy-Baermann covers the story of the race to fill the seat vacated by Klug in Wisconsin, and Robert Kirby Goidel and James McDowell examine the campaign to replace Hamilton in Indiana. These chapters underline the competitive nature of open seat races. Also, these contests demonstrate the influence of retiring incumbents on their party's nominee to succeed them.

Last, in the category of potentially volatile, expensive, and contested contests with incumbents facing strong challenges, two chapters cover the rematch of Loretta Sanchez's narrow and bitterly contested 1996 victory over Robert

Dornan in California and Jo Ann Emerson's reelection effort in Missouri. The Sanchez rematch is examined by Christina Fastnow and Jocelyn Benson, and the Emerson bid is analyzed by Brian Smentkowski, Rickert Althaus, and Peter Bergerson. They show how junior and relatively insecure incumbents work to establish themselves in their constituencies in an effort to fend off strong opposition in their next election and make themselves safe.

Over in the Senate, the safe seats are again considered in the first pair of chapters. Keith Gaddie covers the Don Nickles race in Oklahoma and Sue Thomas and Matthew Braunstein analyze the Barbara Mikulski contest in Maryland. These two safe Senate incumbents sailed smoothly to their reelection victories. These chapters also reveal the significant amount of work that incumbents put in throughout their careers to cultivate their constituencies. Indeed, those efforts make them safe and virtually unbeatable candidates.

The next two chapters cover the open seats in the Senate, left open by the retiring Dale Bumpers in Arkansas and John Glenn in Ohio. Hal Bass takes up the election to replace Bumpers and Stephen Brooks looks at the contest for the seat of the departing Glenn. These chapters illustrate the high quality candidates that run for the Senate. Among other things, they highlight prior political experience and a strong political organization as indispensable tools in running and winning statewide offices.

Finally, the last two chapters cover two contested races for the Senate. These are those of Al D'Amato in New York and Barbara Boxer in California. Indeed, observers long expected these to be two of the most expensive, negative, and hotly contested races nationwide and also the ones most closely followed nationally. The D'Amato contest in New York is examined by Dena Levy and Charles Tien. On the other coast, Boxer's reelection battle in California is analyzed by Jean Schroedel, Marcia Godwin, and Ling Cao. More than any other races, they reveal the competitive nature of contested seats. These chapters underscore the negative tone and high expense of such statewide contests. Moreover, reflecting the heterogeneous population of these two states, these chapters show the multilingual and multicultural bases of these campaigns, likely to be repeated more and more in these and other states in the future.

NOTES

1. For the most recent analyses, see Clyde Wilcox, *The Latest American Revolution? The 1994 Elections and Their Implications for Governance* (New York: St. Martin's, 1995); James Ceaser and Andrew Busch, *Losing to Win: The 1996 Elections and American Politics* (Lanham, MD: Rowman and Littlefield, 1997); William Crotty and Jerome Mileur, eds., *America's Choice: The Election of 1996* (Sluice Dock, CT: Dushkin/McGraw-Hill, 1997); Michael Nelson, ed., *The Elections of 1996* (Washington, DC: Congressional Quarterly, 1997); Gerald Pomper, ed., *The Election of 1996* (Chatham, NJ: Chatham House, 1997); Larry Sabato, ed., *Toward the Millennium: The Elections of 1996* (Needham, MA: Allyn and Bacon, 1997).

2. Norman J. Ornstein, Thomas E. Mann, and Michael J. Malbin, *Vital Statistics on Congress 1995-1996* (Washington, DC: Congressional Quarterly, 1996), 50.

3. Ibid., 55.

4. Ceci Connolly and Ruth Marcus, "Ad Infinitum," *The Washington Post National Weekly Edition,* October 26, 1998.

5. David S. Broder and Claudia Deane, "Both Sides Had Better Watch Out in November," *The Washington Post National Weekly Edition,* October 5, 1998.

6. Ibid.

7. Richard Morin, "A Vote of Less Confidence," *The Washington Post National Weekly Edition,* October 19, 1998.

8. Ibid.

9. Ceci Connolly and Terry M. Neal, "What's a Democratic Candidate to Do?," *The Washington Post National Weekly Edition,* October 12, 1998.

10. Ibid.

11. E. J. Dionne, Jr., "The Democrats' Dilemma," *The Washington Post National Weekly Edition,* September 21, 1998.

12. See Dionne, Jr., "The Democrats' Dilemma"; Dan Balz, "The Shifting Winds of Scandal and Fortune," *The Washington Post National Weekly Edition,* October 19, 1998.

13. Republican pollster Bill McInturff, quoted in Balz, "The Shifting Winds of Scandal and Fortune," 12.

★

PART I

House Campaigns
and Elections

Safe Seats

2

★

Smith Defeats Schneider in New Jersey's Fourth District Race

Joseph R. Marbach

The 1998 election for New Jersey's Fourth Congressional District seat was typical of most House races across the country and highlights the tremendous advantage of incumbency in such contests. The storyline in this race was the same for at least 60 percent of the 1998 House elections: a popular, well-financed incumbent handily defeats a little known, underfinanced challenger.

The Center for Responsive Politics (CRP) reported that going into the final week of the 1998 campaign, in 260 of the 435 House races (60 percent), incumbents had outspent their opponents by a margin of at least ten to one.[1] In fact, in 143 House races, the incumbent faced no challenger. The CRP also reported that incumbency and money were the big winners in the House elections. The reelection rate for House incumbents was 98.3 percent, one of the highest rates ever. In nearly 95 percent of these races, the candidate spending the most money won.[2] In the 1998 election, incumbents who outspent their opponents were nearly invincible. For Representative Christopher H. Smith, this was and has been the case in the past seven elections.

DISTRICT PROFILE

After the 1990 census, the Fourth Congressional District in New Jersey was redrawn in 1992. It stretches from the Atlantic Ocean westward to the Delaware River along a line that essentially divides north and south Jersey. Prior to being reconfigured, the district ran along a north-south axis along the Delaware River. Under the current configuration, the district is cut from four counties, including Mercer, Ocean, Monmouth, and Burlington. The latter three are the fastest growing counties in terms of new housing starts in the state, according to the U.S. Census Bureau.[3] There are 39 municipalities located in the district, the largest of which are Trenton and Mercerville-Hamilton Square in Mercer County, and Brick Township, Lakewood, and Point Pleasant in Ocean County. Other than Trenton (population 88,675) and Brick Township (population 66,473), none of the municipalities has a population greater than 27,000 persons. While the district includes these urban areas and a number of rural tracts, the district has been and continues to remain predominantly suburbanized.

The 1990 census reports that the district is overwhelmingly white (83.7 percent). African-Americans account for 12.5 percent of the district's population, while Latinos make up 5.2 percent. The median age of the citizens living in the district is 34.9 years old. Almost one-quarter of the district (24 percent) is under the age of 18, and approximately 17 percent of the district are over the age of 65.

As noted, Trenton is the largest municipality in the district. This once bustling industrial center has suffered from the country's transition to a service economy and the resulting de-industrialization that has occurred. Like many American cities, the loss of manufacturing jobs combined with the phenomenon of "white flight" has eroded the city's tax base. African-Americans and Latinos now account for nearly 63 percent of the city's population. This large minority population, combined with a sizeable number of state employees, produces a Democratic vote in most elections.[4] The suburban vote in Mercer County tends to be more independent and Republican-leaning and is usually sufficient to offset the Democratic vote coming from Trenton.

Ocean County usually provides the largest voter turnout of the Fourth District's four counties. The county usually votes Republican, although both President Bill Clinton and Senator Robert Torricelli (D-NJ) narrowly won there in 1996. Ocean County has one of the heaviest concentrations of senior citizens in the Northeast.[5] These voters are well informed and the turnout rate among these retirees is above the state average.[6]

The Monmouth County portion accounts for less than 15 percent of the Fourth District's population. This fast-growing section has attracted middle- and upper-middle-class families, which have increasingly supported Republican candidates.

The portion of the Fourth District located in Burlington County includes a number of river towns, including historic Burlington City, the capital of colonial West Jersey. The communities located along the Delaware River are older, industrial towns with tightly spaced suburbs, where Democrats tend to do well. In some of the rapidly developing sections of the county further east, Republicans have been able to make some inroads in recent years.

To the casual observer of New Jersey politics, the Fourth District is usually considered a Republican stronghold. Much of this perception is due to Smith's electoral dominance in the district since the early 1980s. However, as table 2.1 indicates, the district is actually much more competitive than one might think.

**Table 2.1 Election Results for
Selected Fourth District Races in the 1990s**

	Burlington	Mercer	Monmouth	Ocean	Total (%)
1992					
Clinton (D)	13,503	41,286	13,475	37,071	105,355 (39)
Bush (R)	12,097	28,788	20,863	48,159	109,907 (41)
Perot (I)	NR	NR	NR	NR	50,768 (19)
Smith (R)	18,560	42,611	28,400	59,524	149,095 (63)
Hughes (D)	10,948	31,344	10,873	31,349	84,514 (37)
1994					
Lautenberg (D)	10,204	24,859	10,614	27,903	73,580 (46)
Haytaian (R)	9,731	20,672	16,435	39,025	85,863 (54)
Smith (R)	13,994	30,214	19,912	45,698	109,818 (68)
Walsh (D)	6,608	16,132	6,912	19,885	49,537 (32)
1996					
Clinton (D)	17,152	45,901	17,361	46,467	126,881 (51)
Dole (R)	10,351	21,120	19,611	41,353	92,435 (37)
Torricelli (D)	14,445	39,358	15,900	45,160	114,863 (52)
Zimmer (R)	12,466	25,586	20,986	45,071	104,109 (48)
Smith (R)	17,719	39,251	27,758	61,676	146,404 (64)
Meara (D)	9,094	27,875	10,169	30,427	77,565 (34)
1998					
Smith (R)	12,487	22,860	17,777	39,867	92,991 (62)
Schneider (D)	7,701	18,200	7,209	19,171	52,281 (35)

*NR = Not reported.

SOURCE: *Manual of the Legislature of New Jersey.*

Ticket-splitting is common, especially when Smith, the most popular elected official in the district, is among the candidates running.

In recent presidential elections, Clinton narrowly lost the district to Republican nominee George Bush in 1992, but handily defeated Republican nominee Bob Dole in 1996. Likewise, in recent U.S. Senate elections, district voters supported Republican Chuck Haytaian over incumbent Democrat Frank Lautenberg in 1994. However, Democrat Torricelli outdistanced Republican Dick Zimmer in the 1996 election to fill the seat vacated by retiring Bill Bradley.

THE INCUMBENT

Representative Christopher H. Smith, who has represented the Fourth District since 1980, has quietly acquired a reputation as being one of the most influential and powerful members of the New Jersey congressional delegation. He was identified by *New Jersey Monthly* magazine as the eighth most powerful person in the state.[7] The magazine called Smith the "Energizer Bunny" of the state's congressional delegation for his activities on behalf of refugees and human rights.[8] Smith was also profiled by *Congressional Quarterly Weekly Report* as one of a dozen key individuals who shaped Congress' legislative record in 1997.[9] The basis for this recognition was Smith's unwavering opposition to abortion and his insistence that foreign operations spending bills restrict aid to international family planning groups performing or promoting abortion. His stand frustrated both Senate Republicans and the Clinton administration and propelled Smith to national attention.

Smith gained further national notoriety in August 1998 when he traveled to Myanmar in Southeast Asia to assist in the release of 16 activists detained by authorities for handing out pro-democracy literature. Smith got involved in the incident because one of the activists was a constituent. Later that year, his subcommittee (Subcommittee on International Operations and Human Rights of the House International Relations Committee) held hearings on human rights abuses in Myanmar. Smith has also used his committee assignments to take up the issue of human rights abuses in Northern Ireland. In addition to travelling to Northern Ireland on a fact-finding mission, he convened the first congressional hearings ever on this matter. Both activities play well in a district where more than 20 percent of the constituents claim an Irish heritage.[10]

Though his opponents often portray him as a staunch conservative because of his strong opposition to abortion, Smith's voting record is actually rather moderate on social and fiscal policy (see table 2.2 for his 1996 voting record). While his positions are sometimes at odds with the House Republican leadership, these positions appeal to the moderate and independent voters of his district. For instance, Smith voted against the final 1999 budget and was the lone Republican voting against the 1995 deficit-reducing budget reconciliation act.[11] The former included significant pork barrel projects for his district and the state, while the latter included provisions to restructure the Medicare program and to reduce the growth in Medicare spending. Both provisions would adversely affect senior citizens that make up a significant voting bloc in the Fourth District.

Smith's committee assignments provide little opportunity to directly enrich his district through pork barrel projects; thus, he must stay in touch with his constituents in other ways. Smith serves on the House International Relations Committee and chairs its Subcommittee on International Operations and Human Rights. The subcommittee has oversight and budgeting jurisdiction over the Department of State, the U.S. Information Agency, the Arms Control and Disarmament Agency, and the Agency for International Development. The subcommittee is also responsible for allocating funding for the United Nations. Smith additionally is second-ranking Republican on the House Veterans' Affairs Committee. Moreover, he has been appointed chair of the Commission on Security and Cooperation in Europe, also known as the Helsinki Commission.

Smith's committee assignments have given him a forum to advocate human rights abroad. Early in his career, this led him to criticize the former Soviet Union and Eastern European communist regimes. More recently, this stance has pitted him against the People's Republic of China. Smith has led an effort

**Table 2.2 Smith's 1996
National Journal Ratings**

Issue Type	Liberal %	Conservative %
Economic	47	53
Social	35	62
Foreign	28	71

SOURCE: *The Almanac of American Politics 1998,* 920.

to revoke China's "Most Favored Nation" status due to that nation's record on human rights.[12]

As noted, Smith has been one of Congress' most vocal opponents of abortion. He led the 1996 and 1997 House efforts to ban "partial birth" abortions. While Congress twice approved this bill, the Senate failed on each occasion to produce the two-thirds majority needed to override President Clinton's veto.

Smith has also attempted to restrict abortions outside the United States. As noted, his committee and subcommittee assignments allow Smith to influence foreign operations spending, including funding for international family planning activities. Since 1995, when the Republicans took control of the House, Smith has attached provisions restricting aid to international groups advocating abortion practices. His efforts are aimed at reinstating the "Mexico City" policy established by the administration of Ronald Reagan in 1984. This policy denied funding to groups unwilling to promise not to promote or perform abortions overseas. In 1993, President Clinton issued an executive order that overturned this policy.

Smith's efforts have not eliminated family planning aid, but they have reduced the level of spending. Smith and his allies have also used this position to force the Clinton administration to compromise on other foreign spending commitments, such as denying funding to pay the U.S. debt to the UN and the U.S. contribution to the International Monetary Fund (IMF).[13]

Representative Smith's work on behalf of his constituents is almost legendary in the Fourth District.[14] His office has developed a reputation for resolving constituent disputes with federal agencies, explaining confusing federal rules, and clearing up confounding regulations. Providing excellent casework is essential for Smith, since his committee assignments offer him scant opportunity to directly influence the lives of his constituents.

As vice chair of the House Veterans' Affairs Committee and senior Republican on its Health Subcommittee, Smith has been able to bring an outpatient health care clinic to Brick Township and a veteran's primary health care clinic to Trenton. In addition, communities throughout New Jersey, such as East Orange, Lyons, Menlo Park, and Arneystown, have received increased federal funding for veterans' facilities due to Smith's efforts.

Smith is also credited with saving the naval base at Lakehurst. This facility had been targeted for closure by the Defense Department's 1995 base closing commission. Smith's intervention on behalf of the base was one of the factors that convinced the BRAC Commission to reverse the Defense Department's recommendation for closure. The naval base is Ocean County's largest employer. By keeping the base open, Smith and other community leaders saved approximately 3,000 jobs in the district.

Smith has also secured federal funding for many projects in the district. Trenton was the first city in the country to receive funding under the "Weed and Seed" anti-drug program. He has also secured funding to assist in building the Hamilton Transit Station in Mercer County, for beach erosion projects in Ocean County, and for senior and low-income housing throughout the district.

SMITH'S CHALLENGERS

Smith first campaigned for the Fourth Congressional District seat in 1978. Running against Representative Frank Thompson, Jr., a 24-year incumbent, Smith's campaign was underfinanced and relied upon a pro-life network of groups for support.[15] Smith drew less than 40 percent of the vote. In a 1980 rematch, Thompson's indictment in the ABSCAM bribery scandal propelled the 27-year-old Smith to victory. Smith was then able to fend off serious Democratic challenges in 1982 and 1984. Despite redistricting that has completely redrawn the district, he has not faced a serious challenger since and has won each election with more than 60 percent of the vote.

Larry Schneider of Mercer County, the Democratic challenger in 1998, is a vice president at Morgan Stanley Dean Witter. The Wall Street executive had held no previous elected position. His political experience was limited to serving as chair of the East Windsor Transportation Advisory Committee that reports to the township council. Schneider is also a member of the board of directors for Better Beginnings, Inc., a nonprofit day-care center serving low-income families in Mercer County.

Schneider's motive for running was his dissatisfaction with Smith's policies and his perception that the incumbent was out of touch with the constituency. Among the concerns that Schneider cited were Smith's residency (Smith maintains his family's primary residence in the Washington area) and Smith's insistence of linking his pro-life stand to American foreign policy.[16]

Three minor party candidates also ran in the general election. They were Morgan Strong of the New Jersey Conservative party, Keith Quarles of the Libertarian party, and Nick Mellis of the Green party. None of these candidates received more than 1,800 votes in the general election.

THE CAMPAIGN

Neither Smith nor Schneider faced any opposition in their party's primary. This was due in large part to Smith's tremendous popularity in the district. Loyal Republicans were hesitant to contest what has become a "safe" Republican seat and were discouraged by state and county organizations from offering any serious challenge. As a result, Smith has faced no primary challenge during the 1990s. Would-be Democratic challengers, especially those with long-term political career goals, realize that it would take a tremendous amount of resources and exposure to overcome Smith's visibility and high favorable rating among voters, and so are hesitant to serve as their party's sacrificial lamb. This usually leaves the Democratic nomination open to political novices and quixotic crusaders.

Schneider fit into the first category, that of political novice. He was the only individual seeking, and therefore readily received, endorsement from all four Democratic party county organizations. This endorsement short-circuited any potential primary challenger Schneider might have faced, because primary candidates officially endorsed by county party organizations are clearly identified by the "regular" party label on the ballot. This identification gives voters a clear indication of the party's preference for the nomination.

Unlike previous challengers, and despite reports to the contrary, Schneider did not make Smith's opposition to abortion the central issue of the campaign. Schneider directed his criticism at the incumbent's use of anti-abortion requirements as a condition for authorizing foreign operations funding, paying America's UN debt, and providing the U.S. contribution to the IMF. This position in Schneider's view made Smith an obstructionist in foreign affairs.

Schneider also criticized Smith as being a career politician, out of touch with his constituency. Citing the incumbent's position on education, Social Security, and health care, Schneider promised to make these issues his top priority, if elected. He also expressed his concern that Congress had not adequately dealt with the Y2K (Year 2000) computer problem.

For his part, Smith defended his pro-life stand as part of his larger concern for and advocacy on behalf of human rights. He stated: "Abortion, the right to live, the right to vote . . . these issues are all part of a seamless garment."[17] For most of Smith's constituents, the abortion question was not the litmus test they used to judge the representative. Job performance, which equated to casework in the district, was a more pressing concern. Smith knew this and, as noted, made constituency service a high priority.

Schneider challenged Smith to four debates during the campaign, one in each of the district's counties. Both the League of Women Voters (LWV) and New 12 New Jersey (a New Jersey cable television station) invited all the candidates running to separated debates as well. Despite a promise to debate his opponent, Smith declined to participate in any public forum with his challengers, citing a lack of time due to Congress' consideration of the 1999 budget and President Clinton's impeachment proceedings. Smith said that the final budget vote on October 20, 1998, left him with less than two weeks to campaign and that the timing of the proposed debates did not fit into what little time was left in his schedule. In a number of candidate forums, surrogates for Smith faced off against Schneider and some of the other minor candidates. All five congressional candidates did meet to participate in two editorial meetings sponsored by the *Burlington County Times* and *Asbury Park Press,* two of the local newspapers serving the district.

Both the *Burlington County Times* and the *Asbury Park Press* endorsed Smith for reelection. These newspapers were joined by every other daily serving the district, including the *Philadelphia Inquirer, Trenton Times, Trentonian,* and the *Courier Post.* In most of these endorsements, the editorial boards decried their disappointment with Smith's stand on abortion, but cited his work on behalf of his constituents and his opponent's lack of political experience as the main reasons for backing the incumbent.

The Smith campaign also won the battle for endorsements from various organizations. Law enforcement groups, including the New Jersey State Lodge of the Fraternal Order of Police, the National Association of Police Organizations, and the Port Authority Police Benevolent Association, supported Smith. The Veterans of Foreign War (VFW) Political Action Committee and the National Vietnam and Gulf War Veterans Coalitions were among the veterans associations endorsing the incumbent. Other organizations pledging their support to Smith were the National Small Business United, the National Committee to Preserve Social Security and Medicare, and state and national pro-life groups.

Planned Parenthood, the National Organization for Women (NOW), Voters for Choice, and Americans for Democratic Action (ADA) endorsed Schneider.

From the outset, the Smith campaign was well positioned to make short work of any Democratic challenger. Federal Election Commission (FEC) reports indicate that Smith started the campaign with a little more than $100,000 cash-on-hand left over from his 1996 race.[18] He soon raised an additional $247,049 from individual contributions and $173,027 from political action committees (PACs), bringing the total amount of cash available to more than $530,000. PACs representing unions were among Smith's strongest supporters, providing him with $81,500. Others that supported the campaign included the health-care professions; human rights advocates; pro-life organizations; conservative groups; and real estate, builders, and construction companies.[19]

The Schneider campaign was only able to raise a fraction of the money Smith received. According to FEC reports, the challenger took in $39,036, including $24,798 from individuals and $6,500 from PACs.[20] The groups that supported Schneider included Morgan Stanley (his employer), traditional liberal organizations, and pro-choice advocates.

Perceiving no real threat from the challenger and following a philosophy of not spending money if one does not have to spend it, the Smith campaign spent the money judiciously. It prepared one general and two targeted mailings, rented billboard space and, for the first time, used both volunteer and paid telemarketing, also known as "phone banking." The Smith campaign also ran no television advertisements and only a few radio spots during the last ten days of the campaign.

The reason for not using the electronic media was simple. Due to New Jersey's location, sandwiched between New York and Philadelphia, two of the nation's largest and most expensive media markets, campaigns in the Garden State can be costly. In 1998, the total costs of New Jersey's congressional campaigns ran from approximately $343,000 to more than $3.2 million.[21] The average House election in New Jersey cost more than $975,000. New Jersey's lack of a single, state-oriented television station usually works to the advantage of better-known incumbents.

Much of New Jersey's Fourth District is located in the Philadelphia metropolitan region and serviced by that area's media outlets. Advertising rates in Philadelphia, the fourth-largest media market in the country, are expensive, costing between $5,000 to $25,000 for a 30-second commercial.[22] Such ads are not cost effective because the Fourth District makes up only a small portion of the Philadelphia media market. Advertisements run by any congressional candidate in the region reach many more non-residents than residents of the district. Thus, a television ad campaign may not be the most efficient way to reach voters. In recent years, candidates have used less expensive cable television ads that allow them to more directly target likely voters.

The Smith campaign was also concerned over voter turnout and employed the "Lincoln" polling technique, which identified likely voters and tracked their attitudes throughout the campaign. This relatively inexpensive campaign cost Smith approximately $304,000 and was the least expensive campaign run by an incumbent in New Jersey in 1998. It left about $226,000 cash-on-hand for Smith's next electoral contest.

The Schneider campaign used the limited funds it had available to print lawn signs, a staple in grassroots in New Jersey politics, and 40,000 brochures, which were distributed by the candidate and volunteers. The state and county Democratic organizations provided Schneider with advice on how to run a campaign, but gave him no financial backing. Lacking the financial resources to mount any type of media or mass mailing campaign, Schneider ran no television or radio ads. He took advantage of any media exposure offered to him, making himself readily available to the press. He also relied on good, old-fashioned "shoe leather" to take his message to the voters. This strategy included visiting all 39 municipal council meetings to talk and to listen to officials and citizens. He also campaigned outside supermarkets, malls, and shopping centers in an attempt to personally reach as many voters as possible.

In the end, even with a lower than expected voter turnout, Schneider could not overcome Smith's name recognition and favorable image among voters. Smith took 62 percent of the vote, compared to Schneider's 35 percent. The representative was returned to Washington for his ninth term, placing him second in seniority behind fellow Republican Marge Roukema in the New Jersey House delegation.

CONCLUSION

The campaign in the Fourth District was typical of the overwhelming majority of "safe" House seats in New Jersey and across the nation: a well-financed, popular incumbent easily defeated an obscure, cash-poor opponent. In many ways, this campaign provided ammunition to those calling for congressional term limits or significant campaign finance reform. Those arguing against term limits might also cite this race in support of their position. They would argue that Representative Smith was reelected so easily precisely because he effectively represented and served his constituents' interests.

The argument for significant campaign finance reform is less easily countered. The combination of the intangible benefits associated with incumbency and the ease in raising campaign contributions means it is unlikely that many members of Congress will face a credible challenger. This has certainly been, and will likely be, the case for many years to come in New Jersey's Fourth Congressional District, unless the way in which elections are conducted is drastically altered.

NOTES

1. Press release, Center for Responsive Politics, October 26, 1998.
2. Press release, Center for Responsive Politics, November 4, 1998.
3. www.census.gov.
4. www.voter96.cqalert.com.
5. Ibid.
6. *Manual of the Legislature of New Jersey 1997* (Newark, NJ: Skinder-Strauss, 1997), 882.
7. Stephen Barr, "The 25 Most Powerful People in New Jersey," *New Jersey Monthly* 23 (July 1998): 42–43.
8. Ibid.
9. Donna Cassata, *Congressional Quarterly Weekly Report,* December 6, 1997, 2972.
10. Tom McGinty, "Schneider in Uphill Battle to Unseat Smith," *Trenton Times,* November 1, 1998, 9.
11. Michael Barone and Grant Ujifusa, *The Almanac of American Politics 1998* (Washington, DC: National Journal, 1997), 918.
12. Ibid.
13. www.voter96.cqalert.com.
14. "For Congress: Chris Smith in the Fourth," *Trenton Times,* October 29, 1998, A16; "A Congressman Getting Better with Age," *Trentonian,* November 1, 1998, 22.
15. www.voter96.cqalert.com.
16. www.larryschneider.com.
17. Jon Blackwell, "Smith: More to Me Than Abortion," *Trentonian,* November 1, 1998, 3.
18. Ibid.
19. www.crp.org/1998elect/dist_total/98NJ04total.htm.
20. www.crp.org/1998elect/dist_contrib/98NJ04contrib.htm.
21. www.fec.gov/1996/states/njhs97.htm.
22. Barbara G. Salmore and Stephen A. Salmore, *New Jersey Politics and Government: Suburban Politics Comes of Age,* 2d ed. (Lincoln, NE: University of Nebraska Press, 1998), 80–81.

3

Clay Defeats Soulade in Missouri's First District Race

Steven Puro
Kenneth Warren

On August 6, 1968, William (Bill) Clay, Sr., easily defeated four other candidates in the Democratic primary in Missouri's First Congressional District. A few months later, on November 5, 1968, Clay trounced his Republican rival, Curtis Crawford, in the general election, capturing 68 percent of the vote, allowing Clay to become the first African-American ever to represent Missouri in the U.S. Congress. On November 3, 1998, 30 years after Clay first won his seat, he won for the sixteenth straight time by another comfortable margin, winning with 73 percent of the vote. In all 16 races, regardless of the particular circumstances of the various campaigns, Clay never faced any serious challenges in the Democratic primaries or general elections. In fact, Clay often faced only token opposition or, on a few occasions, no opposition at all.

Clay holds what is known as a "safe" seat, meaning that challengers have no realistic chance of defeating the incumbent congressman because the district has socioeconomic and political characteristics that strongly favor one political party or one individual. It must be stressed that Clay's safe seat situation is not unique. Safe congressional seats require candidate development. In addition to socioeconomic and political characteristics that favor a particular individual, the representative must maintain a strong political organization, discourage primary and general election opponents, maintain loyalties to key organized groups within the district, and establish strong constituent relationships. This chapter will discuss Clay's activities in these areas.

Since Clay is typical of safe seat representatives who have been elected for long periods of time, a lot can be learned about the safe seat phenomenon by focusing upon the political career of Clay. As with the other representatives holding safe seats, Clay's congressional district had to be suited for him. That is, the district had to have socioeconomic and political characteristics that would provide Clay with an opportunity to win and continuously hold on to his district. Conversely, Clay, as is the case with other U.S. representatives in safe districts, had to have the background and personal characteristics that would "fit" his district. Simply put, to win and serve a legislative district with a safe seat, as we shall explain in subsequent sections, the district has to be "made" for the politician and the politician has to be "made" for the district.

THE HISTORY AND CHARACTER
OF MISSOURI'S FIRST DISTRICT

St. Louis, the base of Bill Clay's congressional district, was once a large, thriving city that hosted the 1904 World's Fair. In the 1890s, St. Louis had a population around 600,000 and its new Union Station was the largest train station in the world. Its white, heavily German population was hard working and quite prosperous, developing such successful businesses as the May department stores, the Anheuser Busch brewery, and *The St. Louis Post-Dispatch*. In those days, St. Louis was truly an affluent and trendy city, where "Meet Me in St. Louis" had a strong appeal. In fact, in 1904, around 600 million people met in St. Louis at the World's Fair.[1]

But since its glory days around the turn of the century, St. Louis has fallen on rough times, especially since the early post–World War II years. As with so many older cities in America, but more so for St. Louis, businesses and people, especially the more affluent, have been moving out at a fairly rapid and steady pace. In 1950, at its population peak, St. Louis had a population of 856,000; by 1970, two years after Clay's first victory to Congress, St. Louis's population had dropped to 622,000. By 1980, it had plummeted to 453,000, and by 1990 it declined to roughly 397,000. The population for 2000 is projected to be around 340,000, which would represent a loss of 516,000 people since 1950, or 60.3 percent.[2]

It is this declining city that constitutes the electoral base of Clay's district. Clay represents the northern half of St. Louis city, an area that is in even worse economic shape than its southern half. This area once consisted of affluent families living in large, beautiful homes; the area now is largely a ghetto with low-income families, predominantly black, living in deteriorating housing, often beside boarded up houses and abandoned businesses. Property values, incomes, and educational levels are low, while statistics for crime, unemployment, and residents living on welfare are high.[3]

North St. Louis city has remained the heart of Clay's electoral power, even though the St. Louis city part of Clay's First Congressional District now accounts for only about 29 percent of the total vote in the district. When Clay first won his congressional seat in 1968, the city part of Clay's district constituted 72 percent of the total votes cast in the district. In each census since 1968, Clay's district has expanded out into the suburbs of St. Louis County. After the 1970 census, the city's part of the district dropped to about 53 percent of the total vote of the district; after the 1980 census, it declined to only 41 percent of the district's total vote; and after the 1990 census, the city part of the First District's vote plummeted to approximately 29 percent.

Nonetheless, Clay continues to win by comfortable margins districtwide because he has won by lopsided margins (usually by 80 percent plus to even 90 percent plus of the vote) in the heartland of his district—the city—while doing reasonably well in the St. Louis County part of his district, usually winning with 40 to 65 percent of the vote. Clay has fared fairly well in the county, not only because of the advantages of incumbency, but because the St. Louis County suburbs within his district are heavily Democratic. These immediate northern and northwestern suburbs of North St. Louis are populated by racially mixed, less affluent blue-collar workers, while the more affluent communities of Clayton and University City, just west of North St. Louis, tend to be populated by more liberal professionals, many of them Jewish, and many of them professors teaching at neighboring universities—Washington University, Saint Louis University, Fontbonne College, Webster University, and the University of Missouri-St. Louis.

CLAY'S WINNING STATISTICS

Before examining more closely why Clay has been so successful as an incumbent, it is important to scrutinize in relative detail his electoral record since he first won his seat in 1968. Such scrutiny helps us comprehend and appreciate the awesome power of incumbency. Table 3.1 displays how well Clay has done in every general election since 1968. The general conclusion is that Clay has never faced a tough challenge in his reelections.

Regarding the Democratic primaries, Clay has won with better than 60 percent of the primary vote in every election except his first primary contest in 1968. He still won that primary easily with a 48 percent plurality; the remaining 52 percent was divided among four other candidates. In six primary elections (1970, 1984, 1988, 1990, 1994, and 1998), Clay faced no opponents. Because incumbents tend to become more unbeatable the longer they serve, it is not surprising that Clay has only faced opposition in the Democratic primary twice since 1988. As an incumbent, Clay has won those primaries with an average winning percentage of a little more than 80 percent.

In the general elections, Clay has fared almost as well. In 1968, he won an impressive victory as a non-incumbent for an "open" seat with 64 percent. As an incumbent, however, he has won much more impressively, with an average victory of 69.3 percent. In the past three general elections, he has captured nearly 72 percent, providing further evidence that the electoral prowess of incumbents usually increases as the incumbent's tenure in office lengthens.

Clay has won by these landslide margins because he has broad appeal throughout his district. However, Clay's base has always been the city portion of his district where the African-American population is well over 90 percent

**Table 3.1 Summarized Winning
Percentages for Bill Clay in General Elections
as an Incumbent, Missouri's First Congressional District**

Election Year	St. Louis City Area	St. Louis County Area
1968	74*	39*
1970	94	82
1972	82	42
1974	85	48
1976	84	44
1978	87	44
1980	85	48
1982	84	44
1984	86	55
1986	87	44
1988	87	61
1990	80	53
1992	87	60
1994	87	61
1996	89	61
1998	90	66
Average Percentage Win	86.3%	54.2%

*Computed average percentage win excludes 1968, since Clay did not run as an incumbent in 1968.

SOURCE: Percentages were calculated from election results found in Secretary of State, *The Official Manual: State of Missouri* (Jefferson City, MO: Von Hoffman, Inc., 1968–1998 publications).

in most of the North Side wards. Clay wins among this predominantly African-American area in the city by enormous margins, averaging a winning percentage of 86.3 percent. Fortunately for Clay, this huge victory margin in the city has been enough to allow him to win reelections, even though he normally lost in the St. Louis County portion because the county portion of his district represented only 23 percent of the total district vote in 1970 when he first ran for reelection as an incumbent and about 47 percent of the total district's vote when he ran for reelections until 1982. After the 1980 census, Clay's St. Louis County part of his district jumped to 59 percent of his district's total vote, but his lopsided winning city margins still enabled him to win comfortably districtwide. After the 1990 census, the city's share of Clay's district plummeted to only 29 percent of the total vote, yet Clay had by now started to win even in the St. Louis County component because his county area had become, due to redistricting, increasingly blue-collar and Democratic.

What these victory percentages suggest, as will be shown below, is that few people dare challenge incumbents, because politically savvy people understand that the electoral advantages for incumbents are just too great to overcome under most campaign conditions. Consequently, the reality is that most incumbents rarely face politically powerful challengers. Most challenges are merely token challenges, often mounted by the major opposition party just so the party can have someone on the ballot in case something happens to the incumbent (e.g., unexpected major scandal, death, etc.). Third-party and independent candidates may also file to run against incumbents, but such candidates in the American two-party system represent only minor irritations to incumbents since they normally receive less than 2 to 3 percent of the vote.

CLAY FITS HIS DISTRICT

Clay has "owned" the First Congressional District for more than 30 years, winning easy reelection victories every two years, because he has an excellent fit with his district. Clay was born poor on April 30, 1931, in St. Louis in a small apartment without any plumbing or hot water. He was one of seven children. As a minority growing up on St. Louis's declining North Side, an area he would eventually represent in the U.S. House, he observed firsthand the discrimination and racism that would eventually shape his political perspective and make him the civil rights activist that he became. But, unlike so many of his childhood peers, it was clear during his youth that Clay had the natural personal attributes to become a leader in his community. Clay was and is smart, aggressive, focused, and well organized. Full of energy and determination, Clay became determined to fight racism and the social injustices inflicted upon blacks. He prepared himself for "battle" and entered politics by earning a political science degree at Saint Louis University and learned "street politics" from both black and white political leaders of the day.

Clay won respect for his civil rights protests while in the military and during his early career years in St. Louis during the 1950s and early 1960s. But he irked older, "establishment-type Blacks" in the National Association for the Advancement of Colored People (NAACP) because he felt that they were not aggressive enough in opposing the discriminatory treatment against African-Americans. Tim Poor suggests that by the late 1950s, Clay had emerged as a fiery orator, speaking out for all sorts of civil rights causes.[4] By the end of the 1950s, Clay had become a credible, respected spokesperson for black causes in St. Louis, especially for the more "impatient," younger African-Americans.

His formal political career started in 1959 when he decided to run against the white power structure to capture a seat on St. Louis Board of Aldermen. To defeat the white incumbent who held the aldermanic seat in a ward that by now had a black majority, Clay had to put together a solid campaign organization and campaign hard. As noted in the *St. Louis Post-Dispatch,* Norman Seay, Clay's campaign manager, said this about Clay's campaign style: "He was a *vigorous* and *exciting* campaigner—a tough campaigner. He would attack an issue or an individual *re-lent-less-ly.* He would tear into you and do it with a high degree of finesse. He was able to excite the audience. He could easily get them on his side and get them to do basically what he wanted."[5] His organizational skills and his energized campaigning paid off. He won easily, which was an extraordinary achievement in those days for a black politician.

As an alderman, Clay built a solid political organization based upon patronage, loyalty, and just plain political common sense. Those factors would serve Clay long into his political career. He organized his power base block-by-block, making sure that he had organized supporters on every block who could promote the interests of his friends and undermine the interests of his enemies. Clay knew how patronage politics worked and he built during his aldermanic days a "mini political machine" that would help him win his bid for Congress in 1968. After he was elected to Congress, he would expand the base and power of this political machine, eventually making it the most powerful and durable political machine in the St. Louis area and, possibly, all of Missouri.

As an alderman, Clay continued his vibrant efforts to promote civil rights, successfully pressuring fellow board members to pass St. Louis's first ordinances prohibiting discriminatory practices in jobs and public accommodations. But he earned his greatest respect by protesting the discriminatory hiring practices of the Jefferson Bank and Trust Company in 1963, a bank in the heart of the black community with no blacks in white-collar positions. Clay was sentenced to 280 days in jail for protesting. After serving some of his sentence, the judge was willing to release him if he would simply apologize, but Clay refused, holding that he had nothing to apologize for.[6] Of course, this principled, self-sacrificing stand made Clay a genuine hero in the black community—a hero voters would not forget when Clay decided to run for Congress in 1968.

On March 5, 1968, Frank M. Karsten, a white Democratic member of Congress who had served as the First Congressional District's representative for 11 terms, announced his retirement. Karsten's retirement created an open seat just too hard for Clay to resist. Poor reports that within literally minutes of hearing about Karsten's retirement, Clay decided to run for the seat.[7] Clay's decision to run was made quickly, but it was by no means irrational or politically unsound. The fact was that Clay was more than ready. He had prepared himself well for this campaign. By 1968, no candidate was better suited to win this House race than Clay. He was black in a now predominantly black district. He was born and reared in the district. He had gone through the same experiences that people in this district had. He shared their pain, demonstrated against racism and the discriminatory practices against his "brothers" and "sisters." He was one of them. And by 1968, he was their respected leader. He was just turning 37 years old. He had paid his dues. He had made himself "fit" for the First Congressional District. Consequently, he assembled his already-in-place political machine, broadened its base and power, campaigned hard, and won. He won big by trouncing four other candidates in the Democratic primary and winning over a prominent Republican, Curtis Crawford, in the general election with 64 percent of the vote. Clay was on his way!

CLAY GROOMS HIS DISTRICT

Few, if any, politicians win elections repeatedly because they are lucky, although a little luck doesn't hurt. Once a politician wins, he or she must maintain the electoral advantage by constantly grooming his or her district. Clay knew this and has done an excellent job since 1968 doing what he must to insure victory after victory.

The key to Clay's success has been the maintenance of his organization, his political machine. Clay has preserved and strengthened his political organization, thus his political power, by appointing and nurturing a competent and politically savvy office staff, both in St. Louis and in Washington, D.C., but especially in St. Louis. His political organization and campaign staff in St. Louis was headed by Pearlie Evans, a competent and politically astute woman, for almost the entire time Clay has been in Congress (Evans retired in 1998). Their mutual loyalty to each other helped to insure organizational competence, dependability, and stability in Clay's political machine. Clay also recruited and kept other key aides in his St. Louis and Washington offices for decades. Consequently, Clay's workers have been devoted to him because he has been loyal to them.

With this loyal, experienced core, Clay has been able to make and develop alliances over the years that have functioned to broaden and strengthen his political base in his congressional district, making him virtually unbeatable as an incumbent. Although Clay has been loyal to his staff, he has prospered politically by his motto, "Just Permanent Interests." As Clay explained in his book by the same title, political power can only be secured as long as "just permanent interests" are sought, not "permanent friends" or "permanent enemies." This political philosophy has allowed Clay to be flexible in forming the necessary winning political alliances from campaign to campaign. That is, his political enemies during one political campaign may turn out to be his allies during the next political campaign. Likewise, Clay understood that ties to political allies or friends might have to be severed at some future time if political expediency required it.

Clay has realized that political friends may have to be abandoned at some future date, but he has nonetheless recognized the importance of promoting symbiotic relationships within his political organization and within his political environment. Of course, symbiotic relationships are relationships that prove beneficial to the host (e.g., Clay) and those who become symbiotically involved with the host. Symbiotic relationships are crucial to electoral success for politicians because they involve striking *quid pro quo* deals that make various people and organizations dependent upon each other for their success. When the "deals" prove to be no longer beneficial to the "permanent interests" of the politician, deals fall apart and new *quid pro quo* deals are formed.

To groom his power base, Clay has played this symbiotic game well. This is one of the major reasons Clay has survived as an incumbent without serious challenge to his seat. For example, Clay has never hesitated to use his political machine to back his friends, relatives, and even his "past enemies" to help elect them to political office. He has been successful in helping them get elected to key positions of political power from St. Louis Democratic party committee posts to the mayor of St. Louis to the Missouri governor to seats in the Missouri House of Representatives and Senate. Naturally, once elected, these officeholders remember that Clay's machine helped get them elected, so they are willing to support Clay when he needs their help. On occasion, however, politicians have not returned the favor or "crossed" Clay in some way, usually much to their detriment. For instance, in one infamous example, when the then-mayor of St. Louis, Vince Schoemehl, previously in a symbiotic relationship with Clay, defied Clay by running various candidates against Clay's people, including Clay's son, Clay responded by using his machine to defeat a crucial sales tax that Schoemehl felt St. Louis City needed desperately. Later, when Schoemehl ran for governor, Clay's machine was responsible for making sure that voters in North St. Louis turned out to vote against Schoemehl in the Democratic primary. Schoemehl lost.

Clay has also groomed his power base by forming symbiotic relationships with key organizations. Crucial to his political success has been his alliance with labor organizations in St. Louis, Missouri, and nationally. Clay has always been supportive of labor interests and labor organizations have supported Clay. In fact, Clay has relied upon labor support to do as well as he has in the St. Louis County area of his district, a predominantly white, blue-collar labor class area.

In order to preserve electoral support in the First Congressional District, it has been important for Clay to establish a voting record in the U.S. House of Representatives that is received well by his constituents. This means that Clay must keep in touch with his constituents and vote on bills that support their interests. He has done that. Clay has voted for various social, economic, and political measures supported by the vast majority of the voters in the First District. For example, in the 104th Congress, Clay voted against reducing the minimum wage, voted against a rather conservative welfare reform measure, voted against an attempt to override the veto on partial-birth abortions, and voted for cutting the anti-missile defense system.

CHALLENGERS IN THE DISTRICT

William Flanigan and Nancy Zingale suggest that there are high and low stimulus elections, depending upon such issues as differences in media coverage in the election, importance of issues raised in the campaign, attractiveness of candidates, and competitiveness of the contest.[8] The 1998 election in the First Congressional District of Missouri was clearly within the low stimulus category. This section will explore issues surrounding the challengers for Clay's seat in the 1998 primary and general elections.

Challengers in Missouri's First District

A challenger approaching Missouri's First Congressional District election would ask whether a competitive election campaign could be conducted. Is it possible to win in this election context? The challenger must assess the incumbent and determine whether he or she can match or be competitive with the incumbent in terms of recognition, funds, and political and campaign organizations. In the First District, the challenger will note that Clay is regularly elected with almost two-thirds of the vote. Challengers will see that after 15 congressional terms, Clay has established broad name recognition among voters and created trustworthy relationships with constituents. He has developed a "faithful" electorate and maintained an efficient political organization on congressional, state, and local electoral contests and issues. Moreover, he has played a strong representative role in his district and handles specific constituent needs by a smoothly functioning district organization.

Challengers would recognize that Democratic partisanship has been an important factor in this district. They would see strong long-term support for Democratic candidates, ranging from U.S. president to St. Louis city alderman. The district contains many core constituencies for the Democratic party—poor, minority, and lower-middle-class voters, particularly in the urban areas. In addition, in the St. Louis County (suburban) portion of the district, there are strong black and Jewish voting groups that support liberal voting patterns and Democratic candidates.

Challengers would inquire whether Clay's electoral margin in the general election has changed substantially since the 1992 election, the first election under the 1990 apportionment lines. They would observe that Clay's electoral support has been relatively stable, as noted above. His electoral support places the district in the definitely non-competitive category, i.e., electoral support greater than 60 percent for more than two consecutive elections.

The regular absence of serious primary or general election opponents reflects political leaders' difficulties in recruiting congressional candidates. Republican challengers would note their party's candidates lacked prior public experience and political office, and these candidates had not held any significant appointed or elected political office. Previous Republican First District candidates have been almost absent from the political landscape after the election. No serious, overwhelming political issues existed within the district and there has not been a sustained personal opposition to Clay. The absence of competition promotes low voter turnout, and the presence of Clay's organization guarantees increased voter turnout, if necessary, further diminishing possibilities for opposing candidates.

In general elections from 1992 to 1996, Republicans and other opponents were able to raise only minimal campaign funds. Clay did not engage in aggressive fundraising yet easily raised between $300,000 to $375,000 for each campaign. This context is a difficult one for political challengers, and the low probability of running an effective or competitive campaign lessens the opposing party's ability to recruit strong candidates. In general, challengers to Clay in the 1990s have not waged strong campaigns.

The First District election has been deemphasized in the local media. Since Clay has not faced serious challengers or serious opposition on political and social issues, there have been few campaign news stories. Further, television, newspaper, and radio news directors know that there will not be "hard campaigning" by either Clay or his opponents. The news directors' decisions to not allocate coverage to this election is part of a self-fulfilling series of events. The lack of television, radio, and print coverage adds to the general perception that there is not a good opportunity to challenge Clay.

Challengers will also observe Clay's lawmaking and legislative activities to determine if they could offer the district equivalent or improved legislative authority and lawmaking skills. Clay holds a senior position in the Democratic leadership within the House of Representatives. This seniority is a source of formal power and informal authority within that chamber, the House Democratic Caucus, and the Congressional Black Caucus (CBC). Prior to 1994, when the Republicans regained control of the House, he was the chair of the now-abolished Post Office and Civil Service Committee and ranking majority member of what was then the Education and Labor Committee. In those leadership roles, Clay had significant responsibility for the passage of the 1993 Family and Medical Leave Act and the 1994 reform of the Hatch Act, which allowed federal employees' participation in electoral politics.

In the 104th Congress, as ranking minority member of the renamed Education and Workforce Committee, he played an important role in passing legislation increasing the minimum wage. In the 105th Congress, he retained the position of ranking minority member of this committee. If Democrats regain control of the House in the 2000 election, Clay will likely chair this committee. His power as a senior representative is important in the chamber and in the district. It allows him to affect issues that are important to him and to his constituents, such as national issues that concern blacks and labor unions. Clay is recognized as a "powerful legislator" by many voters in the district, and this acknowledgment weakens the likelihood of serious political challengers.

Opposing Candidates in 1998

Clay had two opponents in the 1998 congressional election: Richmond A. Soulade, Sr., (Republican) and Richard E. Illyes (Libertarian). Soulade is a 39-year-old, black North St. Louis County businessperson who had the campaign slogan of "Choice for a New Generation." He had never held public office. His legislative goals fit within the Republican agenda in the 105th Congress concerning government spending, state and local authority, and tax relief to increase economic growth. Soulade emphasized greater health care affordability and accessibility to working class and poor people. This idea is an attractive argument in the district. He favored the Republican medical savings account plan that would give patients greater choice in health care providers and independence from traditional insurance plans.

Soulade's economic plans would have lowered interest rates and provided tax reductions to spur economic growth. He also favored greater state and local control of social issues, such as returning federal dollars to state and local authorities for education. Soulade agreed with the Democratic ideas that funds derived from the government surplus should save Social Security, a key issue for the districts' constituents.

Illyes is a white, 58-year-old computer professional and an Army veteran. Illyes advocated the classic libertarian view. He was the third Libertarian candidate since 1994 to contest this seat. Illyes would limit government intrusiveness on individual rights to permit a freer society, and would replace state unemployment compensation with a system of private insurance. He opposed candidates that favored the existing big government, and sought a much smaller government to allow broader dimensions of individual and economic freedom. His primary legislative objectives would be downsizing government and removing government monopolies. Illyes did not advocate abortion, but he would keep government completely out of the abortion issue. He further argued that there should be a free market to provide educational services to replace public schools. Schools would be "paid on a performance basis, and tax money is paid only for results."[9]

This campaign was his first attempt at congressional office. He was elected Libertarian Township Committeeman for Hadley Township (St. Louis County) in 1996. This township is near the center of the First District. Illyes also serves on the Missouri Libertarian Party Executive Committee. His campaign did not demonstrate connections with that state organization. There was an absence of campaign coordination among Libertarian candidates.

The Primary

In the 1998 primary, there was no opposition for any of the three candidates from within their party. The Missouri primary occurs in early August and it is one of the last in the nation. There is no political party registration in Missouri; an individual can take partisan or non-partisan ballots. In the absence of opposition, the three candidates did not engage in any significant political efforts, such as television or radio political advertisements, or systematic telephone campaigns. State and county political parties provided minimal political advertising for candidates in the district. As noted below, Clay's opponents did not raise campaign funds, and they did not use the primary as an opportunity to promote their name recognition or political differences with Clay. The August primary was a quiet one for House, Senate, and statewide seats, with the possible exception of the Democratic contest for state auditor.

A SAFE SEAT AND A SILENT CAMPAIGN

Clay sees himself acting as an effective agent for the principal elements of his constituency. Carl McCurley and Jeffrey Mondak suggest that principal-agent theory might be useful in explaining the safe seat phenomena. They say: "Voters as principals, appear to use readily accessible information in forming evaluations of a candidate's ability to act as a reliable agent. . . . [Under] these conditions, we expect that voters will take into account information related to the chances that a particular candidate will deliver faithful and effective representation of their interests."[10] At the beginning of both the 1998 primary and general election campaigns, Clay had substantial advantages over his opponents. He had higher name recognition, greater voter approval, and an extensive con-

Table 3.2 1998 Congressional Election Outcome, Missouri's First District

William Clay, Sr. (D-Incumbent)	91,702	72.8%
Richmond A. Soulade, Sr. (R)	30,746	24.4%
Richard E. Illyes (L)	3,588	2.8%
Total	126,036	100.0%

SOURCE: Compiled by authors.

gressional and political record. Paul Herrnson argues an additional advantage of incumbency has been that "incumbents also benefit from the fact that most constituents and political elites in Washington expect them to win."[11] The Clay political organization worked and continues to work at building bonds of trust with its constituents. Clay's past and current behavior demonstrates an ability to make a difference in national and local political events and represent constituents' interests.

At the start of 1998, Clay had an enormous financial and organizational advantage over his opponents. Both opponents lacked financial and organizational resources to conduct a competitive campaign. Neither at this time nor later in the campaign did opponents take serious action to build a broad base of electoral or financial support. Neither Soulade nor Illyes filed Federal Election Commission (FEC) financial reports. This behavior indicates minimal fundraising activities. FEC reports for funds raised in 1997 show Clay had the smallest amount of fundraising and smallest amount of cash-on-hand of any congressional incumbents in the St. Louis metropolitan portion of Missouri. In the last half of 1997, he did not engage in any extensive fundraising. In the last campaign finance report prior to the election, filed on October 15, 1998, Clay was substantially below other incumbents in the Missouri side of the St. Louis metropolitan region in amount raised and amount on hand. It is significant to note that neither of his opponents engaged in fundraising.

On November 3, 1998, Clay easily defeated his nearest opponent by more than 60,000 of 126,036 votes cast (see table 3.2). Clay received more than 72 percent of the vote, his largest vote percentage since the district was redrawn after the 1990 census. Clay conducted traditional campaign activities with person-to-person contact. He did not rely upon mass media advertising, either television or radio. The main information sources were ads in the predominantly black newspapers and the North St. Louis County section of the *St. Louis Post-Dispatch,* the only mass circulation newspaper in St. Louis. In a diverse urban area, television advertisements are expensive and reach only part of his identified constituency. In the latter days of the campaign, televised issue advocacy commercials did not seem directed at Clay's seat, but rather at the neighboring district and the seat held by the Democratic House Minority Leader Richard A. Gephardt, also a holder of a safe seat.

Soulade, the Republican candidate, conducted few, if any, district campaign events. The absence of campaign funds did not permit any television or radio advertising. He participated in several candidate forums with the other congressional candidates. These forums were usually sponsored by nonpartisan organizations, such as the League of Women Voters or the St. Louis Municipal League. The absence of regular contact and serious confrontation between Clay and his opponents reduced the visibility of this election.

Illyes, the Libertarian candidate, conducted even fewer campaign activities than Soulade. Illyes relied upon his website to explain Libertarian principles to major social problems such as abortion, social security, and education. His low profile campaign did not directly confront or address Clay on issues of the size of the federal government. But, he also participated in several candidate forums with the other congressional candidates.

CONCLUSION

Representatives respond to distinctive constituencies. Clay has taken his representational role seriously, and has been responsive to local and national constituencies and national issues. These major constituencies have included labor, women's groups, civil rights, and national and local black organizations. Part of Clay's electoral support and representational style has been a high level of constituency service. Clay entered his sixteenth term and has maintained a well-designed political organization within the district and the city of St. Louis.

Several interesting characteristics have preserved the First District as a safe seat for Clay. In the 1998 election, Clay discouraged serious challengers through careful district political organization and the advantages of name recognition, political experience, and legislative achievements. He did not find it necessary to aggressively raise substantial campaign funds. His challengers have usually lacked prior political experience or an electoral base. In 1998, Clay conducted a "silent campaign." There was hardly any press attention or televised or radio political advertisements. In an era of extensive political spending on media and related use of negative advertising, Clay maintains a safe seat with a low stimulus campaign that insures support from his core constituencies.

What does the future hold for this seat? Who would be likely to succeed Clay? Will the seat remain "safe"? The First District in Missouri has been drawn as a majority-minority district for a candidate who represents core Democrat constituencies—poor, minorities, lower middle class, labor, blacks, Jews. Is Clay's pattern of electoral support transferable to his son, "Lacy" Clay, currently a Missouri state senator? Will an open seat Democratic primary redefine the structure of the key constituencies in the district?

In this majority-minority district, there are greater divisions among St. Louis's black political leaders in the 1990s than there were in the 1960s and early 1970s. In the past, Clay could be an organizing and centralizing force uniting competing interests. Now, it is less certain whether there is a single unifying political leader in the St. Louis black community. The announcement of an open seat will attract many Democratic and Republican candidates with prior political experience. The St. Louis black electorate was split in the 1997 mayoralty primary between two black candidates, Clarence Harmon and Free-man Bosley, Jr. The Clay organization backed the Bosley candidacy. Harmon won the Democratic primary and the general election. In contrast, Lacy Clay has a political record as a Missouri state representative and a state senator. Moreover, he will have the support of his father's loyal political organization. This organizational strength may be sufficient to win the Democratic primary, and then win the general election in a strong Democratic district.

NOTES

Editors' Note: In May 1999, Representative Clay confirmed long-standing speculation that he would retire from Congress at the end of the current term. He promised to support, but not manage, the campaign of his son, William Lacy Clay, Jr., to succeed him.

1. Michael Barone and Grant Ujifusa, *The Almanac of American Politics 1998* (Washington, DC: National Journal, 1997).
2. Ibid.
3. Ibid.
4. Tim Poor, "Tailoring His Legacy," *St. Louis Post-Dispatch,* January 25, 1998, B4–7.
5. Ibid., B4.
6. Ibid.
7. Ibid., B5.
8. William H. Flanigan and Nancy H. Zingale, *Political Behavior of the American Electorate,* 9th ed. (Washington, DC: Congressional Quarterly, 1998), 35–37.
9. www.illyesforcongress.org.
10. Carl McCurley and Jeffrey J. Mondak, "Inspected by #1184063113: The Influence of Incumbents' Competence and Integrity in U.S. House Elections," *American Journal of Political Science* 39 (1995): 865.
11. Paul S. Herrnson, *Congressional Elections: Campaigning at Home and in Washington,* 2nd ed. (Washington, DC: Congressional Quarterly, 1998), 201.

Open Seats

4

★

Baldwin Defeats Musser
in Wisconsin's
Second District Race

Michelle Brophy-Baermann

From Superior to Sheboygan, from Kenosha to Green Bay, Wisconsinites are opinionated when it comes to the city that hosts their state capitol. To some, Madison—nestled on the twin lakes of Mendota and Monona—is the state's cultural mecca, a city bustling with ethnic restaurants, nightly entertainment, coffee houses, beautiful parks, and a nationally acclaimed farmers' market. To others, it's the home of the University of Wisconsin system's flagship campus, with its Badger football team and first-rate medical facilities. And then there are those who see Madison as something else altogether. "Zoo" and "Fantasy Island" are two of the more colorful terms non-Madisonians use to describe this city of 200,000. Whatever their opinion, the folks in Wisconsin are likely to agree that Madison is a lot more liberal than the rest of the state.

For most residents of this midwestern dairy state, best known for its Green Bay Packers and cheese, what happened in Wisconsin's Second Congressional District on November 3, 1998, isn't difficult to explain. The math is simple. Democratic Madison and its surrounding Dane County simply overpowered the Second District's rural and Republican counties, contributing 71 percent of the votes in the Second District. Democrats have the upper hand, so a Democratic candidate won the district's first open seat election in 42 years. It was just liberal local politics as usual. So what if the winner of the election wasn't so usual?

ONLY IN MADISON

In 1998, 150 years after Wisconsin became a state, Wisconsin voters would finally send a woman to represent them in Washington, D.C. But 36-year-old

Tammy Suzanne Green Baldwin is not just any woman, she is a lesbian, and her arrival at the nation's capital makes her the first openly gay legislator to ever be elected to Congress. The day after the election, citizens of Wisconsin's other eight districts could shrug their shoulders with an "only in Madison," but from the time she declared her candidacy more than a year earlier, political analysts had predicted Baldwin's homosexuality would be a liability. *Congressional Quarterly,* a leading information source for news about Capitol Hill, suggested the Republicans' best-case scenario for November would have Baldwin and a moderate Republican winning their respective primaries.[1] Referring to the September primaries, the National Republican Congressional Committee's (NRCC) communications director said it succinctly: "If [Baldwin] wins, it's fine with me."[2]

Baldwin's sexual orientation wasn't seen as the only impediment to a Democratic win in November. From the spring of 1997, when Baldwin announced her candidacy in the Democratic primary race, up until election day, some local pundits doubted her ability to recapture the seat from the legacy of the retiring, and highly popular, Republican incumbent Scott Klug. The Second District was different now, the editorialists and talk radio jockeys would argue. It had changed substantially from the glory days of progressive politics as practiced by one-time Progressive party presidential candidate Robert M. La Follette in early 1900s and liberal representative Robert Kastenmeier, whom Klug had ousted from office after 32 years. While Madison proper was still the same liberal bastion it had always been, more and more people were heading to the suburbs and rural countryside; these voters were increasingly conservative on economic issues and more likely to vote Republican. To the pundits, Klug was a perfect manifestation of how the Second District had changed. And they questioned whether a leftist, lesbian lawyer, and assemblywoman, whose pet campaign issue was the single-payer system of health care,[3] could hold her own against a moderate successor to the popular Klug.

Baldwin's sexuality and changing district demographics were but two reasons the Second District race received attention not just at the local but at the national level as well. After all, this was an open seat race. And not just any open seat race, but one in which congressional Democrats had a chance to pick up a seat. Historically, the party of the president loses seats in off-year elections, so any race where there was a possible gain for the Democrats was bound to garner national attention. Election prognosticators in Washington labeled the Baldwin-Musser race a toss-up and "one to watch."[4]

I'LL TAKE YOU THERE

Baldwin launched her campaign with the snappy, popular tune, "I'll Take You There." To outside observers, it was questionable whether she could take anyone anywhere. In May, four months before September's primary elections, polls showed that Baldwin was less known than both of her opponents. In June, she became the target of both local and national anti-homosexual campaigns. In

Copyright 1998 by Mike Konopacki in the *Capital Times.* Reprinted by permission.

September, Republicans would get their wish; when their primaries were over, not only had a moderate Republican been nominated, but a woman at that. Yet, when the polls closed on election day, Baldwin had fulfilled the promise of her campaign song. How did she manage to take herself and her followers all the way to Washington?

The well-worn maxim, "all politics is local," goes a long way in explaining Baldwin's success at the polls. Without a doubt, Baldwin's progressive community—her "home-town help"—played a major role in getting her elected. Progressivism, so deeply rooted in Wisconsin, has always revolved around citizen involvement in politics. Volunteerism and high turnout are consequences of progressive politics. In both the primary and general elections, an immense and devoted contingent of volunteers and an unexpectedly large number of voters helped propel Baldwin to victory. But local political forces only partially explain what happened in November.

The largesse of "out-of-town" individuals and groups was another crucial factor in the election outcome. Baldwin's ability to raise significantly more cash than her primary and general election opponents, much of this from places as far away as San Francisco and Washington, D.C., gave her an enormous leg up when it came to advertising herself to the district. On election day, bolstered by both local and national political forces, Baldwin had even more reason to be optimistic. She had two things going for her that her opponent did not: experience as a state legislator and, of course, a Democratic-leaning district.

WISCONSIN'S SECOND DISTRICT

Located at the southernmost part of the state, Wisconsin's Second District is dominated by Madison, the only city in North America built on an isthmus, and surrounding Dane County. In 1998, Madison's healthy economy, housing market, schools, and quality of life, coupled with low levels of crime and pollution, led *Money* magazine to rank it the most livable mid-sized city in the Midwest.[5] Dane County's large, white-collar workforce, and sound economy owe a lot to the state government, including the university, and large private employers such as Oscar Mayer, American Family Insurance, Famous Footwear, and Rayovac. Like that of the rest of the district and state, Dane County's population is largely homogenous and middle class.[6]

Residents in the rest of the Second District had been used to playing second fiddle to Dane County and Madison, its crown jewel. This was especially true at election time. Only 30 percent of the district's votes come from the Second District's other seven, predominantly Republican, rural counties. Here, agriculture and tourism had been the main industries. Signs along the various highways from Madison beckon drivers to such area attractions as the "Midwest's Favorite Vacation Spot" in Wisconsin Dells, "Little Switzerland, USA" and the New Glarus Brewing Company in New Glarus, Frank Lloyd Wright's Taliesen in Spring Green, and mail order giant Lands' End in Dodgeville.

Between Madison's downtown isthmus wards and those in rural Dodge, Columbia, Sauk, Richland, Iowa, Lafayette, and Green Counties, lie the wards of Madison's sprawling suburbs. Suburban Dane County is found not only in the middle of the city and the countryside, but also in the middle of a major political battle between Democrats and Republicans. It is a battle the Republicans appeared to be winning. In just ten years, between 1986 and 1996, the Democratic-leaning towns of Fitchburg, Stoughton, Monona, Verona, Middleton, and Waunakee became Republican-leaning towns. And between Republican Scott Klug's first election in 1990 and his last in 1996, almost every Dane County community became more Republican.[7]

SCOTT KLUG: SIGN OF
THE FUTURE OR FLUKE?

For both parties, the 1998 race was more than an election—it was a test. Was Scott Klug's stunning 1990 defeat of long-time Democratic incumbent Bob Kastenmeier a sign of creeping conservatism in the Second District, or just an anomaly? Not surprisingly, Republicans tended to view Klug's victory and three subsequent reelections as a sign that Wisconsin's Second District had become more moderate, and even Republican. His large wins in 1990 (63 percent to 37 percent), 1994 (69 percent to 29 percent), and 1996 (57 percent to 41 percent) supported this claim. Party strategists also noted that the Republican governor, Tommy Thompson, fared very well in Dane County in 1990. Four years later, Thompson even took liberal Madison.

To the Democratic party, Klug was a fluke. His 1990 upset wasn't so shocking considering who he was. A news anchor with the local ABC-TV affiliate for two years, Klug had a degree of visibility, trustworthiness, and name recognition that made him a high-quality challenger to Kastenmeier. And in an election year noted for its anti-incumbent mood, Kastenmeier was vulnerable. Klug capitalized on this vulnerability by using the number 32—complete with a circle around it and a line drawn through it—as his campaign logo. Though he narrowly lost Dane County in 1990, it was an event he would never repeat.

Of course, Democrats had an explanation for how Klug managed to hold on to the district that gave Bill Clinton 50 percent and 55 percent of the vote in 1992 and 1996, respectively. With the exception of his 1996 challenger, a liberal icon and former mayor of Madison, Klug's challengers were relatively unknown, uninspiring, and underfunded. Why would voters take a risk on questionable challengers when their incumbent had a proven track record?

A pro-choice, pocket-book protector, who wasn't afraid to thumb his nose at his party on occasion, Klug's voting record was moderate enough to keep him in office. Even Madison's liberal newspaper, the *Capital Times,* endorsed him in 1994. In a not-so-subtle message to any Republican who hoped to succeed him in 1998, the paper frequently lauded his independence from the party and his concern for the district. Headlines like "Klug shows GOP a better way," "Klug shines, Neumann dims," and "'Watchdog' group rates Klug, Kohl [Democratic Sen. Herb Kohl] and Feingold [Democratic Sen. Russ Feingold] as 'taxpayer heroes,'" drew attention to his "acceptable" congressional record. Editorialists described his votes against the party on such issues as campaign finance,[8] the ban on assault weapons, abortion restrictions, and funding for the National Endowment of the Arts.[9]

Editorial writers weren't the only people convinced of Klug's moderation. In 1996, the liberal interest group Americans for Democratic Action (ADA) calculated that he voted "the right" way on key issues 40 percent of the time. That same year, the *National Journal* rated his voting record more liberal than conservative in each of three policy areas: economic, social, and foreign.[10]

Klug's tenure showed that Republicans *could* be successful in "the heartland's progressive hotbed."[11] But his eight-year congressional record suggested that not just any ordinary, run-of-the-mill Republican would do. When, in February of 1997, Klug announced his decision to retire at the end of the 105th Congress, both parties began gearing up for the showdown.

SETTING THE STAGE:
THE PRIMARY ELECTIONS

Klug's announcement of his intention to abandon Congress for private business set off a flurry of activity in the Second District. Within weeks, the local media were talking about possible Republican and Democratic candidates for the primaries more than a year away. When September 8, 1998, arrived, voters from each party had to look back at a campaign season filled with unity pledges, countless debates, nasty bickering, and goofy advertisements. When the day was over, Republicans and Democrats alike had chosen their party's most liberal candidate. And, with their selection of women, they guaranteed history would be made in Wisconsin.

THE REPUBLICANS

Where else but Madison would the Republican field of primary hopefuls be more diverse than the opposition's? Not one but two women candidates and an African-American man declared their intention to be the Republican nominee. Even more eclectic were the occupational backgrounds of the six Republicans: a beer distributor, a chiropractor, a professor, a firefighter/pastor, a former congressional aide, and Wisconsin's former insurance commissioner.[12]

What these six candidates had in common was their inexperience. None had held elected office before, and only two had any real experience with politics. Proud to be politically "green," four of the six also vied to present themselves as the most Klug-like and the most liked by Klug. Only two Republicans were willing to stand to the right and admit to their political conservatism. One issue that set these two candidates apart from the others was abortion, and this was an issue that would come to play an important role in both the primary and the general election.

The Candidates

Of all the Republican hopefuls, independent management consultant, Nick Fuhrman, 35, had the most political experience. A former congressional staffer and one-time Dane County Republican party chair, his activism in party politics dated back to the early 1980s and his days as chair of the Wisconsin College Republicans at the University of Wisconsin. The first Republican to declare his intention to run for Congress in June, Fuhrman didn't formally declare his candidacy until July 19, five days after the primary filing, reasoning that no one would really be paying attention until then. Considered by many the most issue-oriented and knowledgeable of the candidates, Fuhrman's campaign stressed his ability to "hit the ground running" come January 1999.

Unfortunately for Fuhrman, however, his campaign never seemed to take off. His status as the lone pro-life conservative in the bunch was challenged when the controversial and attention-grabbing Ron Greer entered the fray in June. The $118,000 he raised put him in fourth place overall in fundraising among the Republican candidates, but Fuhrman came in only after Greer in individual contributions. He was able to cajole more than three-quarters of his funds from friends, family, supporters, and such.[13] Fuhrman spent his limited funds carefully by hiring three paid staff members and a media consulting firm to spread his anti-government, anti-tax, and pro-family message. His one television advertisement, which aired just a little over a week before the primary, featured his wife, Elina. An immigrant from the former Soviet Union, her message was compelling: "He understands freedom."

Beer distributor Don Carrig's election campaign shows how money doesn't always determine the outcome of an election. On declaring his candidacy for the Republican nomination in July, Carrig, 54, went on to spend nearly a half million dollars. The *Capital Times* labeled the businessman a "vanity candidate" for basically funding his own campaign. Indeed, almost 78 percent of his war chest came from his own wallet.[14] With this money, he hired a local campaign manager, paid a staff of five, and found a media consulting firm, which he put to good use. A good deal of Carrig's campaign funds went to advertising himself to the district. Though he put 39,000 miles on his Chevy S-10 pickup driving around the district to 775 public appearances, Carrig was best known for his quirky ads.[15] The first candidate to launch a television advertising campaign, Carrig bought $15,000 worth of television ads in early April, two months before the conventional campaign kick-off in June and three months before the July filing deadline. Carrig quickly jumped on the Klug bandwagon using the congressman's image and quote: "If cutting taxes is important to you, nobody will work harder than Don Carrig," said a short television spot.

In stark contrast to beer kingpin Carrig, John Sharpless, Jr., didn't have a lot of money to spend. Nor did he have much of an organization. But Sharpless, 53, an award-winning history professor, had plenty to say about politics. The only problem was, with just under $60,000,[16] he couldn't afford much in the way of self-promotion. The "poorest" of all the Republicans, Sharpless did manage to hire a media consulting firm and pay two staffers. He even fired off his first 15-second spot within days of the filing deadline, in which Klug's quote "probably our most gifted candidate" was featured prominently. But Sharpless' limited resources meant he had to rely primarily on radio, personal appearances, door-to-door campaigning, and his website to advertise his moderate, pro-choice, pro-labor, pro-environment message.

Months before her December 19, 1997, resignation from the state insurance department, local analysts had expected Jo Musser's candidacy. Her official declaration in early January added another social moderate to the list of party hopefuls. A one-time nurse and former CEO of Employers Health Care Alliance, Musser, 47, was pro-choice and socially liberal. Driving around the district with her puppy, Cleopatra, in tow, Musser's campaign theme was similar to, if perhaps more detailed than, those of her opponents. She emphasized smaller government, fewer taxes, and family values. And, like most of her opponents, Musser stressed her Klug quotient whenever she got the chance. Her 30-second spots highlighted Klug's praise of Musser as "the quickest study on the issues."[17] Though heavily self-supported, Musser received more political action committee (PAC) money than any of her opponents. The $21,000 she filed with the Federal Election Commission (FEC) came mostly from insurance industry PACs.[18] Musser used this money to help hire the usual: a campaign manager, media consultants, and (three) staffers. Like underfunded Sharpless, she used the Internet to reach prospective voters. Her webpage offered photos, press releases, contact information, and dizzying graphics. But, like Carrig, Musser had some money to spend on television ads. According to one local reporter, it was Musser's use of "well-timed" ads in early August that made her the "apparent GOP frontrunner."[19]

Much like Musser, the fifth Republican to enter the race was moderate, from the field of health care, largely self-financed, and a woman. But unlike Musser, chiropractor Meredith Bakke, 52, had no political or policymaking experience. Focusing on the issues of tax reform, health care, social security, and character, she was yet another candidate hoping to paint herself as Klug-like. Evidently, Klug had no problem with this strategy. When he couldn't attend one of her fundraisers, he sent a letter instead. Starting with a base of 6,000 patients, Bakke's campaign had to convince non-patients to vote for her. To do this, she needed money. Luckily, she had some in the bank. She funded almost 60 percent of the nearly $200,000 she spent on her quest for the party's nomination.[20] She was able to hire a campaign staff of five, a media consultant, and a campaign manager whose most recent experience just happened to be getting Klug reelected in 1994. Late to turn to television, Bakke was, nonetheless, one of the first candidates to use paid advertising, in this case, on billboards. Bakke also used a personal webpage to reach "connected" voters.

The Republican party was going smoothly until 42-year-old fireman and pastor Ron Greer decided to crash it. When the conservative Greer announced his candidacy in late June, the local press finally had something to fill all those pages. Actually, Greer was no stranger to the paper readers in Madison, having already commandeered the headlines for nearly two years as a result of an ongoing legal battle with the city. The issue? Homosexuality.

Having begun his campaign with such notoriety, Greer was the proverbial lightning rod that attracted bolts of all types. The local media couldn't get enough of him. Even the national media took note of the fearless firefighter. In July, ABC ran a story about his battle with the city on "The World News with Peter Jennings." He went on to attack Democratic hopeful Baldwin's stances on gay marriage, "partial-birth" abortion, affirmative action, taxes, and welfare.[21] Over the course of the campaign, Greer was endorsed by a variety of prominent conservative Christians, including James Dobson of the Focus on the Family, Gary Bauer of the Campaign for Working Families, Green Bay Packers' defensive lineman Reggie White, and 1996 Republican presidential candidate Alan Keyes. Greer was one candidate who didn't need television to get his name known or his message across. Instead, he focused his efforts on radio spots during religious broadcasts, campaign appearances at local church fellowship groups, and bumper stickers with slogans like: "Annoy the Liberals in Madison: Vote for Ron Greer" and "I'm Here, I'm for Greer, Get Used to It!"[22] In the final weeks of the primary election, some political analysts seemed to heed the pastor's message and suggest that Greer just might be able to pull off a coup.

The Race

Greer's entry into the race was a godsend for those who had dreaded a sleepy primary season full of compassionate moderates and their cordial debates. The remaining five candidates didn't see his campaign in the same light. Suddenly, they had an opponent who seemed to dominate almost all campaign coverage. The best the remaining Republicans could do was to try to fight back and hopefully wrestle a few seconds of the limelight from the former firefighter.

Two candidates were able to do this, at least momentarily, by their use of the "pledge device." Fuhrman, the one conservative who had hoped to target like-minded Republicans, attacked Greer for using Baldwin to try "to scare old ladies into cracking open their checkbooks"[23] and for claiming that he (Greer) was the only 100 percent pro-life candidate. Fuhrman then encouraged his fellow candidates to sign a party "unity" pledge. Carrig took Fuhrman's idea a step further and exhorted his opponents to sign a pledge of tolerance. Greer was the only Republican not to sign.

For one prominent Republican, "unity pledges" by the candidates weren't enough to weaken Greer. Klug turned his attention to Republican voters and demanded they be united in voting against the former fireman. A win for Greer in September would be a loss for the Republican party come November, he warned. "If it's a fight over the agenda of James Dobson, its not enough to win," said Klug. "We're not North Carolina or Louisiana. It's hard to believe that sells around here."[24]

Not until the remaining weeks of the campaign did other candidates join Greer on center stage. In mid-August, Greer dragged Musser into the limelight, accusing her of funding telephone polls aimed at smearing him. "Push polling," as this practice is called, involves pollsters asking respondents biased or leading questions. Greer's campaign manager, Mike Maxwell, alleged that potential voters were asked if they would vote for Greer knowing that he had: served time in a military prison for assaulting an officer, been fired from his job as firefighter for distributing anti-gay pamphlets, received support from prominent religious right leaders. Maxwell felt certain, based on conversations with people who claimed to have taken part in the poll, that Musser's campaign was behind the smear attempt. Musser's campaign manager confirmed that the campaign was doing polling, but denied using push polling against Greer.[25]

Heading into September, Musser continued to receive the bulk of the press attention. With just five days left in the race, her dispute with the Washington, D.C., group, Americans for Tax Reform (ATR), grabbed the headlines. In an independent "issue advocacy" radio spot, the group blasted Musser for her unwillingness to sign its anti-tax pledge. Musser denounced the ad, arguing that she had never seen the pledge and that she believed she could sign it if she saw it. ATR's spokesman countered that Musser had received the pledge "on several occasions."[26]

An even larger issue for Musser was her tussle with Carrig over abortion. Having changed his mind on the so-called partial birth abortion after talking to voters and watching a video on the procedure, Carrig mailed out thousands of postcards attacking Musser for her stance. "President Clinton supports partial birth abortion. So does Jo Musser," read the bold white letters on a black background. In response, Musser accused Carrig of lying and misrepresenting her position. Although she opposed this particular procedure, she argued that

**Table 4.1 Money and the Vote
for Republican Primary Candidates,
Wisconsin's Second Congressional District, 1998**

Candidate	Funds Raised ($)	Funds Spent ($)	Vote Received (%)
Jo Musser	249,400	231,241	10,269 (21)
Ron Greer	114,535	66,218	9,874 (20)
John Sharpless	55,310	46,778	8,448 (18)
Don Carrig	490,131	440,965	8,337 (17)
Nick Fuhrman	118,606	107,249	6,731 (14)
Meredith Bakke	207,801	195,778	4,829 (10)

SOURCES: Fundraising data are taken from the Center for Responsive Politics' reports of August 19, 1998. Vote totals taken from the *Capital Times,* September 8, 1998.

Congress's ban, as passed by the Republican-led Congress, was constitutionally unsound and didn't go far enough to protect the lives of mothers. Then, in her shoot-from-the-hip style, she added, "that's why we shouldn't be sending a beer distributor to vote on complex laws."

Not surprisingly, Musser's "beer distributor" comment provoked a response by the mild-mannered Carrig. Within days, he and a group of supporters, including Brandon Scholz, Klug's chief of staff, complained. "There's no place for that. What she said was stupid," he said. But, despite Carrig's demand for an apology, Musser refused, continuing to attack Carrig for changing his mind on "partial birth" abortion for political gain.[27] With just days to go before the election, Musser, Carrig, and the rest of the Republican gang would have to wait and see what impact, if any, all this attention would have on the district's voters.[28]

In the End

More than a year and a half after Klug announced his intention to vacate his seat, he and the local Republican party got their wish, or at least part of it. In the early morning hours of September 9, moderate Musser declared victory. But nothing ever comes easy. Behind by fewer than 400 votes, Greer vowed he'd demand a recount. Irritated by Greer's tactics, Klug abruptly canceled the "Unity Breakfast" he had planned, just an hour before it was supposed to begin at the downtown Howard Johnson's. When it became apparent Musser's vote margin was large enough that he, and not the state, would have to foot the recount bill, Greer eventually gave up on the idea. Instead, he steadfastly refused to support a pro-choice candidate, and contemplated running as a write-in candidate. Unfortunately for Musser, Greer's actions meant the general election season would start with a disunited Republican party. See table 4.1 for the fundraising and vote totals for the Republican primary candidates.

THE DEMOCRATS

In stark contrast to the Republican field of candidates, the Democratic group seemed a bit bland and somewhat civil. Three of the four were strategic politicians—high quality candidates who had waited for an opportune moment (an open seat) to run for Congress. Having served as elected officials, they already knew a bit about running a campaign and raising money for campaign staff, advertisements, polling, and getting out the vote. Only one Democrat was not a professional—he ran a protest campaign with no resources other than what he could scrape up. All four candidates also ran relatively friendly, issue-filled campaigns. This is not to say they never quibbled; indeed, their biggest sticking point had to do with fundraising. But when September 8 finally came and went, the three losers stood solidly behind the winner. Theirs was a united Democratic front.

The Candidates

One month after Klug announced his impending retirement from government, Dane County Executive Rick Phelps followed his lead. Giving up his position as the head of county government after three terms, Phelps, 51, was toying with the idea of a congressional run. From the beginning, Phelps seemed well-situated to become the Democratic nominee for the Second District seat. High name recognition and political connections helped foster this impression. His top contributors included the National Air Traffic Controllers Association, the New Democrat Network, and County Executives of America. By the end of the season, 91 percent of the nearly $500,000 he raised had come from individuals.[29] The second-best fundraiser of all ten candidates, Phelps could foot the bill for a Washington-based media firm and six campaign staffers. He also hired a professional campaign manager whose most recent race was that of U.S. Senator Max Baucus (D-MT).

Analysts initially criticized Phelps's advertising campaign with its cartoon bubbles and focus on his family as too simplistic. In the waning weeks of the season, however, his 30-second "soccer dad" ads were replaced by more conventional ads, including one showing him hanging out with senior citizens.[30] Another spot, called "Equal," tackled the same issue that rival Baldwin was stressing in her campaign, that of equal pay. But Phelps received the most attention for an ad he was not in. Local pundits praised Phelps's commercial featuring Dane County Executive Kathleen Falk. In the ad, Falk admitted to liking all three major Democratic contenders but argued Phelps was the most qualified for Congress. Countywide political experience and local political connections were the main selling points of Phelps's campaign, so when former representative and liberal icon, Kastenmeier, threw his weight behind Phelps, it was a big deal. This endorsement only furthered the notion that Phelps was the candidate to beat.

Tammy Suzanne Green Baldwin, 36, was born and reared in Madison. Labeled a "conscientious policy wonk"[31] for her State Assembly work on such issues as "drive through deliveries,"[32] "partial birth" abortions, electronic filing for campaign contributions, and same-sex marriage, Baldwin was even better known by her other moniker—"Wisconsin's only lesbian legislator." No reporter could write her name without using the label somewhere in the story. As she embarked on her campaign for the Democratic nomination, Baldwin had to know her sexuality would be up for public discussion. Baldwin, however, refused to make it an issue. Her campaign kept its focus on the issues *she* felt were important: health care, education, social security, and drug policy. But for all her efforts to broaden her message and be seen as more than just the "openly lesbian candidate," her sexuality played a crucial role in her campaign. As much as the issue galvanized Christian conservatives, it had the same effect on gay rights activists and like-minded groups. Though interest groups like the Gay and Lesbian Victory Fund, the Human Rights Campaign, the National Organization for Women (NOW), and EMILY's List (Early Money Is Like Yeast) played a prominent role in Baldwin's campaign, 93 percent of her final receipts came from individual contributors.[33]

By September, Baldwin had raised nearly $700,000, and much of that went into short television spots. Analysts called her early ads on comparable worth, health care, and care for senior citizens "flat" but "interesting" for their appeal to "family values."[34] As election day neared, Baldwin's campaign shifted gears and focused on young people. One ad featured a college-age woman who urged viewers to make Baldwin Wisconsin's first congresswoman. This and other ads were strategically placed around shows like Fox's "Ally McBeal" and daytime soap operas, programming that does well with the 18–24 age group. Despite her vast resources, Baldwin didn't ignore the cheaper ways to reach prospective voters. Using her website, e-mail distribution lists, and a large contingent of youthful volunteers, the candidate was resolved to reach out to voters. She was determined to prove that she could win the support of Democratic moderates. And she was driven to make history.

When state senator and part-time realtor Joe Wineke entered the Democratic race in early spring, he was well-known around the district and especially in the suburbs and more rural areas. Like his constituents, Wineke was a more traditional, even conservative, Democrat. This set him apart from his rivals. However, political philosophy wasn't all that separated Wineke from his primary opponents. Campaign financing did as well. Wineke raised more PAC money than any other candidate in either party (nearly 27 percent of all his contributions came from PACs). Despite his ability to play to the PACs, by late August, Wineke had raised less than half as much as Baldwin and a couple of hundred thousand less than Phelps. Having raised more than $315,000 was no drop in the bucket, but it meant that the candidate could not afford to run the same type of campaign as his opponents.[35] To counter the spending imbalance, Wineke concentrated his efforts on going door-to-door and shaking hands. At one point in August, he estimated that he had put 45,000 miles on his car and had knocked on 9,000 doors. His staff had knocked on another 16,000. His heavy reliance on door-to-door campaigning did not mean that Wineke ran an amateur campaign. Like his major opponents, he too hired a professional cam-

paign manager and staff. Nor did Wineke sit out on the air wars. His Washing-
ton-based media firm made humorous commercials that showed him out-and-
about, discussing the issues with voters on their doorsteps. For some, a Wineke
win in the primaries would improve the Democrats' chances of winning back
the seat in November.[36] He was the ideal candidate. Not too liberal. Not a lesbian. Not a Friend of Bill. Just a hometown guy.

A self-described househusband and occasional freelance writer, Patrick
O'Brien, 35, was a virtual nonentity in the Democratic race. It's not that he
was totally without political experience. After all, just two years earlier he had
come in second, taking 21 percent of the vote, in the Democratic congressional
primary. Next to Republican candidates like Bakke and Carrig, O'Brien was
politically experienced. But he was no vanity candidate. The last Democrat to
enter the race, O'Brien raised no funds and eschewed contributions of any
kind. Instead, O'Brien took to the streets, knocking on doors and handing out
his homemade campaign literature. Spending all of about $30 (on ink car-
tridges and gas for the car) O'Brien was described by the *Capital Times* as "Don
Quixote rid(ing) a rusty Cavalier."[37] He drove that Chevy across the district,
nobly battling the campaign financing system and hoping to expand the
Democratic base of voters. But, for the most part, his message fell on deaf ears.
The local media didn't really ignore O'Brien, but neither did they take him
seriously. The papers dutifully profiled him, as they did all the candidates, and
usually mentioned his name in articles about the primary race. But he was
always "the other candidate," never in the headlines, never the newsworthy
candidate.[38]

The Race

The *Capital Times* was right, the race did come down to the three major contenders. And, at least for a while, it looked as though Phelps, Baldwin, and
Wineke might wage a friendly battle. But, it didn't take long for cracks in the
camaraderie to surface. As is true with so many relationships, money was the
main cause in the Democratic dissension.

It all began in late September 1997. Phelps initiated the flak when he
proposed a three-way, voluntary agreement on campaign spending. This agreement would ban all soft money and would limit PAC and out-of-state contributions to 25 percent of total receipts. Likening his proposal to the McCain-
Feingold campaign finance reform bill winding its way through the Senate,[39]
Phelps argued, "I think the goal should be to finance our campaigns through
the families in our community. . . . I'm trying to state a reasonable position."[40]

Reasonable as it seemed, Phelps's proposal appeared to be targeted at his
opponents. Baldwin was already receiving significant contributions from out-
of-state individuals, while Wineke was doing well with PACs. Wineke quickly
lashed out at Phelps: "I find it ironic that the person who was bragging (in July)
about raising $100,000 now wants to limit spending," he said. "Mr. Phelps can't
have it both ways." Wineke upped the ante, challenging his opponents to agree
to a primary spending cap of $250,000.[41]

Just a few months later, Wineke challenged Baldwin and Phelps again. This time he wanted them to agree to run a clean campaign. "[W]e pledge to run a clean campaign on *our own records* of achievement and stands on the issues," read part of the proposal. The other two candidates consented to the idea, but their campaign managers worried such a pledge might be seen as forbidding discussion about their opponents' records. Baldwin's campaign manager made this clear, "If a comparison becomes necessary, we're proud to compare Tammy's record." Wineke maintained that he wasn't trying to stifle debate. Rather, the main target of his pledge was the candidates' paid advertisements. "We're heading toward the point where India and Pakistan are," he warned. "It becomes mutually assured destruction."[42]

Back at the Phelps campaign, the candidate couldn't let his own campaign spending pledge go. In a locally televised debate nearly ten months after he had first proposed the spending agreement, Phelps criticized Baldwin for not signing his campaign spending pledge. Baldwin, who had raised over $300,000 at this point, countered by saying she was forced to raise more money to defend herself against Republican Greer's attacks.[43] As the season heated up, Phelps would continue to lead the way in charges against his opponents.

Phelps enjoyed a narrow lead in the polls when Baldwin aired her first television spot in early August. His campaign quickly attacked the ad on health care because it didn't explicitly discuss her support of the single-payer system. The implicit message, according to Phelps, was that Baldwin had moderated her stance on health care because voters didn't like the single-payer system. Phelps's suggestion that Baldwin was somehow turning to the center to win votes didn't hold much water. Not only did she continue to advocate universal health care, but also she took some less-than-moderate foreign policy stands at an August debate at the State Historical Society.

During this basically friendly foreign policy forum in mid-August, each candidate stressed different issues. Wineke focused on trade; Phelps, the global economy; O'Brien went with military spending. One *Capital Times* writer claimed that O'Brien's performance stood out the most because he came across so well. Another suggested that Phelps had "won" the debate by "scor(ing) most regularly."[44] But it was Baldwin who surprised many when she told of her desire to end the war on drugs. Baldwin stated that she had added her signature to a letter to the United Nations Secretary General. This letter, which was also signed by business, political, and academic leaders from around the world, requested an international discussion on "whether the way we have been conducting the war on drugs has been doing more harm than good."[45]

At the same time Phelps was accusing Baldwin of moving to the center to gain votes, his campaign battled her on a second front. Few political analysts were surprised when he started focusing on Baldwin's out-of-state campaign contributions. In fact, the local media themselves ran stories on the analysis of campaign reports done by Wisconsin's chapter of Common Cause. This "good government" group noted that 56 percent of Baldwin's $514,000 in receipts from individuals had come from out of state, while 20 percent of Phelps's and only 2 percent of Wineke's funds originated outside Wisconsin.[46]

All three campaigns tried to put a good "spin" on the Common Cause figures, with Baldwin's campaign manager stating that much of her out-of-state money came from women who were excited about helping send the first Wisconsin woman to Washington. A spokeswoman for Phelps mentioned he was the only candidate abiding by the spirit of McCain-Feingold and that the interest group's analysis favored him. For his part, Wineke could just point to the numbers. One analyst, former campaign manager for one-time presidential candidate Gary Hart, suggested that Wineke's near-total reliance on Wisconsin contributions might make the difference in a tight three-way race. The spokesperson for Wisconsin's Common Cause lent credence to that idea when he said that Madison-area voters were much more concerned than others about the influence of money on politics.[47] *Capital Times* editorial page writer John Nichols offered a slightly different take on the issue of fundraising. Criticizing candidates who would use analyses of contribution patterns as a way to attack their rivals, Nichols wrote:

> None of the major candidates brings so clean a bill of financial health to the process that voters will necessarily take the charges and counter-charges seriously. And as the television ads that are the dark spawn of all this fund-raising turn into a cacophony, voters may well decide that campaign money (and what it buys) is evil no matter what the source.[48]

While much of the focus in the last month of the race was on out-of-state contributions, another out-of-state phenomenon took place in the Second District. Within two weeks, celebrities and prominent people alighted in Madison to stump for their favorite Democrat. Phelps's campaign first welcomed singer Judy Collins, who performed a mini-concert at a $100-a-plate fundraiser in the palatial home of a supporter. Days later, U.S. Representative Danny Davis, a Chicago Democrat from one of America's poorest congressional districts, accompanied Phelps as he campaigned in South Madison. The two had met a year before when they both sat on a panel on welfare reform. Davis explained his support of the former county executive in terms of his experience in county politics, adding that "county government is often the government of last resort . . . for those who need the intervention of government in their lives."[49] A few days after the Davis visit, another prominent politico arrived in Madison, this time on behalf of Baldwin. Candace Gingrich, the openly gay half-sister of the Speaker of the House Newt Gingrich who had become famous for her attacks on his policies, had a simple message for Madison voters. "I met Tammy then (1995) and I was so impressed with her," Gingrich said. "It's not just that she's sincere and deeply committed, she's also courageous enough to address difficult issues."[50]

At the same time the "celebrity stumpers" were doing their thing, Phelps fired off one last salvo. This time, he sent out two mailers accusing his rivals of having raised taxes on Social Security and pension benefits while in the state legislature. This attack hadn't come without warning. About a week earlier Wineke's campaign manager reported rumors that the Phelps's campaign was testing negative messages about his opponents. But Phelps's campaign denied the rumor and the *Capital Times* noted that Wineke had accused Phelps of the same thing ten years earlier, when the two opposed each other for the office of Dane County Executive.[51]

Phelps's last minute mailings came within a week of the signing of a "unity" pledge by all three candidates. Both Baldwin and Wineke fought back, in different ways. Baldwin called the Phelps mailing "misleading," while Wineke was a bit more animated. "This is a desperate act of a desperate campaign," he said. "I think Mr. Phelps should be embarrassed, should be ashamed, and I hope the voters remember who started the negative campaigning."[52]

Entering the last days of the race, the local pundits were having a tough time deciding what effect all the money and advertising and negative campaigning might have on the final outcome. Phrases like "neck and neck," "no clear front runner," and "three way dead heat" dotted the newspapers. Who would emerge victorious, nobody knew. But as one respected progressive said of the candidates, "There is no lemon among the four of them."[53]

In the End

I never had an interest in politics before this campaign. But I just realized that Tammy's campaign was different. Young people were welcome. These adults with all this experience, people like Paul (Devlin, campaign manager), treated me with more respect than a lot of my peers and teachers do. They made it obvious from the start that young people were going to be a part of this campaign. And when the votes were counted downtown, it was obvious that they responded.

—A 16-year-old Baldwin campaign volunteer[54]

Noting the long lines of young people in "Students for Baldwin" T-shirts who stood waiting to vote, John Nichols, the *Capital Times* editorial page writer, attributed Baldwin's victory to a "youthquake." She had beat Phelps, who came in second, by margins of over 1,000 votes in each district with heavy student populations. On September 8, high student turnout was, no doubt, crucial to her victory. But how did Baldwin go from a less-known long shot to the Democratic nominee for Wisconsin's Second Congressional District?

In some perverse way, Greer and the religious right may have actually helped Baldwin win her party's nomination. Their attempts to raise money and activate voters by demonizing Baldwin and homosexuality helped Baldwin raise money and activate voters by groups who demonized them right back. Not only did Baldwin benefit from all of the advertisements and organization her healthy war chest could provide, the press's focus on Greer and anti-homosexual activism meant more time in the "free" media spotlight for her as well. Confounding the prognosticators who said she was too liberal, too much a feminist, and, of course, too lesbian, on September 8, Baldwin emerged victorious.

At the very same time Greer's demand for a recount was fracturing the Republicans, Baldwin's primary opponents were busy healing the wounds from the last weeks of the election. Wineke even managed to show up at her victory party at Fyfe's restaurant, declaring her "the next Democratic congressman from this district."[55] Just a day after Klug canceled the Republicans' Unity Breakfast, Phelps stood behind Baldwin at the Verona Senior Citizens Center and said, "She'll do an outstanding job in Congress. I want to make it clear that I'm going to do whatever I can to get her elected in November."[56]

The candidates weren't the only ones changing their tune about Baldwin. Suddenly, the same pundits who had called her "managed" and her campaign "tepid" and "cautious" proclaimed that she embodied "a new politics of expanded dialogue and empowerment." Said a staff editorialist for the *Capital Times:*

> Whether she faces Musser or Greer, Baldwin should not be underestimated. She has broken through a wall of apathy and disenchantment that for too long has weakened the Democratic Party in this region. If she continues to draw young people, working women, and other "left out" citizens into the electoral process, she will not merely be a formidable contender, she will redefine Wisconsin politics in much the same way that Feingold did.[57]

See table 4.2 for the fundraising and vote totals for the Democratic primary candidates.

THE MAIN EVENT:
THE GENERAL ELECTION

In some ways, the Second District's general election fight was anticlimatic. Republican Musser and Democrat Baldwin had just two short months to make their cases to the voters. The race itself would be a condensed version of the primary battles: lots of money, a few key issues, agreements, disagreements, negative advertisements, and celebrity endorsements. Just a week after the primary election, *Capital Times* columnist Rob Zaleski forecast a political yawner. Pining for the Baldwin-Greer match-up that would never be, he wrote:

> What this (the Baldwin-Musser race) means, I guess, is that we can expect a relatively clean campaign—one that's free of cheap shots and name calling, and, most important, actually focuses on the issues. . . . But I admit it. A part of me was rooting for the Ronnie-and-Tammy Show—largely for its entertainment value, but also because it would have been an intriguing commentary on where we're at today. I mean, think about it. Baldwin wants to save us from the HMOs. And Greer wants to save us from the homos. How much more '90s can you get?[58]

**Table 4.2 Money and the Vote
for Democratic Primary Candidates,
Wisconsin's Second Congressional District, 1998**

Candidate	Funds Raised (%)	Funds Spent (%)	Vote Received (%)
Tammy Baldwin	673, 914	560,775	24,226 (37)
Rick Phelps	536,750	345,666	22,713 (35)
Joe Wineke	315,792	269,409	17,446 (27)
Patrick O'Brien	0	0	1,036 (2)

SOURCES: Fundraising data are taken from the Center for Responsive Politics' reports of August 19, 1998. Vote totals taken from the *Capital Times*, September 8, 1998.

With a united Democratic party and key endorsements by Kastenmeier and the AFL–CIO just weeks into the race, Baldwin started the race in better shape than her opponent. It wasn't until the end of September that Greer called off his write-in campaign, after a trip to Washington to meet with national conservative leaders yielded fewer financial commitments than he had hoped. Though he declared that Baldwin's policy stands "amount to a direct assault on American culture," he refused to throw his weight behind Musser, citing her positions on such issues as abortion.[59]

Greer's departure left the two candidates alone to duke it out. Just as Zaleski had warned, Musser and Baldwin seemed off to a lame start. Had they been polar opposites, divisiveness would have come easily. But Musser and Baldwin were indistinguishable on some important issues. They were both pro-choice. They both opposed a constitutional amendment barring flag desecration. They both saw the need to protect Social Security. They both opposed a ban on gay marriages. And, at their first joint appearance, both candidates reacted in a similar way to the sexually explicit Starr report[60] released earlier in the day. On the Wisconsin Public Television's "Weekend" show, both Musser and Baldwin agreed that the House should hold an impeachment inquiry to investigate whether the president had perjured himself and obstructed justice. But it was also on this program that the major difference between the two candidates became clear. And this difference would set the tone for the rest of the race.

The issue was health care. Though there would be other issues, Musser's and Baldwin's opposing views on health care came to symbolize their opposing views on government. Since her primary race, Baldwin had advocated universal health care, the so-called single-payer plan, for all Americans. Not surprisingly, the former insurance commissioner had a different take on the issue. While Baldwin argued that no person should be left uncovered and that the current system's administrative costs were too high, Musser claimed her opponent's plan made the government a "two ton gorilla" in the marketplace, arguing that universal health care would mean more bureaucracy and less choice in doctors.

When the "Weekend" moderator asked her a provocative question, Musser couldn't have been more civil. But she made clear her philosophical disagreement with her rival. Mentioning that he had recently seen an NRCC publication saying that Musser was "perfectly positioned to defeat the radical, far-left campaign of Tammy Baldwin" the moderator asked, "Do you consider Ms. Baldwin a radical far-lefter?" To which Musser replied: "I do think that we differ greatly on our approach to achieving our goals. . . . I see a less intrusive government. I see a smaller government. I see lower taxes. . . . I want to see services, but I want to see them to be effectively provided for people." Later, Musser explained her view of government in more detail:

> I believe that there are services and a role for the government in peoples' lives. I think the government is doing a poor job at doing that effectively and efficiently. I would like to see us provide those services much, much better with less intrusion in our lives and less big buildings full of people who are stuck in their ways of doing things.

Baldwin saw things differently. Her response to Musser was to the point:

> I believe we live in a democracy and that the government *is* the people. And so, a criticism of what we can do when we work within government is a criticism of the people. I actually am very hopeful about what we can do as communities when we work together.[61]

During the next two months, she would return to this theme—that the race was a battle between hopefulness and cynicism—again and again.

For a while at least, the Baldwin-Musser debate seemed destined to take the higher ground. But then began the clash of the commercials. A month into the race both candidates were accusing each other of running misleading and untruthful ads. Musser was incensed over Baldwin's ads on health care that suggested she was "incompetent and uncaring," while Baldwin was upset when a Musser ad accused her of having voted, as a state legislator, against putting repeat sex offenders behind bars. Next, the Musser campaign watched as Baldwin's ads suggested she was a tool of the insurance industry, while Baldwin's crew saw a short spot with outgoing Representative Klug saying: "If you're thinking about voting for Tammy Baldwin this fall, one piece of advice—Hold onto your wallet."

The candidates had to fork over big bucks to smear their opponents, and that's what they raised. Between August 20 and September 30, Baldwin took in another $230,000 from individuals, PACs, and the Democratic party, including a check for $500 from Hollywood's Barbra Streisand, $10,000 from the National Association of Trial Lawyers, and $5,000 from the PACs of both House Minority Leader Richard Gephardt (D-MO) and Vice President Al Gore. Musser raised nearly $108,000 during that same period, much of that while fundraising in Washington D.C. with Governor Thompson and Representative Klug. Most of her PAC money came in chunks of $5,000 from the committees of top Republican House members like Speaker Newt Gingrich (R–GA),[62] Majority Leader Dick Armey (R–TX), Representative Bob Livingston (R–LA), and Representative John Boehner (R–OH). Five insurance industry PACs also contributed to her campaign during this period. Mid–October showed Musser loaned her own campaign $300,000, bringing her total spending to nearly $600,000. Baldwin's war chest had surpassed the $1 million mark by this point, and pundits predicted this race would eventually pass the $1.8 million record for Second District spending set two years earlier.[63]

The pundits were right. By election day, the two candidates had together raised nearly $2.4 million and spent more than $2.3 million. Baldwin out-raised and out-spent Musser nearly two to one. Both candidates' receipt patterns looked quite a bit like they had during the primaries, with approximately 78 percent of Baldwin's war chest coming from individuals, 22 percent from PACs, and just one-tenth of a percent coming from the candidate herself. Musser wasn't nearly as blessed with individual contributions. Just 30 percent of her funds came from individuals and 35 percent from PACs. Musser gave or loaned herself one-third of her total receipts.[64]

Out-of-state money had been a big issue for the Democrats in the primaries, but the candidates didn't stress it as much in the general election. Once again, Baldwin received slightly more money from out-of-staters than she did from Wisconsinites. Forty-seven percent of Baldwin's contributions were from Wisconsin residents, while 84 percent of Musser's money was home-grown. Again, Baldwin's top contributors were ideological groups like the Gay & Lesbian Victory Fund and Emily's List and their members, while Musser's biggest donors were businesses like American Medical Security Inc. and Northwestern Mutual Life and their employees.[65]

So much money. And so much of it poured into nasty, little 30-second spots. By the end of October, even the candidates had had enough. Said Musser, "I think we should get off TV entirely."[66] But even if Baldwin and Musser had pledged to run an attack-ad free, perfectly clean campaign, their goal would have been thwarted. Though both candidates *did* sign a pledge to support a legislative ban on soft money if elected, these very same candidates were the targets of the opposing party's "issue ads" paid for by . . . soft money.

"Soft money" is the largely unregulated money individuals and PACs contribute to political parties. While the purpose of soft money is ostensibly for education efforts and get-out-the-vote drives, increasingly it has been used for "issue advocacy." Both the national and state parties create and run ads that look a lot like campaign commercials. Unlike regular political ads, the issue ads don't explicitly ask viewers to vote for or against a candidate. Instead, they "educate" voters about a particular issue or "problem," mentioning the name of the candidate they support or oppose. These ads usually end with a phone number for that candidate, so voters can "call" and "inform" the candidate.

In the 1998 elections, the NRCC actually had a name for its nationwide campaign to hurt Democrats and help Republicans, known as "Operation Breakout." Baldwin was the target of NRCC ads on taxes, welfare, and health care. Baldwin was also the beneficiary of soft money. In her case, the Democratic party of Wisconsin paid for a series of mostly negative campaign ads. Amazingly, with just under two weeks to go until election day, the local NBC-TV affiliate refused to air a Democratic issue ad that criticized Musser's relationship with the insurance industry. The ad began with the question, "Why are the insurance company lobbyists giving Jo Musser thousands of dollars in contributions?" But it was the imagery of a man's hands stuffing hundred dollar bills into a briefcase that caused the station to refuse it.[67] Dave Trabert, general manager of WMTV-TV, argued that the image implied that Musser's campaign had received illegal cash contributions from insurance company executives. "The ad portrayed potentially illegal activity," Trabert said. "It could easily have been interpreted that she took cash."[68]

If the Democrats were having a little bit of trouble attacking Musser, Musser was doing a pretty good job at hurting herself. New to partisan politics, Musser was prone to being impolitic from time to time. Some analysts called her "blunt." In her own words, she was "difficult to manage," (which may explain why she went through four different campaign managers). And, she tended to shoot from the hip. In the middle of October, Musser's political inexperience got her into a heap of trouble over the issue of abortion.

It all started with a simple interview. Musser told the *Capital Times* Editorial Board that she was not sure if she could bring herself to vote for Republican Mark Neumann, who was challenging incumbent Feingold for his Senate seat. One of the biggest issues the former First District representative was using against Feingold was the senator's stance on "partial-birth" abortions. In 1997, Representative Neumann had even pushed for the recall of Feingold and Wisconsin's other senator, Democrat Herb Kohl, after they voted to sustain President Clinton's veto of the Republican measure to ban the procedure. Neumann was against all late-term abortions, even those meant to save the life of the mother. To Musser, this was just wrong. "Russ Feingold and I disagree on fiscal issues. But Mark Neumann and I disagree on protecting abortion rights, which I think is a very important issue. I don't know what I'm going to do."[69]

Musser's comments appeared in John Nichol's October 13 column, and soon thereafter the candidate found herself in the middle of a political maelstrom. A day after the piece ran, Musser issued a press release saying that her comments to the *Capital Times* had been manipulated and that she intended to support Neumann. "Mark and I agree on many more issues than we disagree, and I look forward to working with him when we are elected to our new posts," she said. "I'm proud to be on the Republican ticket with Mark and will be equally proud to serve with him in Congress."[70]

If Musser had hoped the clarification would end her problems, she was wrong. The same day her support for Neumann made the news, Republican activists and conservative commentators blew a gasket. The party's chair of the First Congressional District wrote a letter to the state party chair asking that Musser be cut off from state party funds. That same day a Milwaukee talk-radio host even went on the air to endorse Baldwin. Later, he explained his action: "Tammy Baldwin is an honest left-wing crackpot. Jo Musser is a duplicitous left-wing crackpot. I'll go with the honest one."[71]

Not only had Musser infuriated the local Republican Right, she had irritated the progressive *Capital Times* as well. Nichols vehemently denied Musser's charges that he had somehow manipulated her words. She had spoken in front of a large group, after all. The editorial staff accused her of trying to backtrack and of sending a mixed message.[72] In yet another column on the topic, Nichols suggested she was having a political identity crisis and that she should determine what sort of a Republican she wanted to be.[73]

Most Republicans decided she was the right kind of Republican, or at least the party's only hope. The state party chair refused to cut off her funds. The NRCC chair, Georgia Representative John Linder, attended a Musser fundraiser. Klug went on the campaign trail for her, as did Governor Thompson. Former presidential candidate Bob Dole made a brief campaign appearance. Even Neumann eventually told the press he would "absolutely" support Musser.[74] Still, some strategists suggested she had mortally wounded herself with her Neumann comments and stance on abortion. Greer's former campaign manager suggested she could not win without the support of conservative voters. NRCC chair Linder only managed to reinforce this idea when he reached out to alienated conservatives, urging them to support Musser despite her liberal social views. And one top Republican staffer commented, "I've never seen a candidate create such a mess."[75]

While Musser spent the last weeks of her campaign trying to patch up her relationship with her party, the Baldwin campaign was busy trying to energize its base. On a mission to get voters to the polls, 3,000 (mostly) young volunteers stuffed envelopes, passed out leaflets, knocked on doors, distributed yard signs, made election day calls, and stood around street corners wearing Baldwin sandwich boards.[76] At the local zoo, in one of Baldwin's final campaign appearances, a supporter asked how her campaign was doing. Confirming that she was pleased with how things were going, Baldwin added, "the real challenge is making sure people go out to the polls. Turnout is absolutely critical."[77]

Baldwin and Musser met for one last debate just two days before the election. The tone of this debate was a 180-degree departure from their first. They stressed their philosophical differences as before, but this time they attacked each other relentlessly for their advertisements. Many in the audience were made uncomfortable by what they saw. Said one debate-watcher, "I felt sorry for both of them. It's a sorry situation when this is what they have to go through to get their ideas out . . . like a boxer going 15 rounds." Another audience member described the negative ads as "a third persona, upping the level of tension."[78] This race may not have had the entertainment value of a Baldwin-Greer match-up, as the *Capital Times* columnist had lamented weeks earlier. Yet, it wasn't entirely the cordial, issues-oriented race that Zaleski had predicted. And in the final hours, it was too close to call.[79]

IN THE END

When Tuesday, November 3, finally arrived, Baldwin and Musser had to be exhausted. In just eight short weeks, the two candidates had met for 28 debates and had made countless campaign appearances. They had attacked and counterattacked one another. They had welcomed such political dignitaries as House Minority Leader Gephardt and First Lady Hillary Clinton, Wisconsin Governor Thompson and former Senate Majority Leader and Republican presidential candidate Robert Dole. And they had raised hundreds of thousands of dollars between them. Now, all they could do was wait.

In the wee hours of November 4, Baldwin declared victory. Later in the day, when all 399 precincts had reported their vote totals, the actual outcome was finally known. Baldwin had beaten Musser by a relatively small margin, 53 to 47 percent. It was also later in the day that the voter turnout stories began to circulate. It seemed the Baldwin campaign's attempts to motivate students had paid off. Across Dane County, turnout was about 55 percent, up from below 50 percent in the last mid-term election. Turnout was even higher in Madison, 57 percent compared to 52 percent in the rest of the county.[80] So many voters had decided to hit the polls that many precincts ran out of ballots. The problem was especially acute in the student-dominated wards, where many students waited hours after the 8 p.m. closing time for their chance to vote. See table 4.3 for the Second District's vote totals by county.

ALL POLITICS REALLY IS LOCAL

Through our activism and hopefulness, we . . . made a bit of history.

—Tammy Baldwin[81]

The outcome of the November 3 election can be interpreted in a couple of ways. For the Republicans who believed the district had become more competitive, Musser's win is proof that the Second District is no longer the liberal bastion it had been for decades. In spite of her problems with Greer, in spite of her lack of political experience and her tendency to be impolitic, in spite of her much smaller war chest, Musser did remarkably well, losing to Baldwin by just six percentage points. The Democrats could, of course, remind the Republicans that Baldwin was not your typical Democrat and that a heterosexual candidate might have done even better. Besides, Musser was not your typical Republican. In fact, she was more liberal than some *Democrats* in other Wisconsin districts!

Was Republican Klug's eight-year tenure in Wisconsin's Second District a sign of an increasingly conservative electorate or just an anomaly? A few more elections may be needed to answer that question. But Baldwin's victory makes one thing clear. Although her huge volunteer effort and fundraising advantage helped land her in Congress, all the hometown help and out-of-state money

**Table 4.3 Wisconsin's Second
Congressional District Vote, 1998**

County	Baldwin	Musser
Madison	54,986	28,285
Fitchburg	3,065	3,314
Middleton	3,240	2,891
Monona	2,088	1,659
Stoughton	1,879	1,715
Sun Prairie	2,657	3,458
Verona	1,185	1,367
Rest Dane Co.	22,706	24,911
Total Dane Co.	91,806	67,600
Columbia Co.	6,846	9,693
Dodge Co.*	1,045	1,947
Green Co.*	2,592	4,017
Iowa Co.	2,992	3,928
Jefferson Co.*	304	343
Lafayette Co.	1,899	3,079
Richland Co.	2,667	3,132
Sauk Co.	6,746	9,647
Total	116,897	100,686

*includes partial area of county.
Preliminary totals.

SOURCE: *Capital Times,* November 4, 1998.

in the world wouldn't have meant much if Baldwin had run in say, Cobb County, Georgia. Baldwin *couldn't* win just anywhere; she could only prevail in a progressive place like Madison. In that sense, all politics is indeed local.

NOTES

The author would like to acknowledge the University Personnel Development Committee at the University of Wisconsin–Stevens Point for its financial support of this project and Bryan Brophy-Baermann for his technical and emotional support. She is especially grateful to David J. Rothamer for his excellence and dedication as both research assistant and student.

1. Gregory L. Giroux, "Wisconsin Democrats Hope to Capture Open 1st, 2nd Districts," *Congressional Quarterly Weekly Report,* August 22, 1998.
2. Mary Mead Crawford, quoted in "Republicans Will Walk Some Fine Lines to Hold the House," *Milwaukee Journal Sentinel Online,* May 3, 1998.
3. The single-payer system of health care provides universal coverage to all citizens. The "single payer" is the government. Canada operates under this system. With more than 40 million uninsured, the United States is the only industrialized nation that has not developed a system for making sure all of its citizens receive quality health care.

4. See Chris Murphy, "Race Tight to Succeed Klug," *Capital Times,* October 7, 1998, 4A. See also Stuart Rothenberg, "House Races to Watch: Most Vulnerable Open Seats," *CNN AllPolitics,* August 5, 1998.

5. "The Best Places to Live in America '98," *Money.com.* Or see "Best Places to Live: Clean air and water . . . low crime and taxes . . . good public schools," *Money,* July 1998, 27, 7.

6. According to the 1990 census, whites constitute 92.9 percent of the county, the next largest group is blacks at 2.8 percent, then Asians at 2.4 percent. Median household income is $32,715.

7. Chris Murphy, "County's Shift to the Right Shapes Strategy," *Capital Times,* October 5, 1998, 1C.

8. "Klug Shines, Neumann Dims," *Capital Times,* August 5, 1998.

9. "Klug Shows the GOP a Better Way," *Capital Times,* July 24, 1998, 12A.

10. *The Almanac of American Politics 1998,* Wisconsin's Second District, Representative Scott Klug (R).

11. "Madison Dubbed 'Heartland's Progressive Hotbed': Utne Reader Ranks Our Town Among the Nation's Best for 'Enlightened Politics,'" *Capital Times,* April 2, 1997.

12. At one time, the list of possible Republican candidates also included an editorialist for the *Madison State Journal,* a former pro-football player, the owner of a public relations firm, the state Commerce Secretary, and an interior designer. None of these individuals actually declared his or her candidacy, however.

13. "Total Raised and Spent: Wisconsin District 2," *Center for Responsive Politics,* September 14, 1998.

14. Staff, "GOP Won't Find Klug II, But Can Opt for Brains, Moderation," *Capital Times,* September 3, 1998.

15. Chris Murphy, "Carrig Runs a No-Nonsense Race," *Capital Times,* August 29-30, 1998, 2A.

16. "Total Raised and Spent," *Center for Responsive Politics.*

17. John Nichols, "GOP Loyalist Looks Hard, Picks Sharpless," *Capital Times,* July 16, 1998, 10A.

18. "Total Raised and Spent," *Center for Responsive Politics.*

19. Jeff Mayers, "The 30-second Campaign," *Wisconsin State Journal,* September 2, 1998.

20. "Total Raised and Spent," *Center for Responsive Politics.*

21. Paul Norton, "Anti-gay Attack by Greer Ignites Campaign Battle," *Capital Times,* July 10, 1998, 2A.

22. John Nichols, "Tomorrow is Election Day and the Primary Colors Have Started to Run," *Capital Times,* September 7, 1998, C. The second slogan is an altered version of the gay rights chant, "We're here, we're queer, get used to it!"

23. Staff, "Greer's Greed and Bigotry," *Capital Times,* July 11-12, 1998, 13A.

24. Jeff Mayers, "Ten Candidates Vie in Rare, Incumbent-Free Congressional Race Certain to be Congested, Contentious, and Nationally Noticed," *Wisconsin State Journal,* August 12, 1998.

25. Chris Murphy, "'Push Polling' Charges Heat up GOP Primary," *Capital Times,* August 19, 1998, 4A.

26. Jeff Mayers, "Musser Fights Abortion, Tax Charges," *Wisconsin State Journal,* September 3, 1998, 5C.

27. Ibid.

28. A WMTV-Channel 15 poll of likely voters had Musser in the lead, with 18 percent and Carrig after her with 12 percent. Thirty-eight percent were still undecided. The

poll, done by Opinion Dynamics, had a large margin of error (8.4 percent). These polling data were reported in the *Capital Times'* "Campaign Notebook," under the heading "Kastenmeier for Phelps; Soglin for Baldwin," September 4, 1998, 4A.

29. "Total Raised and Spent," *Center for Responsive Politics.*

30. Mayers, "The 30-second Campaign."

31. Staff, "Choose a Democrat Worthy of Holding Kastenmeier's Seat," *Capital Times,* September 2, 1998, 8A.

32. Baldwin supported a bill to require insurance companies to pay for at least a 24-hour hospital stay for new mothers.

33. "Total Raised and Spent," *Center for Responsive Politics.*

34. Mayers, "The 30-second Campaign."

35. Ibid.

36. Staff, "Choose a Democrat Worthy."

37. Chris Murphy, "Don Quixote Rides a Rusty Cavalier," *Capital Times,* August 25, 1998, 2A.

38. The only exception was reporter Chris Murphy's "Outsider Impresses Dems in Debate," *Capital Times,* August 19, 1998, 4A.

39. The McCain-Feingold bill, named for Republican Senator John McCain of Arizona and Democrat Senator Russ Feingold of Wisconsin, proposed a constitutional amendment to ban soft money. This bill was eventually defeated in the Senate. Federal law limits how much money individuals and PACs can contribute to candidates' campaigns. The soft money "loophole" has come about because individuals and PACs are not limited in what they can give to parties. The parties are supposed to use these funds on educational and get-out-the-vote efforts, but soft money is increasingly used to produce so-called issue ads that implicitly support or oppose certain candidates.

40. Scott Russell, "Phelps Pushes for Gift Limits in 2nd District," *Capital Times,* September 29, 1997.

41. Ibid.

42. Melanie Conklin, "Dirty Laundry," *Isthmus,* June 5, 1998, 7.

43. Chris Murphy, "Democrats Hold Off On Attacks in Debate," *Capital Times,* July 10, 1998, 2A.

44. John Nichols, "Dem Hopefuls Impressive, Especially Phelps," *Capital Times,* August 20, 1998, 12A.

45. Ibid.

46. Chris Murphy, "Out-of-state Campaign Money: Does It Matter?," *Capital Times,* August 8–9, 1998, 2A.

47. Ibid.

48. John Nichols, "Can Knocking On Doors Trump TV Ads?," *Capital Times,* August 6, 1998, 12A.

49. John Nichols, "Outside Stars Stump for Candidates," *Capital Times,* September 5, 1998, 1.

50. Ibid.

51. Chris Murphy, "Wineke Aide: Phelps' Campaign May Go Negative," *Capital Times,* August 27, 1998, 9A.

52. Chris Murphy, "Phelps Draws Flak from Two Primary Rivals," *Capital Times,* September 5–6, 1998, 2A.

53. Staff, "Choose a Democrat Worthy."

54. John Nichols, "Youthquake Erupts in Baldwin's Victory," *Capital Times,* September 10, 1998.

55. Staff, "The Tammy Phenomenon," *Capital Times,* September 9, 1998, 10A.

56. Aaron Nathans, "Dems Fall in Behind Baldwin," *Capital Times,* September 11, 1998.

57. Staff, "The Tammy Phenomenon."

58. Rob Zaleski, "Ron vs. Tammy Promised to Be Ugly but Still Fun," *Capital Times,* September 14, 1998, 1D.

59. Chris Murphy and David Callender, "Greer Calls off Congressional Campaign, Cites Lack of Funds," *Capital Times,* September 23, 1998, 2A.

60. Independent Counsel Kenneth Starr's impeachment referral to the House of Representatives, September 11, 1998.

61. Weekend Transcript of September 11, 1998, "The First Debate Between the 2nd Congressional Candidates, Tammy Baldwin and Jo Musser," October 27, 1998.

62. PACs are limited to $5,000 per candidate per election cycle, so the most they can give is $5,000 for the primary race and another $5,000 for the general. Gingrich handed over $10,000 total to Musser.

63. Jeff Mayers, "2nd District Record Likely," *Wisconsin State Journal,* October 17, 1998.

64. "Total Raised and Spent: Wisconsin District 2," *Center for Responsive Politics,* December 21, 1998.

65. Ibid.

66. Jeff Mayers and Rick Barrett, "In Your Face: People Are Gagging on Negative Ads," *Wisconsin State Journal,* October 31, 1998, 1.

67. Chris Murphy, "TV Station Rejects Dems' Attack Ad on Musser," *Capital Times,* October 21, 1998.

68. Amy Rinard, "Madison TV Station Rejects Ad Ripping Musser's Fundraising," *Wisconsin State Journal,* October 22, 1998.

69. John Nichols, "Neumann's Abortion Stand Scares Musser," *Capital Times,* October 13, 1998.

70. Jeff Mayers, "Musser Changes Her Stance on Neumann," *Wisconsin State Journal,* October 15, 1998, 5C.

71. Chris Murphy, "GOP Pledges Support Amid Call for Fund Cut," *Capital Times,* October 16, 1998, 1.

72. Staff, "Jo Musser's Mixed Message," *Capital Times,* October 15, 1998.

73. John Nichols, "A Political Identity Crisis," *Capital Times,* October 20, 1998.

74. Jeff Mayers, "When Pressed, Musser, Neumann Close Ranks," *Wisconsin State Journal,* October 27, 1998.

75. Nichols, "A Political Identity Crisis."

76. Chris Murphy and Jon Segal, "Volunteers Turn the Tide for Baldwin," *Capital Times,* November 4, 1998, 1.

77. Gwen Carleton, "Baldwin, Musser Show the Toll of Punishing Ads," *Capital Times,* November 2, 1998, 6A.

78. Ibid.

79. Chris Murphy, "Race Tight to Succeed Klug," *Capital Times,* October 7, 1998, 4A. See also Chris Murphy, "New Poll Favors Baldwin, but Race Still Looks Close," *Capital Times,* October 31, 1998.

80. Scott Milfred, "Baldwin's Army May Have Put Feingold In," *Wisconsin State Journal,* November 5, 1998.

81. Jeff Mayers, "Baldwin's Win Over Musser Historic," *Wisconsin State Journal,* November 4, 1998, 1.

5

★

Hill Defeats Leising
in Indiana's
Ninth District Race

Robert K. Goidel
James L. McDowell

There is general agreement that incumbents have an advantage in elections to the U.S. House of Representatives, but there is considerably less agreement as to the source of this advantage. Various works have cited the importance of casework, pork-barrel politics, name recognition, fundraising advantages, and (re)districting.[1] Whatever the source, incumbency is clearly a benefit in U.S. House elections. Incumbents win reelection more than 90 percent of the time and run approximately 10 percent ahead of nonincumbent candidates.[2] But if incumbents have an advantage when they are running for elected office, what about after they have retired? Are there any lingering effects of incumbency in an open seat race?

The question itself may seem odd, but in Indiana's Ninth Congressional District the retirement of 34-year incumbent Lee Hamilton raised the issue of whether a last-minute appeal by a popular incumbent can sway the district in favor of his hand-picked successor. Throughout the campaign, polls indicated that Democrat Baron Hill trailed Republican Jean Leising, whose lead was estimated at anywhere from five to ten percentage points. In the campaign's waning days, however, Hamilton asked that his long-term service to the district be rewarded with the election of the Democratic candidate to the House of Representatives. But was the appeal, described as heartfelt by at least one source, in itself strong enough to carry the district?[3]

Several other factors also appeared to be working in Hill's favor. Unstable throughout the election year, national tides turned in the Democratic direction just prior to the election. Defying predictions of most oddsmakers and historical norms, Democrats picked up five seats nationally, despite (or perhaps because of) a president deeply immersed in a scandal that would eventually lead to his impeachment by the House of Representatives.[4] In the Ninth District, the Republican nominee struggled with the same issue Republicans grappled with nationwide: Why weren't the president's sexual escapades and their aftermath translating into Republican support at the district level?

For some time, political observers had noted the rightward leanings of the district, often commenting that "on paper" the district should elect a Republican. In this context, Hamilton's long tenure was generally considered a personal success more than a party victory. This observation, however, only partly reflected the partisan realities of the Ninth District. In terms of partisan identifiers, the district actually leaned Democratic, as indicated by its tradition of sending Democrats to the Indiana General Assembly. The partisan lean, however, was made up of the sort of conservative, "Reagan Democrats" generally found in the South, rather than the Midwest. As the Democratic nominee, Hill was playing with a modest home-field advantage in terms of partisan identification, but only if he could convince voters that he was a "Lee Hamilton" Democrat.

Hill likely also benefited from the presence of popular former Governor Evan Bayh at the top of the Democratic ticket. Running for the seat held by retiring Republican Senator Dan Coats, Bayh was a virtual shoe-in as a U.S. senator over the underfunded survivor of a bitter three-way Republican primary. In fact, with Indiana's early poll closings of six o'clock, Bayh's was the first Senate election called by the major networks on election night (at 6:01 p.m. EST). Yet, if Bayh's victory over his underfunded opposition was convincing, it was unclear whether his personal victory would translate into greater Democratic support further down the ballot.

In this chapter, we analyze the roots of Hill's successful run for the House of Representatives in Indiana's Ninth Congressional District. His election, despite trailing by as much as ten points in early polls, tells us a great deal about the nature of congressional politics, particularly regarding the importance of endorsements, national partisan tides, and district-level partisanship. Hill benefited from an electoral context that proved to be surprisingly favorable to Democratic candidates and from a district that leaned in his party's direction. He also proved to be a hardworking and aggressive campaigner, as well as an attractive and formidable candidate. Yet, in the end, the election boiled down to two factors: Hamilton and the Democratic tilt of the Ninth District.

BACKGROUND

Indiana's Ninth Congressional District occupies the southeastern portion of the state, nestled in an elbow formed by the Ohio state line on the east and the meandering Ohio River on the south. Its northern and western borders have varied occasionally—but relatively little—during the past 35 years, modified only when congressional mapmakers were forced to add territory to maintain

Table 5.1 County Per Capita Income, Ranking in State (92 Counties)

	1986	1996	Change in Rank
Bartholomew	7	9	-2
Brown	70	48	22
Clark	40	29	11
Crawford	91	90	1
Dearborn	26	48	-22
Dubois	5	10	-5
Fayette	46	59	-13
Floyd	18	20	-2
Franklin	79	84	-5
Harrison	64	57	7
Jackson	55	43	12
Jefferson	80	74	6
Jennings	89	62	27
Ohio	81	60	21
Perry	82	85	-3
Ripley	48	23	25
Scott	87	81	6
Spencer	59	66	-7
Switzerland	92	91	1
Union	76	69	7
Washington	85	82	3

SOURCE: Compiled by authors.

population equity among the districts. In the 1990s, the Ninth District covered an expanse of 20 counties plus several townships in Bartholomew County (Columbus). Its area of just over 6,700 square miles is larger than the state of Connecticut and nearly as large as New Jersey. The majority of the district's population, however, is concentrated in Clark and Floyd counties, bedroom suburbs of Louisville, Kentucky, and two of the more Democratic areas of the region.

A politically and socially conservative district, the area is also one of the state's most economically depressed, despite the presence of Hillenbrand Industries, a Fortune 100 company. In the mid-1980s, five of the state's poorest counties, as measured by per capita incomes, were located within the district, including four of the lowest six rungs on the state's economic ladder. Though the economic situation improved by the mid-1990s, the district still contains four of the state's ten poorest counties (see table 5.1).

Residents of this southeastern corner of Indiana often feel isolated from and neglected by the rest of the state. For example, the Ninth District has only one state-supported four-year institution of higher education, a branch campus of

Indiana University at New Albany in Floyd County. As a result, many residents are more oriented toward Cincinnati and Louisville than Indianapolis. Perhaps the most obvious indication of this sense of being cut off from the rest of the state is Indiana's infamous time situation. One of three states that does not adopt Daylight Savings Time, Indiana is permitted three time zones: six northwestern counties and five southwestern counties always keep their clocks with Illinois; the remaining 81 counties legally are on Eastern Standard Time all year, the net effect being the same time with New York in the winter and Chicago in the summer. However, five southeastern counties (all in the Ninth District) defiantly remain on the same time as Cincinnati and Louisville all year.

Like its neighboring states of Illinois and Ohio, Indiana was settled by migration from the South. As Vice President Thomas Marshall, an Indiana native, remembered it, his state was bisected culturally and politically by the old National Road, which crossed the state from Richmond on the east to Terre Haute on the west: "South of that line the vast majority of the people who came in were from Virginia, the Carolinas, and Kentucky."[5] V. O. Key, Jr., noted that areas of settlement from the South, generally in Indiana's southern reaches, continued to constitute an important element of the state's Democratic party.[6] John H. Fenton concurred, observing that not only was Indiana more nearly a "border state" than other midwestern states but also in the mid-1960s, more of its population had been born in Kentucky and other southern or border states than was true of other states in the Midwest.

These settlement patterns would continue to influence Indiana politics well into the twentieth century. By the 1950s, however, the Ninth District was marginally Republican, voting for President Dwight Eisenhower and sending Representative Earl Wilson to Washington for 11 terms from 1940 through 1964. Wilson's tenure was interrupted only once, in 1958, when he lost by fewer than 800 votes. Wilson regained his seat in 1960 and retained it in 1962, although by only 52 percent of the vote. It was within this setting that the long (17-term) tenure of Representative Lee Hamilton would begin.

Florida-born but Indiana-educated, with degrees from DePauw University and Indiana University's law school, Hamilton was an attorney in Columbus when he made his first bid for Congress in 1964. Riding the lengthy coattails of Lyndon Johnson in only the fourth—and last—Democratic presidential victory in Indiana in the twentieth century, Hamilton upset the longtime Republican incumbent, gaining 54 percent of the vote in a district with otherwise Republican tendencies. Hamilton, however, was not given much chance to survive his initial bid for reelection.

All things being equal, the district at the time leaned Republican but not so strongly that a Democratic candidate could not run and win, provided there was a strong Democratic trend at the national level. Yet, the partisan slant of the district was strong enough that it seemed unlikely that a Democratic candidate would win in the Ninth for more than a couple of election cycles. The next national trend favoring Republicans would, in all probability, wash any successful Democratic candidate from the Republican congressional banks into the Ninth District's bordering Ohio River.

Had Hamilton been less skilled as a politician, the seat could have easily returned to Republican control. However, Hamilton proved to be adept both at campaigning and governing. But political skill was not the only factor working in Hamilton's favor. Hamilton's initial victory had come in a congressional district originally drawn for the 1942 elections, following the state's loss of a seat in the 1940 census. Indiana politicians were as loath as any to redistrict and had failed to draw new boundaries following the censuses in 1950 and 1960. By this point, Indiana's Ninth District, with just over 290,000 residents, was by far the state's smallest in population.

In early to mid-1964, the Supreme Court handed down several redistricting decisions, requiring that congressional districts reflect the principle of "one person, one vote," and Indiana was forced to redraw its congressional boundaries. At the time, for the first time since the early 1930s and the last time in the twentieth century, Democrats controlled the governorship and both chambers of the Indiana state legislature. In an effort to maximize the Democratic congressional delegation, the legislature added strongly Democratic Clark County (Jeffersonville) to the Ninth District from the neighboring Eighth District in southwestern Indiana.

The logic was that the Eighth District Democratic incumbent, Winfield K. Denton, was in a safe district and would survive the redistricting, while freshman Hamilton, now with a more substantial Democratic base, would win election as well. As anticipated, Hamilton won reelection with 54 percent of the vote in 1966. There was no sophomore surge, but he had survived an election in which Democrats lost 47 seats nationwide. One of these Democratic losses was in the "secure" Eighth District, where Denton was swept from office by more than 4,000 votes. Adding to the irony was the fact that Hamilton would have won reelection without the additional voters.[7]

In both 1966 and 1968, Hamilton won competitive races, each time matching the 54 percent of the vote won in his original 1964 campaign. By 1970, Hamilton moved the district out of the "marginal" category by winning with a more substantial 63 percent. Conceding that Hamilton would be difficult to beat, a Republican-dominated state legislature in 1971 included Floyd County (New Albany) in the Ninth District, including additional Democratic voters and augmenting Hamilton's electoral base.

Republicans were not so kind following the 1980 census, though Hamilton would manage to prosper despite Republican designs. In one of the more innovative and controversial redistrictings on record, Republicans redrew the congressional map so radically that they were able to place three Democratic incumbents, including Hamilton, into the same district. Hamilton simply took up residence in the new Ninth District, moving some 20 miles west, from Columbus to Nashville, and coasted to an easy reelection victory.

From 1972 through 1992, Hamilton easily won reelection, never dropping below 63 percent, and almost always running ahead of national and statewide Democratic candidates in the district. Without redistricting, it is likely that Hamilton would have still won reelection, although not by the secure electoral margins posted throughout the 1970s and 1980s. Seen in this light, redistricting

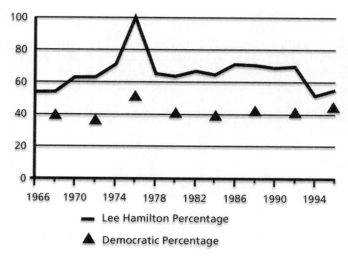

FIGURE 5.1 Democratic Percentages of the Vote for House and Presidential Elections, 1966–1996

played a part in turning a marginal seat into a safe Democratic seat. Yet, redistricting was only part of the story. The other part of the story involved Hamilton himself. Without a popular incumbent, it is hard to imagine that Democrats would have controlled the Ninth District for more than 30 years. Hamilton proved to be politically adept both at home and in Washington, so much so that he was frequently mentioned as a potential candidate for the U.S. Senate (particularly in 1976 and then again in 1990). Each time, Hamilton opted for electoral safety and congressional seniority over statewide office. As figure 5.1 shows, Hamilton was electorally secure in the district.

Hamilton's hold on the district remained firm until the "Republican Revolution" of 1994. That year, Hamilton was almost swept from office in the same manner he had been swept in. With a strong national tide favoring the Republican party, State Senator Jean Leising held Hamilton to only 52 percent of the vote, his poorest showing in three decades. This "near upset" was so surprising that it made national news during an election cycle in which Democrats lost 53 House seats nationwide, including the seat of then–Speaker of the House Thomas Foley of Washington State. At the risk of oversimplification, national news coverage of the Ninth District in 1994 could be summarized by the rhetorical question: How bad was 1994 for Democrats? Lee Hamilton almost lost.

For Republicans, especially for challenger Leising, Hamilton became the "big one" that got away. After a late October poll showed Leising trailing Hamilton by 45 percent, Republicans opted to funnel party support into other, more competitive districts.[8] While it is hard to fault a party that won 53 House seats and control of the House of Representatives for the first time in 40 years, in hindsight, the decision appears to have been a major strategic blunder. As it turned out, the race was far more competitive than the polls indicated. Additional Republican party support, particularly in terms of fundraising, might

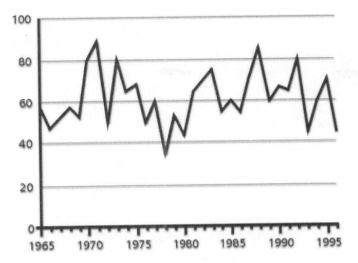

FIGURE 5.2 Lee Hamilton ADA Scores, 1965–1996

have been enough to reverse the approximately 7,000-vote differential that separated Leising and Hamilton in 1994.

Leising tried again in 1996, raising nearly $200,000 more than in the 1994 race. But by 1996, the window of electoral opportunity had been slammed shut. A prosperous national economy renewed the electoral value of incumbency, while national partisan tides favored the reelection of President Clinton and, by extension, the Democratic party. The context of the election provided little hope for challengers of any partisan stripe but was particularly disadvantageous for Republican challengers, such as Leising. In addition, Hamilton, who may have been caught off guard in 1994, would not be caught unprepared a second time around. During the 105th Congress, Hamilton not only raised more money than he had during any past election cycle but also voted more conservatively. As can be seen in figure 5.2, Hamilton's Americans for Democratic Action (ADA) score for 1996 was 45, ten points higher than his low of 35, but 35 points lower than his 1992 score.

In many ways, Hamilton's reign over the Ninth District was textbook congressional politics, reflecting the triumph of incumbency over district partisanship. In Washington, Hamilton secured public works projects for southern Indiana, while bucking party lines often enough to defray charges of political liberalism. Yet, despite his skilled use of incumbency, Hamilton also distinguished himself as an expert on foreign policy, an issue unlikely to resonate much with voters in southern Indiana. His expertise in the foreign policy area earned him a level of recognition and respect from colleagues that often translated into direct political influence over U.S. foreign policy. Hamilton was also willing to tackle the often unseemly topic of congressional ethics and defended Congress as a representative and lawmaking assembly, even as most members were running against the institution they served in. Overall, his reputation for hard work, policy expertise, and personal integrity created a level of personal popularity for Hamilton that transcended party and, with 1994 as the notable exception, virtually assured the Democrats control of the Ninth District. Hamilton's retirement, however, meant that the seat was literally up for grabs.

CANDIDATE SELECTION

Because of the tremendous resources available to incumbents and the inherent difficulties challengers face in raising money, open seats have played a critical role in transforming the party composition of the House of Representatives. In 1994, Republican party gains came primarily in open seat contests; in 1996, Republicans were able to minimize losses by winning a number of such contests.[9] In both years, Republican gains came primarily in districts with a history of voting for Republican presidential candidates.

Districts won by Republicans in 1994 and 1996 looked in many ways similar to Indiana's Ninth District. In both 1992 and 1996, Bill Clinton won a bare plurality of the district's presidential vote, by 622 votes in 1992 and by 1519 votes in 1996. However, the district had given majorities to both Ronald Reagan and George Bush during the 1980s. Reflecting at least in part the competitiveness in presidential voting, both parties believed the Ninth District to be "winnable" in 1998. Republicans targeted the seat as one ripe for takeover, while Democrats marked the seat as one they must hold if they were to narrow the 11-seat gap separating them from majority control of the House of Representatives.

Without the foreboding presence of an incumbent, open seats often draw a wide and deep field of candidates vying for the nomination. As a general rule, the better a party's electoral prospects in November, the more competitive the primaries. From the perspective of a strategic candidate, the retirement of an incumbent may present the best possible opportunity for winning elective office. From the perspective of the party organization, however, divisive primaries not only waste resources but also can create fractures in existing party loyalties and limit its general election prospects. In the Ninth District in 1998, both party organizations successfully identified and united behind a single candidate. As a result, despite the presence of an open seat, the primaries were remarkably uncompetitive.

Both parties also settled on candidates with deep roots in the district. Republicans again chose Jean Leising, their nominee in 1994 and 1996. Leising, born in Lawrenceburg on the Ohio River, now lived near Oldenburg in the northeast part of the district where she managed the family farm. Hill, a former high school basketball and track star, was a life-long resident of Seymour except for his four years at Furman University in South Carolina.

Leising emerged from her party's primary with 68 percent of the vote. Her closest competitor was the 1992 Republican nominee Michael Bailey, whose chief claim to national fame resulted from his unusually grotesque anti-abortion commercials. Bailey, however, received just 25 percent of the vote this

time around. The Democratic primary was even less competitive. Hill, a former state representative and Hamilton's personal choice as a replacement, surfaced from the Democratic primary with a comparable 71 percent of the vote
against even weaker competition.

In the world of politics, Hill had achieved some recognition by running a
strong race against incumbent Republican Senator Dan Coats in 1990. At the
time, Hill was virtually unknown outside his legislative district, although he
had served four terms as a state representative. He had been recruited largely
because bigger Democratic guns, including Hamilton, had opted out of the
race. Senator Coats, however, was also relatively little known statewide at that
time. The former Fourth District congressman had been appointed to the Senate in 1988 following the election of Senator Dan Quayle as Vice President
and was making his initial statewide race. Hill proved to be an aggressive and
innovative campaigner, walking the state while attacking Coats for his use of
the franking privilege. While Hill failed in his upset bid, he held Coats to only
54 percent despite being outspent by a three to one margin.

Thus, perhaps ironically, both party nominees for the Ninth District seat in
1998 had achieved fame—and credibility—by coming close in elections they
were never supposed to win. In 1998, running for an open seat, close wouldn't
count for much. On paper, the candidates were evenly matched running in a
district roughly balanced in terms of its partisan composition. Most major publications, including *Roll Call, Campaigns and Elections* magazine, and *Congressional Quarterly,* listed the district as too close to call.

If one candidate appeared to have an advantage, however, the nod would
have gone to Leising. Early polls indicated she led by as much as ten percentage points, though this lead appeared to reflect name recognition from her
1994 and 1996 campaign efforts.[10] Over the course of the campaign, at least
two additional polls were released by the Republicans. Not surprisingly, both
showed Leising leading the race, although in one of the polls the lead was
within the poll's margin of error.[11] Despite the apparent lead, as many as 28
percent of voters remained undecided less than a week prior to the election.[12]

CAMPAIGN FUNDRAISING

Campaign fundraising is critical in any House district but perhaps more important in districts like Indiana's Ninth. The district is not only large—a four-
hour drive between its northeast and southwest corners—but also contains no
television station within its boundaries. Five television markets—Indianapolis,
Evansville, Louisville, Cincinnati, and, to a lesser extent, Dayton—serve the district. For candidates, this means any mass appeal to voters via television will be
extremely costly, and, by extension, that advantages in campaign fundraising
may translate into advantages in terms of getting one's message out.

If Leising was faster out of the gate in terms of public support, the benefits
of name recognition failed to translate into a campaign fundraising advantage.
Hill dominated the race for dollars from the very beginning of the campaign,

Table 5.2 Candidate Campaign Finance by Reporting Period

	Cash on Hand	Receipts	Disbursements
1997 Year End			
Hill	245,809	192,868	51,058
Leising	16,668	22,989	17,292
April Quarterly			
Hill	330,006	123,199	38,921
Leising	17,249	36,223	35,643
July Quarterly			
Hill	391,522	166,102	94,186
Leising	63,751	108,392	61,564
October Quarterly			
Hill	276,966	208,411	322,767
Leising	205,197	214,841	73,395
Total			
Hill	12,288	1,013,758	1,001,569
Leising	38,326	668,088	630,072

SOURCE: Federal Election Commission.

outpacing Leising during critical early fundraising periods and among almost every type of contributor. For example, at the end of 1997, Hill reported $254,809 cash-on-hand, while Leising had only $16,668. Hill maintained this early advantage in fundraising throughout 1998. During the first quarter of 1998, Hill reported receipts of $123,199, more than three times as much as Leising ($36,223). Also during the first quarter, Hill reported $330,006 cash-on-hand compared to only $17,249 for Leising.

From July to October, Leising outraised Hill but was never able to overcome the early advantage in fundraising enjoyed by her Democratic opponent. As in her prior efforts, Leising raised substantially more money during the final weeks of the campaign. According to Federal Election Commission (FEC) reports, in fact, she raised nearly twice as much money as Hill during the final week. But Leising's inability to translate name recognition and strong poll showings into an early fundraising advantage raised questions about her campaign, particularly given that at least one prior effort at the House languished because of insufficient campaign funds. Table 5.2 lists campaign dollars available to both candidates during this election cycle.

It is unclear why the Leising campaign failed to raise more money earlier in the campaign season. Perhaps the campaign believed its own polling numbers and simply failed to exert the effort until the later stages of the campaign. The early fundraising gap may also have reflected expectations of strategic contributors that the Ninth would remain in Democratic hands. In this respect, Hill's fundraising base showed support from labor and business, as well as substantial support from political organizations. In fact, Hill even outpaced Leis-

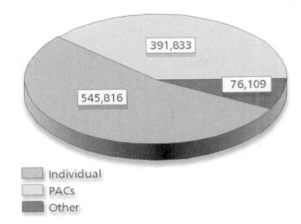

FIGURE 5.3
Source of Contributions
for Democratic
Candidate Baron Hill

Individual
PACs
Other

ing in contributions from business-oriented political action committees (PACs) and individuals. According to the Center for Responsive Politics, Hill raised $245,135 from business sources, while Leising raised just $79,933. Hill's appeal to business interests did not, however, make him any less attractive to labor groups that contributed $174,100 to his campaign. From the various types of political action committees, Leising raised more than Hill only among ideological and single-issue groups. Even there the difference was fairly negligible.

Hill's fundraising success may have simply reflected his attractiveness and aggressiveness as a candidate. Though he was outspent and eventually beaten as a Senate candidate in 1990, Hill had raised more than $1 million. Even if Hill was a more aggressive fundraiser, however, he was undoubtedly helped by Hamilton. Not only did the designation as Hamilton's protégé facilitate his fundraising appeals, but also Hamilton contributed his own time, effort, and contacts to assist Hill in the pursuit of campaign funds. In this respect, Hill benefited from a fundraising organization largely bequeathed to him by his predecessor. Given the size and scope of the district, Hill's success in fundraising provided a clear electoral edge, particularly in the final days of the campaign when Hill closed the gap and then surpassed his Republican opponent.

Leising did benefit from a Republican party issue advocacy campaign entitled "Operation Breakout" that extolled the accomplishments of the 105th Congress. The advertisements implored voters to "call Jean Leising and tell her to continue working to help American families."[13] For example, the *Washington Post* noted the weekend before the election that Republicans intended to spend millions of dollars in eight House districts in Indiana, Kentucky, and Ohio. Indiana's Ninth Congressional District was on the list of targeted races.[14] As with many of the competitive races in 1998, much of the election money was spent by organizations other than candidate committees, and much of that money was not disclosed. Most of this support came from labor organizations (for Hill) and ideological groups (for Leising). See figures 5.3 and 5.4 for overall sources of contributions to both candidates.

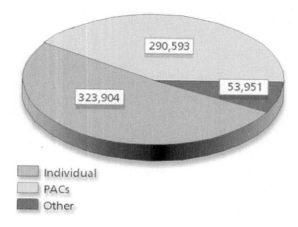

Individual
PACs
Other

FIGURE 5.4 Source of Contributions for Republican Candidate Jean Leising

THE CAMPAIGN

While Hill had an advantage in terms of campaign fundraising, there was no reason to suspect that it would necessarily translate into votes, particularly given Leising's apparent lead in the polls. Recent electoral history, after all, is replete with candidates who failed to buy their way into elected office. Successful campaigns not only raise and spend money, but also spend it in a way that invigorates the partisan base and turns out the vote, while also presenting a message that appeals to independents and weak partisans.

Turning Out the Vote

While the academic literature has questioned the importance of turnout to electoral outcomes, candidates, consultants, and parties see voter turnout as a critical component of electoral strategy. Elections, it is believed, often hinge on which side is more successful in motivating voters to exercise their right to vote. With a looming impeachment cloud in Washington, combined with voter disapproval of its handling by the Republican Congress, it was unclear whether Republicans or Democrats would be more motivated to vote. Because of the heightened competition, open seat elections also tend to attract more voters to the polls.

With Hamilton's name not on the ballot for the first time in 34 years, voter turnout in the Ninth District did increase marginally over previous midterm elections (see table 5.3). In 1990, Hamilton won with 69 percent of the vote, but only 37.4 percent of eligible voters turned out on election day. In 1994, when Hamilton was held to only 52 percent of the vote, 43.4 percent of eligible voters turned out to vote. In 1998, without Hamilton on the ballot, 45.2 percent of the eligible electorate turned out to vote. As the turnout figures illustrate, voter turnout is closely associated with electoral competition. More competitive elections attract additional voters, though it is often unclear which party or candidate is advantaged by the increase in electoral activity.

Table 5.3 Voter Turnout in Midterm Elections in the Ninth District, 1990–1998

	Percent Turnout	Total Votes Cast
1990	37.4	155,851
1994	43.4	175,774
1998	45.2	183,176

SOURCE: Compiled by authors.

In 1998, Republican nominee Leising received 87,797 votes, nearly 3,500 more votes than her 1994 total. In fact, Leising's increase accounts for nearly half of the 7,402 additional votes cast in 1998. Libertarian candidate Diane Feeney, who was not on the 1994 ballot, received 2,406 votes, accounting for 32.5 percent of additional voters. Finally, Democratic nominee Hill received 92,973 votes, just over 1,500 more votes than Hamilton in 1994, accounting for 20 percent of new voters.

Looking just at these numbers, Leising seems to have been the prime beneficiary of increased voter turnout in 1998. In this respect, Leising increased her total vote by nearly 4 percent over the 1994 midterm election. Such calculations, however, assume that increases in vote totals reflect mobilization of new voters rather than conversion of existing voters. Running in an open seat election, Leising's vote totals probably would have increased over her 1994 showing, even if voter turnout remained constant. Without an incumbent on the ballot, Leising should have been able to appeal to a larger share of existing voters, many of whom probably supported Hamilton during past election cycles, but may have had doubts about his potential Democratic replacement. For the Democratic nominee, Hill, had turnout remained constant, one would have suspected a drop in total Democratic votes cast. Having paid the cost of failing to mobilize their base in 1994, Democrats increased efforts to turn out their partisans and attract independents in 1998. These efforts paid off, allowing Hill to surpass the 1994 benchmark for Democratic support in the district.

Invigorating the Partisan Base

Earlier in the chapter, we noted that the district leaned Democratic in terms of its partisan affiliation, but that much of the Democratic base was composed of conservative, blue-collar Reagan/Hamilton Democrats. Geographically, the Democratic vote is concentrated in Clark and Floyd counties, the most heavily populated counties within the district. For a Democrat to win districtwide in an open seat election, the candidate needs to win convincingly in these counties. In 1998, Hill did just that, winning by 4,836 votes in Clark County and by 2,686 votes in Floyd County.

While Hill won in 10 of 21 counties across the district, it was his margin of victory in these two heavily Democratic counties that made the critical difference in the election outcome. In fact, in the remaining counties in the district, Leising defeated Hill by more than 2,000 votes. But in Floyd and Clark counties, Hill out-polled Leising by more than 7,500 votes. For Hill, the victory in 1998 owed much to redistricting done in 1966 as a result of "one person, one vote" ruling and in 1970 due to the census. In these redistricting cycles, first Clark and then Floyd counties were added to the Ninth District, fundamentally altering the partisan makeup of the district. While Hamilton would have won in 1966 without the help of redistricting, 32 years later, Hamilton's successor could not have won had congressional mapmakers not added Democratic voters from the neighboring Eighth District.

The partisan voting behavior of the district in 1998 is best illustrated by considering the performance of other statewide candidates. On the Democratic side, the leading vote-getter in 1998 was clearly Bayh. Across the state, Democrats running for lower level offices did their best to attach themselves to the former governor and U.S. Senate candidate. Bayh, for his part, was more than willing to campaign for his fellow Democrats through television and radio ads, yard signs, and direct mail solicitations. The ads implored voters to vote for Bayh and an assortment of other Democratic candidates, though they rarely mentioned that Bayh was, in fact, a Democrat.

For Republicans, the task of carrying the party label fell into the hands of Secretary of State Sue Anne Gilroy. Then thought to be prepping for a possible gubernatorial candidacy in 2000, Gilroy campaigned statewide for Republican state legislators. Her ads were rarely directed at her opponent in the race, Cheryl Little, but instead targeted current Indiana Governor Frank O'Bannon.

For our purposes, the percentages of the vote won in each of these elections provides a benchmark of the district's support for the strongest Republican and Democratic candidate statewide. As table 5.4 demonstrates, Bayh won convincingly in each of the district's 21 counties. While it is impossible to provide any precise calculation, his impressive showing in the district undoubtedly provided a boost to the Hill campaign, particularly given that Bayh ran about 4 percent stronger in the Ninth District than he did statewide.

What is more interesting, however, is that Gilroy, considered the state's leading Republican, failed to win a plurality in the Ninth District. With a Libertarian candidate on the ballot, Little was able to attract a thin plurality of voters in the Ninth District, despite widespread perceptions that she had little chance to win statewide. By all accounts, Gilroy's showing in the 1998 election was disappointing. In 1994, Gilroy won election with 60.4 percent of the vote, leading the state Republican ticket. In 1998, she won with just 55 percent of the vote, running about even with other statewide Republican candidates. As a result, Gilroy opted out of a run at the governor's mansion in 2000, declaring instead for mayor of Indianapolis in 1999. Regardless, her failure to win a plurality in the Ninth District says a great deal about the opportunity available to a Republican during the 1998 election cycle. A strong candidate might

Table 5.4 Democratic Voting Percentages for Various Offices by County, Indiana's Ninth Congressional District

	Baron Hill (U.S. Representative)		Evan Bayh (U.S. Senate)		Cheryl Little (Indiana Secretary of State)	
Bartholomew	46.6	(1,226)	60.9	(11,937)	35.6	(6,801)
Brown	46.7	(2,633)	64.6	(3,670)	42.7	(2,362)
Clark	58.6	(15,491)	71.8	(18,747)	56.3	(13,879)
Crawford	56.3	(2,207)	70.0	(2,673)	54.1	(1,873)
Dearborn	36.7	(4,342)	57.1	(6,650)	42.9	(4,812)
Dubois	47.4	(5,630)	71.1	(8,623)	47.8	(5,136)
Fayette	44.9	(3,617)	71.9	(5,717)	41.4	(3,087)
Floyd	55.6	(12,366)	68.1	(15,150)	54.3	(11,174)
Franklin	37.4	(2,262)	64.3	(3,813)	41.2	(2,326)
Harrison	51.0	(6,100)	69.4	(8,245)	51.6	(5,839)
Jackson	54.0	(6,856)	68.1	(8,557)	45.3	(5,495)
Jefferson	53.7	(5,212)	64.9	(6,134)	48.6*	(4,321)
Jennings	47.8	(3,423)	63.8	(4,507)	45.1	(3,031)
Ohio	44.0	(911)	59.6	(1,208)	46.3	(909)
Perry	64.0	(3,546)	76.2	(4,218)	64.4	(3,461)
Ripley	38.8	(3,304)	61.1	(5,105)	42.4	(3,261)
Scott	62.5	(3,903)	75.2	(4,492)	63.7	(3,431)
Spencer	49.6*	(3,678)	68.9	(5,121)	49.4*	(3,615)
Switzerland	51.4	(1,443)	67.7	(1,847)	55.0	(1,337)
Union	37.7	(902)	60.6	(1,451)	35.8	(820)
Washington	48.1	(3,921)	65.7	(5,282)	42.9	(3,313)
Total	50.8	(92,973)	67.1	(133,147)	48.1*	(90,283)

*Indicates that the candidate won a plurality but not a majority in the county.

Though only a portion of Bartholomew County is in the Ninth District, voting totals for the Secretary of State and U.S. Senate race include the entire county.

SOURCE: Compiled by authors.

make the race competitive, but it would be difficult for any Republican to win in the Ninth with Bayh at the top of the Democratic ticket.

Presenting a Message

As a candidate, Hill used the resources available to his candidacy. Putting his fundraising advantage to good use, Hill reiterated a simple, basic Democratic message while emphasizing endorsements from Hamilton, Bayh, and Governor O'Bannon, a native of the district from Corydon. Because Hill had not run for elected office since 1990, endorsements from the state's leading Democrats were critical. For voters who might have been uncertain about Hill, appeals from O'Bannon, Bayh, and Hamilton made voting for Hill much easier.

Employing a tactic from his unsuccessful 1990 Senate campaign, Hill also walked across the district, no small feat given the geographic range of the district. Hill's walk was not only symbolic of his aggressive and energetic campaign style, it also challenged an assertion by Leising that Hill did not know the district well enough to represent it. It also illustrated that Hill was not going to simply rely on television advertising and fundraising to win, but would instead combine traditional and modern campaigning.

Discussion of the issues in the Ninth District was a microcosm of what was happening in national politics. Leising attempted to turn the election into a referendum on honesty and integrity. Like Republicans nationally, she believed the scandal involving President Bill Clinton would drive outraged conservative voters to the polls. As the campaign wore on and the impeachment issue began wearing thin, Leising altered her rhetoric, saying she would follow the decision of the House Judiciary Committee.[15] Other than the impeachment issue, Leising appealed to the district's socially conservative voters with pro-life, anti-gun control, and smaller government messages. Her campaign was, by and large, textbook Republican politics.

While Leising emphasized impeachment and conservative values, Hill stressed traditional Democratic themes of education, Social Security, and health care reform. As much as possible, Hill avoided discussion of Monica Lewinsky and President Clinton, other than to say that he would have voted for the Democratic alternative on the impeachment inquiry. Typical of Democratic campaigns in recent years, Hill portrayed his opponent as a potential threat to Social Security. In this respect, he claimed his central purpose in Washington would be to save Social Security both for his parents and his grandchildren.[16]

At least as important as actual stands on issues are perceptions of candidates. Leising attempted to portray herself as a social conservative. Had voters been as outraged at President Clinton over impeachment as they were in 1994 over Clinton's failed health care reform proposal and the proposal to allow gays to serve openly in the military, her strategy might have paid off with a victory. Unfortunately for Leising, the context of the 1998 elections was much different than that of 1994. As a result, her third attempt at the House, modeled after her nearly successful 1994 run, failed, even though Hamilton was no longer on the ballot.

While Leising veered to the right, Hill took the road of moderation, both in terms of issues and personal style. Still, it is unclear whether moderate issue positions, a walk across the district, or an advantage in campaign fundraising would have been sufficient without Hamilton's help. During the campaign's final week, the Hill campaign released an ad in which Hamilton implored voters to keep the seat in Democratic hands. Prior to airing of the ad, polls indicated that Leising was ahead by anywhere from 5 to 10 percent. Yet, importantly, the polls also indicated that as much as 28 percent of the electorate was undecided less than a week before the election.

In combination with several personal appearances, the ad, as well as endorsements from Bayh and O'Bannon, removed any lingering doubts these undecided voters may have had regarding Hamilton's designated successor. As a result, Hill won by a surprisingly large margin in a district believed to be ripe for a Republican takeover. He did so not only by appealing to the partisan nature of the district, an appeal that may have yielded a narrow plurality of the vote, but also by convincing these voters that he was a Democrat in the mold of his predecessor.

CONCLUSIONS

As with most elections, the race to replace Hamilton was decided by a range of factors, only one of which was Hamilton's personal involvement in the race. Yet, in the final count, Hamilton's involvement in the race was critical to Hill's success as a candidate. First, as Hamilton's preferred successor, Hill was able to raise more money than his Republican opponent despite the fact that he had not run for elective office since 1990. While Hill outpaced Leising in virtually every category of fundraising, his most impressive fundraising efforts involved his appeal to business-oriented sources. In this respect, with Hamilton's blessing, Hill was able to raise money in a fashion more akin to Democratic incumbents than to an open-seat candidate trailing in the polls.

Second, despite Leising's lead in the polls, a substantial portion of the electorate remained undecided just days prior to the election. Large numbers of undecided voters often spell trouble for leading, better-known candidates, but this is particularly true when the underdog has plenty of money to spend on advertising during the last week of the campaign. The money spent by Hill during the final week, however, was not spent just on typical campaign advertising, attacking his opponent or extolling his own virtues. Certainly, there was some of this "politics as usual" advertising, but the dominant message during the week was delivered not by Hill, but by Hamilton. It was positive, it was from a trusted, well-known political figure, and it apparently moved substantial numbers of undecided voters into the Democratic column.

Any conclusions regarding the ability of retiring incumbents to translate their own popularity into an electoral advantage for their party's nominee are necessarily limited. What worked for Hamilton may not work for other retiring incumbents. Despite the limitations, there are several conclusions that can be derived from this chapter. First, for incumbents to influence future elections, they must leave office relatively popular. Hamilton influenced the outcome not because he was the retiring incumbent, but because he remained well-known, well-liked, and well-respected within the district. When he appealed to voters to reward his 34 years of service, the appeal was genuine and was well-received. Second, incumbent endorsements may mean less if the incumbent does not take an active role in the campaign. Hamilton not only endorsed Hill, he helped in fundraising, made personal appearances, and appeared in television

Table 5.5 County Population Estimates, 1996

	1990 Population	1997 Population Estimate	Percent Change 1990–1997	Rank of Percent Change
Bartholomew	63,657	68,734	8.0	32
Brown	14,080	15,591	12.7	20
Clark	87,774	93,212	6.2	46
Crawford	9,914	10,499	5.9	49
Dearborn	38,835	46,576	19.9	4
Dubois	36,616	39,139	6.9	41
Fayette	26,015	26,133	0.5	81
Floyd	64,404	71,465	11.0	19
Franklin	19,580	21,582	10.2	23
Harrison	29,890	33,999	13.7	11
Jackson	37,730	40,884	8.4	29
Jefferson	29,797	31,292	5.0	53
Jennings	23,661	27,217	15.0	8
Ohio	5,315	5,458	2.7	63
Perry	19,107	19,306	1.0	76
Ripley	24,616	27,177	10.4	22
Scott	20,991	22,818	8.7	27
Spencer	19,490	20,690	6.2	47
Switzerland	7,738	8,636	11.6	16
Union	6,976	7,272	4.2	59
Washington	23,717	27,143	14.4	10
All Counties in District*	609,903	664,823	9.0	—
Indiana State Totals	5,544,156	5,864,108	5.8	—

*Only a portion of Bartholomew County is in the Ninth District, but entire county figures were used in the estimate. Computing district level population change without Bartholomew County, the estimated percentage is 9.1.

SOURCE: Compiled by authors.

ads. Hamilton's endorsement was itself important, but his active role in the campaign was even more important. Third, Hamilton was able to impact the race in part because some 28 percent of the electorate remained undecided until the final two weeks of the campaign. While Leising was better-known, many potential supporters, presumably weak Democrats and independents, were uncomfortable voting for her. Had Hill been better known in the district, or had voters been more committed in their early preferences, Hamilton's appeal might have been less effective and perhaps less necessary. Finally, Hamilton's appeal also fit well within the broader electoral context. In the state of Indiana, voters were already giving overwhelming support to the Democratic Senate candidate, Bayh. With a conservative Democrat at the top of the ticket and a moderate, independent Democrat endorsing his election, questions whether Hill would fit the district ideologically were easier to resolve in Hill's favor.

While Hamilton played a prominent, perhaps critical, role in Hill's initial election to the House, his future as a representative will be decided by his own record and perhaps by redistricting after the census of 2000. In terms of ideology, Hill will have to be careful not to stray too far to the left of his district. Elected as a "Hamilton" Democrat, his voting record will have to be consistent with his predecessor's—that is, moderate and independent. As a member of the minority party in the 106th Congress and without seniority, Hill may find it difficult to attract federal spending to the district. If so, maintaining support among conservative Democrats will be critical to his ability to win reelection.

Like his predecessor, Hill's fate may be affected by redistricting. As can be seen in table 5.5, the district has grown at a rate (9 percent) faster than the state (5.8 percent) as a whole. In fact, three of the state's ten fastest growing counties are in the Ninth District (Jennings, Dearborn, and Washington). Yet, the highest rates of growth in Indiana have occurred in five of the six counties surrounding Marion County and Indianapolis, the state capital.

Indiana is not projected to lose a House seat following the census of 2000, but the growth in counties surrounding Indianapolis may require some tinkering with district lines. While this potentially could adversely affect Hill's chances at reelection, the boundaries of the Ninth District cannot move much further north without affecting Republican incumbents in the Second and Sixth districts. If Republicans control redistricting, they appear unlikely to add Democratic territory to the neighboring Eighth District where the Republican incumbent had difficult reelection battles in 1996 and 1998. Similarly, if Democrats are in charge of new congressional maps, they are not likely to reduce Hill's chances of continuing in office.

Given that the more Democratic counties in the district are on the Indiana–Kentucky border, it is difficult to see how redistricting is going to have much of an impact. Unless mapmakers decide to radically redesign Indiana's congressional districts (which traditionally has occurred only when a seat was lost), the Ninth District should remain pretty much intact. As such, unless a strong national partisan tide in 2000 or 2002 forces Hill from office, his future as the representative from the Ninth District will likely depend in large part on his ability to emulate his predecessor.

NOTES

1. For a recent review of the literature on the incumbency advantage in House elections, see Gary W. Cox and Jonathan N. Katz, "Why Did the Incumbency Advantage in U.S. House Elections Grow?" *American Journal of Political Science* 40 (1996): 478–497.

2. Using the Gelman–King index, Jacobson estimated the incumbency advantage at 10.1 percent in 1994. See Gary C. Jacobson, "The 1994 House Elections in Perspective," in *Midterm: The Elections of 1994 in Context,* ed. Philip A. Klinkner (Boulder, CO: Westview, 1996).

3. Karen Merk, "Hill's Decisive Victory Keeps Hamilton's Seat," *Louisville Courier-Journal,* November 3, 1998.

4. *Congressional Quarterly* was a notable exception here, predicting a Democratic gain of 2 seats.

5. Thomas Marshall, *Recollections of Thomas R. Marshall: Vice-President and Hoosier Philosopher* (Indianapolis, IN: Bobbs–Merrill, 1925), 56.

6. V. O. Key, Jr., *American State Politics: An Introduction* (New York: Knopf, 1956), 220.

7. Michael Barone, Grant Ujifusa, and Douglas Matthews, *The Almanac of American Politics* (New York: E. P. Dutton, 1973).

8. Philip D. Duncan and Christine C. Lawrence, *Politics in America 1998* (Washington, DC: Congressional Quarterly, 1997), 535.

9. Ronald Keith Gaddie and Jonathan D. Mott, "The 1996 Open-Seat Congressional Elections," *Social Sciences Quarterly* 79 (1998): 445–455.

10. "Race to Fill Open 9th Congressional Seat Will Garner National Attention," *Electnet: The State Election Watch* (www.electnet.org, April 27, 1998).

11. National Republican Campaign Committee Press Release, "Indiana's Howey Report Notes Strength of Leising Campaign for U.S. House Seat," September 18, 1998.

12. Merk, "Hill's Decisive Victory."

13. National Republican Campaign Committee Press Release, "Indiana Targeted in Nationwide 'Operation Breakout' Campaign," October 6, 1998.

14. Thomas B. Edsall, "GOP Spends Millions in Key House Races in Ohio Valley," *The Washington Post,* October 31, 1998.

15. Merk, "Hill's Decisive Victory."

16. In her post-election comments, Leising complained that Hill had distorted her record on the issue. See Merk, "Hill's Decisive Victory."

Contested Seats

6

★

Sanchez Defeats Dornan in California's 46th District Race

Chris Fastnow
Jocelyn Benson

> Are, then, [representatives] in a position to do anything about getting reelected?. . . [I]f an answer is sought in their ability to affect the percentages in their own primary and general elections, the answer is yes. . . . [I]t will be argued that they think they can affect their own percentages, that in fact they can affect their own percentages, and furthermore that there is reason for them to try to do so.
>
> DAVID MAYHEW
> CONGRESS: THE ELECTORAL CONNECTION, 33

"Defeated by a Novice," "Overcome by an Underdog," read the headlines in November 1996, shortly after newcomer Loretta Sanchez ousted long-time incumbent Robert K. Dornan from his seat as representative from California's 46th Congressional District. The winning margin was slim—only 984 votes—and was contested by Dornan for more than a year. He insisted that voter fraud cost him the seat, although a congressional investigation determined that the number of fraudulent votes were not enough to overturn the results. Thus Dornan, on February 14, 1998, stood in front of an American flag on his front lawn and declared his intentions to seek reelection. "This [campaign] is about faith, family, and freedom," said Dornan, even attempting a little Spanish in his speech: "Juntos si se puede" ("Together, it can be done"), he declared.[1] Dornan, who had served 18 years in Congress before his controversial defeat, joined the 46th District race despite being urged not to run by influential Republican activists. His announcement was a declaration of war: "I treated her [in 1996] as one of my children, with a basically positive, hands-off campaign. No more. I'm entitled to the last hurrah. Win or lose, I'm going out with my best shot."[2]

Over the course of the next ten months, Democrat Sanchez and Republican Dornan engaged in a bitter, personal, and high-profile grudge match. In between their harsh criticisms and biting attacks, both candidates behaved like incumbents, acting just as David Mayhew predicted in his 1974 book, *Congress: The Electoral Connection*. Addressing what he saw as their proximate goal, Mayhew argued that members of Congress who want to be reelected should engage in three kinds of behavior: position taking, advertising, and credit claiming. Position taking requires no action, simply a declaration of an issue stance with which the voters presumably would agree. Advertising requires no real content—the goal instead is to increase recognition of the incumbent's name and a positive reaction to it among likely voters. Mayhew's third tendency, credit claiming, requires content, action, and credibility. Members, often gearing their messages toward certain constituencies, attempt to claim credit for policy initiatives, for delivering federal funds and other benefits to the district, and for individual constituent services.

The Sanchez-Dornan race was essentially a race between two incumbents trying to get reelected. Dornan used the 1998 campaign to revisit his past successes on behalf of the district, while Sanchez took advantage of her single-term incumbency to establish a credible foothold in the campaign. Both candidates engaged in position taking, advertising, and credit claiming. In the end, Sanchez was more successful at all three.

THE 46TH DISTRICT OF CALIFORNIA

The 46th is a community in transition, and a difficult one in which to build a strong and loyal constituency base. It is the geographic and economic center of Orange County. Half of the district's population lives in Santa Ana, but the district lines also include most of Garden Grove and Anaheim—including Disneyland and the area nearby, Knott's Berry Farm, John Wayne Airport, and Anaheim Stadium. There is no single industry that sets the economic tone for the area, and thus employment opportunities are in a constant state of flux, leading to frequent shifts in population trends.

The northern part of the 46th is centered around the city of Garden Grove. Perhaps most popularly known as the home of the "positive thinking" television ministry of Robert Schuller and the Crystal Cathedral, Garden Grove has traditionally been divided into three sections: an affluent, predominantly white, residential area to the west, a center region inhabited by a mix of Vietnamese, Koreans and Hispanics, and an eastern portion, where the vast majority of the city's Hispanic citizens reside. Further south is the city of Santa Ana, dubbed the "area's hub and seat of Orange County."[3] As its name implies, Santa Ana is a historic Mexican-American community, and it has also experienced the more recent immigration patterns of the rest of the county. The district also includes the southern tip of Anaheim. Just over 150,000 Anaheim residents live in the district, which has the look and feel of bordering Garden Grove but does not include the wealthier area of Anaheim Hills.

The district has long since undermined the stereotype of white, middle-class, Republican Orange County. The 46th District has the largest minority population in the county—50 percent Hispanic and 12 percent Asian.[4] The California legislature crafted it as a Democratic district as far back as 1962, until Vietnamese-Americans tilted the balance toward the Republican party in the 1980s. The recent growth of Hispanic voters, mobilized by the perceived threats of anti-immigration and affirmative action propositions in 1994 and 1996, along with the existing voting base of blue-collar workers, have now tipped the scales to the political left. Currently, 47 percent of the registered voters in the district are Democrats, with 40 percent registered Republican, earning the 46th the title of "least Republican" in Orange County.[5]

Recent Elections

Dornan, the six-term representative of the 46th District, has long been known for his sharp tongue and feisty rhetoric. Nicknamed "B-1 Bob" for his support of the bomber (and many other military planes), Dornan is a former Air Force fighter pilot and later a civilian radio and television talk show host. He is one of Rush Limbaugh's favorite substitutes, sitting in for the conservative host on many occasions. Like Limbaugh, Dornan is not afraid to call his opponents names. His campaigns are peppered with attacks on his foes, not all of which bear close scrutiny. He has suffered his own share of attacks, which were also not all true. The same combative style has characterized his campaigns in favor of defense spending, against communism, and against abortion.

Dornan served the bulk of this district since 1984, when he defeated the Democratic incumbent in an upset victory.[6] He won the next three races comfortably and withstood a redistricting in 1992 that nearly pitted him against another conservative Republican incumbent, Dana Rohrabacher. Instead, Dornan ran in the leaning-Democratic 46th and was challenged in the primary for the first time by moderate Republican Judith Ryan, a retired Superior Court judge who favored abortion rights. The Dornan-Ryan primary received national attention but drew only 27,000 Republican voters, three-fifths of whom opted for the incumbent. In November 1992, Dornan earned a slim reelection, with just 50 percent of the votes over Democrat Robert John Banuelos, a "hapless Democrat who raised and spent almost nothing" in the general elections.[7] Despite his slim victory, Dornan out-polled George Bush, who received just 40 percent of the district's votes. Even so, in light of the influx of Latino voters into the district, influencing the growing registration advantage of the Democratic party, it became apparent that Dornan would soon have to actively court Orange County's newest constituency or face rejection at the polls.

In 1994, Dornan was challenged by Democrat Mike Farber. Perhaps sensing the indifferent political attitudes of the booming Hispanic and Asian populations, neither Dornan nor Farber courted the district's non-white communities. As had been the case in the past, turnout among the two groups was relatively low. When the predominantly Democrat Hispanic and predominately Republican Asian voters stayed home on election day, Dornan's white followers came out to reelect him with a 20-point lead.

THE ELECTION OF 1996

The story of the 1998 election in the 46th District begins three years earlier, with the candidacy of Democrat Loretta Sanchez. As a young, Hispanic, female Democrat, Sanchez believed she could beat the older, white, male, conservative Dornan. When Sanchez launched her grassroots campaign to represent the 46th District in late 1995, she was widely ignored by the media, the electorate, the Democratic party, and her opponent. Her experience in politics up until that point had been minimal. In fact, she only registered as a Democrat in 1992 and had run just one unsuccessful city council campaign. Nevertheless, from her November 1995 announcement through her victory in the June Democratic primary, Sanchez waged an extensive grassroots campaign through the use of direct mail. The use of persuasion mail to advertise her message was a relatively inexpensive way to reach out as an unknown to a heterogeneous community. "Direct mail is an especially powerful medium for challengers . . . because it is ideal for negative advertising or making appeals that stir voters' emotions."[8] Presenting herself as the "candidate to beat Bob Dornan," Sanchez's pre-primary mail pieces were "designed to take full advantage of suspicions about Dornan's record in Congress, while ensuring that they also would define [Sanchez] as the right alternative."[9]

During this time, Dornan had been running for the Republican presidential nomination, a bid that failed despite his vigorous attention to issues of national defense and abortion. Campaigning for the presidential nomination took him away from the district at the same time that it highlighted his strongest issue positions. His attempt to be president also cost him dearly in terms of campaign resources. Any money he raised went to the national campaign rather than to his House candidacy.

Sanchez began to emerge as a serious threat to the incumbent in the end of June, when she announced she had raised a total of $189,000 to Dornan's mere $24,000. She then used her funds to dive into a unique advertising medium that Dornan and past Orange County campaigns failed to use: cable television spots. In three weeks, Sanchez went from claiming 25 percent of the electorate to 43 percent—putting her in a virtual dead heat with Dornan.[10] This rapid movement caught the eyes of Washington, and leaders in both parties began to wonder if Dornan was in fact in serious danger.

In the final weeks of the campaign, the two candidates scrambled to get out their vote. Sanchez rallied her anti-Dornan troops, especially environmentalists, abortion rights groups, gay activists, and the president of the United States, while Dornan attacked them and rallied the National Rifle Association, abortion foes, and members of the Christian Coalition. Five hundred evangelical Christians stumped door-to-door for Dornan, while more than 100 school-teachers and abortion rights and environmental activists did the same for Sanchez.[11] Sanchez's efforts also included working with other candidates to organize a considerable absentee mail program. "Out of concern for voter intimidation, we figured the best way for Latinos to vote was by absentee," Sanchez's campaign manager John Shallman said, referring to worries that Hispanic voters might be discouraged from voting by being challenged for citizenship.[12]

When the 6,000 absentee ballots were finally counted days after the election, the virtually unknown Sanchez had trumped Dornan by just 984 votes to become the first woman and first Hispanic that Orange County sent to Congress. Dornan challenged this outcome for more than a year, pointing to the large percentages of new citizens who had voted by absentee and claiming that he was the "first U.S. Congressman voted out of office by non-citizens."[13] In March 1998, a House committee announced that while some illegal ballots had been cast, there were not enough invalid ballots to overturn the election results.

THE 1998 PRIMARY

When Dornan announced he would seek the seat again in 1998, some in the party tried to convince him to drop the challenge. He faced three other Republican candidates in the June primary and found many local Republican organizations and leaders shifting their support to his challengers. The high profile Lincoln Club of Orange County, for example, endorsed Lisa Hughes and pledged to actively oppose Dornan. "We're concerned about the health and welfare of the Republican party and its slate of candidates in Orange County," said Howard J. Klein, Lincoln Club vice president, in defense of their decision. "We had to do what was in the best interest of the party and not any one individual."[14] Seasoned Republicans like State Senator John R. Lewis joined the Hughes campaign. "[Dornan] has gone from somebody you laugh with to somebody you laugh at," Lewis said at the time.[15]

But Dornan remained undaunted and went on to win the Republican nomination under the new primary ballot rules. As of 1998, all the candidates for office in California are placed on the same ballot, regardless of party affiliation. Voters choose just one candidate, and the top two vote-getters face off in the general election. In this race, the outcome was similar to what would have been predicted under the old party ballot system. Sanchez received 44.7 percent of the popular vote in the June primary. Three Republicans split much of the remaining vote. Twenty-six percent favored Dornan, while 15 percent and 11 percent voted for his Republican opponents, Hughes and James Gray. A fourth Republican received less than 2 percent. Dornan received nearly half of the votes cast in favor of Republican candidates.

Hughes explained her loss to Dornan as evidence of the "power of incumbency."[16] Dornan agreed, saying his win was the result of "two words: my record."[17] But although his record was enough to secure the nomination, it was not enough to win the general election.

THE 1998 GENERAL
ELECTION CAMPAIGN

Position Taking

In the 1998 general election campaign, both candidates practiced what Mayhew called position taking, or the "public enunciation of a judgmental statement on anything likely to be of interest to political actors. . . . The [representative] as position taker is a speaker rather than a doer. The electoral requirement is not that he make pleasing things happen, but that he make pleasing judgmental statements."[18] Position taking requires no real activity on the part of the incumbent, only the public pronouncement of a stance. All candidates take positions throughout the campaign. Most also follow through on their positions with action of some kind, both before and after the election.[19]

For years, Dornan's position taking remained consistent, revolving around the theme of "Faith, Family, Freedom." He made his active Catholicism known, and he was clear about the political positions associated with some of the issues that the Catholic Church cares about. He comfortably filled his speech with religious rhetoric and quotations from the Bible. Dornan took positions on several social issues like abortion, local school control, and public prayer. He continued his long-held positions against communism, in favor of defense, against taxes, and in favor of a balanced budget.

The 1998 Dornan campaign also contained some new positions. Throughout the campaign, he reminded supporters, the media, and residents in the district of the 1996 voter fraud investigation, taking the explicit position that Sanchez was a liar and a cheat. And, though many in his party distanced themselves from it, Dornan campaigned on the pending impeachment investigation against President Clinton.

Sanchez, meanwhile, had to switch her strategy from the previous election. In 1996, she ran a largely anti-Dornan campaign, needing only to highlight what was unpopular about Dornan's positions rather than forcefully stake out her own. As the incumbent in 1998, however, she had to establish her own positions. She took positions on many of the same issues that Dornan did, but she placed herself on the opposing end of the spectrum. Indeed, many observers suggested that this race gave evidence that the two parties differed substantially. Sanchez retained her ardent pro-choice position and continued to endorse gay rights, as she did in 1996. Sanchez also worked to position herself as the pro-business candidate, employing her previous experience as a financial analyst and owner of the small business, Amiga Advisors.

Both candidates positioned themselves as tough crime fighters. Both promised to work for the district's economic interests. Both also favored strong schools, though their approaches differed along traditional party lines.

Advantage: Sanchez For successful position taking, voters must favor the position taken. In the end, the position taking strategy Dornan played may have backfired. An October poll of the district conducted by Chapman University found that voters tended to be pro-choice (55 percent to 32 percent pro-life) and to separate their votes in this race from the issues surrounding the president (two-thirds). A plurality did consider the voter fraud charges to be valid (44 percent to 37 percent invalid), which may have helped him gain the votes he did secure. But, as Southwest Voter Registration Education Project coordinator Ruben Villareal said, "the Hispanics in the 46th perceived that Dornan, with his constant denunciations of voter fraud after the '96 election, was and is anti-Latino."[20] That position choice likely hurt Dornan among Latinos.

Although smaller numbers supported Dornan's positions on two of his most visible campaign positions—abortion and the impeachment process— Dornan believed these groups would be more active. For example, Dornan said, "We're not losing ground on abortion. The pro-lifers are the ones who are passionate about it and will get out and vote for it."[21] "However, the abortion issue [did] not appear to be a key determinant of voting intentions, since both candidates [drew] support from voters who do not share their views on abortion."[22]

Finally, in an earlier July poll, 36 percent of the registered voters believed that Sanchez cared more about economic problems in their income bracket, compared to 22 percent who believed that Dornan cared more.[23] Sanchez's pro-business positions seemed to carry more weight than Dornan's.

Advertising

Another of Mayhew's behaviors, advertising, is quite costly. Advertising involves not only the kinds of political ads we are used to seeing and hearing but also anything that gets a candidate's name in front of the voters. Mayhew defines advertising as "any effort to disseminate one's name among constituents in such a fashion as to create a favorable image, but in messages having little or no issue content."[24] All press is good press. The goal of advertising is to raise name recognition among the voters and to create an image of experience, sincerity, responsiveness, and concern.

In the 46th District, both candidates were well known from the beginning after their headline-grabbing 1996 match-up. In fact, as early as July, only 26 percent of the registered voters were undecided, although 30 to 40 percent expressed uncertainty about questions specifically evaluating the candidates' performance and promises, a discrepancy that could mean name recognition carried no image content in many voters' minds.[25] The candidates worked hard to advertise in order to capture the undecided vote.

The Incumbency Advantage Incumbents generally have an advantage over challengers in advertising.[26] First, the franking privilege that every member enjoys allows for a number of mailings to the entire district at the taxpayer's expense. These constituent newsletters give officeholders ample opportunity to print their names and faces, and the news is always positive. Sanchez was able to use this privilege during her first year of office, but Dornan maintained a high profile from his mailings to the district over the past several congresses.

Second, incumbents, as policymakers and national figures, are often newsworthy, so they receive free positive and negative coverage in the local press. Since all advertising raises awareness of the candidate, almost any story is seen as good. Sanchez, as the current officeholder, would ordinarily have the advantage here, but both candidates enjoyed press attention during the voter fraud investigation. Even later, the main newspaper for the district, the *Orange County Register,* covered the race extensively. More than 20 percent of the election stories published in the three-month period leading up to the election featured the Sanchez–Dornan race, despite the presence of dozens of other races in the county, including several major statewide candidacies and initiatives, five other U.S. House races, out-of-state races of national prominence, and dozens of local campaigns. This heavy coverage served as free advertising for both candidates.

Third, incumbents usually enjoy a fundraising advantage, allowing for paid television, radio, and print advertising. In Southern California, these things are especially costly, and in 1998, Sanchez and Dornan each raised more than $3 million in what was the most expensive House race of the year.

Fundraising Challenger Dornan, contrary to the trend, raised more money than his incumbent opponent.[27] This is perhaps unsurprising, as Dornan used the fundraising methods he developed during his own time as an incumbent. Most of Dornan's money, nearly 90 percent, came from small individual contributions from all over the country. Dornan used a national direct mail effort to raise most of his funds, a method he had used to solicit campaign contributions for many years. The process is costly and slow, but it paid off for him. Many of his donors sent a check for $25 whenever they could during the campaign, amounting to thousands of total contributions of $100 or less. Twenty-six percent of Dornan's contributions came from outside California.[28] By the final reporting period before the election, he had amassed just under $3.4 million. Only 11 percent of those funds came from political action committees (PACs) or party organizations.[29]

By contrast, about 78 percent of Sanchez's $3 million came from party organizations and PACs. She also differed from Dornan in where the money came from. Sanchez raised about 80 percent of her funds from California donors.[30] Sanchez even received a contribution from across the aisle. New York Republican Representative Michael Forbes bucked his party's efforts against Sanchez by contributing $1,000, a donation soundly criticized by Dornan, who complained, "I know of no precedent in this half a century, and it screams out for written condemnation by the [National Republican Congressional Committee]. Anything else will breed more such disloyalty."[31]

Because of the expensive battle over the voter fraud charges, Dornan had less to spend even though he raised more. He paid his legal fees out of his campaign fund, and was only partially reimbursed by the government after the investigation. Sanchez, who was also partially reimbursed, paid her legal fees out of her personal funds and as a result, she had more campaign money to spare in the final weeks.[32] She even donated some of her campaign money to other Democratic candidates nationally in the final week of the race.[33]

With more than $6 million in the race, each candidate blanketed the district with paid mail, radio and cable TV ads, and public rallies. The campaigns worked hard to create both a positive image of the candidate and a simultaneous negative image of the opponent.

Positive Advertising To create a positive image within one constituency, both candidates advertised in Spanish, a practice that was uncommon before the 1998 elections. In fact, throughout California, Spanish-language advertisements filled the airwaves, and candidates learned new or brushed up on old Spanish skills. The major parties spent about $1 million on outreach efforts to Hispanics statewide, while the gubernatorial candidates also spent $1 million on Spanish language advertising.[34]

These efforts spilled into the 46th District. Dornan's Spanish-language advertising doubled over that of 1996. He printed fliers in Spanish and mailed them to households with Hispanic surnames as targeted advertising efforts. Sanchez, who had dropped her husband's Anglo last name, Brixey, before the 1996 election, also campaigned in Spanish. Campaign literature from both camps prominently featured Latino-Americans standing in front of their businesses or homes. Dornan's literature especially highlighted the Latino presence in the district. Most pictures (that were not of Dornan family members) were of minority children or businesspeople.

Both candidates also appealed to the growing Vietnamese population in the 46th District. Dornan had enjoyed Vietnamese support in the past for his tough anti-communist positions and personal experience as a civilian journalist in Vietnam. Many of the Vietnamese-Americans who moved to the 46th were angry not that the U.S. had gotten involved in Vietnam, but that the U.S. pulled out of Vietnam.[35] To continue building Vietnamese support in 1998, Dornan hired a campaign staffer specifically as a liaison to the Vietnamese community. His campaign printed a thick, four-color magazine in English and Vietnamese, featuring photos of Dornan with Vietnamese-Americans and letters from and to Dornan concerning POW/MIA legislation, compensation for South Vietnamese commandos, and other issues of interest to the Vietnamese community.

Sanchez also courted the Vietnamese vote. She appeared at every event in the Vietnamese community that she reasonably could, participating in community activities, and even donning a traditional costume to celebrate Tet, the Vietnamese New Year. According to Sanchez, courting the vote of a single community was not the plan. "I don't target any particular group. I work on issues that cross ethnic lines. . . . You cannot be everything for everybody at all times."[36] Still, her regular presence in Little Saigon was seen as strategic and helped her among some voters in this growing community. One young Vietnamese-American voter applauded Sanchez's efforts; "She took the time to understand the culture."[37] Her success in doing so paid off on election day, when she captured several predominantly Vietnamese precincts that had voted for Dornan in 1996 as well as every precinct with a substantial number of Hispanics.[38]

Although Sanchez moved campaigning ahead with the new cable television medium in 1996, Dornan was the more innovative in the 1998 election. He employed a state-of-the-art web page for the campaign, complete with high quality downloadable audio and video clips.[39] He used the site to push his campaign theme and showcase photos of himself and his family. Sanchez's website was not nearly as comprehensive or sophisticated.

Despite this electronic disadvantage, Sanchez used another perk of office to advertise and boost her recognition. Members of Congress receive an administrative budget allocation that can be used, in part, on travel to their districts. Sanchez used all of these government-funded trips and more at her own expense, appearing in the district almost every weekend of the year. During those trips home, she held "office hours" in informal locations around the district, like local supermarkets. She used these events to meet more voters than would typically come to her district office.

Dornan accused her of using these events as campaign functions, claiming that, for example, Sanchez was registering volunteers for her campaign while listening to constituent concerns.[40] Because her district congressional staff, not campaigners, staffed the office hours, campaigning should have been strictly forbidden. But these office hours became visible for another reason entirely. One Saturday morning at the Santa Ana Ralph's supermarket, Dornan appeared at Sanchez's office hours to challenge her to a debate. Sanchez had refused to debate him, much as Dornan refused a debate in 1996.[41] The challenge somehow turned into a scuffle, with both camps claiming the other had gotten physical. Dornan's campaign manager caught the mishap on video. The local press seemed to favor Dornan's interpretation when the story told by Sanchez's campaign manager was not supported by the video.[42]

Negative Advertising Both candidates repeatedly attempted to cast the other negatively. For instance, Dornan's literature featured a photo of Sanchez next to medical drawings of a late-term abortion procedure. The mailer was sent to households with Hispanic surnames in an attempt to capture Catholic voters who may be opposed to abortion. His campaign also circulated a list of the 14 "high crimes, misdemeanors, and lies" of Loretta Sanchez, largely though not exclusively surrounding the voter fraud investigation. Dornan tried unsuccessfully to get the press to pick up the list.

Sanchez fired back fairly late in the campaign with a mailer accusing Dornan of abusing the system at the taxpayer's expense with his voter fraud investigation, though there was no mention that her own expenses had also been partially reimbursed. The front of the mailer shouted, "The only thing WORSE than a SORE LOSER is . . . a loser who makes YOU pay for his loss." The mailing highlighted Dornan's subpoenas of records where several people registered to vote with the same residential address. While some of these records showed illegal registration, some were records of people who legitimately lived in group settings. Sanchez played this to her advantage. The literature claimed that "Dornan's witch hunt wrongfully accused thousands of Americans, including Catholic nuns [in convents], U.S. marines [in barracks] and seniors [in retirement homes]."[43] Further, though most of its content was positive advertising, Sanchez's campaign website also attacked Dornan. "The embittered Dornan's allegations of voter fraud smack of racism."[44]

Advantage: Sanchez Like position taking, advertising worked to Sanchez's advantage. An October poll conducted for the *Orange County Register* showed, "Among likely voters polled, Sanchez received a 50 percent favorable rating and Dornan 38 percent."[45] Sanchez's unfavorable ratings were lower than Dornan's, but to her disadvantage, "[v]oters cite[d] dishonesty as a top concern with Sanchez (19 percent), more often than with Dornan (12 percent)." Still, Dornan himself may have advertised too much. "Many voters said they have had enough of Dornan's personality. His abrasive and controversial manner generated the most dislike among voters. It was named by 23 percent of registered voters polled."[46]

And all of the targeted advertising? Republicans in general suffered from a long-term image problem, at least among Latinos. Dornan was no exception. A survey by the Southwest Voter Registration Education Project, an organization dedicated to increasing Latino political participation, "shows that despite [GOP gubernatorial nominee Dan] Lungren and a few other GOP candidates spending record amounts on Spanish-language media, they did not address the issues that are of concern to Latinos: public education first and foremost, along with better jobs and public safety."[47]

Credit-Claiming

Like all incumbents, both candidates attempted to take credit for the actions they had taken while in office. Mayhew suggests that credit may be claimed by "acting so as to generate a belief . . . that one is personally responsible for causing the government, or some unit thereof, to do something" that the constituents desire.[48] Candidates claim credit for constituent casework, localized district benefits or projects, and pushing policy initiatives that, while not bringing direct benefits to the district, are widely favored by the voters in the area.

Policy Credit The Dornan campaign touted a "partial" list, posted on their website and in various campaign mailings, of "What Congressman Dornan Has Done for the 46th District and Orange County." The list detailed federal funds he had secured for the district, small area businesses he had helped to survive, and major policy initiatives (Medicare and Social Security) that he had voted for. "I did it all, and I'm glad" signed Dornan at the bottom of the flyer. Dornan earned a national reputation for his fiery stance on conservative planks, although he was often criticized for allowing his concern over national issues to take precedent over district concerns, climaxing in his failed bid for the presidency in 1996. He claimed his greatest policy legacy was "the tens of thousands of Americans walking around today because I saved them from abortions by cutting off abortion funding at military bases, federal prisons, Indian reservations, and the District of Columbia. A lot of black children and Indian children are alive because of that."[49]

Particularized Benefits Sanchez, known nationally not for issues but as the "darling of the Democratic party," chose to do her credit claiming while spending time with constituents in office hours to show that she focused on issues that directly affected their lives. In particular, she secured $6.75 million for improvements on the Santa Ana Freeway, and $2 million for the Orange County Transportation Authority, and thus managed to convince local officials that she worked hard to push an Orange County agenda in Washington.

As a result of her district-focused activity in Congress, Sanchez also gained support from organizations that had supported Dornan in 1996. Most significant was an endorsement from the three largest police officer organizations in Orange County. At the time, a wounded Dornan remarked: "If this is a general election endorsement, it is incredible because there was no interview of any other candidates." Previously, endorsements were "a very structured process with a full board hearing. This is unprecedented." He later attributed the shift to one word: "unions."[50] The police associations, however, claimed to have good reason for breaking from precedent and supporting Sanchez: "We think Sanchez is responsive to our needs and interested in what we do," said the head of the Santa Ana Police Association's political action committee. "She meets with us and talks to us, and we haven't gotten that in the past. The endorsements are validation of the work that Loretta has been doing on one of her principal areas of concentration: crime."[51]

Representation Both campaigns continued to reach out to Hispanic and Vietnamese communities by highlighting actions they had taken to represent these communities while in Congress. Dornan often claimed "In spirit, I'm the real Latino," or that he better represented a diverse district: "I'm Mr. Immigrant Man. Every community sees me as their Irish brother."[52] Dornan's campaign team compiled and distributed a brochure entitled "How Bob Dornan Has Represented Americans of Hispanic Heritage," while he circulated a list of accomplishments noting that he "saved the Ace Muffler Shop for a 4th generation Hispanic-American Santa Ana family." His literature also spoke to the Vietnamese community, claiming that he secured back pay for Vietnamese commandos placed in North Vietnam in 1964. Interestingly, Sanchez also claimed that she had secured the same compensation through legislation she had written and passed during her first term. In reality, her bill was merely a modified version of one that Dornan had proposed before his ousting in 1996, and similar to one that had already passed in the Senate.

Sanchez was a strong pro-labor advocate in Washington, and thus supported a critical issue to the Hispanic and Vietnamese voters in her district. These actions were not forgotten by the labor unions, which helped secure Sanchez endorsements and funds from organizations that are highly visible in non-white communities.

Claiming to represent Latino and Vietnamese concerns helped Sanchez specifically and Democrats generally in 1998. As one Orange County voter explained, "I voted for the Democrats. They listen to us, and I feel they are on our side. They are working on behalf of the immigrants, and they listen, and they seem to want to make things better for Latinos."[53] Conversely, Dornan's actions had many negative reverberations within the Hispanic community, based primarily on the Republican record. "How can Dornan use [the Virgin of Guadalupe, a revered icon among Hispanics worldwide] in his campaign when the Republican Party constantly hammers at the Hispanic community?" asked Sam Romero, owner of St. Teresa's Liberia Catholica in Santa Ana.[54]

Aware of the fact that the 46th District, due to a large Hispanic Catholic population, is the most Catholic district in Orange County, the candidates repeatedly wore "their religion on their sleeve" in an attempt to claim credit for better representing Catholic voters.[55] Sanchez sidestepped the abortion issue as she visited a variety of Catholic churches in the district throughout the campaign: "I am devoted to giving some time to God," she said, "and I'm always interested in all aspects of my constituents' lives. . . . But I don't discuss politics unless I'm asked." She also admitted: "I don't agree 100 percent with what the church advocates."[56] The Reverend Norman McFarland, Bishop of Orange, even wrote to Sanchez in March 1998 to ask her not to visit churches in the district, as those visits appeared to be "motivated by partisan and personal ambitions associated with the upcoming primary and general elections."[57] The letter was selectively leaked to the press in July.

Neither candidate succeeded in receiving the support of the Catholic Church, however. Dornan emphasized his common cause with the Church, calling his opponent "another Catholic for abortion and sodomy rights."[58] But Dornan's own positions on nuclear arms, land mines, and universal health care placed him outside the Church's teachings. "The bishops look at the world as countries without borders, which is good," said Dornan. "But they don't have to defend our borders. They don't have to create jobs. They could all be socialists—and many of them are."[59] For some, the claims of Catholic representation rang somewhat hollow. "It almost comes down to the lesser of two evils," according to one voter.[60] Reverend Allan Deck, director of the Loyola Institute for Spirituality and a Jesuit priest, summed up the Catholic credit claiming activity: "Both of them are trying to get leverage from their Catholic backgrounds. Both of them are inconsistent in their support of Catholic policy."[61]

Advantage: Sanchez   In the end, actions spoke louder than words, as credit claiming appeared to work more effectively for Sanchez than for Dornan. In the October *Orange County Register* poll, "the top reason cited for picking Sanchez, named by 29 percent of backers, was that she better represented people like them."[62] Sanchez was highly visible in the district throughout her two years in Congress, while Dornan could not shake the image that he had neglected his district for national interests throughout his 18 years in Congress. Sanchez spent two years in Congress and wrote one bill that passed. Although he wrote sections of or amendments to successful bills, Dornan was in Congress for 18 years and left without having authored a single bill that became law. "The voters have seen Bob Dornan for 18 years," remarked his primary opponent, Hughes. "Four weeks of acting on your best behavior is not going to erase years of Bob Dornan rhetoric."[63]

CONCLUSION

"Latina Swamps Dornan in Rematch," "Sanchez Crushes Dornan," blared the headlines the day after the election, the day after Sanchez solidly beat Dornan. Instead of the close race Dornan predicted or the razor-thin margin of 1996, Sanchez won 56 percent to Dornan's paltry 39 percent. Sanchez captured 200 of the 265 precincts in the district. She won every precinct in which Hispanics accounted for at least 25 percent of registered voters, also winning a number of predominantly Vietnamese precincts that voted for Dornan in 1996.

"On Feb. 14, Bob Dornan announced that he was giving the 46th District a valentine by running again—well, here I am," Sanchez gleefully announced to supporters on election night. Dornan, on the other hand, refused to concede the election. "She lied about my record to steal this race two years ago, . . . she smeared my record for two years, cost the taxpayers millions of dollars stonewalling the voter fraud investigation, which was her fault, we proved, . . . and then my party betrayed me, no guts, because of gender and ethnicity. . . . She has raised dirty money from Hugh Heffner, Johnny Chung, abortion mills, and homosexual activist groups. . . . She's the dirtiest candidate in the country and the biggest fraud. I will never concede to her."[64]

Religion and ethnicity certainly played roles in the 1998 race. As a majority-minority district, the 46th was interested in the change a Latina candidate presented in 1996 and eager to give her another term in 1998. The decisive factor in the race, however, was the way that each candidate treated religion and ethnicity in order to win votes. Although both candidates acted like incumbents, Sanchez took successful positions, advertised effectively, and claimed credit that was credible. From 1996 through 1998, Sanchez was in Orange County shaking hands with constituents in diverse neighborhoods every weekend, while Dornan was in Washington working to overturn the 1996 election results. And while Dornan may have done a great deal for the district while serving in Congress, he was not effective in convincing his constituents of that, both while in office and while campaigning. Sanchez, through her office hours, her mailings, and her endorsements, was able to capitalize on the services she had provided her constituents during her two-year term.

NOTES

1. Greg Hardesty, "Dornan's Off and Running Again," *Orange County Register,* February 15, 1998.

2. Ibid.

3. Congressional Quarterly, *Congressional Quarterly Almanac,* Vol. 4 (Washington, DC: Congressional Quarterly, 1998), 220.

4. Michael Barone and Grant Ujifusa, *The Almanac of American Politics 1998* (Washington, DC: National Journal, 1997), 259.

5. Congressional Quarterly, *Congressional Quarterly Almanac,* 220.

6. Dornan was first elected to Congress from a fairly liberal Westside (Los Angeles) district in 1976. He won expensive and bitter reelection victories there twice, serving until his unsuccessful 1982 Senate bid. After two years out of politics, he returned to the fray in Orange County, where he has been a potent force ever since.

7. Michael Barone and Grant Ujifusa, *The Almanac of American Politics 1994* (Washington, DC: National Journal, 1993), 198.

8. Paul S. Herrnson, *Congressional Elections: Campaigning at Home and in Washington,* 2nd ed. (Washington, DC: Congressional Quarterly, 1998), 189.

9. Bill Wachbob and Andrew Kennedy, "Beating B-1 Bob: How Underdog Loretta Sanchez Ended Bob Dornan's Congressional Career," *Campaigns and Elections,* 18 (February 1997), 32–36.

10. Ibid., 34.

11. James Grimaldi, "Dornan, Sanchez Take Race to the Streets," *Orange County Register,* October 26, 1996.

12. Wachbob and Kennedy, "Beating B-1 Bob," 36. Orange County has had something of a history of voter intimidation through the use of "poll guards." According to the *Orange County Register,* then–Assembly candidate Curt Pringle won a narrow election to the Assembly in 1988 after his Republican party allies posted uniformed guards at polling places in 20 heavily Hispanic Santa Ana precincts. The guards carried signs with messages in English and Spanish warning noncitizens not to vote. "The tactic was widely viewed as an attempt to intimidate Hispanic voters, including new citizens who were entitled to vote but might have been frightened by a symbol of authority they did not understand." See Daniel M. Weintraub, "Pringle Can't Shake Poll-Guard Controversy," *Orange County Register,* October 26, 1998. The specter of polling irregularities continues to haunt Orange County politics. Pringle faced the allegations again in his 1998 statewide race, renewing ill-will among some voters. Further reminding Orange County of the event, about 40 federal polling observers were expected to watch both for voter intimidation and for illegal voting. Martin Wisckol, "Observers Expected at the Polls in County," *Orange County Register,* November 3, 1998.

13. Ana Menendez, "Furor in the 46th District: Some Think It's a Circus," *Orange County Register,* November 21, 1996.

14. Jean Pasco, "Zemel Drops Out of Congressional Race," *Los Angeles Times,* February 27, 1998.

15. Ibid.

16. Dena Bunis, "Dornan Defeats Hughes," *Orange County Register,* June 3, 1998.

17. Ibid.

18. David R. Mayhew, *Congress: The Electoral Connection* (New Haven, CT: Yale, 1974), 61–62.

19. Thomas E. Patterson, *Out of Order* (New York: Vintage, 1994), prologue.

20. Guillermo Garcia and Ronald Campbell, "Sanchez Wins All Hispanic Districts," *Orange County Register,* November 5, 1998.

21. Martin Wisckol, "Dornan Stands Behind Three-Pronged Strategy," *Orange County Register,* October 7, 1998.

22. Chapman University Henley Social Sciences Research Laboratory, "The Chapman Poll: Sanchez v. Dornan 1998," July 9, 1998.

23. Chapman University Henley Social Sciences Research Laboratory, "The Chapman Poll #2: Sanchez v. Dornan 1998," October 6, 1998.

24. Mayhew, *Congress,* 49.

25. Chapman University, Poll #2.

26. For a good overview of the incumbency advantage generally, see Herrnson, *Congressional Elections;* Gary C. Jacobson, *The Politics of Congressional Elections,* 4th Ed. (New York: Longman, 1997); Mayhew, *Congress.*

27. Federal Election Commission, "Financial Activity of House Campaigns 1997–98," accessed November 5, 1998.

28. Martin Wisckol, "Sanchez, Dornan Have 2 of Biggest War Chests," *Orange County Register,* October 30, 1998.

29. Ibid.

30. Ibid.

31. Laurence Arnold, "GOP Rep. Gave Money to 2 Democrats," Associated Press, December 9, 1998.

32. Wisckol, "Sanchez, Dornan have 2 of Biggest War Chests."

33. Dena Bunis, "Sanchez Could Reap Rewards of Generosity," *Orange County Register,* November 5, 1998.

34. Mark Katches and Guillermo Garcia, "Hispanics See a Political Sea Change," *Orange County Register,* October 22, 1998.

35. Michael Barone and Grant Ujifusa, *The Almanac of American Politics 1996* (Washington, DC: National Journal, 1995), 210.

36. Vik Jolly, "Both Parties Hunt for Ethnic Voters," *Orange County Register,* October 24, 1998.

37. Ibid.

38. Garcia and Campbell, "Sanchez Wins."

39. Robert K. Dornan, "Dornan for Congress Official Website," accessed November 1, 1998.

40. Martin Wisckol and Dena Bunis, "Taking Off the Gloves in the 46th," *Orange County Register,* August 7, 1998.

41. Debates tend to help the candidate who is behind by lending credibility to a failing campaign or by giving the losing candidate a forum for press and public recognition. Therefore, frontrunners (usually incumbents) often try to avoid debating.

42. Wisckol and Bunis, "Taking Off the Gloves." Sadly, both the press and the public were not surprised at the Ralph's tussle. In 1996, Dornan's son and campaign manager, Mark, performed a citizen's arrest on Sanchez's husband. Sanchez's husband was later fined for tearing down two Dornan campaign signs. That event was followed by additional incensed rhetoric on both sides, which was only echoed in the 1998 campaign. The Ralph's incident seemed to be just one more in a string of bad behavior by the candidates.

43. Dena Bunis, "Dornan Pro and Con the Issue in the GOP Race," *Orange County Register,* May 21, 1998.

44. Loretta Sanchez, "Loretta Sanchez for Congress—46th CD," accessed November 5, 1998.

45. Martin Wisckol and Dena Bunis, "Voters Tell What They Dislike About Hopefuls," *Orange County Register,* October 31, 1998.

46. Ibid.

47. Ruben Villarreal, quoted in Ronald Campbell and Guillermo Garcia, "Hispanic Voters Give Democrats Boost," *Orange County Register,* November 5, 1998.

48. Mayhew, Congress, 53.

49. Martin Wisckol and Teri Sforza, "Dornan's Next Stop: Radio, TV," *Orange County Register,* November 5, 1998.

50. Peter Warren, "Sanchez, Dornan Trade Barbs But Not Face to Face," *Los Angeles Times,* November 3, 1996.

51. Ibid.

52. Jolly, "Both Parties Hunt."

53. Quoted in Campbell and Garcia, "Hispanic Voters."

54. Ibid.

55. Martin Wisckol, "Religion, Politics Mix in 46th District," *Orange County Register,* October 27, 1998.

56. Ibid.

57. Norman McFarland, "Bishop McFarland's Letter to U.S. Representative Loretta Sanchez," *Diocese of Orange Bulletin* (August 1998), 2.

58. Wisckol and Sforza, "Dornan's Next Stop."

59. Wisckol, "Religion, Politics."

60. Ibid.

61. Ibid.

62. Wisckol and Bunis, "Voters Tell."

63. Bunis, "Dornan Pro and Con."

64. *Orange County Register,* "Bob Dornan at 7:10 p.m.," audio clip, November 5, 1998.

7

★

Emerson Defeats Heckemeyer in Missouri's Eighth District Race

Brian Smentkowski
Rickert Althaus
Peter J. Bergerson

The 1998 election in the Eighth District of Missouri featured a first-term Republican congressional widow who the Democratic party leaders felt never actually resided in the district easily turning back a challenge from a conservative Democratic judge who had farmed and lived in the district his entire life. Early in the election cycle, speculation, particularly in Democratic circles, centered on how the race might be competitive. Democrats clung to the idea that past voter loyalties would resurface to elect a strong local candidate. Popular sentiments suggested that a "home grown" Democrat with political connections, governmental service, and campaign experience could make this a competitive race. The district is in a rural but diverse region that had historically been thought of as a Democratic district, but which through reapportionment and realignment has become a Republican one. In this chapter, we tell the tale of the contest in Missouri's Eighth Congressional District in 1998.

DISTRICT CHARACTERISTICS

Missouri's Eighth Congressional District is economically diverse, politically idiosyncratic, and socially homogeneous. It covers 26 counties in the southeast quadrant of the state. The Mississippi River forms the eastern boundary, the river valley and foothills the west, the coal mines in the north, and the Arkansas state line in the south. Agriculturally based, the district has some of the largest and most productive farms in the state. Historically, the district was considered a "safe seat" for the Democratic party until the 1980 election.

The southeastern corner, popularly known throughout the state as the "Bootheel," includes seven counties that look like and vote like the Old South. Long characterized as "Yellow Dog" Democratic territory, the Bootheel was originally populated by migrants from Mississippi, Alabama, and Tennessee who came north to escape the boll weevil infestation and to farm the area's rich delta land for cotton. They brought with them an ideology rooted in a peculiar mix of conservatism, Democratic party allegiance, and skepticism. As Willard Duncan Vandiver, who served in the U.S. House of Representatives from 1897 to 1903, put it: "I come from a state that raises corn and cotton and cockleburs and Democrats, and frothy eloquence neither convinces nor satisfies me. I am from Missouri. You have got to show me."[1]

Today, the spirit of skepticism, conservatism, and agriculture remain in this region, despite the increasingly conspicuous lack of fidelity to the Democratic party. Indeed, Gary Jacobson's observation that "the Republican Party is on its way to building the kind of strong congressional base in the South that once gave the Democrats a formidable head start in the battle to control the House and the Senate" is well at work in the Eighth District.[2] Conservative Democratic party loyalties still have deep roots in the area, particularly in local elections, but in 1998, 25 of the district's 26 counties voted Republican in the congressional election. Consequently, the Bootheel of the state is, for all practical purposes, more "southern" than "midwestern."

The southern label fits not only the region's politics but also its agricultural base. Thirty-five percent of Missouri's cash crops come from the counties of Mississippi, New Madrid, Pemiscot, Dunklin, Butler, Stoddard, and Scott. These counties are the northernmost regions of the United States where cotton and rice grow, and Dunklin County presently ranks as the nation's third largest watermelon-producing county in the country.

The area above the Bootheel, along the Mississippi River, is served by agriculture, retail businesses, light industries, and a medical service center. The agriculture is based on dairy, beef cattle, timber, and fruit production. Cape Girardeau, the largest city in the district and hometown of national radio personality Rush Limbaugh, is a strong Republican area, as are the surrounding counties of Perry and Bollinger.

The vast majority of the nation's lead ore is included in the riches of Missouri's Eighth Congressional District. The northernmost area of the district is referred to as the "Lead Belt" in Iron and Reynolds counties. In the 1980s, Washington and St. Francois counties had double-digit growth as commuters from metropolitan St. Louis settled into bedroom communities. Both counties solidly backed President Bill Clinton in 1992 and 1996, and now the region's claim to fame is its controversial attempt to transform approximately 32 acres of lead deposits into a safe foundation for public parks.[3]

The Ozark forest region to the west once provided the timbers that built St. Louis. The timber economy today includes small wood mills that produce pallets and other wood products, but travel, tourism, and recreation have become the new foundations for economic development and diversification. The Current and Eleven Point rivers, part of the Ozark National Scenic Riverways, provide canoeing, fishing, and leisure time attraction.

The past 20 years have seen a migration from the district as low wages, mechanization, and depleted ores became uneconomical to extract. The population of the Eighth District is mostly nonurban, with 63 percent classified as living in rural areas. The largest city, Cape Girardeau, has a population of 35,000. The population is slightly older and more homogenous than the national average, with 16 percent aged 65 years or older, 94 percent white, 4 percent black, and 1 percent Hispanic. The median household income is $18,207 and per capita income is $9,300, making this area one of the 25 poorest congressional districts in the country.[4]

Politically, the district has been undergoing realignment. As late as the 1970s, the district was considered an invincible Democratic stronghold. Voting patterns today present a far different picture. In 1982, 43 percent of the district's population identified themselves as Democrats, while only 26 percent thought of themselves as Republican. By contrast, 1998 polling data reveal a three way split of 35 percent Democrats, 35 percent Republicans, and 30 percent independent.[5] The most significant aspect of the data is the conservatism evident in the political values of those who think of themselves as independents. As a result, the uncommitted voters may more accurately be defined as "professed" independents but "behavioral" Republicans.

THE 1996 AND 1998
ELECTIONS IN PERSPECTIVE

The 1996 Election

The events surrounding the 1996 campaign effectively sealed the fate of the 1998 election. Indeed, the dynamics of the congressional race in Missouri's Eighth District were inextricably linked to the opportunities that emerged after Representative Bill Emerson died from lung cancer on June 22, 1996. His death caused immediate problems for the Republicans, who had been counting on the proven vote-getter to retain the seat in November. The sudden void in Republican leadership and the party's admittedly weak default candidates created a window of opportunity for the Democrats to reclaim the seat.

Two little-known Republican mavericks, Earl Durnell, a farmer/rancher from the deep Ozarks in the far western edge of the district, and Richard Kline, a retired member of the Coast Guard from a rural area in the east-central part of the district, had filed against Emerson in what most observers expected to be only token opposition. Emerson's death fairly late in the primary season left these two relative unknowns as the only Republicans contesting the nomination.

Upon Emerson's death, Republican party strategists and others were surprised to read the election statutes and learn that due to a revision the previous year, the filing period could not be re-opened to allow the party to run a stronger candidate. Emerson's death had occurred about a month after the final deadline for re-opening, leaving late entrants two options: (1) a write-in ballot, itself surrounded by legal questions, and (2) a signature drive, which required the acquisition of at least 3,700 signatures.

Also complicating matters was the call for a special election to fill the remainder of Emerson's term to be held on the same date as the general election. Under state law, party congressional district committees were authorized to meet and select nominees for the special election. Paradoxically, Missouri statutes created this dilemma for Republicans: they could rally behind a strong successor to Emerson and enter that person's name on the special election ballot, but they were going to be "stuck" with either Durnell or Kline representing their party in the regular election for the full term. This posed a logistical problem of major proportions.

The Democrats, of course, had to deal with the same laws and requirements. Back when the original filing period was open in February and March, three potential Emerson challengers filed: a perennial candidate and retired music store owner, Thad Bullock; real estate and insurance broker, Gene Curtis; and, from the northwest part of the district, a tree farmer and former publisher, Emily Firebaugh. Bullock had actually won the Democratic nomination in 1992 against weak competition, but had been soundly defeated by Emerson in the general election. Curtis was virtually unknown within the party, and lacked districtwide support despite having run once previously. Firebaugh was known by quite a few Democratic activists at the congressional district level, and also had some family-based name recognition in Cape Girardeau. Despite being named early (and correctly) by Democratic pundits as the likely nominee, Firebaugh was not thought by most of them to have what it took to unseat Emerson. Upon his death, however, it looked as if she "might be in the right place at the right time," according to a representative of a Democratic state officeholder.[6]

Faced with the likelihood of losing a cherished seat in Congress, it was incumbent upon the Republican party to recruit a more stellar opponent than the one the electorate had selected in the primaries. The problem, however, was that any candidate recruited into the process would have to have a recognizable name, political clout, and the unique ability to create a campaign on short notice. The pool of such candidates included State Senator Peter Kinder, Bill Emerson's chief of staff Lloyd Smith, State Representative Mark Richardson, Missouri's Farm Bureau President Charles Kruse, Rolla attorney David Steelman, and Jo Ann Emerson, wife of the late congressman.

Despite the credentials of her rivals, Jo Ann Emerson brought to the campaign field two attributes that she alone could offer: a slogan that stressed not only a professional but also a deeply personal commitment to a "legacy" and a close relationship with the Republican congressional leadership. For the party, the choice was clear: Jo Ann Emerson was the preferred candidate. The difficulty, however, was in approaching the would-be candidate while at once respecting her right to grieve and reminding her that time was of the essence.

The ice was broken during a public visitation on the eve of Emerson's funeral. Within days of the funeral, the state party chair, Woody Cozad, contacted Jo Ann Emerson to explain the political "lay of the land."[7] Cozad made it clear that the Republican party would endorse her campaign, and that she had a good chance of winning the election. At this juncture, Emerson appeared reluctant, but suggested that she would consider running for office only if "it is the only way to continue the legacy of her husband."[8]

Shortly after her conversation with Cozad, Missouri's two Republican U.S. Senators, John Ashcroft and Christopher "Kit" Bond, assured her that the only way to continue the Emerson legacy, and to keep the seat in Republican hands, was for her to enter the race. By now she had the support of the state and federal parties, as well as prominent Republicans inside the nation's capital. All that remained was the support of her family. In an interview with the *St. Louis Post-Dispatch,* Emerson explained that her reluctance stemmed from the impact her absence might have on her 14-year-old daughter, Katherine. Having just lost a father, the question was whether the demands of campaigning and holding office would only intensify the loss. "But she was adamant about carrying on. She said, 'Mom, you've got to do this.' With her blessing, I said OK."[9] With that, she embarked on her mission to "keep the seat and make it a living memorial to Bill."[10]

Upon her decision to run, her late husband's staff and the party organizations began the work of smoothing the electoral landscape for a fast and furious campaign. Portrayed not only as a "winnable" candidate but also as someone who could identify with the region and deal with the inner workings of Congress, Jo Ann Emerson ran on the campaign that "southern Missouri needs someone who knows how to get things done, someone who knows Missouri, someone who can hit the ground running on day one in Congress."[11] To those inside the national capital, Emerson was well-known not only as the spouse of a 16-year veteran of Congress, but also as a well-established lobbyist with ties as rich as her bloodline. In the district, the Emerson camp would reinforce her role as a dutiful wife who shared her husband's vision and commitment while downplaying the fact that neither the candidate nor her children were life-long residents of the district or the state.

While crafting the campaign that Jo Ann Emerson effectively represented the best of both worlds—experienced in Washington and committed to the eight-term legacy of her husband—the staff worked on officially getting her name on the ballot. This presented a challenge. In light of Secretary of State Bekki Cook's ruling that filing for office would not be reopened for the August primary, and because "Team Emerson" focused on "running an election for Congress [rather] than running a lawsuit," the Emerson staff and the Farm Bureau set to the task of securing the 3,700 signatures needed by July 29 in order to run as an independent.[12] With her official entrance announced on July 10, she had only 19 days to secure the signatures.

Unlike most late entries or challengers in general, Emerson inherited an experienced political organization. Indeed, as the *Washington Post* reported, Bill Emerson had worked behind the scenes, as well as his wife's back, to prepare his organization for his wife's bid for office.[13] The great value of the congressional staff is its ability to assist the campaign organization as it unifies, organizes, and mobilizes its supporters. At the district level, the targeted foundation of the signature drive and electoral support was the Farm Bureau. Between the coordinated activities of the Emerson election staff and the Farm Bureau, Jo Ann Emerson gathered 600 volunteers who procured 9,600 signatures within the span of 18 days. Importantly, the volunteers were able to begin a valuable "voter education" drive as they secured signatures. Specifically, with each signature they exploited the opportunity to remind supporters to vote independent in the general election and Republican in the special election. From there, they continued their grassroots efforts to reduce straight-ticket voting.

Although the calculus and rationale were simple, coordinating a campaign for two races, each attaching different party labels to the same candidate, in one day was both complicated and risky. In order for the Emerson strategy to succeed, loyal Republicans would have to abandon the party line and vote "independent" at least once in the fall general election. This required voters to distinguish between two of the most potent forces of electoral behavior: party identification and name recognition. The calculated risk was that the combined efforts of Emerson's campaign team and the state and federal Republican party organizations would establish the primacy of the name, with a negligible vote "lost" to the party's primary election winner, Richard Kline. As table 7.1 indicates, this is precisely what happened.

As the election results indicate, the strategy of replacing voter confusion with information generally worked. As an independent candidate for the two-year congressional seat, Emerson carried 50.46 percent of the vote, compared to Firebaugh's 37.28 percent and Kline's 10.53 percent. As a Republican, however, she increased her vote share to 63.3 percent. Although Firebaugh's vote dropped by 3.14 percent between the same-day contests, it is clear that Emerson's special election surge is primarily attributable to the absence of a Republican opponent. Kline's 10.53 percent of the vote effectively became hers in the special election. Therefore, the strategy of voting independent in order to secure a Republican seat ultimately prevailed: the straight-ticket party loyalists who predictably emerged in the general election remained party loyalists when the candidate's name changed.

During the 1996 election, the Emerson team was aware of the fact that the Democratic party considered the Eighth District "winnable" in a genuinely open contest. Knowing that the district could easily revert back to Democratic control, where it had been from the end of the Civil War until 1980, it was incumbent upon the Republican party to not only win the 1996 election, but also to parlay the subsequent congressional term into a second victory and an increasingly safe seat. The newly elected representative began her work toward accomplishing that goal.

Inside the capitol, Emerson demonstrated that she was far from the "typical" freshman. Upon entering Congress, she struck a balance between deliberately avoiding those orientation sessions that would have brought back painful memories of her husband on the one hand, and serving as one of the interim

**Table 7.1 Election Returns for
Missouri's Eighth District, 1996**

	ELECTION		
Candidate (Party)	Primary August 6 (%)	General November 5 (%)	Special November 5 (%)
Bullock (D)	23.90	—	—
Curtis (D)	20.71	—	—
Emerson (I/R)	—	50.46*	63.3**
Firebaugh (D)	55.38	37.28	34.14
Kline (R)	51.05	10.53	—
Durnell (R)	49.05	—	—
Tlapek (LIB)	—	1.20	2.50
Zimmer (NL)	—	0.59	—

*Due to the timing of her entry into the race (after the primary election), Emerson's name appeared on the ballot as an independent.

**Emerson's name appeared on the Special Election Ballot as a Republican.

SOURCE: Compiled by authors.

members selected to help others make the transition on the other. She quickly found herself on the Agriculture Committee, the Small Business Committee, and the Transportation and Infrastructure Committee, as well as the National Republican Congressional Committee (NRCC).

With the 1996 election behind them and the right committee assignments before them, Team Emerson spent the 105th Congress working on her clout in the district. Both the Democratic and Republican parties knew that the "sympathy vote" would dissipate and that the 1998 election would mean greater attention to issues and the work done in Emerson's freshman term. Anticipating such a challenge, she sponsored and signed on to a variety of predominantly symbolic proposals that struck at the heart of the district.

In the votes she cast on the floor of the House, Emerson's conservative credentials and partisan fidelity were clearly represented. In addition to rejecting campaign finance reform, the highlights of her legislative career included votes to impeach the president, release the report on the president by independent counsel Kenneth Starr, provide school vouchers, and oppose labor and environmental legislation.[14] Her legacy may be ultimately linked to the environment. From a property-rights perspective, her opposition to environmental legislation has earned her high regard among past and present Republican leaders as well as her constituents. Indeed, she was the only freshman selected to attend the 1997 conference on global warming in Kyoto, Japan. Her inclusion did not simply emanate from her association with former Speaker of the House Newt Gingrich, but from her outspoken opposition to Clinton administration's environmental policies and environmental groups.

The 1998 Election

Offended by what he considered to be representation by "an absolute out-sider" whose electoral fortunes were owed to "a name and an apparition," Tony Heckemeyer abandoned a 17-year career as a judge for a shot at Congress. Indeed, in an era of anti-governmental attitudes, Heckemeyer pre-sented himself as a fan of government, if not necessarily its contemporary pre-occupations and practitioners. To Heckemeyer, challenging Emerson was a moral obligation. The odds against him, however, were staggering. By 1998, Emerson was not only able to bring to the electorate a commitment to the conservative principles that defined the seat for 18 years, but also a career as a member of Congress. Furthermore, the power vacuum and the special elec-tion that defined the 1996 campaign were absent in 1998, making it easier for the Republican party and the electorate to organize support for a single can-didate throughout the campaign season. Unlike the 1996 election, which wit-nessed a competitive primary without an Emerson name on the ballot, Emer-son ran unopposed in the 1998 Republican primary. In the Democratic primary, Heckemeyer faced challenges from Bullock and Kline. As table 7.2 shows, Heckemeyer easily secured a plurality of the vote, but earned roughly 8 percent less than his predecessor in the 1996 Democratic primary, sending the initial signal that keen competition in the general election would be unlikely.

Between the primary and general elections, Heckemeyer sought to per-suade voters that his qualifications, commonality of interests, and positions on issues not only reflected, but emanated, from his residency in the district. For all intents and purposes, he envisioned himself as the "anti-Emerson." He de-liberately crafted a campaign and a platform that stood in stark contrast to his opponent. Whereas Emerson employed a team of seasoned political consul-tants, Heckemeyer surrounded himself with local volunteers; whereas Emerson emphasized her name and its legacy, Heckemeyer primed his life-long career as a farmer; and unlike Emerson, who offered the voters two years of service in government, Heckemeyer banked on 25 years of combined service in the state legislature and the courts. Most importantly, perhaps, he sought to present a romantic ideal of democracy in action. A self-professed "classic Jeffersonian," he envisioned a race characterized by numerous live, issue-oriented debates.[15]

With 17 years of judicial experience under his belt, he crafted what may be considered a fundamentally "judicial" campaign. Specifically, Heckemeyer's de-bate format would be issue-specific, allotting each participant equal amounts of time, with the last word going to the challenger. Unfortunately for Hecke-meyer, Emerson ran an inherently "political" campaign. She field-tested the is-sues and crafted a media campaign accordingly. Indeed, there were only five fo-rums scheduled, which included three live debates, one of which featured Emerson "live via telephone" from Washington.

While many on the Democratic side decried the Emerson debate tactic as an arrogant attempt to avoid the issues, the Republican response focused on the importance of her work on Capitol Hill. Regardless of the spin, it was clear that Emerson did not consider Heckemeyer a serious threat to her seat.

**Table 7.2 Election Returns for
Missouri's Eighth District, 1998**

Candidate (Party)	ELECTION	
	Primary August 4 (%)	General November 3 (%)
Bullock (D)	28.82	—
Kline (D)	23.46	—
Heckemeyer (D)	47.73	35.69
Emerson (R)	100	62.62
Hendricks (LIB)	100	1.70

SOURCE: Compiled by authors.

Emerson's "political" campaign model fit the expectations of the electorate and the media. A spate of well-crafted surveys was used to identify the salient issues in the district and, consequently, her television commercials, press releases, and public statements broadcast her commitment to social security, family, and property rights. With the aid of an experienced, professional staff, the Emerson political campaign included a scheduled appearance in the Eighth District, while the earned media effort during the off year was directed by the congressional office. Meanwhile, Heckemeyer, who worked his way through three campaign managers, embarked upon a quest to deliver a "courthouse steps speech" in each of the district's 26 counties. Despite his obvious need for media coverage, the amount of "earned" media exposure weighed heavily in Emerson's favor. An analysis of all major newspapers in the district, from January through November 1998, revealed a total of 33 front-page stories dedicated to Emerson, compared to 14 for Heckemeyer. Shunned by the media, Heckemeyer found it impossible to develop an issue, much less an issue-oriented campaign.[16]

Regardless of the quantity and quality of "earned" media exposure, it was clear that Emerson was better situated to wage an effective media campaign. Paid advertising came at a cost, and the financial resources and groups committed to the Emerson campaign completely overshadowed those of her opponent. As Heckemeyer later explained, "No matter how much we raised, she could raise more; no matter how much we could spend, she could spend more."[17] Frustrated with constantly calling for support, and contrary to his campaign manager's insistence that fundraising be continued, Heckemeyer decided instead to "press the flesh" for support.

In addition to the campaign spending differential, there was also an enormous difference in party support for each candidate. While Emerson was in the fortunate position of being able to turn away support from the Republican party, the Heckemeyer campaign, which desperately needed an infusion of money and voter mobilization, received nothing. The Heckemeyer campaign began with a call for support to Democratic party leaders in all 26 counties and ended with returned calls from only three party chairs. Similarly, the support he counted on from House Minority Leader and fellow Missourian Richard Gephardt never materialized. As with his romanticized notions of debates and personal politics, Heckemeyer longed for an equally obsolete party machine—an apparatus that would throw its money and votes behind its candidate. Unfortunately for Heckemeyer, his conservatism probably cost him the endorsement and political action committee (PAC) support that Gephardt could have offered.[18]

By the general election, it was clear that the seat would remain in Emerson's hands. Indeed, Heckemeyer carried only 35.69 percent of the vote (see table 7.2) and mustered a majority in only one of the district's 26 counties.

DETERMINANTS OF THE 1998 ELECTION OUTCOME

In this campaign, four themes emerged as the determinants of the election outcome: name recognition, organization and preparation, money, and the message. Despite the agreement on the significance of these factors, there are noticeable differences of opinion about how they played out during the 1998 campaign.

Name Recognition

Within the Eighth District, both Heckemeyer and Emerson names were well-known but not equally so. Heckemeyer was a life-long resident of Scott County, on the northern fringe of the Bootheel. Though he served as a member of the Missouri House of Representatives during the 1960s and early 1970s, for 17 years he had been Circuit Judge in Scott and neighboring Mississippi counties. An admittedly conservative Democrat, he earned the nickname "Hang 'em High Heckemeyer" for his tough sentencing standards as a judge. He describes himself as "pro-balanced budget, pro-life, and a classic Jeffersonian."[19]

Heckemeyer had an intense devotion to the district. During his campaign, he emphasized his family roots, noting that he lived 100 yards from where his father had lived and farmed, and 100 yards from where one of his sons was living and farming. Though Democratic activists knew his name and were anticipating his announcement of candidacy, few voters in the distant reaches of the vast Eighth District knew the Heckemeyer name before the campaign. It is probable that his name recognition was highest in the area surrounding the two counties that made up his judicial circuit (and where his son Joe was serving his second term as a state representative).

Unlike Heckemeyer, whose ties to the community extend quite literally into the dirt, Emerson had been associated with the Eighth District through marriage alone. She grew up in a political household in Bethesda, Maryland. Her father, Ab Hermann, was a prominent member of the Republican National Committee (RNC), and the family owned property adjoining that of former Louisiana Democratic Representative Hale Boggs. Between the social events sponsored by both families, which obviously crossed party lines, Emerson came of age in the company of politicians, activists, and lobbyists. Indeed, it was her mother, Sylvia, who introduced her to then–lobbyist Bill Emerson. From there, her inside track to Congress and lobbying flourished.

In 1996, most voters throughout the Eighth District probably didn't know Jo Ann Emerson herself or even recognize her name before the campaign. What was clear, however, was that the voters knew the name of her late husband, Bill.

Throughout his 16 years in Congress, Bill Emerson had carefully cultivated an active presence in every corner of the district. Soon after he became congressman, his office purchased a van to serve as the "mobile congressional office." It was driven throughout the district on an announced schedule, and constituents were invited to drop by its location and conduct business with his staff. Over the course of his eight terms, the Emerson name itself had come to be known by most voters in the district. The fact that Jo Ann also carried that name gave her an instant and obvious advantage in name recognition over her 1996 Democratic challenger, Firebaugh.

Emerson, almost immediately following the 1996 election, developed a strategic plan to prepare for the 1998 election. Throughout 1997, she made a systematic effort to become better known in the district and to define herself as the representative of the "right" groups. These groups were identified as seniors, veterans, working women, farmers, and the Republican base.

To reach out to these groups, Team Emerson organized town hall meetings designed to give her exposure through the district as its representative. In 1997 and early 1998, she held 38 town hall meetings with voters to discuss their needs. She also established a Senior Citizens Advisory Council and an Economic Development Advisory Council to hold meetings to discuss social security issues important to seniors and development issues important to the business community. Four meetings of each committee were held in 1997.

Emerson also took steps to defend her seat against probable opponents in 1998. Early in 1997, Lloyd Smith, her political director, and most political observers recognized that Heckemeyer would be the likely Democratic opponent. Heckemeyer himself inadvertently verified that for the Emerson campaign. In the spring of 1997, Judge Heckemeyer spoke to a high school civics class in Sikeston, Missouri, where he discussed his intention of running for the U.S. Congress. In his remarks, he criticized Emerson as an outsider, someone who knew little, if anything, about agriculture and even less about the district. He was unaware that the daughter of the Emerson campaign's political director was in the class![20]

Thus, the Emerson staff developed a strategy to address her "negatives." One of these identified negatives was her lack of knowledge about the farm issues. She took steps to establish her credibility in the agriculture community during 1998. Toward that end, she was the keynote speaker at the Sikeston Chamber of Commerce Farm banquet, where she spoke to 600 people in Heckemeyer's hometown. This was perhaps the biggest and most important agriculture event of the year. Most significantly, the people who attended the banquet were opinion leaders in banking, agriculture, and related fields throughout the district.

Meanwhile, Emerson also spent the first session of the 105th Congress exploiting her congressional clout to raise her name recognition in the district. Political observers from both parties knew that the "sympathy vote" would dissipate and the 1998 election would be a judgment on her performance in office. With her dedication to salient proposals and the right committee slots, she had positioned herself in the public eye as the better known candidate.

Organization

The campaign organization of the two candidates reflected the professional, seasoned, experienced staff of Emerson and the family, volunteer, self-directed effort of Heckemeyer. The campaign strategies clearly reflected the exposure of the Emerson camp and the insulation of the Heckemeyer team. Heckemeyer was perceived as a man of the soil by political observers but not a formidable opponent. Even his lifelong association with local farmers was insufficient to draw the support of the Farm Bureau and other agricultural PACs. His legal credentials and agricultural acumen were never questioned but also never really discussed. Likewise, his vision of an old-fashioned campaign predicated upon direct exposure and questions, answers, and rejoinders was as meaningless to the voters as it was to his opponent. Finally, the support he counted on from a nonexistent political machine never materialized. Neither the Gephardt office nor the party mobilized voters or money for the candidate.

Emerson, however, inherited a committed staff and the eager support of state and federal party organizations and interest groups. The value of securing a successful, experienced campaign organization and exposure throughout the district cannot be overstated. The political director of Team Emerson's 1998 campaign had been directly involved in seven campaigns as a manager and actively associated with numerous others. As Atalie Ebersole, campaign manager for Team Emerson stated: "We are one of the few congressional districts that has a year-around campaign office. It's staffed full time, computerized and ready to go."[21] Thus, Team Emerson in 1998 ran a seasoned, experienced, and well-organized campaign.

Faced with the Emerson campaign juggernaut, by mid-summer Heckemeyer realized that without a comparable level of organizational support his campaign was doomed. In an interview, he was asked when he realized that his campaign was in trouble and when it appeared that a victory would be difficult. He replied that the turning point was in July at a fundraiser sponsored by Missouri Governor Mel Carnahan in the governor's hometown of Rolla, which only 22 people attended. Sadly, he recalled, he knew then that if the governor in his hometown couldn't draw more people to the Heckemeyer campaign, he was fighting a losing battle.[22]

Table 7.3 Financial Activity of Missouri's Eighth District Candidates, 1997–1998

Candidate	Net Receipts	CONTRIBUTIONS ($)		Candidate Support	Net Disbursement
		From Individuals	From Other Committees		
Emerson	1,109,929	580,029	515,414	0	1,028,585
Heckemeyer	321,070	256,832	44,550	11,905	251,936
Hendricks	298	298	0	0	83

SOURCE: Federal Election Commission Financial Activity Reports, 1998.

Money

The significance of money in congressional elections cannot be overstated. As both a barometer of support and a resource that can be exchanged for media exposure, money matters. The advantage that incumbents have in raising money has been well documented.

In 1996, when the Eighth District seat became open due to Bill Emerson's death, there was no incumbent. Democrats, sensing the opportunity to reclaim the previously Democratic district, responded by investing an unprecedented amount of money for a Democratic candidate in that district. Firebaugh received and spent about $830,000 during the entire campaign period, but Jo Ann Emerson exactly matched that during what for her was only a three-and-a-half month campaign. The unique circumstances and party unity behind Emerson's candidacy immediately earned her RNC's support, which in turn stimulated PAC activity. With old friends in the party, in lobbying circles, and other congressional offices embracing her as ideologically desirable and genuinely electable, she had no difficulty generating financial support.

Once Emerson became the incumbent, however, money raising became even easier. Between the 1996 and 1998 elections, her campaign treasurer David Limbaugh—an established Cape Girardeau lawyer and brother of Rush Limbaugh—recorded a steady stream of capital from individuals and committees previously committed to Bill Emerson. As table 7.3 reveals, the Emerson campaign raised and spent more than $1 million during the 1997–1998 election season, more than four times as much as her opponent.

The sizable difference in financial support received by Emerson and Heckemeyer was attributable to the old rule that money follows success. This is especially true of PAC contributions. According to Federal Election Commission (FEC) disclosure reports, a total of 313 committees and 943 individuals contributed to Emerson's campaign, with in-kind spending provided by the Missouri and National Right to Life PACs.

Heckemeyer, however, received no financial support from the Democratic National Committee (DNC), the state party system, or partisan allies in Congress. Ideologically distanced from the Gephardt campaign, perceived as unelectable by interest groups, and considered a high-risk investment by a party that saw its investment in the Firebaugh campaign of 1996 come to naught, Heckemeyer had to rely mostly on individual campaign contributions.[23]

There was a marked difference between the two candidates in the timing of the campaign receipts. Campaign contributions to Emerson for the 1997–1998 campaign cycle had begun to flow immediately after her 1996 election. By the time Heckemeyer announced his candidacy in early 1998, the Emerson campaign had already raised about as much as he would in his entire campaign. As her receipts continued throughout the period, Emerson was able to outraise and outspend him by almost four to one.

In the end, it was neither Heckemeyer's late start nor his lack of enthusiasm in soliciting contributions that tipped the financial scales against him. It was the fact that he was running, not for an ostensibly open seat as Firebaugh did in 1996, but against an incumbent who strategically used the advantages of incumbency to greatly outspend her challenger. Had the odds looked better to potential Heckemeyer contributors, he would have had more support and received more money with which to communicate his message.[24] The fact that he did not explained why both the money and the support to which it was tied weighed heavily in Emerson's favor from the outset of the campaign.

The Message

The great value of money has been that it buys exposure and enables candidates to determine and appeal to a district's salient issues. Since 1996, the Emerson campaign team had periodically conducted surveys in order to test messages and identify strengths and weaknesses. Based upon poll results, for example, Emerson crafted an agenda around the financial and tax interests of seniors (employing her late husband's mother in television commercials), economic development, and property rights. These issues were not only primed in her electronic "Weekly Columns" and press releases but also in town meetings designed to foster her image as a representative dedicated to the district. The snowball effect of this strategy was that it generated "earned" (as opposed to "purchased") coverage. With the coverage of the local media market well established, her campaign team charted her contacts with the editors and publishers of the print media as a way of detecting, then curing, gaps in coverage.

Heckemeyer, on the other hand, not only suffered from a lack of resources but also from a stubborn dedication to an admirable, yet antiquated, campaign strategy. Committed to a "classic Jeffersonian" ideal of direct contact, both with the voters and his opponent, he articulated an agenda that included a speech and a debate in every county. Because speechmaking is a singular enterprise, it was easy for Heckemeyer to stick to his plan and address the citizens of every county from the steps of its courthouse. Unfortunately for the candidate, his exposure was measured almost exclusively in terms of the size of his live audience; with the exception of the Rolla local press, the media, Heckemeyer felt, failed to cover speeches in the remaining 25 counties. The same pattern held true regarding his requests to address area chambers of commerce—only one issued an invitation for a public speech.[25]

Table 7.4 Breakdown of Representative Emerson's Voting Record, 1997–1998

Issue Area	Number of Votes Cast	Vote Breakdown
Campaign Finance	1	Nay on campaign finance reform
Criminal Law–Related	3	Yea on two impeachment measures and crackdown on sex crimes
Education	4	Yea on two bills supporting school vouchers, IRAs for educational expenses, and denying educational testing
Environment	3	Yea on restricted UN conservation program and nuclear storage bills. Nay on revising parks and public lands regulations
Fiscal/Budgetary	12	Yea on all Republican-led fiscal, budget, and tax measures, including defense
Foreign Policy	3	Nay on increasing visas for high-tech workers and increased trade with sub-Sarahan Africa. Yea on $12.3 billion for foreign aid.
Insurance Related	1	Yea to revamp medical insurance regulations
Labor Related	2	Yea on curbing union organizing methods and repealing labor protection for Amtrak employees
Morality/Discretion	9	Yea on releasing Starr Report, preventing FDA approval of abortion drugs, controlling funding of family planning clinics, religious freedom amendment, prohibition of needle distribution funding, three bills regarding monuments/dedications. Nay on bilingual Puerto Rican state.
Privacy	2	Yea on sexual orientation discrimination prohibition and mandatory drug testing for federal employees

SOURCE: Compiled by authors.

The debate format desired by Heckemeyer never materialized at all. Indeed, only three live debates between the candidates occurred. To Heckemeyer, this suggested that the Emerson campaign team was determined to avoid (1) direct confrontation with an opponent whose skill in oral argument, honed through years of legal practice, was superior, and (2) any opportunity to demonstrate that Emerson was running an issueless campaign. He asserted that although Emerson had exposure, she did not really have an issue.[26]

In her defense, Emerson offered her service during the 105th Congress as evidence of her work. With a total of 12 bills sponsored (five of which were to amend the Constitution), 393 others cosponsored, and a total of 44 high-profile floor votes cast, she successfully conveyed to the voters that she was more than the wife of a deceased representative. To the Emerson campaign, her conservative credentials were apparent in her legislative work, which followed along the path of her late husband. Whereas Heckemeyer emphasized a message of hometown roots and agricultural experience, the Emerson message included such well-tested themes as property rights, senior citizens' rights, economic development, school choice, protection of the flag, and a litany of criticism against environmentalism and abortion rights. See table 7.4 for her issues and her voting record during the 105th Congress.

Heckemeyer believed that television is the most powerful medium, and that the lion's share of campaign funds should be spent on that.[27] Particularly in the Eighth District, purchasing television time can be an excruciatingly expensive undertaking. Not counting cable systems, a congressional candidate wanting to saturate the district might have to buy time in at least four major markets in Missouri, as well as time on stations in Illinois, Kentucky, and Arkansas. The Emerson campaign spent about 70 percent of its television budget in the eastern part of the district, including both the population center of Cape Girardeau and the Bootheel. The Heckemeyer television strategy was approximately the same.

Both candidates considered radio advertising to be of less importance. Heckemeyer criticized the lack of newspaper reporting on the campaign, asserting that he got virtually no coverage and because of that, he was unable to develop the issues.[28] Of course, one of the main advantages incumbents have is the media attention they receive between elections, by virtue of simply holding office. Clearly, the ongoing "earned" coverage in both the print and electronic media about the incumbent's activities can contribute greatly to name recognition by potential voters. A typical challenger can always expect a difficult struggle to overcome the built-in media advantage that incumbency provides. For Heckemeyer, the few brief months of the campaign were not sufficient time, nor did he have enough resources, to communicate his message to the voters through conventional media channels. Emerson had carefully employed a media strategy during 1997, and that gave Team Emerson the upper hand in 1998.

SUMMARY AND CONCLUSION

The 1998 election in the Eighth District of Missouri, while not dramatic or suspenseful, can help us understand something about outcomes of congressional races. We have identified four main factors that contributed to Jo Ann Emerson's victory over her challenger: name recognition, organization, money, and message. These four elements were somewhat like the four legs of a chair. Just as some chairs can be successfully constructed using less than four legs, some candidates may have success even without having all four factors in equal abundance.

Some factors can contribute to the acquisition of others. With sufficient money, for example, a candidate could in essence purchase name recognition and, even in the absence of an extensive organization, could communicate his or her message through the media. Likewise, having strong name recognition and a reputation as a credible candidate could help attract an organization and might also draw financial support.

What about the special case of a surviving spouse running for election to the deceased spouse's seat? Our examination of Emerson's 1998 reelection in the context of her initial 1996 election provides some insight. One possible interpretation of her victory in 1996 was that in a sense the seat never effectively became "open" despite her husband's death. She essentially "inherited" the four factors: recognition of the family name, the "Team Emerson" organization, access to her husband's funding sources, and a message of continuing his work.

In addition to these factors, congressional elections can be affected by changes to the district. In the case of southeast Missouri, changes during the past 20 years have made it easier for Republicans to hold what had been a Democratic district for decades. After both the 1980 and 1990 censuses, the Eighth Congressional District boundaries were redrawn and shifted further south, each time excluding at least one St. Louis metropolitan ring county with a significant number of Democratic votes. In addition to the demographic changes that reapportionment brought, other changes took place in the voters.

The years of President Ronald Reagan and Bill Emerson's success made it much more acceptable to vote Republican. Heckemeyer saw this coming. During the Emerson years, more and more Republican state legislative candidates had been winning, until a significant majority of state house seats within the Eighth Congressional District were held by Republicans. This trend has continued during the Jo Ann Emerson years as well. Indeed, a realignment in the district has been taking place, both contributing to, and resulting from, the Emerson congressional years. The realignment and the four factors identified in this chapter have led to the Emersons' continuously holding the Eighth District seat since 1981. The second Emerson, Jo Ann, was able to combine those factors and her unique circumstances in 1996 to win the seat in 1998.

NOTES

The authors would like to thank Theresa Haug, research assistant in the Department of Political Science, for her analysis of media coverage during the 1998 campaign, and Debbie Devenport, department secretary, for her assistance and technical support throughout this project. We are, of course, grateful to Lloyd Smith, Atalie Ebersole, and Tony Heckemeyer for their willingness to participate in the interviews for this chapter.

1. http://mosl.sos.sate.mo.us/rec-man/slogan.html.

2. Gary C. Jacobson, "The 105th Congress: Unprecedented and Unsurprising," in *The Elections of 1996,* ed. Michael Nelson (Washington, DC: Congressional Quarterly, 1998), 164.

3. Tom Uhlenbrock, "Toxic Lead Dump in Bonne-Terre, Missouri, May Become Recreation Site," *St. Louis Post-Dispatch,* February 6, 1999, A3.

4. Congressional Quarterly's candidate (Emerson) and District (Eighth congressional) profile, http://voter96.cqalert.com.

5. Based upon surveys conducted by Jo Ann Emerson's campaign team, 1998.

6. Mark Schlinkmann, "8th District in Turmoil After Death of Emerson," *St. Louis Post-Dispatch,* June 30, 1996, 4B.

7. Erika Niedowski, "Republicans Urge Emerson's Widow to Run for Seat," *The Hill,* July 3, 1996, 8.

8. Ibid.

9. Mark Schlinkmann, "Jo Ann Emerson Makes Race Official," *St. Louis Post-Dispatch,* July 11, 1996, 3B.

10. Lloyd Grove, "The Congresswoman's House of Memories," *The Washington Post,* November 27, 1996, B1.

11. Schlinkmann, "Jo Ann Emerson Makes Race Official."

12. Keith Kirk, as quoted in Tim Curran, "Independent's Day: Emerson's Widow Embraced by GOP, But Not Party Line," *Roll Call,* July 25, 1996.

13. Grove, "The Congresswoman's House of Memories."

14. Congressional Quarterly, Inc.

15. Tony Heckemeyer, personal interview, January 18, 1999.

16. Ibid.

17. Ibid.

18. Ibid.

19. Ibid.

20. Lloyd Smith, personal interview, January 12, 1999.

21. Atalie Ebersole, personal interview, January 12, 1999.

22. Heckemeyer, personal interview.

23. Ibid.

24. Ibid.

25. Ibid.

26. Ibid.

27. Ibid.

28. Ibid.

PART II

★

Senate Campaigns
and Elections

Safe Seats

8

★

Nickles Defeats Carroll in Oklahoma's Senate Race

Ronald Keith Gaddie

> Only something like an alien abduction
> will keep Nickles from taking the oath.
>
> JIM MYERS
> *TULSA WORLD*

No aliens landed, Elvis wasn't sited, and Don Nickles, the assistant majority leader of the U.S. Senate, was reelected in a contest that surprised few observers of Oklahoma politics. Senator Nickles won election to his fourth term in the Senate on the basis of his overwhelming popularity and the exploitation of the advantages of his incumbency. His popularity with a variety of moderate and conservative groups in Oklahoma, ability to raise large amounts of money, and position of assistant majority leader in the Senate contributed to the decisions of many potential Democratic candidates to forego the effort to unseat him. Nickles' reelection was virtually assured when no major Democratic candidate emerged to challenge him for reelection. At age 49, the incumbent Republican is the privileged occupant of a safe senatorial seat.

This campaign is difficult to describe because there is so little to describe. No attractive, quality challengers emerged to oppose the senator. Nickles never took the Democrats presented to oppose him seriously. For that matter, no one else took them seriously. He engaged in limited campaigning back home, instead using his time to campaign on behalf of other Republican Senate candidates, such as Georgia's Paul Coverdell.[1] This election was won on the day that filing closed, if not several months earlier.[2]

SETTING THE STAGE

The Politics of Oklahoma

The Oklahoma Republicans enjoyed dramatic growth in the 1980s and 1990s. Republican growth in Oklahoma has had a distinctively different catalyst than in the rest of the South. In most southern states, Republican growth can be linked to race.[3] Race is not such a divisive issue in Oklahoma. Only 6.7 percent of the state's population is black.[4] Instead, religion (the growth of the Christian Right) has been the major catalyst of the Republican upswing in Oklahoma.[5] Empirical analysis of voting behavior at both the individual and county levels indicates that Christian fundamentalism is positively related to both the growth of registered Republican voters and to the tendency of rural Democrats to vote for Republican candidates.[6] Nickles has been a long-time beneficiary of both the schizophrenic political behavior of rural Democrats and the increased political clout of Christian conservatives in Oklahoma.

Oklahoma is one of the most conservative states in the union, and, at the national and congressional levels, is now one of the most consistently Republican. The only Democrat to win the electoral votes of Oklahoma since 1952 is Lyndon Johnson in 1964. Republicans have regularly won governorships and Senate seats since the 1960s. Through the 1970s, Republican success was at best fleeting outside of major statewide offices.

The transformation of politics in Oklahoma is one of the remarkable success stories of the Republican party in the 1990s. Entering the 1994 election, the Republican party held one U.S. Senate seat, two congressional districts, and only one statewide office (corporation commissioner). In 1994, Republicans took control of the entire congressional delegation with the exception of one seat, took both Senate seats, the governorship, and made gains in state legislative seats and statewide constitutional offices. After the 1994 election, the Oklahoma Democratic party was in disarray and without leadership or organization. The current Democratic executive director, Pat Hall, who was hired as the first professional director for the party after the 1994 debacle, summed up the situation: "In 1994 the Democratic Party not only had fallen asleep; it was a party of apathy."[7] The organized efforts of the Republican party, led by chair Tom Cole, and the Christian Coalition laid bare the hollow, brittle nature of the Democrats' state majority. Oklahoma has been transformed from a bastion of one-party Democratic rule into a competitive state in electoral politics.

Party Organizations

The Democratic and Republican party organizations in Oklahoma are decidedly different in their degree of organization, unity, and in their relationships with the national parties. The state Democrats resemble the Democratic parties of so many southern states: fractured, beset with internal conflict, and loosely linked to the Democratic National Committee (DNC). The Oklahoma Republican party was centrally organized in the 1960s by Henry Bellmon.

More recently, the state party followed the "grassroots" development model advanced by former Republican National Committee (RNC) chair Haley Barbour. Christian conservatives have also firmly established themselves in the party, pulling the party organization even farther to the right.[8]

For years, the state Republican party was characterized by a bifactionalism between "moneybags" elements from Tulsa (also called country-club Republicans) and "grassroots" elements from the small towns of the western plain and panhandle.[9] Bellmon, twice elected governor and senator, typified the country-club Republicans, advocating smaller government and lower taxes. It is widely acknowledged that he had no patience for social-issue conservatives. The emergence of the Christian right as a force in the party has therefore reoriented this factionalism to set traditional Bellmon Republicans against the Christian Right.

The most direct evidence of changing allegiances in the electorate is in the voter registration figures. Oklahoma uses a partisan registration system with a closed party primary. The Republican proportion of registered voters has increased steadily from less than 20 percent of voters in 1964 to about 37 percent of voters in 1998. The change in the partisan balance is related to the falloff in registered Democrats, and less related to gains in registered Republicans. Oklahoma has traditionally gained and lost populations with the cycles of sudden economic boom and long, drawn-out decline. A general decline in registrants occurred at the depth of the oil bust and lessened the number of Democratic registrants from 1,400,000 to just over 1,100,000, a loss of 300,000 voters. Since the collapse of the domestic oil industry in 1986, the number of Republican registrants consistently hovers around 600,000.

The Geography of Oklahoma Partisanship

Oklahoma's geographic settlement patterns play a prominent role in explaining the politics of the state. After the Oklahoma Territory was opened to white settlement, the western and northern tier of counties were settled by midwesterners and plainsmen, especially those steeped in the Jayhawker traditions of nearby Kansas. The southern and eastern counties, especially in Indian territory, were settled by southerners from Texas, Mississippi, and Arkansas. Democrats dominated politics in the state after coopting the progressive and socialist movements. The west and north continued as a Republican redoubt. A line drawn from the northeastern corner of the state to the southwestern corner would pass through the urban centers of Tulsa, Oklahoma City-Norman, and Lawton. To the north and west of this line and outside of these cities, voters are predominantly Republican; about 10 percent of the state population is in the region. To the south and east of the line, voters are predominantly Democratic. This is the "Little Dixie" region of the state that contains about 20 percent of the electorate. The remaining 70 percent of Oklahomans live in the urban corridor that encompasses the major cities of the state.[10]

The growth of the urban corridor has not altered the partisan differences that exist between the two major urban counties (Oklahoma and Tulsa) and the rest of the state. Samuel Kirkpatrick, David Morgan, and Thomas Kielhorn observed that, in the 1960s, the major urban counties voted substantially more Republican than the rest of the state.[11] As indicated in table 8.1, the average urban/rural difference in presidential elections is just over 8.5 percentage points. The Republican candidate won a majority of the urban core counties' vote on eight of nine occasions, and carried a plurality of the urban counties on the ninth. Republicans carried the rural vote on only four of nine occasions, including once by Richard Nixon (1972) and twice by Ronald Reagan (1980 and 1984). At lower levels, the urban vote constituted the margin of victory for the last three Republican governors, none of whom won an outright majority of the vote.

The Collapse of the Democrats

The systematic electoral eradication of Democrats in 1994 was based on a creative strategy designed to separate rural, predominantly Democratic, voters from their habits of voting for the Democratic party. Tom Cole, an Oklahoma City political consultant and former state senator, devised a strategy that emphasized the creative use of comparison advertising and biting attacks on wedge issues such as abortion to differentiate the Republican and Democratic candidates for major office. This media strategy was combined with a low-tech strategy of using the major fundamentalist Christian churches to disseminate voter guides that extolled the virtues of Republican candidates.[12] Cole's effort in 1994 was nothing new. Former governor Bellmon's "Operation Countdown" emphasized candidate recruitment and voter mobilization. That grassroots effort won him the governorship in 1962, as well as the moniker of "father" to the modern Oklahoma Republicans. In the 1980s and 1990s, Republicans reinvigorated this strategy, using sophisticated data analysis and polling to target campaigns outside of Republican strongholds.[13]

THE INCUMBENT

Don Nickles started in politics early, winning a seat in the Oklahoma Senate at age 29. However, as the events unfolded that would lead to his election to the U.S. Senate, Nickles' name was not mentioned as a senatorial contender. His initial election in 1980 was not as close or difficult as one might expect for a young, little-known state legislator. His reelections in 1986 and 1992 were hotly contested, based on the perception of many Democrats that Nickles was an accidental senator who could be defeated by a serious Democratic challenger. His trumping of the opposition in 1986 and 1992 finally dispelled doubts that Nickles was anything less than a political force who was popular in a variety of Oklahoma constituencies. Insiders touted him as a serious senator who was capable of successfully campaigning against any of the well-financed, conservative Democrats who dominated most state offices in the early 1990s. Combined with the changing political landscape of Oklahoma in the 1990s,

Table 8.1 The Cities and Republican Presidential Success in Oklahoma

Year	State	OKC/Tulsa	Out-State	Difference
1964	44.3	51.3	40.7	+10.6
1968	47.7*	52.9	44.9	+8.0
1972	73.7	76.3	72.2	+4.1
1976	49.9*	58.8	45.1	+13.7
1980	60.5	66.1	57.5	+8.6
1984	68.6	72.3	66.6	+5.7
1988	58.4	64.0	54.6	+9.4
1992	42.6*	48.9*	39.1	+9.8
1996	48.2*	54.1	45.1	+9.0

*GOP plurality win.

SOURCE: Kirkpatrick, Morgan, and Kielhorn; Morgan, England, and Humphreys. Figures since 1990 computed by authors from data provided by the Oklahoma State Board of Elections.

Nickles' personal popularity and political effectiveness made him a safe bet for reelection in 1998.

Elections in 1980, 1986, and 1992

In 1978, Senator Bellmon went against his constituency and voted to return the Panama Canal to the Panamanians. That vote was subsequently viewed by many observers as an act of conscience, taken by a senator who acted in the inspired role of a "trustee," as articulated by Edmund Burke. However, Bellmon's action was sufficient to call into question his electoral security at the time, and in 1980, he chose to retire rather than seek reelection. A variety of lesser-known Oklahoma politicians stepped into the void left by Bellmon's retirement, all eager to make the move to the prestige of the U.S. Senate. Twenty candidates formed campaign committees and considered succeeding Bellmon. Nickles was one of five candidates to contest the Republican nomination.

Nickles was little known in state politics. As a first-term state senator, he had done little to distinguish himself in the legislature; of course, that is not unusual in the Oklahoma Senate, whose few Republicans are often better known for their golf games than their legislative prowess. However, he was no lightweight in business matters. At age 27, he effectively took over the operation of his family's business and quickly turned it into a profitable enterprise. The energy and creativity he brought to the Nickles Machine Company would soon emerge in his senatorial campaigns and in his climb up the leadership ladder.

Nickles' 1980 campaign was a costly, high-profile affair that left an indelible impression on his future campaigns. His opponent, Andy Coates, outspent him by more than $170,000. Nickles prevailed with 53 percent of the vote and a plurality of almost 110,000 votes, making his election one of the few by a Republican freshman in 1980 that could not be attributed solely to the coattails of President Reagan. According to James Campbell and Joe Sumners, presidential coattails accounted for a dozen Republican Senate victories between 1972 and 1988, including a half-dozen in 1980.[14] Unlike other Republicans, such as Jeremiah Dent (AL) and Paula Hawkins (FL), Nickles at least had the satisfaction of knowing that he ran ahead of his party. Like many of the Republicans from the class of 1980, Nickles was considered by many Democrats to be a lightweight extremist, a neophyte fluke who was carried into the Senate on Reagan's coattails. One Democrat in the Oklahoma delegation was highly skeptical of Nickles on election night, commenting off-camera at an Oklahoma City television station: "Nickles? Oh God, I can't work with him." In the Senate, he often found himself on the opposite side of issues from his senior colleague, David Boren (D-OK), and Boren would subsequently campaign for his Democratic opponents in 1986 and 1992.

Nickles has not traveled an easy trail to reelection. His initial reelection effort in 1986 was characterized by all of the conditions that were to plague other Republican freshmen up for reelection. The Democratic party hoped to exploit the six-year itch of the electorate and to turn out of office the ideologues that rode Reagan's coattails six years prior. In Oklahoma, the Democrats fielded a strong candidate, Representative Jim Jones, the former chair of the House Budget Committee. Jones' emergence as a challenger constituted a real threat to Nickles' incumbency. Jones was initially elected to the House in a Republican-leaning district (Tulsa) during a Republican year (1972): Nixon carried 79 percent of the district's vote. Jones drew no viable primary opposition, enabling him to focus his entire campaign on defeating the 37-year-old first-term Republican.

For Nickles, this would prove to be his toughest election, tougher than his initial victory in 1980. Jones used his connections with political action committees (PACs) and other interests to raise a war chest in excess of $2.5 million. He actually raised more money than Nickles during the election year. However, Nickles was one of the first modern senators to take advantage of the off-year campaign cycles in the six-year Senate term to raise money. When the election was over, Nickles had outspent Jones by more than $650,000 and won 55 percent of the vote.

In his 1992 reelection against state assembly Speaker Steve Lewis, Nickles finally achieved a safe reelection, based on his formidable financial advantage. Lewis was already "damaged goods" by the time he ran against Nickles. He had failed to secure the Democratic nomination for governor in 1990, taking 30 percent of the vote; the top two finishers had 32 percent each. This race was one of the nastiest in a series of nasty political campaigns in Oklahoma during the 1990s. Nickles, who can be characterized as hawkish in his opposition to taxes, painted Lewis as a "Ted Kennedy clone" that would raise taxes. He outspent Lewis by more than $2 million, drawing heavy financial support from oil and gas producers and conservative PACs.

Nickles has run strongest in the traditionally Republican northwestern part of the state and in the major urban areas of Tulsa and Oklahoma City. Even in

1986, when confronted by Tulsa-area Representative Jones, he won a majority of the vote in Tulsa county and the surrounding suburban counties of Rogers and Wagoner, which were part of Jones' constituency in the House. In his 1992 campaign against Lewis, Nickles expanded his support in rural areas, carrying 15 new, traditionally rural counties that did not vote for him in either 1986 or 1980, and also solidifying his vote in the counties surrounding Oklahoma City. These changes in his vote pattern across three elections reflect an incumbent solidifying his reelection constituency on top of the "normal" partisan vote in the state.

Career Track to Power in D.C.

Nickles is the second-ranking Republican in the Senate. The path to power has not been easy. He fought image problems early in his career. During his first term, Michael Barone described Nickles as "obscure" and typified his election as being the product of the support of the religious right in 1980.[15] This characterization was not without merit. At 31, Nickles was the youngest member of the Senate, two years junior to the lightly regarded Dan Quayle (R-IN), and his election was largely attributable to the intense support he received from the religious right in the 1980 primaries and general election.[16] His committee assignments were similarly uninspiring—Energy and Natural Resources and Labor and Human Resources—although the former is important to the energy-based economy of Oklahoma. His profile on these committees was low, but that is not necessarily a bad thing for a young senator seeking to establish a serious identity in the Senate. Nickles pushed legislation that had little prospects of passing (such as the flat income tax), tended to constituency matters, and developed the type of hard-working reputation a senator needs to attain institutional success. His proposals in his first year to get rid of the 55-mile-per-hour speed limit and to eliminate windfall profits taxes did finally pass the Senate during his second term. He took certain risks, however, such as opposing Boren, who sought to hold up Ed Meese's nomination as Attorney General of the United States. As noted above, this lack of deference to Boren did not endear Nickles to his senior colleague.

After toiling in obscurity for almost a decade, Nickles emerged in the 1990s as an imposing force in the Senate. Spotted as an up-and-coming leader, the most durable member of the Class of 1980 grabbed the first rung of the leadership ladder in 1990, when he was elected chair of the Republican Policy Committee over New Mexico's Senator Pete Domenici.[17] Nickles also chaired the National Republican Senatorial Committee (NRSC) in 1990, when the party lost only one seat.[18] In that position, he worked hard to consolidate Republican opposition to new taxes. Although his effort to have Senator Alan Simpson (R-WY) elected majority whip in 1995 failed (by one vote), he was able to succeed Senator Trent Lott (R-MS) as majority whip when Lott was named Majority Leader after the departure of Senator Bob Dole (R-KS) in 1996. Nickles prevailed by a unanimous vote, and the post was rechristened Assistant Majority Leader.[19] He has opposed Lott on occasion, most recently in voting against the October 1998 budget compromise. In the wake of the 1998 election, Nickles considered a challenge to Lott for the Senate leadership, but he ultimately decided against it.

THE DEMOCRATIC PARTY PRIMARY: DEAD CANDIDATE WALKING

It is difficult to understand the reelection of Nickles without also understanding the impact of the political events of the 1990s on the pool of potential Democratic senatorial challengers. In this section, the destruction of the Democratic candidate pool and the implications of that damage for a challenge to Nickles are discussed. I then describe the field of Democrats who did run for the Senate in 1998 and discuss the unique circumstances of the Democratic primary and runoff.

The Diminishing Democratic Candidate Pool

Oklahoma nurtures the political ambitions of aggressive, populist politicians. Oklahoma, like neighboring Arkansas, has a history of being kind to young candidates, especially when the very bright ones run for major office. (For example, see chapter 10 in this volume on the election of Blanche Lambert Lincoln.) A variety of governors were elected while in their early 30s, including George Nigh, Robert S. Kerr, and Boren. The state legislature has hosted a variety of legislators in their twenties, and the congressional delegation is usually made up of former state legislators who had progressive ambition. Nickles was among that group, having been elected to the state senate at age 29.[20]

For Democrats, the problem in Oklahoma is that the pool of potential Democratic challengers has been devastated in the last six years. In 1994 and 1996, the Oklahoma congressional delegation transformed from a 4–2 Democratic advantage to a 6–0 Republican advantage. Of the major statewide offices, only three were held by Democrats entering the 1998 election year. Former Democratic congressmen and statewide officeholders are either aged or suffered recent political defeats in efforts to win statewide office or reelection. For example, David McCurdy, once considered the safest of safe Democrats in Congress, was defeated in his 1994 bid for the U.S. Senate.[21] Mike Synar, another promising Democratic representative, was defeated for renomination in 1994. Most major Democrats in state politics are in the legislature, where they hold 60 percent of the seats. The jump from a constituency of 31,000 to representing a state of 3 million is daunting for many legislators. Any "quality" Democrat will have to introduce him- or herself to about 97 percent of the state's voters.

The collapse of the Democratic pool of quality candidates was a result of the 1994 election. The Democratic party was struck by two blows—one affected the governor's race, the other affected a variety of contests up and down the ticket. In the governor's race, a schism in the Democratic party erupted that divided traditional, rural Democrats from the state party. Those voters supported former Democratic representative Wes Watkins, who bolted the party and ran as an independent, pulling almost 25 percent of the statewide vote. The Democratic nominee, lieutenant-governor Jack Mildren, carried the usual Democratic vote in urban and strong manufacturing areas, but trailed Republican Frank Keating by 17 percent of the vote due to Watkins' 50 percent-plus showing in Little Dixie.

The second blow came from the fundamentalist community. Christian Right voters were strongly mobilized in congressional contests and the Senate contests to succeed retiring senator Boren. The Christian Coalition voter guides were distributed extensively in Oklahoma. The efforts of the churches helped separate suburban and rural white voters from their Democratic past.[22] For the Democrat considering a run for statewide office, the failure of the major party members to win in 1994, the defection of Christian conservatives from the Democratic party, and the daunting prospects of running an expensive statewide campaign limited their ambitions in 1998.

The weakness of the Democratic challenger pool was evident in the 1996 race for the Senate. Short-term incumbent James Inhofe had defeated McCurdy in 1994 to fill the remaining two years of Boren's term.[23] When Inhofe was up for election to a six-year term in 1996, his general election opponent was 70-year-old part-time political science professor and "humorist" Jim Boren, the cousin of former senator Boren. Jim Boren is considered to be something of a gadfly in Oklahoma politics, making mileage off the political success of his cousin. Boren's 41 percent of the vote in 1996 was largely a tribute to name recognition; one in four voters who cast ballots for Jim Boren thought he was, in fact, former senator Boren.[24]

The Candidates

State Democratic party executive director Pat Hall summed up the situation with regard to the Senate campaign at the state party's midterm convention: "As of yet we don't have anybody who has $3.5 million and wants to take on Don Nickles." No state legislator or significant local official decided to run. Instead, a handful of fringe, amateur candidates emerged at the last minute to challenge Nickles.

An air conditioner repairman from Tallequah, Don Carroll decided on the second day of filing that Nickles should not get a free ride for reelection. Carroll drove to the capital, Oklahoma City, and discovered that he had three fellow Democrats who shared his sentiment. Carroll explained his rationale for running: "what sets us apart from other governments" is that we always have two choices. Carroll did not actively campaign for the nomination, due to business demands. Carroll spent less than $1,000 during the primary campaign, and he was arguably the least visible candidate on the campaign trail.

A 44-year-old farmer/rancher from Choctaw, Jerry Kobyluk possessed more political experience than anyone else in the Democratic field. He previously sought statewide office, running far behind the major contenders for the

1994 Republican gubernatorial nomination. Kobyluk switched parties, with the intention of running against Governor Frank Keating in 1998. After participating in candidate forums and interviews as a gubernatorial candidate, he filed for the Senate, most likely because there were no announced candidates at the time he filed. In an interview the day before the 1998 Democratic primary, Kobyluk said that during the 1994 gubernatorial campaign, many voters indicated that they would have voted for him, but he was in the wrong party. So, he changed party for this election. Kobyluk campaigned extensively around the state, attending party events and seeking out support from Democratic activists and officials in all 77 Oklahoma counties. Kobyluk was not an especially engaging speaker, but in the weak field of announced candidates, he constituted a credible challenger for the Senate nomination.

Another candidate, Jacquelyn Ledgerwood, was a 69-year-old socialite from the suburban college town of Norman. The Ledgerwoods are an established Norman family known for philanthropy. Her son, Thomas Ledgerwood II, ran previously for governor and the U.S. Senate, with little success. This was her first foray into elective politics. However, Ledgerwood died seven days after the filing deadline. Under Oklahoma law, only the candidates can remove themselves from the ballot after filing, so Ledgerwood remained on the ballot for the August primary.

Like Carroll, Arlie Nixon decided to run for the Senate because the voters deserved a choice. An 84-year-old retired airline pilot and former vice president of the International Federation of Airline Pilots, Nixon would have made an interesting challenger 30 years ago. He had success in business after retiring from flying, and he was a legitimate war hero. Nixon flew missions over Europe during World War II, and in 1948 flew supplies and foodstuffs in the Berlin Air Lift. Like Carroll and Ledgerwood, Nixon did not actively campaign, noting that "You'd have to be out of your mind to think you could beat Don Nickles. . . . [I]t's a protest campaign. I expect to spend under $5,000. I'm not taking any contributions. I'm not going to do anything."[25]

Finally, Nickles did not draw a Republican primary opponent.

The Democratic Primary

The Democratic primary was a remarkably low-key event, befitting the stature and quality of the candidate field. Media outlets in the major cities dedicated little time or space to the race, which had to compete with the Democratic gubernatorial primary and many local contests for attention. In the two weeks before the primary, L'Affaire Lewinsky again exploded into the national headlines, pushing the Oklahoma Senate race even further into the background. The forecast voter turnout was under 30 percent, and, in fact, voter turnout for the primary was only 22 percent, indicating the lack of interest in the candidates seeking to challenge the incumbents in the major offices (see table 8.2). Every statewide constitutional and congressional office had an incumbent seeking reelection. Despite the lack of quality candidates or significant media coverage, this primary was also one of the great political stories of 1998.

Table 8.2 The 1998 Democratic
Primary and Runoff for U.S. Senate

Candidate	PRIMARY		RUNOFF	
	Vote	**Vote %**	**Vote**	**Vote %**
Jerry Kobyluk	54,196	20.59	—	—
Jacquelyn Morrow Lewis Ledgerwood	56,393	21.43	38,817	24.84
Don E. Carroll	120,759	45.8	117,442	75.16
Arlie Nixon	31,860	12.10	—	—
%Turnout*	22.5	—	13.3	—
Rolloff from Primary to Runoff**	—	—	–59.1	—

*Turnout as a percentage of registered Democrats.

**Increase/decrease in runoff votes as a proportion of primary votes cast.

SOURCE: Oklahoma State Board of Elections.

As noted earlier, only Kobyluk actively campaigned for the office. He was the only candidate who seemed to actually believe that he had a chance of unseating Nickles. Kobyluk campaigned throughout the state and made a serious financial investment, spending more than $40,000 of his own money to seek the Democratic nomination. Watching Kobyluk campaign and listening to him speak, however, was to reminiscent of the politicians whom David Canon has called "hopeless amateurs," candidates who run with little war chest, little qualification, and the earnest hope that lightening will strike and they will be elevated to public office.[26] Kobyluk's two switches (from Republican to Democrat in 1997 and then from gubernatorial candidate to Senate candidate in 1998) indicate that he was driven less by any particular policy imperative or ideological concerns than by just being a nominee and, hopefully, an elected official. These sudden changes suggested a candidate who was not grounded in partisan attachments, political beliefs, or the ability to articulate his qualifications for public service.

No polls exist for the Democratic Senate primary. State Democrats had not actively sought a candidate to run against Nickles. On primary morning, political observers had no idea who would be the nominee. The best guess was that there would be a runoff election. The extent of this uncertainty was reflected by who was invited to appear on local television as the results rolled in. A Tulsa Public Broadcasting System (PBS) station invited Nixon to discuss his candidacy and prospects while awaiting the returns. As the results came in, Carroll quickly established a 40 percent share and a 20-point lead over the opposition that would be sustained throughout the night. Carroll had not actively campaigned. Efforts by major newspapers to contact him were frustrated by the demands of a hot summer. As an air conditioner repairman, the 108-degree heat of the Oklahoma summer had kept Carroll too busy to return calls to the papers. Carroll did not even enjoy the number one ballot position in the Democratic primary. Conventional wisdom of Oklahoma politics is that the top slot in a multi-candidate primary is worth between five and ten points. In an electorate that knows nothing about any of the candidates, Carroll may simply have benefited from having the most WASPish name in a WASPish state, while Kobyluk garnered the top-of-the-ticket benefit.

Throughout most of the evening, Kobyluk ran in second place. His active campaigning had produced significantly more votes than his last-place effort in the Republican gubernatorial primary four years earlier. Kobyluk, however, also demonstrated a bitter edge during primary night. During a live, statewide television broadcast of the election results, Kobyluk was interviewed about his plans. He discussed his reasons for switching parties and expressed dismay that a candidate who failed to campaign would garner more than 40 percent of the vote. Kobyluk's dismay would turn into chagrin, when, at the end of the night, he slipped into third place, behind the late Ledgerwood.

Carroll's victory was difficult for political experts to explain. He carried all 77 counties, including a majority of the vote in Tulsa County. One political activist from Tulsa came up with the most plausible explanation for this implausible outcome when he related to an Oklahoma City reporter, "maybe he's placed a lot of air conditioners in people's homes."[27]

Dead Candidate Walking

When the primary votes were tallied, Carroll had garnered more than 45 percent of the vote. The late Ledgerwood came in second (21.4 percent), and Kobyluk third (20.5 percent). Under Oklahoma law, a party nominee has to secure a majority vote to be nominated; if not, the top two finishers advance to a runoff election three weeks hence. And, under Oklahoma law, as noted earlier, candidates can only be removed from the ballot by themselves. The same law says a candidate cannot be removed from the primary ballot due to death. So, Ledgerwood would appear on the primary runoff ballot on September 15.

The Ledgerwood candidacy attracted far more attention than any other political event in Oklahoma in 1998. National and international news services contacted political pundits in the state to discuss the story. Moreover, it also set off a flurry of activity as the remaining, living candidates, the state parties, and the state attorney general all sought to get an understanding of the consequences of a possible Ledgerwood victory.

More than one Democratic activist confided that they would rather give the nomination to a dead woman than to nominate a living candidate who had no prospect of victory. Democratic party chair Bob Kerr would not confirm any concerted effort to get out a vote for Ledgerwood, though he conceded to a reporter at a campaign event that "certainly that's a possibility." Democratic politicians indicated that they supported a Ledgerwood nomination because that would give the state party central committee the opportunity to choose a replacement nominee. This conspiracy theory made its way into the mainstream press within two days of the primary, and set off a debate among the state party leadership, the state's attorney general, and the press regarding the eligibility of Ledgerwood, should she be nominated in the September runoff.

Republican officials accused the Democrats of exploiting Ledgerwood's death. The chairman of the state Republican party, Quineta Wylie, said Democrats were using the dead candidate for political gain, based on a statement made by Democratic chair Kerr to the *Tulsa World*. Kerr responded, saying that Wylie's charges were "absurd."[28]

In the days immediately following the primary, conventional wisdom argued that the Democratic party would be able to replace Ledgerwood, if she won the nomination. Precedent seemed to say as much. In 1942, the Republican nominee for the U.S. Senate, former senator W. B. Pine (1925–1931), died after the primary election. The Republican Central Committee picked Ed Moore as a substitute. Democratic party officials and journalists assumed that that precedent would apply, should Ledgerwood win the primary runoff.

However, the attorney general and the state election board indicated that the Pine-Moore precedent did not apply to this situation. In an advisory opinion released on August 28, Assistant Attorney General Victor Bird and the state election board indicated that there was no law that allowed for the removal of Ledgerwood's name from the ballot, should she be nominated. State officials anticipated a lawsuit in the event that Ledgerwood won. Lance Ward, secretary of the state election board, observed that "a lot of vested interests" were interested in substituting for a dead person on the ballot. Among the various individuals who requested rulings from the courts were Carroll and Kobyluk. The final ruling, as interpreted by Attorney General Drew Edmondson, was definitive about retaining Ledgerwood on the ballot.[29] In short, if the voters of Oklahoma saw fit to nominate a dead woman for the Senate, her name would appear on the ballot in November.

The Runoff

Despite his concerns about the status of a dead candidate, Carroll had reason to be confident. Runoff election is won by the front-running candidate from the primary more than two-thirds of the time.[30] Carroll was in an especially enviable position, having received more than 40 percent of the vote and leading his nearest opponent by more than 5 percent. Carroll swamped his dead opponent 75 to 25 percent, again carrying all 77 counties.[31] Despite the landslide victory, voters were largely disinterested in the runoff. Turnout fell 59 percent from the primary. The electorate was not interested in determining who would lose to Nickles.

HOW TO OUTSPEND
YOUR OPPONENT 238 TO 1

Studies of representatives and their campaigns consistently find that campaign styles are defined in their initial election. Like the paranoid golfer or baseball pitcher, they keep doing everything exactly the same way as long as it works. Initial elections are typically close, and therefore incumbents often campaign as if they are always in tight races. No matter how large the lead, the surviving incumbent will always work hard to ensure that he or she gets reelected.

One form of paranoid campaigning among Senate incumbents is the rise in "preemptive" expenditures and the building of war chests throughout the six-year term. Since the early 1970s, off-year fundraising has increased among incumbent senators.[32] Part of this increase has to do with the retiring of debt; the other part is an increase in early buildup of a war chest to prepare for a significant challenge or, preferably, to scare away potential challengers.[33] Nickles has faced well-financed opponents on three occasions. In his initial election, he was outspent by his Democratic opponent; in 1986, he and his opponent engaged in one of the year's most expensive Senate campaigns; and in 1992, against a state legislator, Nickles spent more than $3 million compared to his opponent's $1.5 million. Nickles' entire political experience has been expensive campaigns against well-funded opponents.

The Incumbent

It was surprising to learn that Nickles did not engage in extensive early fundraising before the 1998 election. After the 1996 election, he had raised about $250,000 since his last election. By Oklahoma standards, it was about a third of the money that an incumbent representative spends on reelection. In the last 18 months leading up to the election, Nickles' fundraising kicked into gear. He raised nearly $2.7 million. The money was raised roughly equally from political action committees (PACs) and individuals (see table 8.3). An examination of Nickles' Federal Election Commission (FEC) reports reveal substantial amounts of money received from the petrochemical industry, defense contractors, and the financial and health services community. Nickles was especially successful in attracting corporate PAC money. He ended up spending approximately $2.4 million in his reelection effort, or roughly 200 times the combined expenditures of all of his opponents.

So what does an incumbent with a sure-fire reelection do with his money? In Nickles' case, part of the money went into "party-building" efforts, such as get-out-the-vote drives and candidate schools that are designed to "build up" the party at the grassroots. Nickles financed these activities. However, his principal contribution to Republican "party-building" in Oklahoma in 1998 was the financing of candidates. Through his leadership PAC, Nickles contributed more than $85,000 directly into the campaigns of Republican challengers and vulnerable incumbents in the state legislature. These donations were made in the last four weeks of the campaign, and ranged from $500 to the legal limit of $5,000. The candidates and the size of their receipts from Nickles are listed in table 8.4, along with the Republican percentages in those districts for the 1998 election and the previous election. Most of the recipients were either candidates for open seats or challengers. Of the 33 state legislative candidates who received money, only 10 received less than 40 percent of the vote. In the open seats, five candidates won previously Democratic districts; all five who won received at least $3,000 from Nickles' leadership PAC. The *Daily Oklahoman*

Table 8.3 The Cycle of Fundraising

Election Cycle	Receipts	Expenditures	PAC Receipts	Individual Receipts
Don Nickles (R)				
1993–1994	57,394	105,331	8,653	8,045
1995–1996	197,710	76,434	110,295	34,315
1997–1998	2,699,927	2,381,198	1,058,146	1,356,499
Don Carroll (D)	—	No report		—
Jacquelyn Ledgerwood (D)	—	No report		—
Jerry Kobyluk (D)				
1997–1998	26,200	26,050	0	1,400*
Arlie Nixon (D)	—	No report		—

*Jerry Kobyluk contributed $25,050 to his own campaign.

SOURCE: Federal Election Commission.

stated in a September editorial that the "real battle ground in Oklahoma politics this year will be over control of the legislature."[34] This was certainly the perception of the Nickles campaign as it disposed of money down the stretch.

Nickles also engaged in party building by funding other party organizations and committees. The Oklahoma Republican Senatorial Committee, a PAC for state Senate candidates, got $10,000; its counterpart in the state House, the House Republican PAC, received $5,000; the Oklahoma Republican Party, $10,500; Tom Cole's GOP PAC, $5,000. Larger contributions also were made to the Oklahoma Republican Party ($50,000) and the National Republican Senatorial Committee ($300,000). These funds do not include Nickles' fundraising efforts nationwide on behalf of other Republican candidates.

The Challenger

Carroll spent less than $5,000 in his senatorial campaign, which means, by law, he did not have to report his expenditures or receipts. As an amateur, there was little prospect that Carroll would raise significant money or constitute a credible challenge to Nickles. The national Democratic party quickly wrote off the entire state. A source that refused to be identified at the Democratic Senatorial Campaign Committee (DSCC) said that whatever money had been earmarked for Oklahoma would instead go to more competitive races elsewhere.

Before candidates can get major party support, they have to prove their credibility to the party and to potential givers.[35] Carroll certainly hoped to get support from the state and national party. However, the nature of his financial appeals indicated that he either had no concept of the cost of the campaign or that he had no friends who would stake his campaign. In the end, even the state Democratic party decided that the Carroll candidacy was too far gone. In comparing Carroll to the 1996 gadfly candidate Boren, Hall observed that the party

Table 8.4 Nickles' Party Building Activity in Oklahoma

Recipient	Amount ($)	1998 GOP %	Prior GOP %
State House Candidates			
Sue Tibbs (H-23)	2,000	49.2	49.4
John Smaligo (H-74)	2,000	47.8	44.6
Mark Liotta (H-77)*	4,000	56.8	50.6
Bob Henkle (H-5)	3,000	38.1	38.5
Paul Landers (H-10)	3,000	44.4	39.4
Jerry Huffer (H-14)	3,000	42.2	41.0
Lavon Williams (H-3)**	1,000	32.3	No Republican ran
Greg Piatt (H-48)**+	4,000	54.6	45.2
Richard Wolf (H-18)	500	29.1	34.2
Eric Hawkins (H-45)	2,000	49.6	47.5
Ricky Brewer (H-52)	1,500	37.4	37.4
Curt Roggow (H-41)**+	4,000	55.9	49.9
Earl Wells (H-61)	2,000	43.1	45.1
Todd Hiett (H-29)**	3,000	58.2	57.5
David Lancaster (H-12)	4,000	40.0	44.0
Everett Maylen (H-26)	500	33.2	34.7
Susan Winchester (H-47)**+	4,000	53.7	41.9
Kevin Calvey (H-94)**+	4,000	50.1	40.3
Tim Clem (H-96)	2,500	45.1	45.8
Flint Breckinridge (H-78)	3,000	39.5	49.0
Chris Benge (H-68)**+	3,000	55.4	45.4
Fred Morgan (H-83)*	5,000	Unopposed	No Democrat ran
State Senate Candidates			
Kevin Farmer (S-12)	500	36.3	33.0
Ben Curtis (S-4)	5,000	32.9	No Republican ran
Carol Martin (S-24)*	4,000	54.8	55.0
David Myers (S-20)	4,000	49.8	51.0
Glenn Coffee (S-52)**	1,000	71.5	No Democrat ran
Mike Johnson (S-22)**	1,000	64.2	No Democrat ran
Brian McKye (S-46)	1,000	43.0	44.0
Kelly Monroe (S-18)	1,000	29.8	37.0
Scott Pruitt (S-54)**	1,000	63.5	61.0
Michael Robins (S-16)	4,000	39.8	42.0
Gary Banz (S-42)	3,000	45.2	No Republican ran

*Republican incumbent. **Open seat. +Flipped to the GOP.

SOURCES: Federal Election Commission; *The Almanac of Oklahoma Politics*; The Oklahoma Board of Elections.

had raised money for Boren, but that "I don't know this year. Don Carroll has not put together a team that I know of. He is our candidate, and we're going to do everything we can to help him."[36] Everything turned out to be nothing in the case of Carroll, as Oklahoma Democrats acted in the southern Protestant tradition of helping those who help themselves.

MEDIA AND CAMPAIGNING

The question that must be answered about the 1998 reelection campaign by Nickles is: Does the absence of a campaign constitute a campaign? The elections of 1998 in Oklahoma were largely driven by local contests and local issues. The campaigns for major offices on the ballot were not visible. If anything, what characterized this campaign was its general lack of any impression on the voters after the primary.

Themes

The only advertising in the general election campaign was aired by Nickles. His campaign emphasized the classic themes associated with incumbents: integrity, accessibility, and the desire to work hard for the constituency. This approach by Nickles was a tremendous relief to Carroll. In his previous contests, Nickles had engaged his opponents in vigorous, slash-and-burn campaigns. Nickles' campaign manager, Mark Nichols, indicated that unless the race became unexpectedly close, there would be no slash-and-burn, attack campaign against the opposition. That was the case. Unlike previous Nickles' campaigns, the comparative advertising and charges and counter-charges that created some of the most vicious campaigns in Oklahoma history were entirely absent.

Advertising

Any discussion of political advertising in this campaign is, like every other aspect of the campaign, necessarily one-sided. The Nickles camp ran a series of warm, positive ads that featured either Nickles talking about his political accomplishments or a narrator discussing Nickles' incumbency, political position in Washington, and his service to Oklahoma. No mention of party or the opponent was made. Nickles' advertising ran for the last four weeks of the campaign in the major media markets of the state. Carroll ran no radio or television advertising, although he claimed to have purchased cable advertising in northeastern Oklahoma. He purchased no direct mail. The DSCC did not run targeted ads or "issue-advertising" in Oklahoma. There was no interest among state or national Democrats in the challenge to Nickles.

The Media

Coverage of the Nickles-Carroll contest was almost nonexistent. The media only showed interest in the novelty of a dead woman being the Democratic nominee. After Carroll beat Ledgerwood, media interest turned to the governor's race, the congressional campaign in the Third District, and the Clinton scandal. Nickles' reelection was a foregone conclusion, and as such it did not merit significant coverage. The fact that the incumbent spent more time out-of-state, campaigning for his Republican colleagues, than in state, running against his invisible challenger, meant that there were few opportunities for free media coverage.

Hence, local reporters assigned to cover the campaign were quite frustrated. The Nickles campaign was an absentee affair. Despite spending more than $2 million, it was almost an austerity campaign. A *Tulsa World* reporter observed that "the campaign is certainly not wasting money on campaign kits [the packets of press clippings, issue papers, campaign literature, and other information that are often sent to the media]; in response to a request for material [campaign manager Mark] Nichols faxed one page . . . it was a bit short on specifics."[37] The incumbent senator stayed away from the character issues surrounding President Bill Clinton. Instead, he focused on privatizing Social Security and attacking the erosion of American prestige in international affairs.

To Nickles' credit, he is a safe incumbent and a national leader. He spent the 1998 campaign season fulfilling obligations to reinforce the Republican senatorial majority and attain the lofty goal of a cloture-proof 60-vote majority. Therefore, he mortgaged his time and effort to supporting marginal Republican incumbents like Lauch Faircloth (NC) and Paul Coverdell (GA), and in assisting challenges for vulnerable Democratic seats. He even reversed the polarity on campaign finance, giving more than $300,000 to the National Republican Senatorial Committee (NRSC) instead of taking campaign money from them.

As little as Nickles was visible in Oklahoma, Carroll was completely out of sight. Carroll's campaign operation consisted of an answering machine. If you were lucky, he would return your calls. Under these circumstances, it is safe to say that the Senate race was run out of public view, and, in fact, if you went looking for it, you might still not find it.

ELECTORAL OUTCOMES

Nickles' 1998 victory set a record for a Republican Senate candidate in Oklahoma. He carried 66.4 percent of the vote and 76 of 77 counties in a decisive victory over his air-conditioner repairman opponent. Analysis of outcomes indicates that the election conformed to the expected patterns of Oklahoma politics. Nickles carried 70.2 percent of the vote in Tulsa and Oklahoma counties, and 65.2 percent in the rest of the state. While the difference between the traditional urban centers and the rural counties was not as pronounced as in many other elections, it was nonetheless evident even in this landslide.

Nickles' performance was not even the top Republican performance of the election. Although he set a Republican Senate record in Oklahoma with 66.4 percent of the vote, two other statewide officeholders, Lieutenant Governor

**Table 8.5 Nickles' Performance
Compared to Other Republicans in 1998**

Candidate	Vote %
Brenda Reneau (Labor Commissioner, Incumbent)	68.42
Mary Fallin (Lieutenant-governor, Incumbent)	67.55
Don Nickles (U.S. Senator, Incumbent)	66.38
Republican U.S. House Candidates (All Incumbents)	62.70
Denise A. Bode (Corporation Commisioner, Incumbent)	60.14
Frank Keating (Governor, Incumbent)	57.86
John P. Crawford (Insurance Commissioner, Incumbent)	49.85
State House Candidates (Contested Districts only)	49.59
State Senate Candidates (Contested Districts only)	45.60

SOURCE: Oklahoma State Board of Elections.

Mary Fallin and Labor Commissioner Brenda Reneau, both polled a larger percentage and a larger vote total than Nickles (see table 8.5). The senator's statewide percentage was four points better that the total percentage of the all-Republican congressional delegation, and almost nine points ahead of incumbent governor Keating's reelection percentage.

A closer look at the electoral geography of the 1998 election indicates that there is a remnant of the tripartite political strengths observed in Nickles' previous efforts. He was weakest in Little Dixie and strongest in the cities and the northwest. Nickles pulled off a rare trick for a Republican in winning a majority of the vote in Little Dixie. Even in 1972, when Oklahoma cast more than 70 percent of its vote for Richard Nixon, Little Dixie had given Democrat George McGovern a majority. In 1998, the allegiances to the Democratic party were not sufficient to make these Democrats vote for an unknown candidate who did not campaign.

Election Outcome in Context

What characterized this contest was the lack of either surprises or unusual events following the Democratic primary. In table 8.6, the results of a November 3 exit poll are presented. Nickles' vote came primarily from self-identified Republicans, 96 percent of who voted for him. He also ran well among self-identified Democrats, pulling 32 percent of those voters. These exit poll results are bad news either way for Democrats. Almost 60 percent of Oklahomans are registered Democrats, compared to 44 percent Democratic identification in exit polls. If voter turnout was proportional across parties by registration (the more likely case), then a sizeable number of registered Democrats are now identifying as Republicans. If the exit poll figures in fact reflect party registration, then registered Democrats turned out at rates far below that of registered Republicans. Democrats either defected or were demobilized, either of which

Table 8.6 Exit Poll, 1998 Oklahoma Senate Campaign

	All Respondents (Read Down)	Don Carroll (D) (Read Across)	Don Nickles (R)
Vote by Gender			
Men	50	27	70
Women	50	35	62
Party Identification			
Democrat	44	59	38
Republican	40	3	96
Independent	16	27	65
Political Ideology			
Liberal	14	63	32
Moderate	45	38	58
Conservative	41	12	86
White Religious Right Voters			
Yes	33	14	84
No	64	40	57
Vote for Congress			
To Support Clinton	15	78	19
To Oppose Clinton	26	4	93
Clinton Not a Factor	57	30	66
Should Clinton Be Impeached?			
Yes	43	6	92
No	54	52	45
Should Clinton Resign?			
Yes	48	8	89
No	49	53	43
Should Clinton Be Censured?			
Yes	46	23	74
No	48	41	56
How Clinton Handles His Job			
Approve	45	59	37
Disapprove	51	7	91
Opinion of Clinton as a Person			
Favorable	29	68	27
Unfavorable	68	15	83
Opinion of Clinton			
Approve/Favorable	27	69	25
Approve/Unfavorable	16	43	54
Disapprove/Favorable	0	0	0
Disapprove/Unfavorable	50	6	91

Note: Oklahoma Senate (n = 754, 95% confidence +/- 4._%).

SOURCE: AllPolitics.com.

did not bode well for Democratic efforts to unseat Nickles. Voter interest in Oklahoma was at near-historic lows. Hall had predicted such an outcome eight months earlier, noting that "if we [Democrats] don't turn out that base vote, then, in fact, we are going to be in trouble in 1998."[38] A careful analysis of the election results indicates that the highest turnout in Oklahoma was in constituencies that hosted either close state legislative or district attorney contests. Local politics, in other words, determined political interest.

The Impact of the Clinton Scandal

Any discussion of an election in 1998 would not be complete without a visit to the impact of the Clinton scandal, if only to emphasize its irrelevance to most voters, even in a state where Clinton is unpopular. As noted earlier, Oklahoma is a conservative state, both by reputation and in fact. Exit polls of voters in the November election revealed little support for President Clinton. Oklahoma is one of a few states where Clinton had a negative job approval rating entering the November election, with 51 percent of Oklahoma voters disapproving of his job performance. Even among those who approved of his job performance, more than half had a negative personal opinion of the president. About half of the voters questioned in exit polls wanted the president to either step aside or be removed from office. To the extent that the president would be an issue in such a low-stimulus, low-profile election, one would expect Clinton to be of no help to a Democratic senatorial candidate.

The exit poll numbers reflect this proposition. As in much of the nation, most congressional voters in Oklahoma did not cast ballots to support or oppose President Clinton. Their ballots ratified the incumbency of a successful, valuable member of the Senate who avoided attracting any meaningful political opposition (see table 8.6). The impact of the Clinton scandal, therefore, was minimal in Oklahoma.

SUMMARY

Nickles won reelection long before the first candidate filed. His efforts in Washington to attain institutional power and represent the issues of importance to him made him a popular senator who would not be challenged by potential partisan rivals. Nickles has achieved a rare combination in American politics, combining both institutional and constituency popularity and success.

It is possible that Nickles could confront a significant challenge in 2004, should he stand for reelection. One of the "quality" Democrats mentioned above would have to serve as the likely standard bearer; or, a new, vibrant Democrat will have to appear who is as yet unknown to the political class of Oklahoma. A challenge will not only have to be well funded but also require the emergence of a candidate who feels he or she can take on Nickles and separate rural, conservative voters from their new habit of voting for this popular Republican incumbent. Such a task will prove daunting as long as Nickles remains on the ballot.

NOTES

1. Chris Casteel, "Nickles Continues Campaigning—Race Predicted to Be Easy Victory For Senator," *Daily Oklahoman,* October 28, 1998.

2. Jim Meyers, "Nickles Seen as 'Sure Thing' for Reelection," *Tulsa World,* October 4, 1998.

3. See, for example, Charles Bullock III and Mark Rozell, eds., *The New Politics of the Old South* (Baltimore, MD: Rowman and Littlefield, 1998); Earl Black and Merle Black, *Politics and Society in the South* (Cambridge, MA: Harvard University Press, 1987); Edward Carmines and James Stimson, *Issue Evolution* (Princeton, NJ: Princeton University Press, 1989).

4. David R. Morgan, Robert E. England, and George G. Humphreys, *Oklahoma Politics and Policies* (Lincoln, NE: University of Nebraska Press, 1991).

5. Nancy Bednar and Allen D. Hertzke, "Oklahoma: The Christian Right and the Republican Realignment," in *God at the Grassroots: The Christian Right in the 1994 Elections,* eds. Mark Rozell and Clyde Wilcox (New York: Rowman and Littlefield, 1995), 91–108.

6. Ronald Keith Gaddie and Scott E. Buchanan, "Oklahoma: Realignment in the Buckle of the Bible Belt," in *The New Politics of the Old South,* eds. Charles Bullock III and Mark Rozell (Baltimore, MD: Rowman and Littlefield, 1998).

7. Rob Martindale, "State Democrats Gearing Up for Battle with Smugness in Election Cycle," *Tulsa World,* April 4, 1998.

8. Gaddie and Buchanan, "Oklahoma"; Bednar and Hertzke, "Oklahoma."

9. Jon F. Hale and Stephen T. Kean, "Oklahoma," in *State and Party Profiles: A Fifty-State Guide to Development, Organization and Resources,* eds. Andrew M. Appleton and Daniel S. Ward (Washington, DC: Congressional Quarterly, 1996).

10. Morgan, England, and Humphreys, *Oklahoma Politics.*

11. Samuel A. Kirkpatrick, David R. Morgan, and Thomas Kielhorn, *The Oklahoma Voter* (Norman, OK: University of Oklahoma Press, 1977).

12. Bednar and Hertzke, "Oklahoma."

13. Hale and Kean, "Oklahoma."

14. James E. Campbell and Joe A. Sumners, "Presidential Coattails in U.S. Senate Elections," *American Political Science Review* 84 (1990): 513–524.

15. Michael Barone and Grant Ujifusa, *The Almanac of American Politics 1984* (Washington, DC: National Journal, 1983).

16. For perspectives on Dan Quayle's Senate career, see Richard F. Fenno, *The Making of a Senator* (Washington, DC: Congressional Quarterly, 1989).

17. Richard F. Fenno, *The Emergence of a Senate Leader: Pete Domenici and the Reagan Budget* (Washington, DC: Congressional Quarterly, 1991).

18. The president's party typically loses seats in the midterm election. See James E. Campbell, *The Presidential Pulse of Congressional Elections,* 2d ed. (Lexington: University Press of Kentucky, 1997).

19. Jim Myers, "Nickles Elected Whip," *Tulsa World,* June 17, 1996.

20. Youthful origins of successful political careers is a norm in American politics. In 1995, of the 150 governors and U.S. senators, one-third were initially elected to public office before age 30, and more than half were initially elected to public office before age 35. Nickles therefore follows in the tradition of not only the state of Oklahoma but also the tradition of most successful politicians.

21. Gary W. Copeland, "The Closing of Political Minds: Noncandidates in the 4th District of Oklahoma," in *Who Runs for Congress? Ambition, Context, and Candidate Emergence,* ed. Thomas A. Kazee (Washington, DC: Congressional Quarterly, 1994); David Averill, "Fallen Stars: Will the Last Democrat to Leave the Party Turn Out the Lights?" *Tulsa World,* November 10, 1996.

22. Bednar and Hertzke, "Oklahoma."

23. Senator Boren resigned in 1994 to become president of the University of Oklahoma.

24. Allen D. Hertzke and Ronald Keith Gaddie, *The Carl Albert Center Poll: 1996 General Election* (Norman, OK: University of Oklahoma, 1996).

25. Chris Casteel, "Nickles' Challengers Want Change," *Daily Oklahoman,* August 16, 1998.

26. David T. Canon, *Actors, Athletes, and Astronauts* (Chicago: University of Chicago Press, 1990).

27. David Zizzo, "Dead Candidate's Strong Showing Not Easily Explained," *Daily Oklahoman,* August 27, 1998.

28. Paul English, "Demos Exploiting Death, GOP Says," *Daily Oklahoman,* August 28, 1998.

29. John Greiner, "Runoff Victory May Make Dead Woman Nominee," *Daily Oklahoman,* September 9, 1998.

30. Charles S. Bullock III and Loch K. Johnson, *Runoff Elections in the United States* (Chapel Hill, NC: University of North Carolina Press, 1992).

31. Barbara Hoberock, "U.S. Senate: Carroll Defeats Dead Woman in Runoff Vote," *Tulsa World,* September 16, 1998.

32. Richard F. Fenno, *The United States Senate: A Bicameral Perspective* (Washington, DC: American Enterprise Institute, 1982).

33. Peverill Squire, "Preemptive Spending and Challenger Profile in Senate Elections," *Journal of Politics* 53 (1991): 1150–1164; James L. Regens and Ronald Keith Gaddie, *The Economic Realities of Political Reform: Elections and the U.S. Senate* (New York: Cambridge University Press, 1995).

34. "Year of the Elephant?" *Daily Oklahoman,* September 20, 1998.

35. See Linda Fowler and Robert D. McClure, *Political Ambition* (New Haven, CT: Yale University Press, 1989).

36. John Greiner, "Official Vows Democrats Will Help Senate Candidate," *Daily Oklahoman,* September 17, 1998.

37. Myers, "Nickles Seen as 'Sure Thing.'"

38. Martindale, "State Democrats Gearing Up."

9

Mikulski Defeats Pierpont in Maryland's Senate Race

Sue Thomas
Matthew Braunstein

W ith all the turmoil in American politics in 1998, how did an outspoken, liberal, Democratic, feminist, female senator once quoted as saying, "Some people raise flowers; I raise hell," face a no-lose situation? What factors coalesced to give Senator Barbara A. Mikulski an easy ride to reelection to her third term in the U.S. Senate? In this chapter, we explore both the electoral context of 1998 and the distinctive situation of the most popular statewide candidate in the state that is home to Cal Ripken of the Baltimore Orioles as she emerged victorious in what was, for others, a challenging electoral context.

BARBARA ANN MIKULSKI:
THE INCUMBENT'S INCUMBENT

Mikulski was born in 1936, in East Baltimore, the oldest of three daughters of parents who owned a grocery store. After high school, during which time she worked in her parents' store, the senator earned a B.A. at Mount Saint Agnes College and a M.S.W. at the University of Maryland. She came to political notice in the late 1960s, when she used her experience as a social worker to organize her neighbors to stop construction of a 16-lane highway through the historic Fells Point area of Baltimore. This highway not only threatened Fells Point but also would have cut through the first black home ownership neighborhood in the city and would have prevented the later successful development of the Inner Harbor Area. With that victory, Mikulski became known as the street fighter who beat the highway.

Mikulski has been running at lightening speed ever since. Her first bid for office came soon after the highway victory and was successful. In 1971, she won a seat on the Baltimore city council. With strong ethnic roots and history in the community as a strong liberal, she was chosen as the head of the Democratic National Committee's (DNC) Commission on Delegate Selection in 1972.

In 1974, she decided to launch a long-shot race for the U.S. Senate against the incumbent Charles Mathais. She lost respectably but marched forward, winning in 1976 the U.S. House seat previously vacated by Mathais.

Apart from that one early loss, Mikulski has won every race she has entered, usually by a wide margin. After ten years in the House of Representatives, in 1986 Mikulski once again set her sights on the U.S. Senate and ran a historic race in which two women competed for the office. Once again, Mikulski emerged victorious. Former White House aide Linda Chavez garnered 39 percent of the vote; Mikulski won with 61 percent.

In 1976, her first race for the U.S. House, Mikulski attracted a whopping 75 percent of the vote and stayed in the 70s or, in one case, the high 60s throughout her House career. Running for the Senate in 1986, she received 61 percent of the vote, and by her first reelection bid, bested that record by a full ten points, earning a 71 percent vote share.

Out of concern for the people of Maryland, in October 1996 Mikulski celebrated her twenty-fifth anniversary of public service by sponsoring a Day of Volunteerism. More than 300 volunteers from across Maryland helped create a computer learning center at Brehm's Lane Elementary School and removed trash and debris from the Armistead Creek and the Herring Run Stream.

What about Mikulski has brought her such consistently strong electoral victories? One clue is her impressively high name recognition and popularity in Maryland. For example, a poll conducted in the summer of 1998 for the *Baltimore Sun,* the *Montgomery Gazette,* WRC-TV, and WTOP Radio showed that Mikulski had a 67 percent favorability rating, the highest in the state.[1] But the real question is, what makes her so popular? Journalists, pundits, politicians, and voters agree that it's her common touch, her fighter's spirit, and the perception that she is fighting for regular folks, not just to further her own situation. From her first foray into the political world to her current perch in the Senate, Mikulski has shown herself as one of the people and steadfastly maintained that all politics and policy is local and that her job is to serve the people in their day-to-day needs as well as to prepare this country for the future.

> It's the beauty of a Barbara Mikulski, who knows how to sound like a street kid dressed up like a grown-up whenever she lets herself forget she is an Important Person. Remember [her] years ago, standing in front of a crowd after she helped defeat all the geniuses who wanted to run an eight lane highway through Fells point? . . . What's the phrase? The Common Touch? Or is it just the ability to let the human being show behind the political image?[2]

In a recent front-page article in the *Washington Post* (available throughout Maryland), journalist Doug Struck commented on her way with constituents:

... the Maryland Democrat was entertaining businessmen with tales of "fighting off the evil Vaders" of the federal government, saying she was a "little stealth rocket, a heat-seeking missile, under everybody's radar." The audiences loved it. Here was a 62-year-old-fireplug-shaped-4-foot-11 pol with a dockworker's brogue, offering up fanciful and self-mocking depictions, the antithesis of the Somber Self-Puffing Politician.[3]

MARYLAND: A SOLIDLY DEMOCRATIC STATE?

Maryland could be many things at once: northern as well as southern, moralistic as well as libertine, industrial as well as rural, leaving people to their own devices yet with a heavy government presence.[4] Mikulski's popularity as the junior senator from Maryland is in part a reflection of the qualities of the state itself. Maryland is a state of almost 5 million people (ranking 19 out of 50 in population), approximately 70 percent white and 25 percent black. Fifty percent of Maryland's citizens live in and around the Baltimore metropolitan area, the biggest city, about an hour away from Washington, D.C. Its citizens, on average, live fairly well. The state is ranked fifth in the nation on measures of per capita income. Maryland is known for its successful urban renewal of Baltimore; the historic district in Annapolis, which houses the nation's oldest state capitol building in use; its beautiful eastern shore; the Chesapeake Bay; excellent universities and colleges such as Johns Hopkins and the University of Maryland; and, of course, its state bird and namesake baseball team, the Baltimore Orioles.

Politically, Maryland is, by most measures, one of the nation's most Democratic states. As evidence, in statewide elections, Democrats have not lost a contest for senator or governor since liberal Republican Charles Mathais retired from the Senate in 1986. After the 1998 election, the State Senate had 32 Democrats and 15 Republicans; the House of Delegates had 107 Democrats and 34 Republicans. In the U.S. Congress, both senators are Democrats and Marylanders are represented in the U.S. House by four Democrats and four Republicans. The governor is Parris Glendening, also a Democrat. In the 1996 contest for U.S. President, Maryland gave Democratic incumbent Bill Clinton 54 percent of the vote, Clinton's fifth best in the nation; in 1992, they gave challenger Clinton 50 percent, his third best in the nation. In the 1988 Bush race and the 1984 Reagan reelection, Maryland mirrored the rest of the country going for Bush and Reagan, but by smaller margins than most places (51 percent for Bush and 53 percent for Reagan).[5]

Maryland has also been a particularly progressive state with respect to electing women to politics. After the 1998 election, the state legislature was home to nine female senators out of 47 members, and 46 female members of the House out of 141 members. The legislature has a strong and active women's legislative caucus. Moreover, the lieutenant governor is Kathleen Kennedy Townsend.

The trend toward the politics of the Democratic party can be explained by the large number of federal public employees who live in Maryland, people who are natural backers of the party in government. Since the Democrats controlled the U.S. Congress for 40 years, a reign that ended only recently in 1994, support for Democrats is long-standing and has only recently been challenged.

Another reason for the tilt toward Democrats is the fairly large percentage of African Americans in Maryland. At approximately 25 percent, the African American population of the state comprises a sizeable share of votes. Indeed, in the 1998 electoral cycle, incumbent Governor Glendening was successful in keeping his office in part because of high turnout by African Americans, who overwhelmingly supported his candidacy.

MIKULSKI'S COMMITTEE ASSIGNMENTS, PRIORITIES, AND LEGISLATIVE RECORD

Mikulski sits on the powerful Senate Appropriations Committee, which sets the federal budget each year, and is the ranking member of its Subcommittee on Veterans, Housing, and Independent Agencies. This subcommittee oversees funding for the Veterans Administration (VA), the Department of Housing and Urban Development (HUD), the National Aeronautics and Space Administration (NASA), the Environmental Protection Agency (EPA), the Corporation on National Service (CNS), the National Science Foundation (NSF), and 18 other agencies in the federal government. She is also a member of the Labor and Human Resources Committee and ranking member of its Subcommittee on Aging. These assignments reflect her legislative priorities.

In 1994, Mikulski was unanimously elected as Secretary of the Democratic Conference for the 104th Congress. Her responsibilities in this job included leadership liaison with ranking committee Democrats and participating in leadership decisions. She was reelected unanimously again in 1996 for the 105th Congress. The press release she issued following her reelection puts her policy interests into focus:

> In the last Congress, we Democrats put into the law books the values we held in our hearts. In the process, we stopped bad things from happening and made good things happen, like increasing the minimum wage, passing some health insurance reform, and protecting seniors' Medicare and Social Security. We put the interests of the soccer moms, little league dads, the grannies who love them, and the kids who rely on them above partisan political interest.[6]

As the quote above illustrates, legislatively, Mikulski is a self-proclaimed liberal. As she defines that term, liberalism includes rights and responsibilities, and she believes that "being politically effective means helping those who are not in the middle class get there through hard work and practicing self-help."[7]

Consistent with this belief, her voting record is considered by interest groups that rate the legislative records of members of Congress to be moderately to strongly liberal. In 1996, the American Federation of State, County, and Municipal Employees (AFSCME) awarded Mikulski a 100 percent rating. The League of Conservation Voters (LCV) issued a 92 percent rating. However, the American Civil Liberties Union (ACLU) rated her voting record at 39 percent. The Chamber of Commerce rated her record as 23 percent supportive, and the Christian Coalition found her supportive 7 percent of the time. According to the *National Journal,* in 1996, Mikulski voted in the liberal direction 96 percent of the time on economic issues, 80 percent of the time on social issues, and 68 percent of the time on foreign policy issues.

Recent specific examples of her votes in these areas include voting against reducing Medicare growth, in favor of increasing the minimum wage, and in favor of continuing funding for troops in Bosnia. She also voted against the Gulf War Resolution and in favor of the Welfare Reform Act of 1996. Mikulski explained the latter vote by saying: "Without this bill, would poor children be better off? I'm not so sure. The current welfare system is dysfunctional. It needs a big wake-up call. The very nature of the system encourages a culture of poverty."[8] Mikulski has also always been a chief supporter of the space program and has been an enthusiastic advocate of the Space Station Freedom.

Mikulski also has been active from the start in women's issues. In 1991, she defended Anita Hill in her sexual harassment charges against now Associate Justice of the U.S. Supreme Court, Clarence Thomas, and opposed the retirement of Admiral Frank Kelso at the rank of four stars because she believed that his connection with the Navy's 1991 Tailhook convention incident (in which Navy personnel engaged in sexual harassment during a party) should be reflected in his retirement status. This was a courageous position to take because the Naval Academy is located in Annapolis, Maryland. Because she is a senator from Maryland, some may have expected her to vigorously defend Naval personnel. Mikulski has also successfully sponsored the Mammography Quality Standards Act and played a key role in establishing the Office of Women's Health Research at the National Institutes of Health.

Nationally, Mikulski's legislative priorities have focused on a robust economy, seniors' issues, children's issues, science and technology advancement, crime, and women's issues. In her speech at the 1996 Democratic National Convention, she highlighted some of these priorities:

We're not just defending programs, we're defending values. What are those values? Making sure that health care is affordable, portable, and undeniable. Making sure that children get early detection, screening, and immunization. Making sure that young children have food for thought and food to think, and that is why we fought so hard to stop those cuts in school breakfast and lunch programs. . . . In our Democratic framework for the future, each child grows up healthy, safe, and strong, and each child knows the power of parents' love.[9]

Mikulski's spot on the Labor and Human Resources Committee allows her to pursue her long-time advocacy of accessible, safe, and affordable health care. Recently, she has focused on co-sponsorship of the Democratic Patient Protection Act, which is meant to address problems in operations of health service providers. Says Mikulski, "The pendulum has swung too far. Quality of care and access to care have suffered terribly in this Brave New World of managed care. The Democratic Patient Protection Act will give Americans a health care Bill of Rights. It will give them the right to chose their doctors, the right to hold HMOs responsible, and the right to access to emergency care."[10]

Among Mikulski's legislative sponsorships in the 105th Congress are bills to fund the Older Americans Act of 1965; amend the Public Health Service Act to increase employment opportunities for women scientists; revise and extend mammography quality standards; protect spouses and surviving spouses of Social Security recipients; amend the Federal Food, Drug, and Cosmetic Act to provide for improved safety of imported foods; and provide increased funding for Empowerment Zones, America Reads, and Disaster Mitigation programs.

One of the reasons Mikulski has been the most popular politician in her state is that, from the beginning of her career, she has been an aggressive legislative advocate for Maryland, especially concerning job growth. In working for Maryland's citizens, Mikulski has been effective in "bringing home the bacon." As a result of the 1997 Intermodal Surface Transportation Efficiency Act (ISTEA), she is responsible for an increased amount of federal dollars for Maryland's highways, bridges, and bus systems. Maryland's proximity to the District of Columbia means that it has some of the busiest highways in the nation and the second-highest per-vehicle congestion rate, along with long commutes as many residents travel to D.C. to work. So, the seemingly mundane topic of road funding takes on added significance in Maryland.

Mikulski and Paul Sarbanes (Maryland's senior senator) have worked together over time to provide substantial federal funds to the state for enhanced law enforcement and child protection. The state has benefited from such programs as Community Oriented Policing Services (COPS); Innocent Images, which fights pornography and child predators on the Internet; and Police Corps, which provides advanced police education and training. Mikulski has also fought for funds to further Maryland's environmental initiatives, including protection of the Chesapeake Bay, Brownfields, or polluted and abandoned industrial sites, and pfesteria research (pfesteria is a toxic microbe found in the waters along the eastern shore of Maryland).

Funding programs is one way to earn the respect of the people of Maryland; another is protecting programs threatened with cutbacks. Says Struck of the *Washington Post:*

> She helped block cutbacks at the Goddard Space Center in Greenbelt [Maryland], NASA's Wallops Island, the Patuxent River Naval Air Station and the Curtis Bay Coast Guard Yard. And she has squawked at any threat to the appropriations for the space station, the Hubbard Space Telescope or defense contracts for Westinghouse or Northrop Grumman, all staples of Maryland's burgeoning high-tech industry.[11]

In sum, Mikulski has mastered the art of protecting her state's interests while pursuing the policy interests that are her political passions.

MIKULSKI VERSUS
HER 1998 CHALLENGERS

The Primary Election

The story of Mikulski's reelection reveals few obstacles in the path to a third term. Although ten Republicans and two Democrats ran against her in the primary held in September, the contest was less than challenging for her. Few opponents in either party raised any significant amounts of money, and their name recognition levels were low as were their favorability ratings.

Indeed, in April 1998, *National Journal's The Hotline* printed an article titled, "Senate Report—Maryland: Yet More Proof This Race Is No Race." In it, a poll of registered voters matched Mikulski with a few of her challengers. The results were overwhelming, with Mikulski garnering more than 60 percent of each matchup. Similarly, when voters were queried about favorable or unfavorable impressions of each candidate, Mikulski earned a more than 60 percent favorability rating, with none of her challengers topping 7 percent.[12]

In July 1998, the *Baltimore Sun* reported that Mikulski's Republican primary challengers said they were running because "they are fed up with high taxes, excessive government regulation and social programs, and the decline in the quality of public schools."[13] The challengers also faulted Mikulski for having "alienated people with a partisan, pork-barrel approach to legislating."[14]

Before the September primary, the *Baltimore Sun* endorsed Mikulski and Republican George W. Liebmann, a 59-year-old Baltimore lawyer who once worked as a gubernatorial aide but had no experience in elective office. The vote tallies showed the winners to be Mikulski with 84 percent of the Democratic vote, and long-time failed candidate Ross Pierpont as the unexpected winner of the Republican primary with 19 percent of the vote. See table 9.1 for the primary results.

Pierpont was an 81-year-old health care consultant and retired surgeon who had run 14 times since the mid-1960s and, while sometimes winning nominations, lost each general election. He ran for the Republican Senate nomination in 1986 and lost. He had also run for the U.S. House, the governorship, and mayor of Baltimore. The frequent runs gave him name recognition levels in excess of his Republican challengers, and in a crowded field, this recognition allowed him to carry the day on September 15.

Pierpont believed he should be elected because Mikulski:

> . . . promotes divisive policies that undermine our social structure and waste billions of dollars. Example: our failing health care system. Years ago, I warned health plans supported by Mikulski could never deliver what they promised, would undermine health care, and waste billions. Mikulski was on the wrong side in health care as in other policies she promotes. The Pierpont Healthcare Program covers everyone—that's everyone!—cradle to grave with freedom of choice while saving $500 bil-

Table 9.1 Primary Opponents of Barbara Mikulski

Candidate*	Hometown	Age	Occupation	Vote Share (%)
Republican Opponents				
Barry Asbury	Parkville	46	Political Organizer	7.1
Michael Gloth	Finksburg	42	M.D.	11.1
George Liebmann	Baltimore	59	Lawyer	8.2
Bradlyn McClanahan	Annapolis	47	Social Worker	9.7
Thomas Scott	Baltimore	52	Construction	6.9
John Taylor	Crofton	33	Information Systems	13.5
Kenneth L. Wayman II	Ellicot City	51	Computer Executive	9.7
Howard D. Greyber	Potomac	75	Physicist	9.7
Ross Z. Pierpont	Timonium	81	Health Care Consultant	18.9
John Stafford	Laurel	57	Lawyer	5.2
Democratic Opponents				
Kauko H. Kokkonen	Towson	60	Transit Administrator	5.3
Ann L. Mallory	Silver Spring	53	Dentist	10.5
Barbara Mikulski	Baltimore	62	Incumbent	84.2

*Qualifications: registered voter, 30 years of age, citizen nine years, inhabitant of the state at time of election.

SOURCE: *Congressional Quarterly Weekly Report,* September 21, 1998.

lion every year. For a forward-looking agenda, including health care for everyone, put Mikulski out, put Pierpont in.[15]

Pierpont's limited television commercials contained the tag line "Pierpont: For the Health of America."

In addition to his primary theme of better health care, Pierpont also advocated smaller government, especially in terms of a reduction in government regulations and increased local control of schools, lower taxes, including significant property tax reduction, harsher sentences for drug dealers, and increased support for the military. State Republican leaders said diplomatically that Pierpont faced an uphill battle. "It's a difficult race to take on," acknowledged Joyce Terhes, Republican party chair. "I wish him luck."[16]

In part the political experts were referring to the chances of beating an incumbent who has performed relatively well and is free of any particular charges of scandal. It is difficult enough for a quality challenger to win against an incumbent; winning against a popular incumbent is almost impossible without an extremely strong and visible record. While Pierpont had some name recognition in Maryland for his almost constant quests for electoral office, he had not won any general election, had little public realm governing experience, and had a weak record at fundraising.

The General Election

Mikulski's campaign themes and priorities emphasized her long-term legislative goals. She said she wanted to continue with her agenda of (1) keeping the economy strong, (2) fighting for a safety net for seniors, (3) getting behind our kids and our teachers, and (4) working for safe streets in a safe world. Campaign commercials emphasized these themes while touting her "one of the people" approach and her success in working for the citizens of the state. One of the commercials showed her with a Baltimore Orioles cap saying that she had to buy the cap in the children's section and, therefore, Marylanders can feel secure that her head had not swelled like typical politicians. The tag line of each of the commercials was "Common Sense; Uncommon Courage."

The Mikulski camp felt they had an excellent chance to repeat the high vote share of her immediate previous race. Political elites agreed. Early in the 1998 electoral cycle, state Democratic party chair Peter Krauser said of Mikulski: "She is one of the most popular political figures in Maryland," and that he "was unconcerned about her re-election to a third-term."[17] The polls agreed with the pundits. In an election preview, *Roll Call* noted that, on September 20, Mikulski was leading Pierpont by 69–19 percent.[18] Interestingly, Mikulski had the highest poll rating of any senator running in this cycle.

The campaign financing highlights were also suggestive of a race without drama, suspense, or uncertainty. As table 9.2 shows, Mikulski far exceeded Pierpont in campaign cash gathered in 1998.

In light of Mikulski's apparent safety, she spent a lot of her campaign time working on behalf of the incumbent Democratic governor, Parris Glendening, who was running a tight and costly race against repeat challenger Ellen Sauerbrey. The governor was ultimately reelected, and conventional wisdom says that having a popular public figure such as Mikulski in his corner was a help.

On November 3, 1998, the people of Maryland voted and the result looked much like Mikulski's first Senate reelection race. She re-won her seat by 71 percent to 29 percent and returned to Capitol Hill with a strong mandate. This may have significant implications for the next election cycle. By winning big, Mikulski is likely to have staved off a heavily competitive race in 2004.

THE INCUMBENCY ADVANTAGE: A WINNER FROM THE START?

How can Mikulski's easy victory be explained, especially in light of such a volatile election year? First, a bit of conventional wisdom about members of Congress is that, absent a terrible scandal, those who want to retain their seats are likely to do so. While truer for the House than for the Senate, the average incumbent reelection rate of senators in the modern era stands at 78 percent.[19] In 1998, 93 percent of senators and 98 percent of representatives who stood for reelection won. This means that while absolute safety is by no means guaranteed, incumbents who do their jobs well (by all accounts, Mikulski certainly does) have good chances of staying in their job.

Table 9.2 1998 Campaign Finance Figures for the Maryland U.S. Senate Seat*

Candidate	Party	Total Receipts ($)	Ending Cash on Hand ($)
Mikulski	Democrat	2,755,737	598,537
Pierpont	Republican	66,325	10,910

Funding Sources ($)

Mikulski

Donations from PACs	862,021
Individual Donations	1,780,103

Pierpont

Donations from PACs	0
Individual Donations	275
Loans from Candidate	66,000

*Totals through October 14, 1998.

SOURCE: Federal Election Commission.

Incumbents are highly successful in their reelection bids because voters are happy with the hard work they do for them. Those in office generally work carefully and constantly to maintain contact with their constituents, solve problems citizens may have with federal programs and agencies, gather information about constituents' policy preferences and vote accordingly as much as possible, and make sure that their constituencies get a fair share of federal dollars.[20] Everything we have learned in this chapter suggests that Mikulski is a stellar example of providing this kind of attention to her constituents.

Hard work on the part of sitting legislators translates into what is called in legislative literature the "incumbency advantage." If a senator does her job right, constituents are aware of her record or voting and service and are generally pleased with it. For voters to want to chose a challenger over a sitting incumbent, they have to be displeased with some aspect of the job the incumbent is doing and find a reason to believe the challenger would do a better job.[21]

More than anything else, getting a message out depends on a great deal of money. Name recognition takes advertising, and advertising takes money. For Mikulski and other senators, the exercise of incumbency advantage through vehicles such as speeches and other appearances in the state, news coverage, newsletters sent to state residents, constituency service, and the like are all paid for by the federal government as part of the job of a senator.

For challengers to get visibility and name recognition that approaches the incumbent's (unless, of course, the challenger already has name recognition for some other endeavor such as acting, sports, or business), vast sums of money have to be raised. While sitting members of Congress also raise money for their reelection races, the task is much easier for them. As Mikulski's campaign finance figures for the 1998 year alone indicate, donors are more likely to give large amounts to those who are a fairly sure bet and have already been in a position to cast supportive votes. Raising money is simply much easier for those already in office. Challengers have a harder time convincing donors that they have a viable race, that they are right on the issues, and that should they win, their low level of seniority in the office can be overcome by hard work. Indeed, since the average U.S. Senate race costs $3.3 million, matching and exceeding what an incumbent can raise is a serious obstacle to challengers.[22]

Moreover, fundraising is not something that one can start just a few months from an election. With today's campaigns centered on television and other media outlets, a person needs to accumulate funds long before the actual campaign season begins. Without funds, political parties and possible donors tend not to take a candidate seriously and are reluctant to give any money. This situation is analogous to saving for college when a child is 17 years old as opposed to when she is born.

Smart politicians are also strategic politicians. Sitting senators attempt to discourage serious opposition to their reelection bids by raising a great deal of money early, generally referred to as "preemptive spending." Opponents of incumbents will look at war chests gathered early and weigh whether they have a chance of raising enough money for a reasonable challenge. In fact, in the case of Mikulski, the preemptive strike strategy was quite successful this electoral season. A pre-primary *Washington Post* feature on her noted that "Mikulski's ephemeral opposition has not stopped her from raking in campaign contributions like a leaf sweeper in autumn. Mikulski set a goal of raising $3 million for this campaign—100 times what any of her opponents has raised. It scared off more serious Republican challengers."[23]

In sum, in addition to being an excellent match with the state, Mikulski had all the advantages of incumbency and she used them wisely. The reward for her strategic sense, hard work, and luck in drawing a weak challenger was a reelection rate that will once again give pause to anyone considering a challenge in six years.

POSTSCRIPT: A WOMAN OF FIRSTS

In the end, the story of Barbara Mikulski cannot be told without mention of one other intriguing aspect of her career. She achieved so much, so quickly, and so successfully being something of an outsider. By this, we mean, women in politics, particularly at the level of the U.S. Senate, are still rare. For example, only nine women serve in the Senate and only 27 have ever held a Senate seat.[24] In short, Mikulski has sought, competed for, and won victories that have been difficult for women in politics to achieve.

As testament to her unique situation, with her first Senate victory, Mikulski became the first Democratic woman to hold a Senate seat not previously held by her husband, the first Democratic woman to serve in both houses of Congress, and the first woman to win a statewide election in Maryland.

This record is also compelling in that Mikulski has focused her attention and political advantage on helping other women win office. For instance, during the 1992 electoral cycle, not content with only her own success, she campaigned on behalf of the Democratic women running for the U.S. Senate (a Senate that, prior to that election, contained only two women) and helped elect five new Democratic women.[25] After the election, she was dubbed the unofficial "Dean of the Senate Women." In 1994, as noted earlier, Mikulski was unanimously elected as secretary of the Democratic Conference for the 104th Congress, the first woman to be elected to a Democratic leadership position in the Senate. She still holds this position.

Quite possibly another first, one that illuminates the range of her interests and talents, are the mystery novels that she has co-written with Marylouise Oates. While other senators have written books in office, even novels, she probably is the only woman in Congress to have penned murder mysteries. The two novels to date focus on the career of Senator Eleanor Gorzack, who is confronted with not only unexpected murders, but the day-to-day difficulties of being a woman in a place where so few have gone before and so few inhabit today. From the seemingly trivial problems of a lack of bathrooms for women close to the Senate chambers to being a novelty in the "Old Boys Club," Mikulski and Oates tell it like it is, as illustrated by the following examples:

New Senator Gorzack speaking to a senior female senator:

The Senate Wives' Lounge? "Don't you, ah don't we, the women senators, have our own lounge?" I asked as we raced up the stairs. "No," Hilda said crisply. "We have a powder room off the Senate floor. 'Powder room' is what a mind as euphemistically damaged as Foxy's would call two stalls and one sink. And can you understand we were all thrilled to get that?"[26]

Fictional Vice President Baxter addressing Senator Gorzack:

"It's not the conventional wisdom, but I am from the old school," Baxter began, looking somewhere over my head, like in the direction of Virginia. "Maybe it's unfair, but women just don't have the kind of experience in legislative matters that's called for on the federal level. Certainly not in the United States Senate."[27]

A fundraiser speaking to Senator Gorzack:

"You just don't know how hard it is for women candidates. You've never been through an election. A primary election, in which you see your friends line up against you. A general election, in which every intimate detail of your personal life gets dragged through the papers. A campaign where women are held to different standards from men. . . . I'm talking about a woman candidate. Any woman. Who comes under scrutiny for her hairstyle, and her clothes, and whether or not she wears a scarf around her neck, and if she spends enough time with her kids, and why doesn't she have kids anyway? Just get ready. It's a lot harder than you can imagine."[28]

Undoubtedly, the insight for some of these fictional experiences came from the political life lived by Barbara Mikulski. It makes her achievements both a rarity in American politics and events to be celebrated.

CONCLUSION

In a year of fits and starts, surprises, and individual and collective party upsets, Mikulski was elected to her third Senate term with ease. Her hard work, one-of-the-folks image, fit with the state political culture, and strategic smarts ensured that as others worried about their political future, she could focus on her post-election agenda. We hear that a movie made from her mystery novels is on her non-political priority list. Her political priorities are likely to be more of the same—protecting Maryland, serving her constituents' needs, and working for legislation on health care, education, and economic development.

NOTES

1. A telephone poll was conducted from July 9 through July 13, 1998, by Potomac Survey Research of Bethesda for the *Baltimore Sun* and three Washington-area news organizations: the *Montgomery Gazette,* WRC-TV, and WTOP Radio. Results are based on interviews with 1,204 registered voters who said they would likely vote in the upcoming primary and general elections. The margin of error for the overall results is plus or minus 2.8 percent. That figure is higher for the subgroups, such as likely Democratic or Republican voters. Published July 24, 1998, no author cited.

2. Michael Olesker, "A Perfect Mix of Showbiz and Politics," *Baltimore Sun,* July 7, 1998.

3. Doug Struck, "Barbara Mikulski: Fact vs. Fiction," *Washington Post,* September 8, 1998.

4. Michael Barone and Grant Ujifusa, *The Almanac of American Politics 1998* (Washington, DC: National Journal, 1997).

5. Philip Duncan and Christine Lawrence, *Politics in America 1996* (Washington, DC: Congressional Quarterly, 1996).

6. Barbara Mikulski Press Release, January 31, 1997.

7. Ibid.

8. Barone and Ujifusa, *The Almanac.*

9. Kathleen M. Vick and Kelly Fagan, eds., *Official Proceedings of the Democratic National Convention* (Chicago: Democratic National Convention, 1996), 252–253.

10. Barbara Mikulski Press Release, July 16, 1998.

11. Struck, "Barbara Mikulski."

12. "Senate Report—Maryland: Yet More Proof This Race Is No Race," *National Journal's The Hotline,* April 10, 1998.

13. David Folkenflik, "Novices Run for Mikulski Seat," *Baltimore Sun,* July 4, 1998.

14. Ibid.

15. Kathryn Miller, ed., "*The Washington Post* Maryland Voter's Guide," September 15, 1998.

16. Raju Chebium, "Will 15th Try Be the Charm for Ross Pierpont?" Associated Press Baltimore Bureau, September 17, 1998.

17. Hill Briefs, *Congress Daily* (Washington, DC: National Journal), July 7, 1998.

18. John Mercunio, Norah O'Donnell, and Rachel Van Dongen, "Election Preview: *Roll Call's* In Depth Look at the Important Races, Key Districts in 1998 House and Senate Contests," *Roll Call,* October 12, 1998.

19. Roger H. Davidson and Walter J. Oleszek, *Congress and Its Members,* 6th ed. (Washington, DC: Congressional Quarterly, 1998).

20. Richard Fenno, *Home Style: House Members in Their Districts* (Boston, Little Brown, 1978). See also Thomas A. Kazee, ed., *Who Runs for Congress: Ambition, Context, and Candidate Emergence* (Washington, DC: Congressional Quarterly, 1994).

21. Gary C. Jacobson, "You Can't Beat Somebody with Nobody: Trends in Partisan Opposition," in *Controversies in Voting Behavior,* 2nd ed. (Washington, DC: Congressional Quarterly, 1993). See also Gary C. Jacobson, *The Politics of Congressional Elections,* 4th ed. (New York: Longman, 1997).

22. Davidson and Oleszek, *Congress and Its Members.*

23. Struck, "Barbara Mikulski."

24. "Factsheet: Women in the U.S. Senate 1922–1998," Center for the American Woman and Politics (New Brunswick, NJ: Rutgers University Press, 1998).

25. Elizabeth Cook, Sue Thomas, and Clyde Wilcox, *The Year of the Woman: Myths and Realities* (Boulder, CO: Westview, 1994).

26. Barbara Mikulski and Marylouise Oates, *Capitol Offense* (New York: Signet, 1996), 43.

27. Ibid., 145.

28. Ibid., 192–193.

Open Seats

10

★

Lincoln Defeats Boozman in Arkansas's Senate Race

Harold F. Bass, Jr.

In 1932, Arkansas voters made history when they elected Hattie Caraway to a full term in the U.S. Senate. The previous year, Caraway had been named to succeed her late husband in the Senate. She became the first woman popularly elected to senatorial office, and she served two full terms. Sixty-six years later, in 1998, her seat was vacated by the retirement of four-term incumbent Dale Bumpers. Once again, Arkansas attracted national attention when it elected the youngest woman senator to date, Democratic nominee Blanche Lincoln, who had recently celebrated her thirty-eighth birthday.

Bumpers' retirement had endangered the long-standing Democratic lock on the seat. Indeed, with the exception of two terms during Reconstruction, it had been safely in Democratic hands since Arkansas entered the Union in 1836. In 1998, it appeared vulnerable to a Republican takeover.

A former representative from eastern Arkansas, Lincoln soundly defeated her Republican adversary, State Senator Fay Boozman. In accounting for her impressive victory, her gender proved beneficial, though not decisive. Rather, factors of region, ideology, and experience loomed larger. An ideological centrist, Lincoln demonstrated statewide appeal, enhancing her established regional reputation as an attractive, disciplined, enthusiastic, and well-funded campaigner. In turn, Boozman never advanced significantly beyond his regional and ideological bases among northwest Arkansas's conservatives. Lincoln's victory also contributed to a surprisingly strong senatorial showing by the Democrats nationally, enabling them to maintain their 45–55 minority in an election year when most commentators anticipated a net gain of up to five seats for the Republicans.

STATE PROFILE

Arkansas is a border South state with an estimated 1998 population of 2,538,303 divided into four congressional districts. The population is more than 80 percent white. African Americans constitute by far the largest minority group, with slightly more than 15 percent of the population. Hispanics are a rising, but still relatively small, proportion of the population. Long caricatured as a poor, rural state, Arkansas remains near the bottom in state rankings of per capita income. Its rural roots also persist, although more than 53 percent of Arkansans now reside in urban areas.[1] The population is overwhelmingly Protestant, with Baptists and Methodists dominating. Catholic and Jewish adherents are a negligible presence.[2] As in the rest of the South, the Democratic party has long dominated the political landscape, but it now confronts an increasingly competitive Republican party.

Little Rock is the state capital. Located in the geographic center of the state, it is by far the largest city, with a 1990 population of 175,727, as well as the largest metropolitan area, with more than 500,000 residents. The state's most significant media market, all four major television networks have affiliates located there; and it is home of the only statewide newspaper, the *Arkansas Democrat-Gazette*. Indeed, most of the other substantial media markets that serve the state lie outside its boundaries, in such nearby cities as Memphis, Tennessee; Tulsa, Oklahoma; Joplin, Missouri; and Shreveport, Louisiana.

Central Arkansas comprises one of the state's four congressional districts, each of which constitutes a definable region with distinctive cultural, socioeconomic, and political patterns and traditions.[3] Anchored by Pulaski County, the Second District is geographically the smallest, the most urban, and affluent. Once reliably Democratic, this district's growing suburban population, whose counterparts have fueled the Republican progress elsewhere in the South, has similarly been proving increasingly hospitable to the Republicans.

To the northwest lie the Ozark Mountains and the Third Congressional District, the fastest growing sector of the state in population, urbanization, and economic development. The traditional haven of mountain Republicans, and augmented by substantial in-migration from the Midwest, this region has remained the geographic base of the Republican electoral coalition in the state.

To the east is the Mississippi River Delta, the state's poorest region, where the declining agricultural sector continues to dominate the economy. The region's generally rural population includes a significant minority presence. The northern two-thirds of eastern Arkansas makes up the First Congressional District, where traditional Democratic loyalties have most clearly persisted, albeit with a profound demographic shift over the past three decades. The civil rights revolution undermined, but did not completely erode, the hegemony of the conservative, white planter class within the Democratic party. In turn, the newly enfranchised African American population has become the foundation for continued electoral success for the Democrats.

The last region is southern Arkansas, home of the Fourth Congressional District. Here, the rural tradition and substantial minority presence also per-

sist. Heading west, the substantial forest products industry augments the traditional agricultural economy of the Delta. Long considered one of the most
solidly Democratic districts in the United States, its growing Republican base
resides in the relatively urbanized Union and Garland counties, where the
cities of El Dorado and Hot Springs have begun to provide a hospitable suburban environment.

These relevant regional variations should not obscure the reality that
Arkansas is a small, relatively homogeneous state. Its political culture embraces
strong expectations of familiarity between candidates and voters. Successful
candidates tend to be known throughout the state by their first names: Dale
(Bumpers), David (Pryor), Bill (Clinton). As such, the political culture also
places a premium on traditional, personal campaigning, even as it has accom-
modated the increasing reliance on mass media that has become the national
norm.

Statewide candidates in Arkansas simply don't have the luxury of structur-
ing their campaign appearances as media events. Rather, they must allocate a
considerable portion of their time and effort traveling throughout the state,
typically concentrating on the county seats. Such institutions as the Gillette
Coon Supper, the Mount Nebo Chicken Fry, and the Slovak Oyster Supper
have been standing stops on the campaign trail for serious candidates.

PATTERNS OF PARTY COMPETITION

Appreciating the events and outcome of the 1998 Senate race in Arkansas requires a more detailed assessment of the evolving patterns of partisan competition.[4] At the end of World War II, Arkansas was the site of "pure one-party politics."[5] Within the long-dominant Democratic party, "policy consensus and
factional fluidity"[6] prevailed amid "a politics of personal organization and ma-
neuver."[7] The Republican party was neither an organizational presence nor a
factor in statewide electoral competition, although it did exhibit a long-
standing pocket of regional strength in the mountains of northwest Arkansas.[8]

This one-party setting meant that the Democratic party organization was
also by definition weak.[9] Its largely unchallenged electoral dominance made
party identification essentially untested and thus potentially vulnerable. Indeed,
by virtue of long-standing practice, Arkansas voters were well-prepared to enter the modern age of candidate-centered politics.[10]

Since the mid-1960s, the once moribund Republican party has been la-
boring, with growing success, to break the entrenched monopoly of the
Democratic party. Its successes, largely limited to the upper echelons of the
party ticket, have been sufficient for it to now aspire to supplant the Democrats
as the majority party in the state. From the Democratic perspective, the challenge has been to hold on to the established position of dominance in the face
of increasing Republican competitiveness.

Initially, the broader Republican realignment that swept across the South in
the latter half of the twentieth century met strong resistance in Arkansas. How-

ever, as the twentieth century neared its end, Arkansas voters were demonstrating increasing signs of joining the ranks of their fellow southerners in succumbing to Republican allures. The Republican advance was unmistakable, and it appeared to be gathering momentum. These developments proceeded erratically, and at distinctive paces with regard to electoral competition in presidential, gubernatorial, congressional, and senatorial races.

Presidential

At the presidential level, Arkansas voters remained steadfast in the Democratic camp through 1964. Four years later, Arkansas abandoned the Democratic fold to support a third-party nominee from the region, Alabama Governor George Wallace. Since their initial abandonment of the Democratic presidential standard in 1968, Arkansans have voted Republican in 1972, 1980, 1984, and 1988. The Democrats reasserted their time-honored hegemony only in 1976, 1992, and 1996, with the voters embracing regional and state favorite sons, Jimmy Carter and Bill Clinton, on all three occasions.

Gubernatorial

Spearheading the Republican advance at the state level, in 1966 Republican Winthrop Rockefeller won the first of two consecutive terms as governor. Rallying behind newcomer Dale Bumpers, the Democrats recovered the statehouse in 1970 and held it for a full decade, encompassing two terms apiece for Bumpers and his successor, David Pryor, who then passed the torch to Bill Clinton.

In 1980, public disenchantment with Governor Clinton's first-term performance led to his reelection defeat at the hands of Republican Frank White. However, White's tenure was short-lived, as Clinton soundly defeated him in a rematch in 1982. Clinton went on to win convincing general election victories in 1984, 1986, and 1990.[11] When Clinton was elected president in 1992, he passed on the governorship to Lieutenant Governor Jim Guy Tucker, who won his bid for a full term in 1994.

However, the Republicans returned to power in 1996, when Governor Tucker resigned following his felony conviction at the hands of the Whitewater special prosecutor. On becoming governor, Tucker had called a special election for his vacated office of lieutenant governor. Republican Mike Huckabee prevailed in that 1993 contest and went on to win the next general election in 1994. Thus, Tucker's resignation elevated Huckabee, making him the third Republican to hold gubernatorial office over the previous three decades.

Congressional

At the congressional level, the same year that Rockefeller won his first term, 1966, the Republicans elected John Paul Hammerschmidt to the House in the Third District in northwest Arkansas. Hammerschmidt held on to the congressional seat for more than a quarter-century, and the Republicans have maintained party control since his retirement in 1992, with the Hutchinson brothers, Tim (1992–1996) and Asa (1996–   ), as their standard bearers.

More than two decades later, in 1978, the Republicans succeeded in electing Ed Bethune to an open seat in the House from the Second District, in central Arkansas. Bethune gave up his congressional seat in 1984, and the seat returned to the Democratic camp, albeit with a strident conservative, Tommy Robinson, prevailing in the primary and general elections. Subsequently, after winning reelection twice, Robinson changed his partisan allegiance and proclaimed himself a Republican. However, he did not seek reelection in 1990. The Democrats reclaimed the seat for former Fourth District representative Ray Thornton, who relocated in central Arkansas, and has held it since then, with Thornton giving way to Vic Snyder in 1996.

In the Fourth Congressional District, spanning southern Arkansas, the long-standing Democratic dominance came to an end in 1992. That year, the seven-term incumbent, Beryl Anthony, failed to survive a primary challenge from Secretary of State Bill McCuen. In the general election, the scandal-plagued McCuen lost to an obscure, lightly regarded Republican, Jay Dickey. Extraordinarily attentive to constituency interests, Dickey weathered a strong challenge to his initial reelection in 1994, and then won an easy third-term election in 1996. In addition to his expected suburban support, Dickey has demonstrated surprising strength in the rural counties in the southwest that were once overwhelmingly Democratic.

Only in the Mississippi Delta setting of the First District has the Democratic party sustained its time-honored hegemony. In 1992, 11-term incumbent Bill Alexander lost a primary contest to Blanche Lambert, who went on to win the general election and reelection in 1994. A new mother of twins, she gave up her seat in 1996, when it was won by Democrat Marion Berry.

Senatorial

At the senatorial level, the traditional Democratic dominance was sustained in recent decades by the formidable tandem of Bumpers and Pryor. Bumpers, a popular two-term governor, went to the Senate in 1974, having bested five-term incumbent J. William Fulbright in the Democratic primary and received an 85 percent majority in the general election.[12] In winning three additional terms, Bumpers never again faced a primary challenge and out-polled his Republican opponents by landslide margins of 59 percent (1980), 62 percent (1986), and 60 percent (1992) in the general elections.[13]

Pryor, who succeeded Bumpers as governor in 1974, won election to an open Senate seat in 1978. He survived a heated primary contest with Fourth District Representative Thornton and Second District Representative Tucker, besting Thornton in the runoff, and then won 77 percent of the general election vote.[14] Like Bumpers, he never again faced a primary challenge. The Republicans positioned themselves to mount a strong challenge to Pryor's bid for reelection in 1984, putting forward the popular Second District Representative Bethune to run on President Ronald Reagan's coattails, but Pryor coasted to a comfortable 57 percent majority, signaling the end of Bethune's political viability. In 1990, Pryor faced no opposition to his reelection.

Six years later, Pryor retired, opening up the seat. For the first time since 1978, the Democrats had a contested senatorial primary. Their nominee was Attorney General Winston Bryant, who was slated to face popular Lieutenant Governor Huckabee. However, Huckabee ascended to the governorship following the resignation of Tucker. The Republican State Executive Committee then turned to Third District Republican representative Tim Hutchinson. In a tight but rather lackluster race, Hutchinson emerged victorious, with 52.7 percent of the vote, even as President Clinton easily carried the state in his own reelection bid. With these additions, the Republicans now held one of two Senate seats, two of four congressional seats, and the governorship.

Thus, as the end of the twentieth century neared, the Republicans could claim to have made dramatic inroads over the previous three decades on the traditional Democratic dominance, and momentum appeared to be on their side. The northwest quadrant of the state had been clearly secured. The Republicans were growing in strength in the heavily populated suburbs of central Arkansas, and southern Arkansas was proving to be increasingly hospitable. Only eastern Arkansas was consistently continuing to withstand the Republican tide.

AN OPEN SEAT EMERGES

These electoral developments and trends set the stage for Bumpers' announcement in the summer of 1997 that he would not seek election to a fifth term in 1998. That decision had been awaited with great interest in both Arkansas and Washington, D.C., and it provoked distinctly different partisan reactions. In the state and national Democratic camps, the atmosphere was one of apprehension. Another term would likely have been forthcoming for the widely respected incumbent, though he surely would have had to endure a substantial general election challenge. Bumpers' decision to retire left the state Democratic party rightly fearful that it might lose its remaining Senate seat to the upstart Republicans. Nationally, the Democrats had to confront the distressing possibility of exacerbating their existing minority position in the Senate with the loss of a once-safe seat.

Nor was there an obvious heir apparent within the party. Indeed, because extraordinary durability of the popular triumvirate of Bumpers, Pryor, and Clinton had blocked access to top political offices in the state, the governorship and the two Senate seats for over two decades, the Democratic party had experienced a degree of stagnation within its ranks.[15] This problem was exacerbated by the recent downfall of Governor Tucker.

In contrast, the Republicans viewed Bumpers' retirement with anticipation. His announcement whetted Republican appetites for the capture of a second Senate seat and an almost wholesale reversal of the traditional partisan pattern. Moreover, they dared to hope that their electoral successes might now begin to trickle down to the lower-level contests across the state, where the Republicans had yet to make significant inroads outside of northwest Arkansas and the Little Rock suburbs.

From their perspective, one significant reason why Republican fortunes in Arkansas lagged well behind their gains elsewhere in the region was to be found in the aforementioned durability of Bumpers, Pryor, and Clinton. Clinton had ascended to the national stage, Pryor had retired, and now Bumpers was doing likewise. Nationally, the Republicans aspired to expand their 55–45 Senate majority to a filibuster-proof 60–40 margin. The now-vulnerable Arkansas seat afforded them an excellent opportunity to move toward that ideal. In addition, they hoped again to embarrass President Clinton on his home turf by securing the remaining Senate seat, so that the Democrats would have lost both Senate seats on his watch.

PARTY PRIMARIES

State law provides that parties designate nominees through primary elections. It further requires a runoff primary should no candidate get a popular majority in the first primary. Technically, the state's primaries are closed, or restricted to party members. However, since Arkansans do not register to vote as partisans, they officially declare their party affiliation only at the primary election sites, where they request and receive their ballots. As such, a prospective voter has considerable discretion in deciding which party primary to participate in, and crossover voting is a distinct possibility. State law sets the time frame of March 17–31 for candidates to file to participate in the parties' primaries on May 19.[16]

Historically, the dominance of the Democrats meant that its primaries provided the only meaningful contests. The winners of its primary nominations were virtually guaranteed victories in the general elections, frequently without challenge. Before World War II, voter participation was often greater in the Democratic primaries than in the general elections that followed. With the rise of two-party competition, voter participation has been in decline in Democratic primaries and on the rise in general elections, a pattern seen throughout the South as the region comes more into line with the rest of the country.[17]

For example, the Democratic primary in 1978 attracted 569,702 voters to the polls, sending Pryor and Thornton to a runoff where Pryor prevailed. Four years earlier, 585,378 people voted when Bumpers bested Fulbright. In 1996, only 323,387 voters participated in the primary that sent Winston Bryant into a runoff with Lu Hardin, won by Bryant. This dramatic decline is only partially attributable to rising numbers of Republicans voting in their own primary. Indeed, contested Republican primaries have been exceedingly rare. The first real Republican senatorial primary in the state's history occurred in 1992, when a total of 52,238 votes were cast.[18] Thus, the rise of party competition in Arkansas, like in the rest of the South, has diminished the perceived importance of the Democratic primary, once the real election, while heightening the significance of the general election.

This clear shift notwithstanding, the Democratic primary continued to attract a hugely disproportionate share of voters, including tens of thousands who would likely vote for at least some Republican nominees in the fall general election. It has done so because to date most of the Republican electoral successes have been concentrated at the top of the party ticket. Northwest Arkansas has been a growing exception to his generalization. Elsewhere, most state legislative races, as well as county and local contests, did not attract Republican candidates. Thus, voters seeking a voice in the selection of such officials found themselves virtually obliged to participate in the Democratic primary. In 1998, the rare open seat opportunity generated primary contests in both parties, minimizing any temptations for crossover voting.

Democratic Primary Field

The Democratic race initially attracted five aspirants: Bryant, Nate Coulter, Scott Ferguson, Patrick Henry Hayes, and Lincoln. Hayes, the mayor of North Little Rock, subsequently reconsidered and never formally filed for the primary competition.

Three of the remaining four were attempting to revive their political careers. Bryant, 59, and a native of Donaldson, in southwestern Arkansas, was a fixture in state politics. For more than two decades, he had been winning lesser statewide races, first for Secretary of State (1976–1978), then Lieutenant Governor (1980–1990), and currently as Attorney General (1990–1998).

However, Bryant had faltered when he sought top-level offices. In 1978, he lost in a runoff primary to Anthony for the Fourth District congressional seat. More recently, in 1996, Bryant won the party nomination for U.S. Senate, but he fell in the general election to Republican Tim Hutchinson. Anxious for redemption, he had high name recognition and general good will throughout the state. His populist rhetoric and policy orientations struck a responsive chord for significant segments of the electorate, most notably organized labor. Balanced against those assets, he had antagonized entrenched business interests, his campaigning skills were substandard, and many Democrats held him responsible for the loss of the Senate seat they had so long taken for granted.

Coulter, 38, was similarly hoping to jump-start his stalled political career. Born in Nashville, in southwestern Arkansas, Coulter had returned to Arkansas after law school at Harvard. While practicing law in Little Rock, he had become active in Democratic politics. Bright, articulate, and ambitious, he developed ties to the disparate political organizations of Bumpers, Pryor, and Clinton. Most notably, he had managed Bumpers' successful reelection effort in 1992.

The next year, Coulter made his initial foray into elective politics, seeking the vacated office of lieutenant governor in a special election. Coulter parlayed his mildly progressive politics and his considerable connections with the Democratic establishment into a primary runoff victory, putting him up against

Republican Huckabee, a Southern Baptist minister who had recently lost a Senate bid to Bumpers. In a low-stimulus election, Huckabee prevailed by a narrow margin. Coulter resumed his law practice and cultivated his connections with Democratic party organization activists, while angling for an opportunity to reenter the political fray. The open Senate seat afforded him that prospect.

Lambert, 37, had earned state and national notice in 1992 when she emerged from obscurity as a congressional aide and Washington lobbyist to challenge the entrenched First District congressional incumbent, Alexander, for his seat in the Democratic primary. She capitalized on her deep roots in the agricultural community of eastern Arkansas, but even more so on rising public disenchantment with Alexander to win that race. She went on to prevail in the general election in the traditionally Democratic district.

In Congress, she associated herself with the "Blue Dog" coalition, a group of moderate and conservative Democrats, while antagonizing some more liberal pressure groups in the Democratic coalition, most notably organized labor. Following her marriage during her first term, she styled herself Blanche Lambert Lincoln; and she weathered a strong challenge to her reelection in 1994. With the Republicans now in control of Congress, Lincoln proved accommodating to many of their policy proposals, exacerbating her estrangement from the liberals in the Democratic camp. During her second term, she became pregnant and gave birth to twins. Citing maternal responsibilities, she declined to seek reelection in 1996. Two years later, she was determined to pursue the open Senate seat, now referring to herself as Blanche Lincoln.

Ferguson, 46, was a little-known, second-term state representative from eastern Arkansas. A radiologist from a prominent family, Ferguson was clearly willing to commit substantial amounts of his own considerable financial resources to his electoral quest. Much like Lincoln, he portrayed himself as an ideological centrist.

Thus, the Democratic field divided rather neatly on regional lines. It consisted of two easterners, Lincoln and Ferguson, going up against two southwesterners, Coulter and Bryant, both of whom had relocated to central Arkansas. Ideologically, all were relative centrists, but the Lincoln-Ferguson tandem leaned more clearly in the direction of conservatism, while Bryant and Coulter were heirs to the more liberal populist and progressive traditions in state party politics.

Republican Primary Candidates

In the Republican camp, Governor Huckabee figured prominently in the initial speculation regarding a nominee. After losing his Senate race against Bumpers in 1992, his political career skyrocketed. He became lieutenant governor in the 1993 special election, and he went on to win easy reelection in the 1994 general election. With Pryor retiring from the Senate, the popular Huckabee secured the Republican senatorial nomination without primary opposition in 1996, and he was accorded a good chance of winning the upcoming general election. However, Governor Tucker's mounting legal difficulties intervened, and prior to ascending to the governorship in June 1996, Huckabee decided to abandon his Senate bid that fall to provide stability in the office of chief executive.

Governor Huckabee now had to decide whether he would run for governor or senator in 1998. He was considered the clear favorite for either post. Eventually, he opted to seek election as governor. This decision left the party without an obvious frontrunner for its senatorial nomination.

State Senator Fay Boozman, 51, was the first to announce his candidacy. A prominent northwest Arkansas ophthalmologist, Boozman was a close friend, neighbor, and political ally of the Hutchinson brothers (Senator Tim and Representative Asa). In his reputation and his rhetoric, Boozman represented the rising tide of social conservatism associated with the Religious Right.

Another state senator, Joe Hudson, of Mountain Home, proclaimed his intention to contest the Republican primary, but he later withdrew his candidacy prior to the onset of filing. Several other party notables figured in speculation, but ultimately declined to run.[19]

Tom Prince, 48, the former mayor of Little Rock, eventually rose to oppose Boozman in the Republican primary. Prince had initially attained political prominence as a Democrat. Subsequently, like many traditional Democrats in the region, he drifted into the Republican camp. Prince emphasized his economic conservatism and his central Arkansas roots, staking his claim to the nomination on the assertion that he was the more electable of the two. Prince's belated entry into the race meant that for the second time in their history, and the second election in succession, Arkansas Republicans would have a contested senatorial primary.

As the election year dawned, conventional wisdom in the state presumed Lincoln and Boozman to be the respective frontrunners. Between the two, Lincoln was considered to be simultaneously the more vulnerable to a primary upset and the more likely to prevail in the fall general election.[20]

The Democratic Primary Campaign

The campaign did not generate a great deal of public interest and attention. Throughout the spring, little movement took place. In all the polls published in advance of the May primary, Lincoln and Bryant consistently maintained clear separation from Coulter and Ferguson.

Lincoln's demonstrated fundraising ability contributed strongly to her frontrunner status. The only candidate with national experience, she parlayed her connections with national political action committees into a formidable financial advantage over her opponents. She also appealed to conservative Arkansans by recalling her ability to work constructively with a Republican Congress. Unlike Bryant or Coulter, she had never run a statewide campaign. Nevertheless, she had a strong personal following in the electorate in her native east Arkansas. She had significant support within the agricultural sector, and she was the most enthusiastic and effective personal campaigner.

Her primary opponents, along with media critics, labeled her "an insubstantial lightweight" who lacked the capacity to comprehend and confront serious policy questions. She also suffered the animosity of organized labor, in response to some controversial congressional votes.

Bryant joined Lincoln as a leading Democratic contender, with Coulter and Ferguson lagging behind. Poorly funded and abandoned by his long-time allies in organized labor in the months leading up to the May primary, Bryant pursued a minimalist campaign strategy that relied almost exclusively on his widespread name recognition. His bet was that it would be sufficient to put him in the runoff with Lincoln, required by state law if no candidate received a majority of the vote. At that point, he hoped to draw the necessary support from regional and ideological constituencies to best her in a two-person race.[21]

Coulter appealed to "establishment" Democrats, based on his previous associations as a subaltern with Bumpers, Pryor, and Clinton. In addition, he hoped to build support among two traditional constituencies of the national Democratic party: organized labor and minorities. Finally, Coulter systematically sought to make a campaign issue of Whitewater Special Prosecutor Kenneth Starr, attacking both Starr's conduct in the office and the propriety of the office itself. Coulter hoped that this tactic would generate support among voters who were outraged by Starr's ongoing investigations and prosecutions of so many noteworthy Arkansans, including their president and former governor.[22]

Ferguson positioned himself as the fresh face in the campaign. Ideologically, he pitched his appeal toward traditional conservatives who lingered in the Democratic ranks. In addition, he hoped to attract significant east Arkansas support, at Lincoln's expense.

The formidable shadows of Bumpers and Clinton loomed over this race to choose Bumpers' successor. None of these candidates appeared likely to rise to the high standard Bumpers had set in almost three decades at the center of state politics, with his iconoclastic integrity, rhetorical skills, and command of policy issues. In addition, the tumultuous events of the Clinton presidency had important consequences for Arkansas politics. It had proved exhausting, sapping energy from statewide politics. Moreover, it had shifted the attention of many Arkansans to the national stage, where their long-time favorite son found himself embattled in a controversy that attracted their concern. The Senate race took a backseat to this drama.

Lincoln's campaign was the only one that appeared to generate much enthusiasm, deriving from her effective personal campaigning and fundraising prowess. Her high standing in the polls persisted even as she committed a handful of widely publicized gaffes in public statements and debates that reinforced perceptions regarding her alleged superficiality. She also came under fire on more substantive issues, notably her willingness to accept campaign funds from tobacco interests. In defending herself against the latter charges, Lincoln made repeated reference to her own agricultural background.[23]

Indeed, Lincoln emerged as the lightning rod of the Democratic primary campaign, attracting the most opposition from the field. The other leading contender, Bryant, ran a virtual stealth campaign, one that effectively insulated

him from assaults from the trailing competitors. This approach impeded the latter's efforts to displace Bryant as the challenger to Lincoln in the upcoming
runoff. Bryant sought to identify himself with such popular issues as a constitutional amendment to outlaw flag-burning, a stance that mollified some conservatives while alienating the liberals that were his more likely constituency.

Ferguson showed himself to good advantage in the series of debates held
among the candidates. On the eve of the primary, he won the dubious Democratic primary editorial endorsement of the *Arkansas Democrat-Gazette,* whose
ideological bent is decidedly conservative, and which could be expected to
back the Republican nominee in the general election.[24]

Coulter also did relatively well in the debates. In something of a coup,
Coulter managed to secure the primary endorsement of the AFL-CIO. Bryant
had been counting on that support, and his failure to secure it weakened his
candidacy.[25] However, Coulter fell short in his effort to secure the endorsement of the Arkansas Education Association, which declined to recommend a
choice, thus effectively benefiting Lincoln.[26] Coulter's campaign proved particularly disappointing to his supporters in its inability to generate anticipated
public enthusiasm and support.

Throughout the primary campaign, Lincoln maintained her fundraising
advantage, eventually receiving more than $800,000. Ferguson ran second, with
almost $600,000, but this impressive total included $225,000 in personal loans
and loan guarantees. Coulter was well behind, with less than $375,000 on
hand. Bryant trailed the pack, falling short of $130,000, although his high name
recognition kept his campaign competitive.[27]

As the primary election neared, Lincoln began gradually distancing herself
from Bryant.[28] Taking advantage of her superior financing, Lincoln mounted
an expensive advertising campaign. On April 13, five weeks before the primary
election, Lincoln began running campaign ads on statewide television that promoted family oriented themes. In one, viewers saw the candidate at home, with
her husband and twin sons. The voiceover intoned, "Blanche Lincoln: daughter, wife, mother, Congresswoman. She lives our rock-solid Arkansas values." In
another, the candidate appeared with a group of senior citizens and schoolchil-
dren, and observed, "There's some tough fights ahead for our families. In the
United States Senate, I'll fight for your family."[29]

Two of the other candidates soon joined the advertising fray. Coulter made
his appearance on the airwaves with an attack on Starr and the law providing
for a special prosecutor.[30] Ferguson put forward an ad showing him with children on a playground, talking about legislation he sponsored in the General Assembly to protect children.[31] Bryant, hoarding his limited campaign funds,
banked on name recognition to get him into the runoff primary.

Late in the primary, the always volatile race issue emerged on the agenda.
News reports threatened to embroil frontrunner Lincoln in questionable activities in two arenas. First, prior to entering the arena of electoral politics in
1992, she was alleged to have registered as a lobbyist on behalf of a puppet
regime in one of the South African homelands of that era. Lincoln initially responded that she could not recall the situation in question. She subsequently

claimed that her lobbying efforts were undertaken in opposition to the cause of apartheid and in support of freedom.

Second, Lincoln was reported to have enlisted campaign workers to buy African American votes in eastern Arkansas, where this constituency is a significant minority of the primary electorate. Both Coulter and Ferguson quickly sought to take advantage of her apparent problems, but they proved unsuccessful in doing so.[32] Coulter also ineffectually played the race card against Bryant, alleging him to be weak in his commitment to affirmative action.

These incidents notwithstanding, the campaigns were all generally positive. None degenerated into the ugly, name-calling practices that increasingly characterize contemporary campaigns across the nation. The frontrunners, Lincoln and Bryant, clearly benefited from the disinclination of Coulter and Ferguson to take the low road.

On May 19, primary election day, the turnout was a disappointing 318,801 voters, fewer than had participated in the 1996 primary. Both the 1996 and the 1998 votes reflected a relative lack of enthusiasm on the part of the traditional party faithful for any of the challengers. The voter turnout was about 25 percent of registered voters.

As expected, Lincoln and Bryant moved on to the runoff. Lincoln led the field with an impressive 45.4 percent of the vote. Bryant trailed with 27 percent. Ferguson slipped into third place with 14 percent, and Coulter, in a disappointing showing, brought up the rear with 13 percent.[33]

Lincoln carried 50 of Arkansas's 75 counties. In her native east Arkansas, she typically piled up healthy majorities of the vote. Her efforts to cultivate the African American vote proved successful. She also carried the more heavily populated counties in central and northwestern Arkansas. Bryant led the field in 23 counties, though majorities were rare. His regional support was strongest in southwestern Arkansas, where he was regarded as something of a favorite son. Coulter won two counties in southwestern Arkansas as well, where he had roots, but he generally fared poorly throughout the rest of the state, rarely running better than third. Ferguson trailed in every county, but his regional support in east Arkansas, perhaps augmented by the endorsement from the *Arkansas Democrat-Gazette,* enabled him to slip past Coulter into third place.

The Democratic Runoff Primary Campaign

Since Arkansas election law requires a party nominee to receive a majority of the votes cast in the primary, a runoff election was scheduled for June 9, three weeks after the primary. In this revised setting, Lincoln enjoyed an overwhelming financial advantage that manifested itself in huge imbalances in campaign fundraising and spending. Indeed, her resources exceeded Bryant's by an astounding five to one, and she outspent him seven to one. Party organization activists, state and national, increasingly impressed by her campaign performance, now generally rallied to her standard.[34]

Seeking to make the best of a bad situation, Bryant endeavored to turn Lincoln's fundraising success against her by making an issue of Lincoln's acceptance of funds from out-of-state political action committees. In keeping with his populist leanings, but incongruously, in light of his extensive statewide office-holding experience, Bryant attempted to portray himself as an outsider, standing for the people against the system. He also regained his typical organized labor support that had gone to Coulter in the primary. At the same time, in his campaign rhetoric and issue stances, he appeared to be positioning himself farther right on the ideological spectrum, vainly hoping to outflank Lincoln in appealing to traditional conservatives in the primary electorate.

In the runoff election, Lincoln won a landslide victory. She prevailed with 62.4 percent of the 215,092 votes cast. This time, she carried 65 counties, with east Arkansas again providing her with tremendous margins. Bryant's base had shrunk to ten counties, mostly in the southwest quadrant of the state.[35] In addition to region, the gender factor apparently provided her with her impressive margin.[36]

The Republican Primary Campaign

On the Republican side, Boozman immediately emerged as the favorite, fortified by his strong regional base of support. In the rare Republican primaries held to date for statewide offices, typically some three-quarters of the votes came from northwest Arkansas. Moreover, Boozman had the endorsement of Senator Tim Hutchinson, in itself a departure from conventional practice in primary contests. Less openly, the National Republican Senatorial Committee (NRSC) in Washington conveyed its preference for Boozman. Boozman also had the support of the Religious Right, drawn to his espousal of conservative social values.

Prince countered by championing economic conservatism and alleging his superior electability in a statewide contest. Generally sharing Boozman's conservative social values, he nevertheless sought to emphasize economic issues, in an attempt to portray Boozman as a captive of the Religious Right. Prince's appeal called attention to the close connection between Boozman and Senator Tim Hutchinson and suggested that Arkansas voters would be unlikely to want a carbon copy, regionally or ideologically, of their junior senator.

Neither candidate enjoyed widespread name recognition. In pre-primary polling, Boozman consistently enjoyed a comfortable advantage, but the number of undecided voters remained sizable.[37] On the eve of the primary election, Boozman received the editorial endorsement of the *Arkansas Democrat-Gazette,* legitimating the statewide base of his candidacy.[38]

Boozman raised about $250,000 prior to the primary, more than three times the amount accumulated by Prince. Apparently confident of victory, Boozman reserved most of this total for the general election contest. He declined to run extensive television ads, focusing instead on identifying and mobilizing likely primary voters.

Prince initiated a media campaign four weeks before the election. His television ads emphasized his commitments to decentralizing education policy making, tax reform, and outlawing partial-birth abortions. His tag line, "Tom

Prince, he can win in November," reinforced his claim to be the more electable candidate.[39]

On primary election day, Boozman emerged as the overwhelming choice of the Republican voters, winning 77.7 percent of the vote and carrying all 75 counties. The Republican vote totaled an unremarkable 54,777. In only 11 counties did as many as 1,000 voters participate. These counties were located in either northwest Arkansas or central Arkansas. Boozman showed surprising strength among party voters in the latter region, trouncing Prince by more than two to one in Prince's home base, Pulaski County.[40] Thus, the anticipated regional division among primary voters did not materialize. Boozman's campaign went into neutral gear for three weeks before Lincoln won the Democratic runoff primary to oppose him.

Thus, the primary campaigns produced no major surprises. The party electorates confirmed the conventional wisdom intact at the outset of the year by nominating the frontrunners. Lincoln and Boozman successfully surmounted the obstacles presented by their primary opponents. Moreover, they were able to unite their respective parties in anticipation of the general election.

However, these primary onslaughts in each party raised issues and concerns regarding the victors that shaped ensuing general election campaign tactics and appeals. Lincoln sought to build on the fears Prince aroused—that Boozman was an ideological extremist and that regional diversity mandated against two senators from northwest Arkansas. In turn, Boozman hoped to demonstrate that Lincoln was the captive of special interests, that his command of policy issues was far superior to Lincoln's, and that he was the candidate of substance who better reflected the conservative values prevalent in the state.

THE GENERAL ELECTION CAMPAIGN

As the fall campaign loomed, conventional wisdom and poll data placed Lincoln in the driver's seat.[41] She was well-financed, had high name recognition, had a strong regional base complemented by demonstrated statewide appeal, and had proven herself to be a vivacious campaigner. Moreover, she had the support of the traditional Democratic party establishment throughout the state. The major concerns regarding her candidacy carrying over from the primary campaign pertained to her reputation as a lightweight who might falter under pressure and demonstrate her relative lack of issue awareness.

Boozman's hopes rested in part on the prospect of widespread voter revulsion with the Clinton presidency, in the wake of allegations and revelations regarding his relationship with former White House intern Monica Lewinsky. Also, Boozman hoped that the general election campaign would reveal Lincoln to be shallow and unprepared intellectually for the demands of a Senate seat. His major challenges were to overcome his image as a nondescript campaigner and ideological extremist whose appeal was essentially regional.

The general election campaign also featured a minor party nominee, Charles Hefley, who was unopposed for the Reform party nomination. Hefley

was a Fort Smith bricklayer. His candidacy, largely symbolic, posed no significant threat to either major party nominee.

Campaign Organizations

Both Lincoln and Boozman entered the general election phase with primary-
tested campaign organizations that blended personal loyalists, experienced
state and national party organization operatives, and nationally renowned
pollsters and political consultants. Reflecting the superior funding her campaign enjoyed, Lincoln's organization was more extensive and elaborate.[42]
Lincoln designated Steve Patterson as campaign manager. A seasoned Capitol
Hill staff assistant, Patterson had previously worked as Lincoln's congressional
chief of staff (1994–1996). Serving in Arkansas as a field consultant for the
Democratic Congressional Campaign Committee (DCCC) in 1996, Patterson advised the successful congressional campaigns of Berry in the First District and Snyder in the Second District. Patterson headed up a group of 17
Arkansas-based campaign operatives headquartered in Little Rock and traveling throughout the state in coordination with volunteers and county party
organizations.

   In this latter arena, Lincoln enjoyed a distinct advantage over Boozman. The
legacy of long-time Democratic domination throughout the state provided an
infrastructure that, if rarely dynamic, nevertheless provided a framework for activity. The campaign organization labeled itself "Friends of Blanche Lincoln,"
a name that evoked the folksy familiarity of her campaign appeal.

   In addition, the Lincoln campaign employed the services of three highly regarded political consulting firms associated with the national Democratic
party: Lake, Sosin, Snell, Perry & Associates for public opinion research;
Strother, Duffy, & Strother for political media and strategy; and the Bonner
Group for national fundraising. The niche occupied by the Lake firm pertained
to electing women to public office. It had previously and successfully worked
on behalf of a number of women seeking election to the U.S. Senate.

   The Strother firm took particular pride in its performance on behalf of
southern Democrats who were able to withstand the rising Republican tide
throughout the region. It had considerable experience in Arkansas campaigns,
having worked for then-Governor Clinton throughout the 1980s and for Lincoln's own congressional campaigns in 1992 and 1994.

   Finally, the Bonner Group was responsible for connecting the Lincoln campaign with potentially sympathetic individuals and political action committees
throughout the nation. It proved extraordinarily successful in doing so.

   Boozman named co-campaign chairs: Sam Sellers and Jeb Wilkinson. Sellers provided the campaign with a familiar Arkansas face. He had considerable
experience in Arkansas campaigns, having directed a successful congressional
campaign for Tim Hutchinson in the Third District and an unsuccessful one
for Bill Powell in the Second District. Wilkinson was an import, having previously directed a congressional campaign and served as political director of the
Virginia Republican party. The two oversaw a comparatively lean campaign

headquarters operation in Little Rock occupied by some ten full-time staff, consisting of a press secretary, an operations director, and a finance director, along with a staff scheduler, a receptionist, two field organization liaisons, and three staff interns.[43]

Like Lincoln's, the Boozman campaign sought to develop systematic links with supporters throughout the state. This effort was impeded by the lack of a Republican organizational presence in much of the state. As such, many of Boozman's more visible and energetic supporters tended to be identified in their communities not so much as Republican partisans but as single-issue advocates. In particular, Boozman drew support from pro-life elements of the electorate who brought intensity to their campaign activity, but who sometimes appeared extreme to their fellow citizens.

Boozman also used the services of the national Republican party and allied political professionals. Unlike the better-financed Lincoln, Boozman did not employ a research director and staff at campaign headquarters. Rather, he relied on the research services of the NRSC.

His principal consultant and pollster was Ed Goeas, affiliated with the Tarrance Group, in Arlington, Virginia. Interestingly, Goeas and Celinda Lake, Lincoln's pollster, cooperated in a nationwide polling operation for the 1998 elections. The Arkansas senatorial campaign was the only race where the partners went head-to-head. The media campaign was conducted by Jimmy Innocenzi, of Sadler and Innocenzi, also based in Arlington. Debby Snodgrass, of Cole, Hargrave, Snodgrass, located in Oklahoma City, Oklahoma, served as print and general consultant. In the battle of outside consultants, the advantage went to Lincoln, whose team was reputed to be the more high-powered.

Campaign Developments

The fall campaign got underway in a relatively low-key fashion. Both nominees pledged to conduct positive campaigns and to avoid temptations to go negative.[44] In their campaign appearances, Boozman and Lincoln demonstrated vastly different personal styles that departed from traditional expectations in Arkansas politics. In particular, neither was given to the flamboyant oratory that once flowed freely from the campaign stump.

Lincoln characterized herself as a conversationalist and listener.[45] Her style featured energy and enthusiasm in keeping with her vivacious personality. In her stump speeches and television ads, she emphasized family values, often appearing with her twin boys in tow. Lincoln also consistently stressed her commitment to preserving Social Security and Medicare. She staked out moderate positions on controversial policy issues. For example, she tempered her pro-choice stance on the abortion issue with an opposition to partial birth procedures. The experience of having conducted two previous congressional campaigns served her well. Indeed, her campaign resembled that of an incumbent, featuring numerous references to her previous stint on Capitol Hill. This theme resonated in an electorate acutely aware that the state's cherished seniority on Capitol Hill had declined precipitously in recent years.

Cast in the role of challenger, Boozman's campaign presence was never-theless much more bland and subdued. Clearly lacking Lincoln's campaign ex-perience and effectiveness, he portrayed himself as a citizen legislator.[46] Knowledgeably but diffidently, he called attention to his mainstream conserva-tive values and policy perspectives, advocating tax reform and local control of schools. His strong pro-life position on the abortion issue evoked the greatest intensity on his part.

The general election campaign proved relatively uneventful. Boozman was unable to make significant inroads into Lincoln's established base of support.[47] Lincoln's financial advantage was formidable. She raised $2,976,086. Boozman trailed badly with $1,082,684.[48] She also had the enthusiastic support of the Democratic Senatorial Campaign Committee (DSCC), which made her elec-tion a top priority.[49] In contrast, Lincoln's consistent 15 to 20 percent lead in polls hurt Boozman's fundraising efforts across the board, but notably with the national party, which hesitated to invest scarce "soft money" resources in what increasingly looked to be a vain attempt to shift party control of the Senate seat. Almost a month before the election, rumors were circulating throughout the state that Boozman was in line for a post-election gubernatorial appoint-ment to head the state Health Department.[50]

Lincoln secured numerous noteworthy endorsements from a wide range of state and national organizations (see table 10.1). She attracted the support of a variety of occupational groups, including farmers, educators, realtors, home builders, and contractors. Having opposed her primary candidacy, or-ganized labor now rallied to her side. Among issue-based groups, the National Committee to Preserve Social Security and Medicare was most visible in ad-vancing her candidacy. Boozman was far less successful in this arena. Prominent among his handful of endorsements were anti-gun control and pro-business organizations.[51]

While Lincoln, in disciplined fashion, avoided committing the gaffes that critical observers and even sympathizers expected, Boozman was less fortunate. One remark on his part in mid-October proved particularly damaging. Re-sponding to a question at a civic club gathering about his strong pro-life posi-tion on the abortion issue, Boozman indicated that he was not particularly worried about an exception to a ban on abortion that would allow such pro-cedures in cases of rape. He suggested that pregnancy was most unlikely to re-sult from such an event, because in that crisis situation, the female body would likely generate a protective shield, inhibiting impregnation. This off-the-cuff remark soon attracted widespread public attention and fueled gender-based concerns that Boozman was an ideological extremist particularly inattentive and insensitive to issues of women's health. Boozman apologized for any hurt he caused, but he pointedly declined to retract his observation, a response that doubtless widened the already substantial gender gap.

This incident also became the catalyst for charges and counter-charges in the waning days of the campaign that both camps were reneging on their mu-tual pledges to avoid negative campaigning. Angry accusations surfaced in television ads, press releases, and speeches. Less than a week before the elec-

Table 10.1 Endorsements

Blanche Lincoln	Fay Boozman
American Hospital Association	Campaign for Working Families
Arkansas Black Farmers Association	Gun Owners of America
Arkansas Credit Union League	National Association of Independent Business
Arkansas Education Association	National Rifle Association
Arkansas Forestry Association	Remington Arms PAC
Arkansas Home Builders Association	60 Plus Association
Arkansas Realtors Association	
Arkansas Recyclers Association	
Arkansas State Council of Machinists	
Association of Community Organizations for Reform Now	
Business and Professional Women of Arkansas	
Business and Professional Women/ USA	
National Committee to Preserve Social Security and Medicare	
National Cotton Council of America	
National Education Association	
National Farmers Union (NATFARM-PAC)	
National Realtors Association	
National Restaurant Association	
National Treasury Employees Union	
New Democrat Network	
United Contractors, Inc.	
United Paperworks International Union	

SOURCE: *Arkansas Democrat-Gazette*, November 1, 1998, 29A.

tion, the Lincoln campaign unveiled an ad that alleged: "Boozman said a women could not become pregnant due to rape. He believes a special hormonal shield protects them." Boozman promptly accused Lincoln of lying. In turn, Lincoln accused Boozman of the same offense, specifically misrepresenting her congressional voting record in an effort to undermine her claim of unqualified commitment to the preservation of Social Security and Medicare.[52] These late-breaking developments attracted substantial public attention, but there is no indication that they significantly altered public opinion and electoral decisions.

On election day, Lincoln received 55 percent of the 700,844 votes cast in the generally low-turnout contest. She carried 60 counties, with her native eastern Arkansas proving most supportive. Her impressive margins in the Delta regions suggest that the African American vote was substantial.

Boozman attracted 41.8 percent of the vote. He won 15 counties, 12 of them were contiguous in northwest Arkansas. The remaining three were scattered throughout the state: one in the west, one in the south, and one in the north central area. Hefley, the Reform nominee, got only 3.1 percent of the vote. Like Boozman, he typically did best in his native northwest Arkansas, suggesting that he probably drew more of his support from the Republican nominee. Thus, Lincoln won a sweeping statewide victory, one in keeping with the once-normal Democratic landslides. The Republican party did not significantly advance its cause outside its traditional regional base in the northwest region and its outlying and isolated southern flank.[53]

National tides undoubtedly played a role in Lincoln's victory. The Democrats did unexpectedly well in the midterm elections, picking up five seats in the House. In the Senate, where the Republican party anticipated improving its 55–45 majority, and even entertained hopes of attaining 60 seats, the elections merely maintained the status quo. The size of Lincoln's victory suggested a home-state backlash against the national Republican attack on President Clinton. Although Boozman distanced himself from these attacks, his party label likely tainted him in the eyes of mainstream Arkansas voters.

Lincoln was a far more experienced and effective candidate than Boozman, whose candidacy suffered from several flaws. He was an earnest but unassuming campaigner, with no personal electoral constituency or campaign experience outside of his solidly Republican state senatorial district in northwest Arkansas. Boozman's close ties to Senator Tim Hutchinson cut both ways. They boosted his primary candidacy, providing it with instant credibility. However, the perception that he was a carbon copy of Hutchinson hurt outside of his base in northwest Arkansas. Regional diversity between the two senators has been a long-standing tradition in Arkansas politics.

An examination of other major state races suggests that Lincoln's victory was more personal than partisan. The Republican governor, Huckabee, won almost 60 percent of the vote in his bid for a term in his own right. The four congressional districts remained evenly divided, with the Democrats easily retaining the first and second districts, while the Republicans comfortably held on to the third and fourth districts.

These outcomes suggest that the major problem facing the Republicans in their efforts to claim dominant status in Arkansas politics is putting forward compelling candidates. When they do, voters appear quite receptive. To date, however, the Republicans lack the critical mass of attractive aspirants to compete across the board. In the face of rising Republican challenges, the Democrats are also finding it increasingly difficult to identify quality candidates with statewide standing to fill vacancies caused by the departures of long-entrenched incumbents.

As such, Lincoln's landslide victory catapulted her into the position of unchallenged leader of the state's Democratic elected officials. The embattled Democrats had found their new champion. In claiming the seat once held by Hattie Caraway, she became instantly recognized throughout the state simply as Blanche, the heir apparent to the legacies of Dale, David, and Bill.

NOTES

1. Erica Werner, "Population in Arkansas grows 0.6%," *Arkansas Democrat-Gazette,* December 31, 1998, 1A, 12A. Relevant census data from 1990 and ensuing updates can be found on the World Wide Web at http://www.census/gov/statab/www/states/ar.txt.

2. Diane D. Blair, *Arkansas Politics and Government: Do the People Rule?* (Lincoln: University of Nebraska Press, 1988), 266.

3. Census data for 1990 for each district are available on the World Wide Web at http://www.census.bov/datamap;www/05.html.

4. Blair, *Arkansas Government and Politics,* ch. 3–5, 14, *passim.* See also V. O. Key, Jr., *Southern Politics in State and Nation* (New York: Vintage, 1949), ch. 9; Boyce Drummond, *Arkansas Politics: A Study of a One-Party System* (Ph.D. dissertation, University of Chicago, 1957); R. E. Yates, "Arkansas: Independent and Unpredictable," in *The Changing Politics of the South,* ed. William C. Howard, Baton Rouge: Louisiana State University Press, 1972), 233–293; Jack Bass and Walter DeVries, *The Transformation of Southern Politics: Social Change and Political Consequences Since 1945* (New York: New American Library, 1976), ch. 5.

5. Key, *Southern Politics,* 183.

6. Ibid., 184.

7. Ibid., 195.

8. Ibid., 280–281.

9. For a discussion of the institutionalization of party organization in Arkansas, see Harold F. Bass, Jr., and Andrew Westmoreland, "Parties and Campaigns in Contemporary Arkansas Politics," *Arkansas Political Science Journal* 5 (Winter 1984).

10. Blair, *Arkansas Politics and Government,* 69.

11. Beginning in 1986, a constitutional amendment provided for a four-year term for state executive officers.

12. Congressional Quarterly, *Guide to U.S. Elections,* 3rd ed. (Washington, DC: Congressional Quarterly, 1994), 817.

13. Ibid.

14. Ibid.

15. See Diane D. Blair, "The Big Three of Late Twentieth-Century Arkansas Politics: Dale Bumpers, Bill Clinton, and David Pryor," *Arkansas Historical Quarterly* 15 (Spring 1995): 53–79.

16. "1998 Election Calendar," Office of the Secretary of State, State of Arkansas.

17. Malcolm E. Jewell and David M. Olson, *American State Political Parties and Elections,* rev. ed. (Homewood, IL: Dorsey, 1982), 131–132.

18. Congressional Quarterly, *Guide to U.S. Elections,* 855–856.

19. This group included former State Senator Jim Keet, former Second District congressional nominee Bud Cummins, and Lu Hardin, head of the state Department of Higher Education, who had joined the administration of Governor Huckabee following his defeat in the 1996 Democratic senatorial runoff primary.

20. John Brummett, "Who's Hot, Who's Not, in Politics," *Arkansas Democrat-Gazette,* November 16, 1997, 5J.

21. John Brummett, "Bryant's Minimalist Plan," *Arkansas Democrat-Gazette,* February 5, 1998, 5B.

22. Rachel O'Neal, "Coulter Enters Race for U.S. Senate; Independent Counsel Needs Reins, Democrat Says," *Arkansas Democrat-Gazette,* January 29, 1998, 1B.

23. Elizabeth McFarland, "Race Heats Up; Lincoln Foes Get Into Tobacco Row," *Arkansas Democrat-Gazette,* May 12, 1998, 1A, 7A.

24. "How We Rank Them: The Candidates for the Senate," *Arkansas Democrat-Gazette,* May 17, 1998, 4J.

25. John Brummett, "Labor Dumps Bryant for Coulter," *Arkansas Democrat-Gazette,* April 21, 1998, 5B.

26. John Brummett, "Senate Choice: Inertia or Real Race," *Arkansas Democrat-Gazette,* April 14, 1998, 5B.

27. Bill Simmons and Dauphne Trenholm, "Favored Lincoln Leads in Cash, Too," *Arkansas Democrat-Gazette,* May 17, 1998, 21A.

28. Bill Simmons, "Lincoln Pushes Past Bryant in Latest Poll: Boozman Leads Prince in GOP Race," *Arkansas Democrat-Gazette,* May 14, 1998, 1A, 8A. This newspaper poll gave Lincoln a 42 percent to 35 percent lead over Bryant.

29. Elizabeth McFarland, "Lincoln Ad for Senate Race First to Hit TV, Emphasizes Family," *Arkansas Democrat-Gazette,* April 14, 1998, 3B; McFarland, "TV Ads Present Strong, Homey Faces of Senate Candidates, Analysts Say," *Arkansas Democrat-Gazette,* April 26, 1998, 1B.

30. Roy Pierce, "Coutler's Senate Ads on TV Take on Starr," *Arkansas Democrat-Gazette,* April 16, 1998, 8B; McFarland, "TV Ads Present Strong, Homey Faces."

31. Elizabeth McFarland, "TV Ad Aims to Show He Puts 'Our Kids' First, Ferguson Says," *Arkansas Democrat-Gazette,* April 23, 1998, 2B; McFarland, "TV Ads Present Strong, Homey Faces."

32. Doug Smith, "Lincoln's South African Connection: It Was Minor and She Forgot, She Says," *Arkansas Times,* May 8, 1998, 13; Elizabeth McFarland, "Lincoln Pays Two to Court Black Vote in East Arkansas," *Arkansas Democrat-Gazette,* May 8, 1998, 8B; McFarland, "Race Issues Ignite Fuss in Primary: Two Criticize Lincoln for South Africa Work," *Arkansas Democrat-Gazette,* May 9, 1998, 1B, 7B; John Brummett, "Blanche Forgets Again," Arkansas Democrat-Gazette, May 9, 1998, 9B; Elizabeth McFarland, "Apartheid Ad a Lie, Lincoln Says," *Arkansas Democrat-Gazette,* May 13, 1998, 1A, 12A.

33. "Summary Totals of Votes Cast at the Democratic Preferential Primary, 19 May 1998," Office of the Secretary of State, State of Arkansas.

34. Elizabeth McFarland, "Voter Turnout Key in Senate Runoff, Experts Say," *Arkansas Democrat-Gazette,* June 1, 1998, 1B, 6B; Ernest Dumas, "Stubborn Winston Bryant," *Arkansas Times,* May 29, 1998, 17; Max Brantley, "Hang It Up, Winston," *Arkansas Times,* May 22, 1998, 18.

35. "Summary Totals of Votes Cast at the Democratic General Primary Runoff Election Results, 9 June 1998," Office of the Secretary of State, State of Arkansas.

36. John Brummett, "Anatomy of a Blanche Sweep," *Arkansas Democrat-Gazette,* June 11, 1998, 5B.

37. An *Arkansas Democrat-Gazette* poll in mid–April gave Boozman 31 percent, Prince 10 percent, and Undecided 59 percent. See Bill Simmons, "Bryant, Lincoln Way Out Front." A month later, the newspaper poll showed Boozman with 39 percent, Prince with 22 percent, and 39 percent undecided. See Simmons, "Lincoln Pushes Past Bryant in Latest Poll."

38. "How We Rank Them."

39. McFarland, "TV Ads Present Strong, Homey Faces."

40. "Summary Totals of Votes Cast at the Republican Preferential Primary, 19 May 1998," Office of the Secretary of State, State of Arkansas.

41. Simmons, "Lincoln Pushes Past Bryant," reports newspaper poll results on the eve of the May primary giving Lincoln a comfortable 51 percent to 29 percent margin, with 19 percent undecided.

42. Lincoln's home page on the World Wide Web provides brief biographies of the members of her campaign organization. See http://www.blanche98.org/html/team.html.

43. Personal correspondence with David J. Sanders, press secretary for the Boozman campaign.

44. Elizabeth McFarland, "Democrats Fast off Block in Senate Race," *Arkansas Democrat-Gazette,* June 11, 1998, 1B, 6B.

45. Robert McCord, "Addressing Lincoln," *Arkansas Democrat-Gazette,* June 12, 1998, 17.

46. Elizabeth McFarland, "Most Polls Put Lincoln Ahead in Senate Race," *Arkansas Democrat-Gazette,* November 1, 1998, 23A, 29A.

47. Max Brantley, "Political Burnout," Arkansas Times, October 9, 1998, 13, refers to late September polling data giving Lincoln 50 percent and Boozman 31 percent, a negligible departure from the May data. See Simmons, "Lincoln Pushes Past Bryant."

48. The Federal Election Commission provides an updated report, "Financial Activity of Senate Campaigns 1997–98," on its World Wide Web site, http://www.fec.gov/1996/states;arsen6.htm.

49. McFarland, "Democrats Fast off Block."

50. Brantley, "Political Burnout." Boozman did in fact receive that gubernatorial appointment following the election.

51. McFarland, "Most Polls Put Lincoln Ahead."

52. Ibid.

53. "Summary of 11/3/98 General Election Results by County," Office of the Secretary of State, State of Arkansas.

11

⭐

Voinovich Defeats Boyle in Ohio's Senate Race

Stephen Brooks

At 7 p.m. in Ohio, the polls closed and election watchers began to settle in to follow Ohio's returns. Bucking the national trend of generally good news for Democrats, in Ohio, the night belonged to the Republicans. With the exception of one Supreme Court justice, Republican candidates took all statewide offices from governor to auditor. The Republicans also retained control of both houses of the state legislature. Even in the U.S. Senate race, Republican candidate George Voinovich won easily over Democrat Mary Boyle, taking the seat held by retiring astronaut-turned-senator-turned-astronaut John Glenn.

Election watchers didn't have to wait long to learn the outcome of this race. As soon as the top-of-the-hour commercials were over, exit polls had confirmed a Voinovich victory. The final tally of votes showed a 56 percent to 44 percent lopsided victory for the popular governor, having completed his maximum two terms as Ohio's chief executive. Early in the election season, some observers had given Boyle a fighting chance to keep the seat for the Democrats. However, her campaign was never able to crack the advantage Voinovich held from the beginning. While this race was technically an "open-seat" contest, the Voinovich campaign never treated it as such. From the beginning, this campaign looked, sounded, and was treated as though Voinovich was an incumbent. Similarly, Boyle's campaign was always in "catch up" mode. She was always a challenger.

INCUMBENT AND
FRONTRUNNER CAMPAIGNS

For political scientists, practitioners, and commentators, incumbency is believed to have special powers. Certainly election statistics seem to support this view. In the 1998 election, 98 percent of U.S. House incumbents won reelection while 93 percent of their Senate incumbent colleagues kept their positions. While somewhat higher than previous years, the percentages are typical of most election years and make most incumbent candidates appear invincible.

In attempting to explain this invincibility, scholars have long described the advantages incumbents bring to elections.[1] In elections where name recognition is a good first start, those already in the office have the advantage of having been on the ballot before and having received press coverage simply by holding that office. By using their positions to inform voters of their work and to directly help constituents, incumbents can be seen as active, helpful, and important.[2] Because of their position, many incumbents also have a fundraising advantage, which can both discourage quality opponents and provide needed resources to produce winning margins.[3]

Practitioners cite many of the same factors in describing the advantages incumbents bring to elections. Most incumbents as candidates have a quasi-campaign operation in place throughout their term in office. In addition to the benefits of office cited above, incumbents have practical campaign experience. While existing officeholders can make campaign mistakes, most have been through the campaign experience at least once, reducing the possibility of "fatal" miscues.

Attempts to describe the "incumbency advantage" have dominated research on elections, while providing little understanding of why challengers may occasionally win, or evaluating the dynamics of open-seat elections. Lack of research can be blamed in part on the small number of cases where challengers were successful or open-seat races that were actually competitive. In recent years, challengers have used their lack of incumbency or "outsider" status to their advantage. Through the use of "opposition research," challengers try to use an incumbent's voting record, attendance records, or some disliked aspect of the incumbent's term in office as the basis of a negative campaign.[4]

The distinction between incumbent and challenger is not limited to explaining success or defeat—it is also used in understanding the nature of campaigning itself. Judith Trent and Robert Friedenberg describe three campaign communication styles: incumbent, challenger, and incumbent/challenger, although they note that an incumbent may choose a challenger style, a challenger may run an incumbent style campaign, or candidates may mix styles.[5] Campaign practitioners urge potential candidates to assess the degree of incumbent advantage (or disadvantage) when developing a campaign strategy.[6]

However, just because incumbents are likely to win elections does not mean that their candidacies are somehow unique or different. Table 11.1 presents an analysis of the margin of victory for the 34 Senate races in the 1998 election, where 29 races involved incumbent candidates and five were open-

**Table 11.1 Winning Margins (%) for
Incumbent and Open-Seat U.S. Senate Races, 1998**

	Smallest	Largest	Mean	Median
Incumbent races	0	62	19.0	13.0
N = 29	Nevada	Hawaii		
Open-seat races	0	41	25.7	27.0
N = 5	Kentucky	Idaho		
All races	0	62	24.7	32.5
N = 34				

SOURCE: Compiled by author.

seat races. For both the mean and the median, incumbent races were closer than open-seat contests. This can also be seen in the eight races with victory margins of less than 10 percent. All but one of those races (Kentucky) involved incumbent candidates. Likewise, one open-seat race (Idaho) ended with an incumbent-like victory margin of 41 percent.

These results suggest that making distinctions between candidates simply because one may be an incumbent is not useful in understanding campaign behavior. It is more likely that an incumbent candidate in a close race will act more like his or her counterpart in a close, open-seat election than an incumbent with an easy race. Likewise (and more useful for analysis), an open-seat candidate with a safe lead will likely act more like a traditional incumbent.

What is being suggested, then, is that the analytical framework be moved from incumbent versus open-seat races to ones distinguished by the competitiveness of the race. The distinction being suggested is that campaigns can be distinguished by a "frontrunner" style and a "challenger" style. Making such a claim is not a challenge to previous understanding; it is just an expansion of current view of open-seat elections. Because, almost without exception, when the incumbent is running, he or she is the frontrunner. Therefore, there is no difference between the concept of frontrunners and the concept of incumbents. However, this framework allows for an understanding of those leading open-seat races (and their challengers) as well as suggesting that incumbents in close contests will likely not run a traditional "incumbent campaign."

What, then, are the characteristics of a "frontrunner" campaign? More than likely, these campaigns will be well-financed and will be able to raise money early in the campaign season.[7] Even if the race begins to close (as most races invariably do), the frontrunner will be able to raise money fairly easily if he or she does not already have sufficient funds on hand.

The style of a "frontrunner's" campaign combines using the trappings of his or her existing office or position to stay above the fray of the campaign and maintaining a conservative approach based upon a defensive strategy.[8] The "rose garden" strategy of pretending there is no campaign is an often-used technique of presidential frontrunners, campaigning from the White House.

Advertising for frontrunners is more positive, not wanting to risk losing current supporters in a backlash from a negative campaign. Frontrunners, knowing they will be attacked by their challengers, can also design inoculation strategies against the inevitable. They also can prepare counterattacks to the negative campaign. A popular theme to these counterattacks is to portray the challenger as a "dirty campaigner."

A "challenger" campaign is likely to be more innovative. Except in unusual circumstances, challengers have limited funds, so they must find innovative ways to get recognized and be taken seriously. Many operate under a "catch-22" of campaign finance—financial support does not come to those with little chance of winning but one has little chance of winning without financial resources.

A "challenger" campaign is one driven by the need to "catch up."[9] This need, which is often identified early, produces a campaign that is willing to take risks, to be more creative, and to be more aggressive. A campaign behind in the polls has little to lose by trying something different. We would then expect a "challenger" campaign to use a broader range of issues and techniques than a "frontrunner" campaign. The challenger is more likely to use attack advertising and use it earlier in the campaign. In general, then, the "challenger" campaign is trying hard to "punch holes" in the opponent's lead. Often, too, when a breakthrough is made, it only encourages the challenger to be more aggressive, to push even harder.

The 1998 Senate race in Ohio between Voinovich and Boyle is a classic example of an open-seat frontrunner versus a challenger campaign. As this chapter shows, Voinovich's lead never shrank below 55 percent and the Boyle campaign was in a constant battle to gain enough exposure, momentum, and money to be a serious contender for the seat. Although he was not an incumbent, Voinovich ran the traditional frontrunner (incumbent) campaign and the race was his to lose.

OHIO POLITICS AND THE RACE
FOR THE SENATE: A BRIEF HISTORY

Ohio is frequently referred to as one of the nation's "battleground states," as the state is narrowly divided between the two major political parties. In the recent history of presidential elections, the state has been a "must win" state for at least one candidate, if not both. The winning president has taken the state in all elections since 1960, although the largest winning vote was 63 percent by President Lyndon Johnson in 1964. Similarly, the governor's seat has been shared by both parties. Since 1908, Ohio has had a Republican governor for 40 years and a Democratic governor for 40 years.

This political division has its roots in the settlements in the south by Virginians and in the north by New Englanders.[10] Growth and development only strengthened the partisan differences. The north became, and has stayed, a center for heavy industry, especially steel, rubber, automobiles, and chemicals.

These industries became unionized and fostered migration of minorities and already union-friendly miners from Appalachia, laying a foundation for the core of the Democratic party. At the same time, southern and central Ohio developed as a leading agricultural region, largely supporting Republican candidates. Traditionally, the formula for a Democratic victory was ensuring turnout from the populated north, while encouraging independent moderates from the southern part of the state to tip the balance. The Republican formula was essentially the reverse. In addition, Ohio voters have a reputation for caution in casting their ballots. Beyond party, voters want to know something about the candidates. Ohio political observers are quick to point out that winners of most statewide political contests have been successful only if they have previously lost a statewide race.

Most of these lessons can be seen in the two Senate races that preceded the 1998 Boyle-Voinovich contest and set the stage for this race. In 1992, former astronaut and three-term Democratic incumbent U.S. Senator John Glenn was challenged by former four-term Republican member of the U.S. House of Representatives as well as Ohio's then-lieutenant governor, Michael DeWine. Because of their careers in politics, both candidates were well known, although DeWine had not yet lost a statewide campaign.

In 1992, voters were in an anti-incumbent, anti-Washington mood, putting Glenn in the most vulnerable position for defeat of his senatorial career. DeWine was in a strong position to take full advantage of Glenn's weaknesses. DeWine tried to portray himself as an "outsider" versus the long-time senator. He attacked with ads parodying an "Energizer Bunny-style" rabbit to remind Ohio voters that Glenn still owed $3 million from his unsuccessful 1983–84 presidential candidacy and ads reminding voters of Glenn's link to the Charles Keating savings and loan scandal. The campaign portrayed Glenn as out of touch with Ohio and called for a change.

The relationship between Glenn and DeWine took an unpredicted turn from maintaining the tenuous "insider-versus-outsider" balance and dialogue. DeWine found himself targeted as a participant in the U.S. House bank scandal, accepting speaking honoraria, and taking "exotic" junkets paid for by interest groups. The Glenn campaign took full strategic advantage of DeWine's "incumbent disadvantages." Glenn also responded by attacking the DeWine campaign and its "sleazy mudslinging tactics," as Glenn called them. Despite higher voter discontent, Glenn survived what he acknowledged to be the toughest of his three senatorial campaigns.[11] Glenn received 51 percent of the vote, DeWine 42 percent, and virtually unknown socialistic candidate Martha Kathryn Grevatt garnered 7 percent. A record-breaking 76 percent of the 6.5 million Ohio registered voters turned out to vote, which no doubt helped Glenn.

Having now lost his statewide race, two years later, in 1994, DeWine returned to run again for Senate, although he had a difficult primary fight with former director of the National Institutes of Health, Bernadette Healey. DeWine's opponent in the general election was Joel Hyatt, a newcomer to politics as a candidate but not to political campaigns. These candidates were running for the seat vacated by retiring Democratic Senator Howard Metzen-baum, Hyatt's father-in-law. While Hyatt was seen as Metzenbaum's hand-picked successor, he also had to survive a difficult primary challenge by Boyle, a Cuyahoga County commissioner.

The well-financed DeWine campaign developed an "outsider-insider" strategy. For most of his commercials and many public appearances, he donned a plaid shirt and casual pants (two years before the Lamar Alexander plaid shirt) to show himself as "one of the people." At the same time, the campaign slogan of "A Proven Fighter for Ohio Families" was used in his commercials, speak-ing of his successful experiences in government. The campaign and commer-cials focused upon issues like welfare, crime, and "family values," paying almost no attention to Hyatt. The exceptions were two commercials questioning Hy-att's trustworthiness.

The Hyatt campaign ran an "outsider" strategy, playing up the candidate's business background and lack of government experience. Portraying Hyatt as someone who started his legal clinics to help the "little guy," his positive com-mercials focused on his position on issues like abortion rights, welfare reform, and congressional reform. They also contrasted Hyatt with DeWine by using DeWine's former congressional experience as the topic of "comparison" ads. To maintain the outsider image, the campaign had to maintain a delicate bal-ance concerning Hyatt's father-in-law, Metzenbaum. To acknowledge the close link would make Hyatt look like an insider, but to deny any link would alien-ate hard-core Democrats who supported Metzenbaum. This and other issues produced an image of a campaign that was not well disciplined. Falling behind in the polls, Hyatt replaced his Ohio-based consulting team with a national firm, which projected more confusion to analysts and voters.

DeWine benefited from the highly successful national Republican cam-paign and even more from being on the ballot with Voinovich, the popular governor running for reelection. In the end, DeWine became a part of the Re-publican sweep (with the exception of one Supreme Court seat) of all statewide offices on the ballot. The final vote was 53 percent for DeWine, 39 percent for Hyatt, and 7 percent for independent candidate, Joseph Slovenic.

THE 1998 SENATE CAMPAIGN

The Candidates

The stage was set for the 1998 campaign when rumors began to fly that Glenn would be retiring. When he made it official in February 1997, the contest be-gan. There was little doubt that the Republican candidate would be Voinovich, who was barred from running for a third term as governor. In fact, even if Glenn had not retired, Voinovich was expected to run.

Voinovich was an ideal candidate for the Republicans and could be iden-tified as a "frontrunner" from the beginning. Hailing from Cleveland, the heart of the Democratic base, Voinovich enjoyed unprecedented popularity as governor. He had held political office most of his adult life, working his way from assistant attorney general to the Ohio House of Representatives to Cuyahoga County (Cleveland area) commissioner to lieutenant governor for a year.

In 1979, he ran for and won the mayor's race in Cleveland, a major accomplishment for a Republican in the solidly Democratic city. When he arrived, the city was in fiscal and political disarray. Nationally, Cleveland was known as "The Mistake on the Lake." During his ten years as mayor, the city underwent a major turnaround with a rejuvenated downtown, economic stability, and most of the tarnish removed from its national image. Voinovich was given credit for bringing the diverse interests of the city together to make the change possible.

Building upon this success, Voinovich tried a run for the Senate in 1988, challenging incumbent Metzenbaum, but lost by 14 percent, thereby losing his obligatory statewide campaign and becoming a future contender. Two years later, he won his first term as governor and, four years later, easily won a second term against weak opposition. Voinovich is known as a moderate, practical politician who measures success more by what gets accomplished than ideological litmus tests. As governor, he won high approval ratings, with consistently 60 to 70 percent of respondents approving of his job performance. His campaigns are usually a mix of promoting his accomplishments in office and practicing "ethnic politics"—touring the variety of ethnic festivals held each summer and visiting churches and community centers. While not overly charismatic or dynamic, he feels comfortable on the campaign trail.

His opponent was Boyle, a perfect candidate for the "challenger" role. Unlike Voinovich, Boyle came late to political office. While she had not run for office early in life, she had supported her husband's political career as city council member and mayor of a Cleveland suburb, as well as running other candidates' campaigns. In 1976, when her husband decided to not run for the state legislature because he needed to tend the family business, Boyle said, "Why not me?" She ran and won.

While she liked her time in the legislature and was quickly moving to leadership positions, she disliked the time away from her family. So, in 1984, she decided to take on a well-financed Republican incumbent for Cuyahoga County Board of Commissioners, winning that post. During her eight-year tenure, the County Commission faced a number of difficult problems, ranging from a human services workers' strike to helping bring new sports facilities to Cleveland to the collapse of a leveraged investment fund. Throughout these problems, she gained the reputation of a "straight shooter" and a policy maker who analyzed all the details.

In 1994, she entered into the Democratic Senate primary campaign against Joel Hyatt and, although not victorious, gained the attention of Democratic party activists because she nearly upset Hyatt, the party- and union-endorsed candidate. She was seen as a tireless campaigner with campaign savvy. In 1996, she decided not to seek her fourth term as county commissioner and set her sights on the Senate seat likely to be vacated by Glenn. She spent the time traveling the state to attend Democratic events and developing a fundraising base.

When Glenn retired, no other candidates came forward, leaving the race to her. Many Democrats tried to convince her to run for state offices, especially secretary of state, realizing she would have a good chance to be a Democratic influence on the 2000 state reapportionment board. She resisted, claiming she wanted to be a legislator. While most observers gave her little chance of victory, they also acknowledged that a woman candidate had the best chance to exploit Voinovich's few weaknesses.

The Beginnings

While neither candidate officially declared his or her intentions until late summer and early fall 1997, their announcements were not a big surprise. Voinovich had been thinking about this race since his last victory as governor and, as described above, Boyle had been running for the seat since leaving the Cuyahoga County Commission. However, her delay in making the final decision only increased her fundraising disadvantage.

Early polls demonstrated the hill Boyle would have to climb to win in September. For example, a September 1997 poll gave Voinovich a 29-point lead, 52 percent to 23 percent with 25 percent undecided or not planning to vote. In the May primary, Boyle was unopposed while Voinovich was challenged by David McCollough, a Cincinnati-area high school teacher who, as a conservative, challenged Voinovich's more moderate positions on taxes and social issues.

With the large difference in potential votes, the Boyle campaign decided to attack early and ran a set of television commercials during the primaries. Voinovich was seen as vulnerable in three areas. First, while he had not been directly linked to scandal, there had been problems in his administration. His chief of staff was forced to resign and later was convicted for receiving reduced rates from a state contractor for a remodeling project on his then-girlfriend's home. In addition, Voinovich's brother owned a major construction firm, which built county jails, state prisons, and other government facilities. This firm, The V Company, had been involved in a number of questionable practices.

More problematic for Voinovich, however, were the challenges the state was facing in education. In his 1990 campaign, Voinovich had promised to become the "Education Governor." Midway through his second term, the state lost a Supreme Court case that found the state system of funding in violation of the Ohio Constitution, which calls for "fair and equal education." During the court case and the ensuing news coverage, examples were given of schools still using outhouses, schools with condemned classrooms, and schools that could not take advantage of the governor's premier lead program to have a computer in every classroom because they had inadequate electrical service. Although Voinovich pointed out the large funding increase for schools during his tenure, the perception was that he was not accomplishing what he had promised.

Adding to the difficulty was Voinovich's support for a ballot measure to increase the state sales tax by 1 percent, half of which would go to the schools and the other half for property tax reduction. As with any tax proposal, this ballot initiative was controversial and, in the end, was overwhelmingly rejected by voters in the May primary by a four-to-one margin.

Ohio has had a long history of punishing politicians who increase taxes or even support the idea of a tax increase. Instead of focusing exclusively upon education, the Boyle campaign decided to link the education issue to support of the tax issue. Although she was unopposed, during the May primary the campaign used $400,000 to run ads linking Voinovich to the unpopular tax increase proposal. "George Voinovich's $1 billion tax increase just isn't the answer," the ad claimed.

To a limited degree, the campaign worked. In the aftermath of the commercials, Voinovich's lead had shrunk by six points, but he still held a good lead of 57 percent to 34 percent. In addition, the Boyle campaign was encouraged by Voinovich's primary opponent's showing. In what was expected to be a rout, McCollough received a surprising 28 percent of the vote. These and other factors had the Boyle campaign arguing that she was a respectable contender. With the primary activity over, both camps returned to fundraising (although Voinovich had much less need) and planning their strategy for the main event.

The Main Campaign

As with most campaigns, Labor Day signaled the beginning of the visible-to-voters campaign. Although Boyle had advertised early, she hadn't been back on television. The main reason for this lack of visibility was obvious. The mid-October financial filing with the Federal Election Commission (FEC) showed that, at the beginning of the month, Voinovich's campaign had $2.5 million compared to Boyle's $107,000. One non-political advertising executive suggested that these funds could buy Voinovich more than 2,000 gross rating points on television (a measure of the estimated viewership of the ads) compared to 600 gross rating points for Boyle. She went on to say, "If I had $107,000 and I were Boyle, I would go to Jamaica."[12] The Boyle campaign pointed out that more money was coming in daily and that they would focus on television beyond Columbus.

With limited funds, the Boyle campaign concentrated upon grassroots activity, crisscrossing the state talking with anyone and everyone willing to listen. She was especially interested in Democratic organizations to ensure her "base" supporters turned out to vote. This tactic was also linked to a general Democratic strategy. Of all statewide races, Democrats had the best chance at winning the gubernatorial contest. That could only be done by ensuring a strong turnout of loyal Democrats and winning over independent voters. The hope was that a victory at the top of the ticket would provide coattails for other Democratic candidates. For this strategy to work for Boyle, she needed to convince Democratic voters to cast their ballots for her, along with other Democrats.

Although he had a sizable war chest, Voinovich was not a television campaigner. He, too, enjoyed a grassroots campaign style, participating in ethnic festivals, speaking to groups of voters, and taking part in campaign rallies. So, during the campaign, he too was out on the road. During the trips, however, he had a shadow from the Boyle campaign—a campaign worker in a chicken suit. This was part of Boyle's attempt to engage Voinovich in debates. As a fron-trunner, he had little incentive to debate. Debates would only increase the chal-lenger's visibility and name recognition. Moreover, the campaign was his to lose, and a misstatement during a debate could be costly.

The result of extensive subsequent negotiation between the camps was one televised debate in mid-October. During the debate, the candidates concen-trated on the themes of their campaigns. Boyle attacked Voinovich's record on education and the environment and promoted her image as one concerned about "people issues." Voinovich rarely responded to the attacks, except to suggest that the problems began when Boyle was in the legislature or to com-ment: "I'll let the people judge my record on education."[13] The theme of his well-known record of public service that prepared him well for the Senate dominated his comments. It even extended to Boyle's challenge for more de-bates. Voinovich responded, "The people of Ohio know who George Voinovich is. They know my good things and they know my warts. I don't think my getting up for four or five more debates is going to have a big change on whether they're for me or against me."[14]

As expected, the television advertising campaign was rather lopsided. Voinovich began his television campaign in late September, while Boyle waited until the last two weeks to begin hers. Even then, in the Cleveland area, where neither candidate needed name recognition, Voinovich ran more than three times more spots than his opponent did. Boyle's campaign was helped by "is-sue ads" run by the Ohio Democratic Party. Ironically, one of Boyle's campaign issues was campaign finance reform, where she called for an end to just this type of "soft money" advertising. When asked about this apparent contradic-tion, she said: "I can't control the Ohio Democratic Party."[15]

News coverage, or "earned media," of the campaign did not favor Boyle. With the race not being close, most news coverage of the contest focused upon the candidates' background and the struggle Boyle was having in trying to close the gap. This limited news coverage was also prompted by two other, much larger stories. First, the one close statewide contest in the election sea-son was for governor. As this was the one race most pundits felt could be won by a Democrat, political writers focused upon it. The close race also generated more debates, more advertising, and even a finding by the Ohio Elections Commission of "improper advertising." Needless to say, all this activity drew news coverage away from the Senate race.

In addition, just before election, the outgoing Glenn made his historic sec-ond trip into space. While this generated extensive national news coverage, Ohio news organizations played up the "home state" angle with reporters go-ing to Florida for live coverage of the launch and to Glenn's hometown of New Concord to interview friends of the Glenn family. This extensive cover-age, coming less than a week before and lasting until four days after the elec-tion, shifted the focus of the news from the election (which would likely have been the biggest state story) to the outgoing senator.

As the campaign entered its final days, all polls predicted a Voinovich victory. As voters went to the polls on election day, news broke that Ohio Secretary of State (and soon to be governor) Bob Taft had submitted a complaint against Voinovich to the Ohio Elections Commission claiming that he had allegedly illegally laundered $60,000 in campaign funds. He was charged with paying the salary of a campaign worker through his brother's company and another consultant. The Boyle campaign charged that Taft had delayed the announcement so it wouldn't influence the election, a charged denied by Taft, who said that he had passed along the charges as soon as he had received them. He also said that the judge in the case had issued a gag order preventing any public announcements on his part. Although the charges reflected one of the main attacks on Voinovich by the Boyle campaign, the news came too late to be an issue in the campaign. As soon as the polls closed, Voinovich was declared the winner. This was quickly followed by a gracious concession speech by Boyle. At the same time, her campaign was requesting that the Secretary of State not certify the election until the charges against Voinovich had been investigated. The final vote count had Voinovich winning 56 percent to 44 percent.

FRONTRUNNER VERSUS CHALLENGER: AN ANALYSIS

As was argued earlier, the 1998 Ohio Senate race fit the mold of a "typical" modern political campaign, where one candidate enters into the race as the assumed leader and his or her opponent takes up the role of challenger. While in most of these races the leading candidate owes his or her position to incumbency, other open-seat races have a clear frontrunner without the benefit of incumbency. This section will examine the content of these types of campaigns, which have an identifiable frontrunner and a challenger. Drawing from scholarly work on incumbency campaigns, finance, strategy, earned media, and message will be considered in the context of this Senate campaign.

Campaign Finance

One definition of a frontrunner is a candidate who enters into the campaign with a large war chest, and therefore has the potential to run an effective campaign against his or her opponent. The accumulation of a large campaign fund can be an effective deterrent for a credible challenger to appear.[16] In addition, well-financed candidates have an easier job at raising money for their races. Interest groups and large contributors are more likely to support potential winners than those with little chance of victory. This makes raising money a "catch-22" for the challenger. He or she cannot raise large sums of money unless there is a chance for victory, but without money, he or she has little chance of pulling off an upset.

This dilemma can be seen in the contest between Voinovich and Boyle. At the start of 1998, long before the spring primary, Voinovich had already amassed a campaign war chest and was $2.3 million ahead of Boyle, who still hadn't made up her mind about running. After deciding to run, she began to gather funds, but decided to spend $400,000 for an early television campaign during the primaries. While the campaign produced a small dent in Voinovich's poll numbers, the change was not significant enough to encourage a major shift in interest in the campaign.

Boyle also suffered some bad luck on the fundraising trail. A year before the election, she had lined up the endorsement of EMILY's (Early Money Is Like Yeast) List and promises of visits by prominent Democrats. President Bill Clinton came to Cleveland and raised more than $150,000 for her campaign. She also had fundraising visits from Vice President Al Gore, First Lady Hillary Clinton, and former Senator Bill Bradley (D-NJ). However, in mid-October, when the campaign was in the greatest need of funds, Senator Edward Kennedy (D-MA) had to cancel his trip because of the extended congressional session. Only days later, Tipper Gore, wife of the Vice President, had to cancel her visit because of a leg injury.[17]

Boyle also didn't receive help from the man she was hoping to replace. Often in campaigns the outgoing official assists in fundraising and travels the campaign trail with his or her party's candidate. That wasn't possible here because Glenn's schedule was filled with his training to return to space. In addition, he refused to endorse or campaign for Boyle, claiming it was not an appropriate role for an astronaut.[18]

Voinovich, on the other hand, had little need for extensive, overt fundraising. The final campaign finance report filed before the election tells the tale. On the first of October, Voinovich began the final weeks of the campaign with $2.5 million while Boyle had only one-twentieth as much ($107,000).

The result of this disparity can be seen in how the two candidates spent their money in the Cleveland media market. While neither candidate needed name recognition in northeast Ohio, both wanted to ensure a good turnout for their candidacy. Table 11.2 includes information on the television ads purchased by the two candidates during the last five weeks of the campaign on the two stations in the Cleveland market, used most by both candidates. As can be seen, Voinovich started much earlier than Boyle and, even during the final weeks, had purchased many more spots. On one hand, these numbers overstate to some degree the extent of advertising by Voinovich because some of these ads were not exclusively his. Showing his confidence in victory, some of these spots were used by the governor to endorse the Republican candidate wanting to follow him, Bob Taft, who was in a close contest. On the other hand, these numbers do not include the other three major television stations in the Cleveland market, where some had no Boyle ads but on which Voinovich was advertising.

Strategy

In simplified terms, the strategy of any challenger's campaign is to become a viable contender, at minimum having your opponent's poll numbers below 48 to 50 percent. If a victory becomes a possibility, the dynamics of the campaign

**Table 11.2 Purchased Television
Advertising at Two Cleveland Television Stations:
Boyle and Voinovich Campaigns, October/November 1998**

Station	Candidate	9/29–10/5	10/6–10/12	10/13–10/19	10/20–10/26	10/27–11/2	Total
WEWS (ABC)	Boyle	0	0	0	20	20*	40
	Voinovich	35	52	43	63	71	264
WKYC (NBC)	Boyle	0	0	0	11	21	32
	Voinovich	41	39	49	54	73	256
Total	Boyle	0	0	0	31	41	72
	Voinovich	76	91	92	117	144	520

*Estimated based on incomplete report.

SOURCE: Television station purchase files.

change. Money is easier to raise; the press, sensing a real "fight," begins to cover the race; and the frontrunner becomes more willing to engage his or her opponent. However, getting to that point is the struggle for the challenger. While trying to build up one's image, a challenger must produce doubt in voters' minds about the frontrunner. The most effective way to convince those supporting the status quo to change is through attack advertising. Voters must be convinced to change to the challenger. If the attacks are effective, they can also raise issues of interest to the news media, adding to the impression that the challenger is "onto something."

While a challenger may be on the attack, one of the most effective strategies for the frontrunner (especially one holding a political office) is to be an apolitical "statesman," demonstrating his or her competency by doing a good job. While not avoiding campaigning, a frontrunner's campaign appearances can often seem to be a combination of official visits/campaign trips. And, while frontrunners should be prepared to respond to political attacks, they need to be careful in using negative advertising. Under certain circumstances, attacks can have a boomerang effect.[19] This is especially true for a frontrunner with a comfortable lead. He or she runs the risk of being "mean" or "kicking the opponent when he or she is down." As long as the lead is reasonable, frontrunners can focus upon their attributes to keep voters on their side. Advertising, then, stays positive throughout the campaign.

The Boyle and Voinovich campaigns followed these strategies. The focus of the Boyle campaign was the shortcomings in Voinovich's record as contrasted with her record and issue positions. But, to make a dent in the Voinovich lead, the campaign needed to begin early. Her campaign therefore decided to undertake a "spurt strategy," which is "to 'spurt' early in the campaign, often four to six months before the election, purchasing a large amount of television time for one to two weeks. . . . The purpose of this early spurt is to build name recognition and help establish the candidate as a credible contender for the office."[20] It was hoped that the beginning "spurt" would create enough interest in the campaign to provide added funds and public interest. Of course, the danger to this strategy is using extensive funds at the beginning, leaving less money to advertise in the closing weeks of the campaign when voters are more interested in the messages. Boyle's limited ability to use television at the end showed the risk.

The Voinovich campaign, however, held its "ammunition" until the end of the race, not seriously advertising until the final month. The combination of having a sizable war chest, and the luxury of being able to wait, allowed it to strategically determine the time and the place necessary for advertising.

Message

Strategy and message are always closely linked, as political campaigns are always fought over competing messages. According to one campaign consultant, Cathy Allen, successful challengers know and exploit four main weaknesses of their opponents: "they've lost touch, are too arrogant, just don't get it, and are not connecting with voters."[21] It is not sufficient to criticize the opponent; the challenger needs to project a new vision for change. While campaign speeches and debates allow the challenger to develop such a message, it is difficult to project them in a 30-second commercial or in a "sound-byte" that will be picked up by the news media.

To maintain the lead position, the frontrunner's main job is to counter any perception that she or he is out of touch or has views that don't match those of the constituencies. Normally, this can be done by emphasizing one's record and highlighting accomplishments in those areas that the challenger is attacking. If the challenger's attacks are gaining legitimacy, the frontrunner can counterattack by pointing out the opponent's weaknesses (usually lack of experience) in comparative ads. If voters seem truly angry at the frontrunner, he or she can deliver a message of apology. [22] Most of the time, however, simply focusing upon one's accomplishments with occasional jabs at the challenger are sufficient to maintain a lead.

The Boyle campaign's message was a presentation of Voinovich's weaknesses, combined with a promise of caring and compassion by Boyle. The criticism of Voinovich focused on two general areas. The first was education, where the state system had been found unconstitutional and a tax increase supported by the governor was turned down by a large margin of voters the previous spring. Early in the campaign, attention was placed upon his support of a tax increase, but when that message seemed to wear thin and began to have little impact, the attacks spoke directly to the state of education in Ohio and Voinovich's "lack of leadership." Figure 11.1 is the script of one of Boyle's television commercials aired during the last weeks of the campaign. It provides an example of the education message combined with Boyle promising positive change. This is a typical challenger advertisement in that it criticized the frontrunner, while providing an upbeat message about the challenger and trying to demonstrate her competency. It was a fast-moving advertisement because it needed to combine both a criticism of the opponent and positive messages about the challenger.

Video	Graphics	Audio
Boy picks up a lottery ticket, jumps out of seat and does somersaults around a classroom.		*Very soft drumbeat underneath voice* Child: I'm a winner!
Cut to split screen. Rough black and white picture of Voinovich and blue tint picture of school children overlaid with graphics of school paper one after the other.	George Voinovich * Ohio Public School Buildings Rank Last George Voinovich * Classes Are Overcrowded George Voinovich * Drop Outs Doubled George Voinovich * $1 Billion Tax Hike	*Announcer:* For eight years George Voinovich promised to use lottery money for education. Eight years later, Ohio public school buildings rank last in the nation; classes overcrowded; drop outs doubled. And then he pushed for a one billion-dollar tax hike.
Cut back to boy tearing up a lottery ticket, throwing it away and sitting dejected in his seat.	VOINOVICH: LOTTERY BROKEN PROMISES	George Voinovich. Eight years of lottery broken promises that hurt our kids.

Video	Graphics (Bottom left:)	Graphics (Top left:)	Audio
Cut to Mary Boyle with girl looking at homework.	MARY BOYLE	Endorsed by: *fast crawl list:* AFL-CIO	*Change to upbeat music.* Mary Boyle won't gamble with education.
Cut to African American girl raising her hand in class.	MARY BOYLE Smaller Class Sizes	American Nurses Assn. Columbus Education Assn.	She'll work for smaller class sizes, increased standards, and tougher discipline.
Cut to Mary Boyle talking with a teacher in a classroom.	MARY BOYLE Increased Standards	Irish-American Democrats Cleveland Police Patrolman's Assn.	
Cut to Mary Boyle working with a boy on his homework in a classroom.	MARY BOYLE Tougher Discipline	OH Federation of Teachers Sierra Club	
	MARY BOYLE United States Senate		Mary Boyle for Senate so all our children will get a chance to win.

FIGURE 11.1 Script of "Boyle for Senate" Campaign, 1998.

Boyle's second general criticism tried to show how Voinovich was "out of touch" with common voters. It tied together Voinovich's large campaign fund, contributions from large corporations, and hints of corruption in his administration. At the same time, Boyle was promoting campaign finance reform, her support for the "little guy," and her position as the underdog. This route of attack rarely made it into campaign commercials but was taken through the press. In one speech, Boyle suggested independent counsel Kenneth Starr and Voinovich were both "$40 million men," a usable sound-byte reference to his campaign fundraising for his three statewide campaigns and two issue campaigns.[23] Throughout the campaign, her messages made reference to his campaign link with big business and, for example, called for him to return a $7,200 contribution from the Huffy Company after it announced a plant closing in Celina, Ohio.[24] These messages followed the profile of a challenger, attempting to raise questions about the frontrunner's ability to govern and to stay in touch with the common voter.

Just as clearly, however, the Voinovich campaign followed the frontrunner's playbook. The theme of his campaign was summarized by its slogan: "Experience we can trust." The focus was to show that the governor was both competent and in touch with Ohio families. Other than occasional comments on the campaign circuit or responses to Boyle's criticisms coming from his campaign headquarters (rarely from Voinovich himself), the campaign didn't even recognize the challenger. All the advertisements showed the governor as a concerned public official and a caring person by having him play with his grandchildren or speak with factory workers. Figure 11.2 is the script of a Voinovich commercial running at the same time as the Boyle ad. Filled with warm tones, soothing music, and smiling faces, it was serious enough to project an image of professional competence but soft enough to make it clear that the candidate was a compassionate leader. By tying concern about all families with images of the candidate's own family, the ad showed that the candidate understood the issues and had the "right" values to act upon them.

Voinovich's campaign style also assisted in demonstrating how he wasn't one of those "distant politicians." This newspaper report on the governor's visit to Cleveland shows his ability to keep close to his constituency:

> "He's (Voinovich) doing a great job," said Cuyahoga County Common Pleas Judge Ronald Suster, a Democratic candidate for the Ohio Supreme Court and long-time acquaintance of Voinovich. Suster shared the stage with Voinovich this month at Steve Bencic's 37th Annual Oktoberfest in Painsville, an event Voinovich has missed only once, in 1992, "and then," he said smiling, "I sent President Bush to represent me."
>
> Working a crowd gathered under a massive tent for Wiener schnitzel and beer, Voinovich and his wife, Janet, were embraced by an aura of good feeling and warmth, constantly being stopped to be photographed. . . . "It's easy to paint Republicans as country clubbers, but you can't do that with a guy from Collingwood," said Cuyahoga County GOP Chairman James P. Trakas.[25]

Video	Graphics	Audio
Voinovich, dressed casually, walking with his wife, grandchild and other family members.		*Soft soothing piano music in background.*
Cut to front face shot of Voinovich talking into the camera.	George Voinovich	*Voinovich:* To me the most important part of my life is family.
Cut to Voinovich family around the dinner table with grandchild in his wife's lap. Quick close-up of grandchild.		My grandparents were immigrants who taught my folks to be tight with a buck *(slight laugh).* I guess it rubbed off.
Cut back to full face Voinovich talking. Quick shot of family walking.		My mother also taught me you are measured by what kind of life you leave your kids and their kids.
Cut to Voinovich talking on couch with wife and grandchild. Reaches to grandchild when he says her name.		One reason I'd like to go to Washington is to protect Medicare and Social Security, so we can take care of our folks. And our kids and grand kids like Mary Faith don't have to worry about it.
Cut back to Voinovich face, talking.		You can count on me working for my family and yours.
Cut to Voinovich and wife holding and looking at grandchild.	George Voinovich Experience we can trust	*Announcer:* George Voinovich. Experience we can trust.

FIGURE 11.2 Script of "Voinovich for Senate" Campaign, 1998.

This campaign was a true frontrunner's effort. All the messages were designed to deflect any criticism about Voinovich's ability and his concern for voters. Because of his comfortable lead, the campaign didn't need to go on the attack against Boyle but rather just tout the value of the frontrunner. In fact, mentioning the opponent was seen as providing extra exposure to the challenger, something Voinovich didn't want to do.

Earned Media

Because challengers usually do not have the money to the extent that incumbents do, they need to find ways to get their message out without paying for it. That is why they must, as political consultant Mark Weaver has said, ". . . use paid media to raise charges related to the incumbent's strengths, and use earned media to bait him on his weaknesses."[26]

In this contest, the Boyle campaign had difficulty in maximizing its use of the news media. As described above, the challenge to Voinovich never caught on enough to make it a significant "fight" for the press; political writers had a more interesting race in the contest for governor and much of the state was distracted by the launch of Glenn into space. In fact, most Ohio voters likely saw more news coverage of the Senate races in New York, California, and Illinois than the contest in their own state. Unlike the Ohio Senate campaign, those races were often mentioned in the national news. Local news also gave little attention to the Boyle-Voinovich match-up.

A good example was a local Cleveland newscast on the Wednesday night before the election. The 11:00 p.m. news began with almost four minutes of coverage of the Glenn space flight, with one anchor and one reporter broadcasting from Florida and another from Glenn's hometown. The second story covered the debate between gubernatorial candidates and the third story was on an Ohio ballot issue concerning the hunting of mourning doves. The Senate contest was never mentioned.[27]

Without the assistance of the news media, challengers must rely upon their own funds to advertise their message. In this contest, the huge difference in funds available to the two candidates made the challenger's message hard to hear and limited it to the advertised airways.

CONCLUSION

Every two years, more than 1,000 individuals choose to devote almost a year's worth of their time, energy, and finances to run for a position in the U.S. Congress. Less than half get the reward of taking the oath of office as a senator or member of the House. While few enter into this endeavor planning on losing, a majority of them embark on what many would consider a hopeless quest. Like overtime basketball games or soccer game-ending shootouts, attention of the news media is focused upon those races where either of the two major candidates has a chance of winning.

In reality, however, most contests are where one candidate runs the race to keep a winning margin from slipping away, while the opponent fights to find a way to gain attention, raise the profile of the campaign, and put victory within reach. This chapter has focused upon one such race, the U.S. Senate race in Ohio, between Mary Boyle and George Voinovich. In looking at this contest, we've seen the work and struggle of a challenger to make the race interesting and the attention of the frontrunner to keep his victory certain.

Both these candidates played out a typical "dance" during the election, one that typifies modern American politics. Because the contest is the frontrunner's to lose, the main "dancer" in these contests is the challenger because gains by a challenger force a frontrunner to adjust his or her steps. Boyle, the challenger in this race, was well-suited for the job. A scrappy politician and a tireless campaigner, she exhibited the will and the determination to take on a difficult race.

The focus of her campaign fit the challenger profile. The concentration on education and campaign finance, issues that traditionally work well for women, brought together her opponent's weaknesses. These issues positively positioned her underdog status. Her limited success and bad luck in raising money for the campaign was her biggest weakness, not an uncommon one for challengers.

Throughout the campaign, she strove to find a weakness in her opponent's campaign. Attacks on his record in education, environment, and taxes, combined with complaints about his ties to big monied interests, attempted to portray him as out of touch and less competent. In the end, however, she had limited funds to spread that message to voters, and the news media didn't find her message interesting enough to repeat often. What began as a campaign with an outside chance of winning evolved to a finish with inadequate voter support, as had been predicted throughout the campaign.

While Boyle may have been an excellent challenger, Voinovich was an outstanding frontrunner. In addition to plenty of money, he was a well-known and a well-liked politician and, most importantly, had not made any major personal or professional mistakes that could make him seem out of touch with the public. With that foundation, he followed the frontrunner's script by promoting his positives and minimizing any opportunity for mistakes.

He was active on the campaign trail, with appearances that brought him close to the people and ones that demonstrated he took the contest seriously. He limited debates to one, but demonstrated his respect for the importance of the contest. The campaign also saved most of its resources for the final weeks, preparing it for any unexpected Boyle gains and allowing for a final emphasis on Voinovich's positives. The strategy worked and the campaign was able to "stay the course" throughout the race.

The news media played its usual role of nearly no involvement in these types of contests. Political communication scholars have widely documented what is known as "horse race journalism," or the focus of campaign news reporting on who is ahead, who is behind, and the strategies of a campaign. A corollary to this concept is that when there is no "horse race," news media are absent. While it would be unfair to suggest that this race was not covered by the media, the typical newspaper reader or television watcher would had to have paid close attention to gain much information about these candidates, their positions, or even the importance of a U.S. Senate race to Ohio voters. Other, more interesting political contests and other news events overshadowed a campaign in which voters seemingly showed little interest. Some might argue, however, that this race, like many others, received the attention it deserved.

In observing this "typical" frontrunner-challenger race, critics of the American electoral system might suggest that elections like the Boyle-Voinovich contest are nearly predetermined and demonstrate the futility of the process, especially since races like these are common. For others, however, the glass may be half full. This contest produced two excellent candidates, either of whom, as most editorials pointed out, would likely be a good senator. The citizens of Ohio, while not choosing Boyle, saw a candidate who likely will be on the ballot again, and "rewarded" Voinovich, a public servant who had done a good job. In addition, the contest allowed for public scrutiny of both candidates and their policy positions. For Ohio in 1998, this especially meant a forum to continue a debate on education and the role of money in political campaigns.

For these candidates, future candidates, and students of the campaign process, this race supported much of what is known about running for office. The first lesson is that even if you do everything right, although both campaigns could be criticized for certain errors, victory is not guaranteed. Many times external factors in a campaign can have more influence on the outcome than any specific activities by the campaign during the campaign season. Second, there are certain roles that candidates play in campaigns like these. The challenger tries to find a way to make it a close contest, while the frontrunner works to keep his or her lead. While the specific issues may vary, the timing of events and advertising can change the focus of the campaign. The key for the challenger is to put together the right combination of these two factors that shave the frontrunner's lead, and for the frontrunner to make sure the challenger's combination doesn't work. In this case, the right challenger combination either wasn't available or wasn't found. But, in all races, it is this dance to find the right combination that makes elections interesting.

NOTES

The concept of "frontrunner" and "challenger" as well as much of the information on the 1994 and 1996 Senate races are drawn from Marilyn Roberts and Stephen Brooks, "Position, Timing and Attack in Winning Campaign Communication Strategies" (paper presented at the annual meeting of the American Political Science Association, San Francisco, August 29–September 1, 1996). This chapter has benefited from comments and research by Rocky Alderman and Rick Farmer.

1. For a more thorough investigation, see Paul Herrnson, *Congressional Elections: Campaigning at Home and in Washington* (Washington, DC: Congressional Quarterly, 1995); Daniel Shea, "The Resurgent Voter: Incumbent Defeat in the 1994 Midterm Election," (paper presented at the annual meeting of the Western Political Science Association, 1995); Jonathan Krasno, *Challengers, Competition, and Reelection: Comparing Senate and House Elections* (New Haven, CT: Yale University Press, 1994).

2. Richard Fenno, *Home Style: House Members in Their Districts* (Boston: Little, Brown, 1978).

3. David Epstein and Peter Zemsky, "Money Talks: Deterring Quality Challengers in Congressional Elections," *American Political Science Review* 89 (1995): 295–308; Herrnson, *Congressional Elections.*

4. Daniel Shea and Stephen Brooks, "How to Topple an Incumbent: Advice from Experts Who've Done It," *Campaigns and Elections* 16 (June): 21–25.

5. Judith Trent and Robert V. Friedenberg, *Political Campaign Communication,* 3rd ed. (Westport, CT: Praeger, 1995).

6. Ann Beaudry and Bob Schaffer, *Winning Local and State Elections* (New York: Free Press, 1986); Loren Belker, *Organizing for Political Victory* (Chicago: Nelson-Hall, 1982).

7. For more information on the frontrunner's advantage in fundraising, see Frank J. Sorauf, *Inside Campaign Finance: Myths and Reality* (New Haven, CT: Yale University Press, 1992).

8. Trent and Friendenberg, *Political Campaign Communication*.

9. Trent and Friendenberg, *Political Campaign Communication;* Shea and Brooks, "How to Topple an Incumbent."

10. A good description of Ohio political history can be found in John H. Fenton, "Issueless Politics in Ohio," in *Government and Politics in Ohio,* ed. Carl Lieberman (Lanham, MD: University Press of America, 1984).

11. Judith Barra Austin, "Glenn Struggling but Still Leading in Ohio," Gannett News Service, October 16, 1992.

12. Katherine Rizzo, "Boyle Campaign Continues to Trail in the Money Chase," *Akron Beacon Journal,* October 15, 1998.

13. James Hannah, "Voinovich, Boyle Joust Over Education, Environment," *Akron Beacon Journal,* October 15, 1998.

14. Hannah, "Voinovich, Boyle Joust Over Education, Environment."

15. James C. Benton, "Candidates Answer Public's Questions," *Akron Beacon Journal,* October 16, 1998.

16. Edie N. Goldenberg and Michael W. Traugott, *Campaigning for Congress* (Washington, DC: Congressional Quarterly, 1984); Daniel M. Shea, *Campaign Craft* (Westport, CT: Praeger, 1996).

17. John Affleck, "Boyle Hit by Bad Breaks Late in Ohio Senate Campaign," Associated Press, October 15, 1998.

18. John Leavitt, "Glenn Refuses to Endorse Boyle," *USA Today,* October 2, 1998.

19. Gina Garramone and S. J. Smith, "Reactions to Political Advertising: Clarifying Sponsor Effects," *Journalism Quarterly* 61 (1984): 771–775; Ronald Paul Hill, "An Exploration of Voter Responses to Political Advertising," *Journal of Advertising* 18 (1989): 14–22.

20. Trent and Friedenberg, *Political Campaign Communication,* 285.

21. Shea and Brooks, "How to Topple an Incumbent," 23.

22. Campaigns and Elections, "The Classics of Political Television Advertising," video, June 1986.

23. Darrel Rowland, "Voinovich Too Busy Being A Fund-raiser, Boyle Charges," *Columbus Dispatch,* October 24, 1998.

24. Associated Press, "Boyle Says Voinovich Should Return Huffy Contributions," *Akron Beacon Journal,* October 6, 1998.

25. Joe Hallett, "Sights Set on the Senate," *Cleveland Plain Dealer,* September 27, 1998.

26. Shea and Brooks, "How to Topple an Incumbent," 25.

27. Channel 3 News, WKYC-TV, Cleveland, Ohio, October 29, 1998.

Contested Seats

12

Schumer Defeats D'Amato
in New York's
Senate Race

Dena Levy
Charles Tien

Pundits, pollsters, scholars, and other experts expected the 1998 congressional elections to solidify the Republican majority in Congress. The voters were supposed to express their disapproval of President Bill Clinton's behavior by voting against Democrats in U.S. House and Senate elections. Ironically, 1998 turned out to be the first time since 1934 that the president's party picked up seats in a midterm election in the House of Representatives. In the Senate, the Republicans dreamed of picking up five seats to have a filibuster-proof majority of 60 votes, as mandated by Senate rules. This did not occur; Democrats held off Republican gains and maintained their 45 seats. The New York Senate race exemplified the surprising national outcome. Democratic challenger Charles Schumer soundly defeated three-term incumbent Republican Alfonse D'Amato by nine percentage points (54 percent to 45 percent). In this chapter, we use the quality challenger literature to frame our analysis of the race and hypothesize that Schumer won primarily because the conditions necessary to defeat an incumbent senator were present in 1998 in New York.

Gary Jacobson sums up what it takes to defeat an incumbent: a strong challenger, a good reason to vote against the incumbent, and money to acquaint the voters with both.[1] These three criteria were all present in New York in 1998. One key to Schumer's success lies in his status as a quality challenger. Schumer was an 18-year House incumbent with a large campaign war chest. He raised more than $13 million, which gave him the ability to get his message out to the voters. The three-term incumbent senator he was running against was vulnerable. D'Amato was a Republican in a traditionally Democratic state who barely defeated an underfunded challenger in his previous race. Many believed that D'Amato's time was up. Democratic primary challenger Mark Green expressed this view when he talked about D'Amato early in the election year: "Even a cat only has nine lives—and he's in his eleventh."[2] Before developing our quality challenger argument, we first provide a brief introduction to the state of New York, the candidates, and summarize the Democratic primary and general election.

NEW YORK STATE

In New York, the division between upstate and downstate (New York City) cannot be overstated. The political culture of the regions differs considerably. Upstate New York is primarily rural, traditionally votes Republican, is the location of many major corporations, including Xerox, Kodak, and Corning, and is largely homogenous ethnically and racially. In comparison, New York City tends to vote Democratic, is the financial capital of the world, and is more heterogeneous ethnically and racially. The upstate-downstate split was institutionalized in the 1890s after Brooklyn, Queens, Staten Island, and the rest of the Bronx joined current Manhattan and parts of the Bronx to increase the size of New York City. This doubled the population of New York City and heightened upstate fears of being overpowered politically and economically.[3]

Historically, upstaters have seen Democrats as defenders of New York City, and New York City residents have considered Republicans to be the party of upstate interests.[4] Contributing to the current upstate-downstate split is the issue of race and ethnicity. New York City is home for most of the state's African American, Hispanic/Latino, Asian, and Jewish populations. The 1990 census data highlight the racial and economic differences between upstate and downstate New York.[5] In 1990, 72 percent of the state's black population and 81 percent of the state's Hispanic/Latino population lived in New York City. The socioeconomic status for minorities is, on the whole, much lower than it is for whites. For example, in 1988, 38 percent of blacks and 51 percent of Hispanics did not finish high school compared to 22 percent of whites. The unemployment rate in 1991 was 11.5 percent for blacks, 10.4 percent for Latinos, and 6.5 percent for whites. These differences in socioeconomic conditions lead to different policy preferences and different partisan affiliations between upstate and downstate New Yorkers.

In 1998, the traditional upstate-downstate differences persisted. Just as in most other years, the Democratic candidate won the downstate vote in 1998. The margin of victory in 1998, however, was significantly greater than in previous years. Schumer, the Democratic candidate, didn't just win New York City, he won by a large margin. Schumer's 75 percent of the vote in the city was at least ten points higher than previous D'Amato opponents. A key to Schumer's success was winning the large cities by large margins, most notably New York City. Schumer won in only 18 percent of the state's 62 counties, but defeated D'Amato by 219,531 votes in Manhattan, by 128,630 votes in Queens, by 116,412 in the Bronx, and by 162,137 in Brooklyn (with 88 percent of precincts reporting). Schumer's average margin of victory was greater than 65,000 votes in the counties where he was the winner. By contrast, D'Amato's average margin of victory was approximately 6,000 votes in the counties where he won (82 percent of the 62 counties).

To characterize Schumer's victory as merely a downstate victory, however, is incomplete. Schumer not only won big downstate, but he carried upstate New York as well with 54 percent of the two-party vote. Schumer outdistanced all previous Democratic opponents of D'Amato's in upstate New York by at least 10 points. The previous best by a D'Amato opponent in upstate New York was in 1992 when Robert Abrams won 44 percent of the vote in a vastly underfunded campaign. Therefore, Schumer's victory was a complete one.

ALFONSE D'AMATO

New York's junior senator Alfonse Marcello D'Amato entered the Senate in 1980. D'Amato's political career, however, dates back to the 1960s. He served as supervisor of Hempstead (population approximately 700,000) from 1971 to 1977 and vice-chair of the Nassau County Board of Supervisors from 1977 to 1980. To the surprise of most political observers, he decisively defeated Senator Jacob Javits in the 1980 primary by successfully portraying Javits as old (76), liberal, and ill. Benefiting from the anti-liberal mood of the time, he narrowly defeated liberal Representative Elizabeth Holtzman by 45 percent to 44 percent and rode President Ronald Reagan's coattails into the Senate.

D'Amato's voting record shows that he has been one of the state's most conservative senators in the last 50 years. A front-page *New York Times* article said:

> He staunchly opposes abortion and gun control, regularly advocates tougher penalties for criminals and has rarely met a tax cut he did not like. He endorsed major portions of Newt Gingrich's Contract with America in 1995 and hailed the Republican takeover of Congress as a stinging repudiation of liberalism. And he continues to receive among the highest ratings in the Northeast from conservative groups like the Christian Coalition.[6]

The Conservative and the Right to Life parties have endorsed D'Amato in each of his Senate races. As a further illustration of his conservatism, D'Amato's ratings from 1991 to 1996 from the Americans for Democratic Action (ADA) have ranged from a low of 15 to a high of 35, averaging 23.3.[7]

The traditionally liberal New York voters, however, were largely unaware of his conservative views. In a *New York Times/CBS News* survey in October 1998, only 39 percent of respondents considered him to be conservative.[8] Some analysts believed that many voters were unaware of his conservative views because he strategically shifted toward the liberal positions during reelection years. For example, in 1996 he received the lowest rating possible from the

League of Conservation Voters (LCV) as he consistently voted against bills supported by environmentalists. In 1997, his rating shot up to 29 percent as D'Amato started backing environmental legislation such as a proposal to increase federal air quality standards.[9] D'Amato also led efforts to restore food stamp benefits after voting for the welfare reform bill in 1996.[10] D'Amato also was silent on the relationship between President Clinton, who was popular in New York, and Monica Lewinsky. This was surprising given that D'Amato headed the Senate investigation into Whitewater in 1995.

D'Amato was reelected twice and was known as a tenacious supporter of New York interests in the Senate. He recently prevented large reductions in mass transit spending, which is vital to New York. He was able to steer $900 million toward breast cancer research, which is important to his constituents in Long Island where there is an unusually high incidence of breast cancer. During his 18 years in the Senate, D'Amato became known as the go-to guy for New York. He was mockingly called "Senator Pothole," which he quickly adopted as a proud nickname. D'Amato also strategically picked high-profile noncontroversial issues on which to work. D'Amato focused on constituent demands and interests, including AIDS funding, the death penalty for drug dealers, and protection for Wall Street.[11]

D'Amato has also been under suspicion for ethics violations. D'Amato suffers from a reputation of being motivated by self-interest. His ". . . personal manner does not especially inspire confidence or arouse enthusiasm. So he stays in favor by doing favors."[12] He sometimes gets himself into trouble by doing the wrong favors for the wrong people. In particular, he was reprimanded by the Senate Ethics Committee in 1991 for allowing his brother the use of his office while representing a defense contractor. Two years later, D'Amato's brother was convicted of mail fraud for accepting a payment while lobbying D'Amato.[13]

D'Amato's first reelection campaign in 1986 proved little challenge for him. He easily defeated challenger Mark Green, outspending him by almost eight to one. D'Amato was not nearly so sanguine in 1992, when he eked out a victory of 49 percent to 48 percent against challenger Robert Abrams. By all accounts, the 1992 race was an ugly one. Many believe that D'Amato was successful in the general election due to a split within the Democratic party that resulted from their bitterly fought primary. In the Democratic primary, front-runner Geraldine Ferraro faced Elizabeth Holtzman and Attorney General Abrams. Holtzman attacked Ferraro for failing to remove a pornography distributor from a building owned by Ferraro and her husband and accused Ferraro of having mob connections. Holtzman's strategy backfired, leaving Abrams the victor of the primary, winning 37 percent to Ferraro's 36 percent with Holtzman trailing with 12 percent and Al Sharpton receiving 14 percent. The general election was surprisingly close, particularly given that D'Amato was considerably better financed than Abrams ($11.5 million compared to almost $6.5 million). Abrams, already suffering from a difficult primary, hurt himself by calling D'Amato a "fascist" in Binghamton. He further compounded the mistake by refusing to apologize for several days. D'Amato was also able to take advantage of the finding that Abrams was late paying taxes on a country home.[14] The combination of these events provided D'Amato a slight edge and he went on to his slim victory.

CHARLES SCHUMER

Chuck Ellis Schumer has spent his entire adult life in politics. After graduating from Harvard Law School, he was elected to the New York Assembly in 1974 at the age of 23. In 1980, he entered the House as a representative from Brooklyn. Schumer quickly built up a sizable campaign war chest and has faced relatively little challenge during his career in the House. This provided him the opportunity to focus on policy. Schumer prided himself on being an able legislator. He used his House Banking Committee assignment to help put together the 1989 Savings and Loan bailout. Schumer also made the most of his House Judiciary Committee assignment, and as the eventual chair of its Subcommittee on Crime came up with the key compromise on farm laborers in the Immigration Reform Act of 1986 and again in 1990 on employment-sponsored immigration.[15] Other areas of Schumer's legislative interest were funding for tuberculosis control, auto theft law, and violence against women. Schumer, unlike many Democrats, supported the death penalty, but was also a primary supporter of the Brady Bill that would regulate the purchase of guns. Schumer long held statewide ambitions and was considered a likely candidate to run for governor. However, acting as a strategic politician, Schumer recognized Pataki's strong approval ratings and decided instead to run for the Senate against incumbent Al D'Amato. By most accounts, Schumer was the highest quality challenger faced by D'Amato. Among other things, Schumer entered the Democratic primary with a substantial war chest of more than $5 million.[16]

Throughout Schumer's tenure in the House, he never lost touch with his constituents in the Ninth District of Brooklyn. He grew up in Brooklyn and his wife and children continued to live there while he served in the House. Schumer would return home when the House was out of session, and in Washington he shared a house with three other colleagues.

Schumer's ADA ratings are considerably higher than those of D'Amato's. He describes himself as a moderate Democrat, and has drifted towards the political center during his career. While most observers cited Al D'Amato as being the pragmatist in this race, Chuck Schumer gradually positioned himself to appeal to the center of the political spectrum. He promoted himself as being tough on crime and had the 1994 crime bill, which added police officers to the streets and increased the number of federal crimes punishable by death, behind him to support his claim. He has also worked to reduce waste and fraud in the food stamp program to appeal to a wider spectrum of voters. In 1996, Schumer angered many liberals by voting for the Defense of Marriage Act, which defined marriage in federal law as a legal union of one man and one woman, no matter what states may say.

THE PRIMARY

Although D'Amato ran unopposed in the Republican primary, Schumer's nomination was not a foregone conclusion. Nevertheless, the 1998 Democratic primary was not altogether eventful, particularly in comparison to the bloodbath of 1992, where the party was so divided that the eventual nominee was never able to fully recover during the general election. Indeed, the candidates themselves went to great lengths to avoid a repeat of 1992. Three candidates participated in the primary—Geraldine Ferraro, Public Advocate Mark Green, and Schumer. Both Green and Ferraro publicly stated that they would support the eventual nominee during the general election. Schumer alone made no such promise. Instead, his campaign simply insisted that Schumer would win the primary.[17] In fact, Schumer's first ads attacked D'Amato rather than his primary opponents and argued that he would be the strongest challenger against D'Amato in the general election.[18]

Ferraro clearly had the early edge in terms of name recognition, and early polls showed her 30 to 35 points ahead of Green and Schumer. As a three-term representative from Queens and then vice presidential candidate in 1984, Ferraro was a household name with celebrity status. She ran for the Senate in 1992 and was narrowly defeated in the primary by Abrams. However, in 1998 Schumer had the early lead in raising money. He entered the race with $8 million compared to Green's $1.4 million. Ferraro, as host of CNN's *Crossfire,* was prohibited from raising money, thereby putting her at a substantial disadvantage from which she never recovered. Ferraro compounded her problems when she got into an on-air fight with a television host during an interview. When asked why she did not want to participate in televised debates, Ferraro accused the television host both during the interview and later of supporting fellow candidate Green.[19] Green was the most aggressive campaigner at the beginning of the primary. Although he did not personally attack Ferraro, like Holtzman did in 1992, he did charge her of being "silent on the issues."[20] Likewise, Green attacked Schumer as the "big-money political insider."[21]

Despite Ferraro's name recognition and Green's aggressiveness on the campaign trail, Schumer won the primary with 51 percent of the vote, Ferraro followed with 26 percent, and Green with 19 percent. Many cite Ferraro's lack of money as the principal cause of her loss; Ferraro's ads only started airing August 31, forcing her to rely almost exclusively on her name recognition.[22] Green, strapped for money in comparison to Schumer, was also unable to air television ads prior to the end of August.[23] Schumer was able to run television ads almost continuously starting in January 1998 and he spent the lion's share of the $4.5 million spent on television ads during the primary.[24]

GENERAL ELECTION

Both candidates had enough money to take their messages to the voters from the beginning of the campaign to the end, and the messages were overwhelmingly negative. The New York race quickly became one of the ugliest ever seen in the state. Rather than focusing on substantive issues, D'Amato and Schumer waged a campaign of attacks and insults. The day after the primary, D'Amato started running ads calling Schumer too liberal for New York, while Schumer's ads countered by portraying D'Amato as a liar who had served New York for too long.

In the general election, D'Amato chose to employ the same strategy that he so successfully used against his opponents in his earlier elections. To that end, he attempted to portray Schumer as a "tax and spend" liberal. D'Amato's initial strategy was evident in his early campaign ads. Indeed, on the first day of the general election campaign, D'Amato released a television ad that claimed: "Chuck Schumer's a New York City liberal, and he proves it every day."[25]

Playing to his base upstate supporters, D'Amato also tried to portray Schumer early on as interested only in New York City. D'Amato intentionally played up the upstate-downstate division in order to suggest that Schumer would continue to favor downstate interests if elected to the Senate. In one television ad, D'Amato showed New York City Democrats turning into sharks as they swam upstate. In perhaps one of the more humorous ads of the election, D'Amato criticized Schumer for voting against providing more than $25 million of relief for upstate New York after a severe January 1998 ice storm. The ad ended with a picture of camels being herded across frozen tundra, and a voiceover telling viewers, "Schumer votes for Foreign Aid for countries like Mongolia, but votes against upstate New York. If you live in Mongolia, Schumer's your man. If you live in New York, Al D'Amato's there for you."

D'Amato's early attempts to portray Schumer as a liberal who was out of touch with the state did not damage Schumer's campaign as anticipated. This can be explained both by the fact that Schumer simply is not that ideologically distant from the state, and that the word "liberal" simply does not resonate in the same way that it did in past elections, especially in New York, which was among Clinton's best states in 1992 and 1996. Once it became obvious that the "liberal" strategy was not working as successfully as in the past, D'Amato began a relentless campaign of faulting Schumer for missing 110 votes during 1998. At a news conference in Rochester, D'Amato said: "We've got a guy they should dub 'The Phantom.' As a matter of fact, not only does he have the worst attendance record of all the Congressmen in this state, he has the worst record as it relates to his committee assignments. He missed 99 percent of his Banking Committee votes. He made one out of 103. Now that's incredible."[26]

Schumer responded quickly to many of D'Amato's attacks during the campaign. He had enough funding to respond to each attack with television ads, which ensured that his responses would reach the voters. Schumer's response to the Mongolian ad was to point out that D'Amato also voted 11 times to provide funding for Mongolia.[27] The response suggested that D'Amato was being hypocritical and dishonest for criticizing Schumer for voting for foreign aid. When D'Amato scrounged up an 18-year-old federal grand jury investigation into Schumer's use of personal staff from his office in the state assembly on his first congressional campaign, Schumer was quick to fire back. He called D'Amato the "most investigated Senator in New York history."[28] Schumer also responded effectively, if not almost too late, to D'Amato's charges that Schumer was avoiding his duty as a member of Congress by missing so many votes. D'Amato was relentless in his attacks on Schumer for missing many votes while campaigning for the Senate. The attack was so effective that Schumer was forced to stay in Washington for a few votes when President Clinton was in New York campaigning for him. Schumer attended the campaign event by video feed, but missed an opportunity to be seen side-by-side with the president, who was extremely popular in New York.

Some observers began to believe that D'Amato had once again found the key to permanently damaging his opponent. However, D'Amato was ultimately hoisted by his own petard. Schumer's aides learned from *The Village Voice* that D'Amato was also guilty of missing votes (more than 1,000 votes according to *Newsday*) in the Nassau County Board of Supervisors and the Hempstead Town Board when he first ran for the Senate in 1980. "Mr. D'Amato's senior aides were caught completely off guard by the disclosure, and other Republicans expressed astonishment that Mr. D'Amato could have made such a fundamental mistake."[29] Eight days before the election, D'Amato was defending himself against the same accusation that he had tirelessly made about Schumer. Again, D'Amato looked hypocritical and dishonest, exactly how Schumer was portraying him throughout the campaign.

Schumer not only was able to respond effectively to many of D'Amato's attacks, but also often gave as well as he got. Schumer accused D'Amato as being beholden to large corporations and other interest groups, criticizing D'Amato for "lining his pockets" with $390,000 in speaking fees during the 1980s (when accepting honoraria was customary among members of Congress). Schumer noted that he refused to accept any honoraria during his career in the House. Schumer also marked the six-year anniversary of D'Amato's claim that he would not run again if he won in 1992 by showing a giant reproduction of a 1992 *Daily News* headline that read "D'Amato Stunner: My Last Run" in campaign stops around the state.[30] D'Amato's broken promise fit perfectly with Schumer's constant portrayal of D'Amato as dishonest and untrustworthy.

The underlying theme repeated throughout Schumer's campaign ads was "D'Amato—Too many lies for too long." Schumer and his aides decided on this theme once he was confident of winning the primary. Although there was some concern that this approach could backfire since it accused the incumbent senator of being a liar, it "played directly to what the Schumer campaign had concluded were two of Mr. D'Amato's biggest liabilities: voters didn't trust him and thought he had been in office too long."[31] The clear advantage of this theme was that it served as a framework for the entire campaign. It did not hurt when D'Amato seemed to continually act during the campaign in ways that made the "liar" label seem appropriate.

In particular, when D'Amato used a Yiddish vulgarism "putzhead" to describe Schumer and made fun of Representative Jerrold Nadler's (D-NY) weight in a private meeting with supporters, Schumer's campaign manager responded immediately by alerting reporters who were about to attend a D'Amato press conference on breast cancer of the incident. "Mr. D'Amato never knew what hit him. As his aides watched in helpless disbelief, the question suggested by Mr. Schumer's aides instantly eclipsed an appearance intended to highlight Mr. D'Amato's efforts to win Federal funds for breast cancer research and to attack Representative Schumer for missing votes in Congress."[32] Schumer's camp did not stop with hijacking D'Amato's press conference. His campaign went on to place a television ad showing D'Amato's initial denials and a voiceover that said: "New Yorkers can't trust Al D'Amato. Eighteen years is too long." The ad ended with the now familiar tag of "D'Amato—Too many lies for too long."

D'Amato rejected any form of grassroots campaigning, relying solely on a media blitz largely devoid of substantive content. D'Amato's campaign had set aside less than 1 percent ($200,000 out of the more than $20 million) of his budget for getting out the vote.[33] Schumer also relied extensively on using the media to garner support for his candidacy. The television advertising race between D'Amato and Schumer, highlighted above, can largely be characterized as one candidate slinging mud and the other responding with more mud. Even the two debates that occurred late in the campaign can be characterized as mudslinging. Each candidate often tried to drown out the other using the same attacks featured in their television ads. Overall, there was little substance throughout the general election. However, it is not surprising that so much of the campaign avoided discussion of policy issues. After all, in a candidate-centered era, focusing on the weaknesses of the candidates has become commonplace. When a reporter challenged D'Amato about his attacks on Schumer's attendance record, D'Amato fired back, "You mean to tell me I should not point out his missed votes, his poor votes, his votes that hurt people? That's what a campaign is about."[34]

Surprisingly, D'Amato failed to end his campaign on a positive note. Generally, television advertising follows a predictable formula. Candidates begin by identifying themselves and providing voters with an autobiography of their accomplishments. This is particularly true of incumbents who can advertise how they diligently worked on behalf of their constituents. The middle segment of a campaign shifts to using negative advertising against one's opponent. However, toward the end of the campaigning period, candidates usually return to focusing on themselves, leaving the voters with a positive message. D'Amato largely failed to end his campaign on a positive note. Former New York Mayor Edward Koch was surprised by the extent to which D'Amato relied on negative campaigning: "There is nothing wrong with negative campaigns, but they must (a) be true and (b) be a minor part of a campaign that is overwhelmingly positive about the candidate himself. Here it was all negative. I thought that it was a mistake."[35] Further surprising observers, D'Amato rarely appeared in his own advertisements, missing another opportunity to portray himself in a positive light.[36]

Campaign Finance

The New York Senate race was the most expensive Senate campaign ever that did not involve personal money. The two candidates combined spent more than $33 million, all of which came from donors. Although Schumer was considerably better financed than his predecessors running in 1986 and 1992, D'Amato still had a monetary advantage. D'Amato raised more than $20 million, which set a record in fundraising for an incumbent senator. Schumer, however, was by no means a fundraising slouch. He raised more money than any other Senate challenger ever except Oliver North (running for a Senate seat in Virginia in 1994), who raised more than $20 million. Schumer spent more than $13 million, which guaranteed that he was never off the air.

Political Action Committee (PAC) contributions followed the expected pattern of giving the greater portion of funds to the incumbent. Comparing the top five contributors to both campaigns further shows D'Amato's fundraising advantage. Not surprisingly, two of the five (Goldman, Sachs and Company and Bear Stearns and Company) gave money to both candidates. Contributors will frequently hedge their bets this way. However, the amounts differed considerably, with D'Amato getting the lion's share. Goldman, Sachs was Schumer's number one contributor with $41,000. By contrast, they were D'Amato's third biggest givers with $103,800. America Bank, N.A. (MBNA) gave the largest contribution to D'Amato ($128,670). Bear Stearns was second in contributions to both candidates—$35,850 to Schumer and $117,751 to D'Amato.[37] Perhaps most notable is the fact that D'Amato's fifth largest contributor gave more money than Schumer's largest contributor ($47,850 versus $41,000).

The political parties also participated in the Senate election. The Democrats put considerable effort into helping Schumer win, sending the heavy-hitters to campaign with him. First Lady Hillary Clinton appeared with Schumer four times, Vice President Al Gore stumped in New York twice, and President Clinton also campaigned with Schumer on two separate occasions.[38] For the White House, helping Schumer defeat D'Amato was personal, stemming from the period when D'Amato served as chair of the Senate Whitewater hearings in 1995 and 1996. "D'Amato said he wanted 'every child in America to know how to spell subpoena.' That kind of talk helped make this race a presidential grudge match."[39] President Clinton helped Schumer raise $1.2 million for the campaign, and the First Lady helped raise an additional $800,000.[40] Clinton also participated in a telephone conference call with party officials in all of the state's counties, urging them to help get out the vote.[41]

The Republican party helped D'Amato primarily with money. The Republicans considerably outspent the Democratic party in television ads—$1.8 million versus almost $240,000.[42] D'Amato also benefited from the presence of other well-known New York politicians, particularly Governor George Pataki, New York Mayor Rudolph W. Giuliani, former representative and vice presidential candidate Jack Kemp, and Koch.

Senate candidates typically spend more money on advertising than do House candidates. In the House, media markets are less likely to match the geographic boundaries of the district. Thus, representatives from New York City who run television ads will appeal to not only their own but also neighboring constituencies. As a result, these candidates will not get the most out of their resources with television ads. The viewers have to filter through a lot of noise.[43] Thus, House candidates are more reluctant to use much television in their campaigns. Senate candidates, however, almost always have a much larger geographic constituency, which makes it far more efficient to rely on television advertising. This is particularly true for challengers who need to increase their name recognition across the state.[44] On average, Senate candidates can expect to spend around 45 percent of their budgets on political advertising.[45] It has been estimated that Schumer and D'Amato and their respective parties spent at least $15.5 million on television ads. This number increases to $25.5 million, or $6 for every vote, when including all forms of media.[46] According to Competitive Media Reporting, 26,000 ads were run during the New York Senate election, 28 percent alone in the New York City media market.[47]

Campaign Consultants

One of the surprising elements of D'Amato's campaign was the number of judgment errors that he made. This can partly be explained by his choice of campaign consultants. D'Amato continued to rely on the same "brain trust" he had at his side for much of his political career, but many of them were involved in other campaigns and unable to devote their full attention to D'Amato's race. Zenia Mucha ran Governor Pataki's campaign while Arthur J. Finkelstein was dividing his time and loyalty between D'Amato and Senator Lauch Faircloth (R–NC).[48] Although Mucha did shift her focus back to D'Amato toward the end of the campaign, it was already too late.

Bickering among D'Amato's advisers and state Republican officials did not help the situation. Republican leaders were concerned that Finkelstein opted to put too much money into television advertising, and not enough into traditional getting-out-the-vote paraphernalia such as bumper stickers and lawn signs.[49] In contrast, Schumer's team (campaign manager Josh Isay and media consultant Hank Morris) was focused exclusively on Schumer. Isay, Morris, and Schumer were obsessively attentive to all aspects of the campaign and acted quickly whenever they saw D'Amato make a mistake. The senator's "putzhead" comment and his foreign aid vote are just two examples.

Any time a challenger soundly defeats a three-term incumbent, it is surprising. Although D'Amato may have been perceived as vulnerable, he was the incumbent and possessed all the advantages associated with being an incumbent (such as name recognition, more contributions, a strong record of constituent services, and media coverage). On average, incumbents are more likely to win than challengers. However, not all challengers are created equally, and some are more likely to fare better than others. This was certainly the case for Schumer when facing D'Amato in the 1998 election.

Thus far in this chapter we have focused our attention on describing and analyzing the election outcome. A *New York Times* headline after the election went far in explaining why challenger Schumer successfully defeated incumbent Al D'Amato: "Schumer Wins Election Using D'Amato's Tactics."[50] In fact, when the Schumer campaign discovered that swing voters admired D'Amato's abrasive style, they set out to copy it. Many voters said that the type of vehicle D'Amato resembled most was a bulldozer, and Schumer set out to be exactly that—a bulldozer.[51] From political scientists' perspective, however, we argue that the election can be analyzed in terms of the quality challenger literature. Schumer was simply the best opponent that D'Amato had faced in his political career.

QUALITY CHALLENGER

One of the few truisms in politics is that incumbents are difficult to beat. That is particularly the case for the House, but also holds true for the Senate. Incumbents have many advantages that are difficult for challengers to overcome: name recognition, the franking privilege, and constituent service, to name but a few. Senate elections tend to be more competitive than House elections, although the strength of incumbency is wide-ranging. From 1946 to 1996, the reelection rate for Senate incumbents ranged from 55 percent to 97 percent. By contrast, House reelection rates are more consistent for incumbents. From 1950 to 1990, House incumbents were reelected at rates between 79 percent and 98 percent.[52]

One explanation for why representatives tend to be more secure than senators is that Senate elections are on average more costly than House elections. In 1996, individuals running for the Senate spent an average of $3.55 million on their campaigns.[53] The average House race costs around $1 million. According to Jacobson, it " . . . boils down to this: Regardless of their potential, if challengers cannot raise lots of money they can forget about winning."[54]

Related to these factors is the quality of the challenger, which is fundamental to defeating an incumbent. A key element to explaining why Senate elections are more competitive than House elections is that individuals running for the Senate tend to be of higher quality.[55] The pool from which to draw potential Senate candidates is usually larger than is the pool for House candidates. Moreover, senators are higher-profile politicians than House members. The media thus tend to pay more attention to Senate races, resulting in both more and free publicity for challengers. Incumbent senators are also hindered by the difficulty of developing "home styles" that are as effective as those of incumbent representatives, given the differences in their constituency size.[56]

Most scholars measure challenger quality with a simple dichotomous variable to distinguish political amateurs from those who have held a political office. Others, recognizing that some previous political experiences are more beneficial than others, finesse this measure by starting with a six-point scale that captures the range of political offices from "no experience" to "governors."[57] They then multiply that score by the proportion of the state that is covered by the office held. Thus, a governor would receive a score of 600; six for the highest political office multiplied by 100 indicating that the office covers the entire state.

Peverill Squire and Eric Smith add a second component to the concept of challenger quality—campaign skills. This concept captures the individual characteristics of each candidate that either aid or detract from the campaign. Thus, individuals who are considered to be media savvy, attractive, and eloquent will fare better in a campaign than those who are not.[58] This variable is coded "1" for those who are considered to have exemplary campaign skills, "-1" for those without such skills, and "0" for mixed reviews. This two-part measure of challenger quality identifies important elements of a successful challenger. It also provides us a useful framework for analyzing why Schumer was successful in ousting D'Amato.

Schumer, as an incumbent representative, would be categorized as a "5" on the challenger quality measure and by all accounts a "1" on the campaign skills measure. From the very beginning of the race, commentators acknowledged that Schumer was uniquely skilled and savvy about presenting himself to the voters. Indeed, as early as the Democratic primary, Schumer conducted a campaign ". . . that even his rivals described as largely flawless: From the start, he avoided making attacks on his opponents and spoke about his record in Congress."[59] During the general election, Schumer was focused and tireless. In Schumer, Democrats had "an exuberant campaigner with stamina to burn. They got a brawler willing to fight fire with fire, mud with mud. And they got someone whose ambition and skill at self-promotion easily rivaled—and quite possibly surpassed—Mr. D'Amato's."[60] Schumer clearly was D'Amato's highest quality challenger to date. Rating his previous two challengers using the same measure provides one explanation for why D'Amato has been so successful.[61] His first challenger was Green. The Squire/Smith ranking codes Green a "2" for being a locally elected government official. In 1992, D'Amato's challenger was of slightly higher quality. Abrams receives a "3" on the Squire/Smith scale. It is not surprising that the higher the rating received by the challenger, the greater his percentage of the vote.

Quality challengers are able campaigners who already have some political experience and name recognition, can raise the money needed to get their message out to the voters, and therefore get more votes. Other factors, of course, influence the challenger's vote share. Using ordinary least squares regression, Squire examines the challenger's share of the vote and finds that the following variables are significant in explaining challenger vote share: incumbent's primary margin, challenger's party, challenger's quality, challenger's expenditures, and the midterm status of the election.[62] Squire's model estimated that Schumer would win the election, and it helps us see what factors contributed to Schumer's victory. What is noteworthy here is that challenger quality and challenger expenditures have independent effects on the vote share. This means that good candidates must be more than just good fundraisers, and that good campaigners also need money to succeed. If you can raise money but run a bad campaign, you still might lose; and if you are a good campaigner but can't raise enough money to get your message out, you might lose as well. As

Table 12.1 Breaking Down the Vote: Percent Voting for Senate Candidates in 1992 and 1998

	1992		1998	
	D'Amato	**Abrams**	**D'Amato**	**Schumer**
White	55	43	51	48
Black	16	80	13	86
Hispanic	29	68	17	82
Men	56	44	50	49
Women	47	53	40	59
Protestants	49	47	48	51
Catholics	59	38	52	47
Jewish	41	59	23	76
Liberal Republicans	—	—	—	—
Moderate Republicans	75	23	74	26
Conservative Republicans	91	7	87	11
Liberal Democrats	15	85	8	90
Moderate Democrats	31	67	17	83
Conservative Democrats	—	—	—	—
Family's financial situation is:				
Better today	69	30	40	59
Same today	55	43	48	51
Worse today	37	59	49	48

SOURCE: *The New York Times*, November 8, 1998, A42.

we have stressed in this chapter, Schumer was a very good campaigner, and he could raise money among the best of them. A quote from Schumer's House colleague Sam Gejdenson (D–MD) sums up his determination as a campaigner and his tenacity as a fundraiser. Says Gejdenson, Schumer "learned that there were different time zones, and that he could continue making phone calls into the night by working his way west. Chuck has new friends in Hawaii."[63]

THE VOTE

Schumer soundly defeated D'Amato, and his success was not limited to down-state. Table 12.1 compares exit polls from 1992 to 1998, and shows D'Amato's thorough defeat.[64] Not only did D'Amato lose support from the expected groups, including blacks (down 3 percent), Hispanics (down 12 percent), and women (down 7 percent), but also he lost from groups that previously provided him solid support. For example, D'Amato lost four points from conservative Republicans. He also lost ground from self-identified Republican women. Individuals who thought that their family's financial situation was either better or the same overwhelmingly supported Schumer in 1998, although both of these groups were solidly behind D'Amato in 1992. Only those who felt that they were worse off today gave a one-point advantage to D'Amato over Schumer. D'Amato also lost some of the support of white voters, dropping from 55 percent in 1992 to 51 percent in 1998.[65]

D'Amato's decline in support from 1992 to 1998 among women might be partially explained by Schumer's effort to make the former appear defensive about his pro-life position on abortion. In their second debate, Schumer urged D'Amato to "have the decency, the honor and the courage to come clean and say that you are strongly pro-life and you believe in it. And I will say I'm pro-choice and I believe in it. And we'll let the chips fall where they may."[66] The killing of an obstetrician in his own home in a Buffalo suburb during the campaign by a radical anti-abortion protester may also have mobilized pro-choice women more than in other elections.

The scandal involving President Clinton and former White House intern Monica Lewinsky was also a factor in the 1998 midterm elections, especially in New York. Clinton remained extremely popular in New York throughout the election year, and many Democrats may have voted against the Republican D'Amato to express their disapproval of how Republicans in Congress seemed preoccupied with the matter at the expense of substantive issues like Social Security, education, and health care. In 1992, 31 percent of self-identified moderate Democrats reported voting for D'Amato. In 1998, the percent of self-identified moderate Democrats who reported voting for D'Amato dropped to 17 percent. This group comprised 22 percent of all voters in New York in 1998.

The African American vote was also important in 1998. As already mentioned, Clinton is very popular in New York, especially among black voters. Many opinion polls before the election showed that blacks, more than any other group, supported Clinton and felt that Republicans were mistreating him. It is possible that black voters turned out in large numbers to defend the president. Democratic party officials distributed fliers in heavily black neighborhoods that read, "The Republicans want to impeach our president. Say NO and send the Republicans a message." Democratic Representative Charles Rangel from Harlem said: "For black people, this is almost like a Presidential election year."[67] Jesse Jackson also expressed the urgency of the election, using radio spots to get out the Democratic vote. The state Democratic party and labor unions also worked on getting out the vote in heavily black neighborhoods such as Harlem. If the efforts to get out the black vote succeeded, as many believe they did, then the lower overall turnout in New York suggests that it was core Republican supporters who stayed home in 1998 rather than Democrats, giving a clear advantage to Schumer.

The Jewish vote also turned out to be critical to Schumer's success, and the courtship of this group resulted in one of the most embittered moments in the campaign as each candidate attempted to portray himself as the "true friend" of the Jewish voters. D'Amato's use of Holocaust victims to bolster his support among Jewish voters apparently backfired. Few doubt D'Amato's efforts on behalf of his Jewish constituents. D'Amato is largely responsible for the investigation into Swiss bank accounts that contain the proceeds from the Holocaust. However, Schumer has a natural entrée into the Jewish vote and lost family to the Holocaust. He was critical of D'Amato's use of the Holocaust to win votes: "I think it's a shame that Al D'Amato would stoop to using the Holocaust for political purposes. My record on Holocaust, on Jewish issues is second to none. And I think this is just . . . it shows what kind of man he is."[68] Calling Schumer a "putzhead" and initially denying the comment did not help D'Amato's case among Jewish voters either. In the end, only one out of four Jewish voters supported him. In 1992, D'Amato received 41 percent of the Jewish vote.[69]

Perhaps D'Amato's final indignity occurred on election day and is, in many ways, symbolic of a campaign where more went wrong than right. Schumer, breaking with convention, declared victory a full 30 minutes before D'Amato conceded defeat. D'Amato was not being contemptuous of Schumer, in fact he was quite gracious in congratulating the victor. Instead, D'Amato, along with ten others, got stuck in the hotel elevator on his way down to concede defeat. D'Amato later told his supporters, "When they tell you that you should only put six people in an elevator, listen to them. Because we spent 25 minutes trapped between the 44th and 45th floor."[70] National Public Radio's Melissa Block summed it up nicely: "An ironic metaphor for a campaign that seemed to stall as it entered the final stretch."[71]

In the final analysis, Schumer's success rests on the extent to which he was a quality challenger. Important elements of quality challengers are the profile of their previous office, their ability to raise money, and their campaign skills. Schumer had all three qualities in spades. He was an 18-year incumbent member of the House, from where he was able to build a strong legislative record and raise a lot of money for his own reelection efforts. Schumer was able to portray himself as someone who would be able to do as much for the state as D'Amato. He highlighted his legislative accomplishments on the Brady Bill and the assault weapons ban. Indeed, in the exit polls, respondents found no difference between the two candidates in terms of which candidate would get things done for New York.[72]

Perhaps the best example of Schumer's political skill dates back to his initial decision that D'Amato was vulnerable after three terms in office. Schumer recognized that the public generally did not trust D'Amato. This realization formed the basis for Schumer's entire campaign strategy: "Too many lies for too long." Schumer rode this theme throughout his campaign, while D'Amato's actions during the campaign seemed to confirm the claim of dishonesty. D'Amato initially denied the "putzhead" statement; he criticized Schumer for missing votes during the campaign, while he had done the same 18 years earlier; and he pointed out that Schumer voted for foreign aid when he had also done the same. Exit poll results confirmed Schumer's ability to get out his message and make it stick. According to an ABC News poll, 58 percent of respondents agreed that D'Amato had been senator for too long and 31 percent thought that Schumer was honest and trustworthy, while only 18 percent considered D'Amato to be so.[73]

NOTES

1. Gary C. Jacobson, *The Politics of Congressional Elections,* 4th ed. (New York: Longman, 1997).

2. Adam Nagourney and Robert Pear, "At Start of Tough Campaign, D'Amato Runs from G.O.P.," *The New York Times,* March 24, 1998, A.

3. John Kenneth White, "Political Conflict in New York State," in *Governing New York State,* 3rd ed., eds. Jeffrey M. Stonecash, John Kenneth White, and Peter W. Colby (Stony Brook, NY: SUNY Press, 1994).

4. Ibid.

5. Data are presented by Ester R. Fuchs and Phillip Thompson, "Racial Politics in New York State," in *Governing New York State,* 3rd ed., eds. Jeffrey M. Stonecash, John Kenneth White, and Peter W. Colby (Stony Brook, NY: SUNY Press, 1994).

6. James Dao, "A Conservative, D'Amato Learned to Adapt," *The New York Times,* October 23, 1998, A.

7. Interest groups frequently rate representatives based on their voting record on key legislation. The Americans for Democratic Action (ADA), a liberal interest group, employs a 0–100 scale, where 100 indicates perfect support for the ADA and 0 perfect opposition. This rating is frequently used to measure ideology, where the higher the score, the more liberal the member's voting record.

8. Dao, "A Conservative, D'Amato Learned to Adapt."

9. In 1998, D'Amato's rating slipped back down to 13, but was still considerably higher than zero.

10. Nagourney and Pear, "At Start of Tough Campaign."

11. Michael Barone and Grant Ujifusa, *The Almanac of American Politics* (Washington, DC: National Journal, 1993).

12. Ibid., 862.

13. Ibid.

14. Ibid.

15. Ibid.

16. Karen Foerstel, "N.Y. Democrats Try to Avoid Repeat of 1992 Collapse as Rivals Keep Heat on Ferraro," *Congressional Quarterly Weekly Report,* 1998, 2335–2336.

17. Ibid.

18. Adam Nagourney, "Schumer Opens His Ad War in Fight for D'Amato's Seat," *The New York Times,* January, 14, 1998, B.

19. Karen Foerstel, "N.Y. Democrats Try To Avoid Repeat," 2335.

20. Ibid.

21. Ibid.

22. Ibid.

23. Ibid.

24. Rita Ciolli, "TV Ads Made New York Races Costliest," *Newsday,* 1998, A23

25. Adam Nagourney, "Using 'Liberal' as Epithet May Fail D'Amato This Time," *The New York Times,* 1998.

26. "In Their Own Words," *The New York Times,* October 18, 1998.

27. The money was part of the Foreign Aid bill.

28. David Halbfinger, "Candidates Scrutinized During Tenure," *The New York Times,* October 31, 1998, B.

29. Ibid.

30. Adam Nagourney, "Schumer and D'Amato Look for an Edge," *The New York Times,* October 18, 1998.

31. Ibid.

32. Ibid.

33. James Dao and Adam Nagourney, "Recipe for an Upset: Schumer's Sureness, D'Amato's Missteps," *The New York Times,* November 8, 1998.

34. Nagourney, "Schumer and D'Amato Look for an Edge."

35. Dao and Nagourney, "Recipe for an Upset."

36. Nagourney, "Schumer and D'Amato Look for an Edge."

37. www.msnbc.com.

38. Adam Nagourney, "D'Amato and Schumer End Campaign on High, Hoarse Notes," *The New York Times,* 1998.

39. Eric Pooley, "A Wizard Casts His Spell," *Time,* October 26, 1998, 48.

40. Blaine Harden, "Clinton Stumps for Schumer in Tight N.Y. Senate Race," *The Washington Post,* October 31, 1998, A13.

41. Jonathan P. Hicks, "The 1998 Campaign," *The New York Times,* November 2, 1998, A.

42. Ibid.

43. Dena Levy and Peverill Squire, "Television Markets and the Competitiveness of House Elections," SUNY Brockport and University of Iowa, Typescript, 1998.

44. Jacobson, *The Politics of Congressional Elections.*

45. Roger H. Davidson and Walter J. Oleszek, *Congress and Its Members,* 5th ed. (Washington, DC: Congressional Quarterly, 1996).

46. Rita Ciolli, "TV Ads Made New York Races Costliest," *Newsday,* 1998, A23.

47. Ibid.

48. Dao and Nagourney, "Recipe for an Upset."

49. Ibid., 42.

50. Adam Nagourney, "Schumer Wins Election Using D'Amato's Tactics," *The New York Times,* November 4, 1998.

51. Dao and Nagourney, "Recipe for an Upset."

52. Jacobson, *The Politics of Congressional Elections,* 21.

53. Matthew Moen and Gary Copeland, *The Contemporary Congress: A Bicameral Approach* (Belmont, CA: Wadsworth, 1999).

54. Jacobson, The Politics of Congressional Elections, 42.

55. See, for example, Alan Abramowitz, "A Comparison of Voting for U.S. Senator and Representative," *American Political Science Review* 74 (1980): 633–640; and Thomas E. Mann and Raymond Wolfinger, "Candidates and Parties in Congressional Elections," *American Political Science Review* 74 (1980): 617–632.

56. "Homestyle" is the term coined by Richard Fenno to describe the relationship developed between legislator and her constituents.

57. Peverill Squire, "Challengers in U.S. Senate Elections," *Legislative Studies Quarterly* 14 (1989): 531–547; and Peverill Squire and Eric R.A.N. Smith, "A Further Examination of Challenger Quality in Senate Elections," *Legislative Studies Quarterly* 21 (1996): 235–248.

58. Squire and Smith, "A Further Examination of Challenger Quality."

59. Adam Nagourney, "Schumer Wins Nomination to Senate, Beating Ferraro and Green," *The New York Times,* September 16, 1998.

60. Frank Bruni, "How to Succeed in Politics (by Really Trying Hard)," *The New York Times,* November 4, 1998, B.

61. Holtzman, D'Amato's opponent in the 1980 election, would receive the same rating on the Squire/Smith challenger quality ranking as Schumer. When running against D'Amato, she was a representative from Brooklyn. However, D'Amato was not the incumbent in this race, so neither candidate can be considered as the challenger in the election.

62. See Squire, "Challengers in U.S. Senate Elections," for a detailed explanation of how the variables are measured.

63. Bruni, "How to Succeed in Politics."

64. Questionnaires were conducted by Voting News Service and given to voters as they exited polls.

65. Dao and Nagourney, "Recipe for an Upset."

66. Adam Nagourney, "D'Amato and Schumer Focus on Issues in a Feisty Debate," *The New York Times,* October 26, 1998, B.

67. James Dao, "In New York's Tight Race for Senate Black Voters Could Be Decisive," *The New York Times,* October 25, 1998.

68. Adam Nagourney, "D'Amato and Schumer Vie for Jewish Voters' Support," *The New York Times,* October 19, 1998.

69. Dao and Nagourney, "Recipe for an Upset."

70. As quoted in Melissa Block, "Schumer Defeats D'Amato in New York," NPR Morning Edition, November 4, 1998, Transcript # 98110414-210.

71. Block, "Schumer Defeats D'Amato."

72. www.msnbc.com.

73. Buck Wolf, "Vote 98: Senate Races," ABCNews.com, November 4, 1998.

13

★

Boxer Defeats Fong in California's Senate Race

Jean Reith Schroedel
Marcia L. Godwin
Ling Cao

For virtually her entire freshman term, California's Senator Barbara Boxer had been viewed as vulnerable for a reelection bid. Boxer narrowly won her seat in 1992 by much smaller margins in California than either fellow Senate candidate Dianne Feinstein or presidential candidate Bill Clinton. Her mix of liberal ideology and strong ties to the Clinton administration, strengthened by her daughter's marriage to the First Lady's brother, made her an obvious target for both national and state Republicans. As recently as a month before the general election, Boxer appeared to be losing ground in the polls to opponent Matt Fong and seemed on the verge of defeat.

Yet, Boxer cruised to a ten-point victory on election day. What happened? This chapter takes an inside look at the high-expense, all-or-nothing nature of California campaigns. The task of conducting a disciplined and focused campaign in this populous, diverse, and media-savvy state is especially difficult. The story of the Boxer race yields important insights about successful campaign strategies, but also serves as a cautionary tale for campaigners who misinterpret gender issues and the changing demographics of the California electorate. Boxer's victory, especially when viewed in the context of Democratic successes in other California races, should be considered a wake-up call to the rest of the country. We may be entering a new era in California politics, with important implications for both California's leadership role and the future of electoral politics within the United States.

STATE PROFILE AND BACKGROUND

The California Electorate

The California electorate has been notoriously adverse to electing straight-party tickets. A majority of registered voters have been Democrats since the Great Depression. However, higher Republican turnouts and the need for mass media campaigns have resulted in competitive, candidate-centered campaigns for statewide offices. The state's history of progressive political reforms, including the initiative process and cross-filing across parties in primary campaigns, also led to comparatively weak political parties. In Daniel Elazar's classic typology of political cultures, California was categorized as a moralistic state, with a strong individualistic strain and a competitive two-party system.[1]

While the state legislature and congressional delegation had been solidly Democratic over the last 20 years, the gap between the two parties' strength considerably narrowed in the 1990s and policy making became increasing partisan.[2] The State Assembly briefly held a Republican majority in 1995, and the congressional delegation in the 105th Congress (1997–1998) was fairly evenly divided with 27 Republicans and 25 Democrats. Statewide offices, which are contested in even-numbered, non-presidential years, historically have been divided between the two parties. For example, the governor and lieutenant governor have not been members of the same party since 1978. Five Republicans and three Democrats held the eight statewide offices following the 1994 election.[3]

Under the surface of this competitive system has been the potential for serious change in any given election. The simple fact that the Democratic party has maintained about a ten percentage point advantage in voter registration means that shifts in voter turnout and party loyalty can have dramatic results. In addition, the number of voters declining to state a party preference has exponentially increased since 1980 and now stands at about 13 percent of the total electorate. With voters approving an open primary system beginning in 1998, independent voters can critically influence both primary and general elections.

The real sleeping giant has been the Latino/Hispanic vote. Latinos constitute almost one-third of California's population but only about 8 percent of the electorate in 1994, the last statewide election.[4] Much of the discrepancy between the size of the Latino population and their relatively small proportion of the electorate is due to the fact that many Latinos are immigrants; traditionally, the naturalization rates, especially among those from Mexico, have been quite low. That, however, is changing. The 1994 passage of Proposition 187, which prohibited undocumented aliens from receiving basic governmental services—prenatal care, primary school education, and basic medical care—was viewed by many Latinos as a racist attack on the entire Hispanic community and triggered a massive increase in naturalization rates. Between 1994 and 1996, the pool of eligible Latino voters in California increased dramatically. Moreover, by 1996 a staggering 21 percent of the eligible pool of Hispanic voters in the state were individuals naturalized since 1992.[5] The most likely beneficiary of the growth in the Latino electorate was the Democratic party, because Hispanic voters, except for Cuban Americans, have a long tradition of supporting Democrats.[6]

Boxer's First Senate Campaign: Perceptions and Reality

California's senatorial elections have reflected the schizophrenic nature of California voters. Liberal Democrat Alan Cranston was elected to four terms, retiring in 1992 at age 78 with his reputation tainted by the savings and loan crisis. During the same general period, the second seat was held by three different officeholders: Democrat John Tunney, followed by Republicans S. I. Hayakawa and Pete Wilson. Therefore, it was considered somewhat normal in California to have senators from different parties and have fairly frequent turnover in at least one of the seats.

The 1992 election featured the unusual circumstance of having both Senate seats open. Former San Francisco Mayor Dianne Feinstein defeated appointee John Seymour to take over the final two years of now–Governor Wilson's term. Barbara Boxer, a five-term Representative and former Marin County Supervisor, was elected to the full six-year term, replacing Cranston. Through a quirk in Senate rules, Feinstein became the senior senator and won reelection to a full term in 1994, defeating millionaire, one-term Republican Representative Michael Huffington.

The conventional wisdom was that the election of two Democratic, Jewish women from the Bay Area was an aberration, partially due to "Year of the Woman" media hype.[7] Feinstein was the well-known candidate, with more moderate views and statewide campaign experience from her narrow defeat in the 1990 governor's race. Feinstein won her race handily, defeating her opponent by more than 15 percentage points.

In contrast, Boxer won the general election campaign by only six percentage points over Bruce Herschensohn, a television political commentator and former Nixon official, who was perceived as a weaker opponent. Boxer had achieved visibility in Congress by exposing defense procurement problems and through her participation, with other female representatives, in a march to the Senate in 1991 to protest the Clarence Thomas–Anita Hill hearings. However, during the course of the campaign, Boxer received unfavorable press coverage for having the third-worst check bouncing record in the House banking scandal and for missing congressional votes while campaigning. Boxer was perceived as overcoming these negatives only by linking her campaign directly with Feinstein's and by the late revelation that Herschensohn allegedly had patronized both a nude dance club and an adult newsstand.

On the other hand, Boxer exhibited several campaign strengths that indicated that an opponent should not take a reelection defeat for granted. In spite of negative press and no experience in statewide campaigns, Boxer defeated an equally experienced and well-funded congressional representative *and* the incumbent lieutenant governor in the primary. The perky, former Brooklyn College cheerleader campaigned continuously, to the point of deciding to drop out from exhaustion until being talked out of it by her extremely supportive family.[8] Boxer also proved to be a formidable fundraiser, receiving large amounts of funds from EMILY's (Early Money Is Like Yeast) List and a wide range of other contributors.[9] The Boxer campaign was estimated to have outspent her challenger by a two to one ratio in the general election; the overall campaign was the most expensive in the country in 1992.

In the general election campaign, Boxer proved to be both opportunistic and focused. Boxer and Feinstein had no history of working together prior to the 1992 campaign, a fact little known outside of California.[10] Boxer may have benefited from Feinstein's popularity, but both candidates had to consciously decide to campaign as a team. Boxer's campaign also had the fortitude to hold its funds until the last few weeks of the campaign, when it unleashed a barrage of self-described "completely positive" television spots on her opponent's views on issues, noting "that he thought *Roe v. Wade* was a 'crazy' decision; that he thought everyone had the right to carry an Uzi; that he wanted to drill oil off California's magnificent coast."[11] Thus, any future opponent could reasonably expect the following from a Boxer campaign: an energetic and resilient candidate, willing to work cooperatively with other candidates; a well-funded campaign; and the airing of a series of issue-based ads targeting her opponent, running late in the campaign season.

Boxer's First-Term Record

Boxer kept a relatively low profile during her first two years in office. Continuing to work cooperatively with Feinstein, Boxer deferred to Feinstein on sponsorship of legislation such as the California Desert Protection Act and the federal ban on assault weapons so that Feinstein could maximize her legislative record before running for reelection in 1994. Boxer's initial committee memberships included Budget; Banking, Housing and Urban Affairs; and Environment and Public Works. With Republicans gaining a majority in the Senate in 1994, Boxer's opportunities for meaningful legislative activity became limited. However, Boxer was able to obtain environmental protection for the Presidio, a historic military base in San Francisco; solidify her leadership position on sexual harassment issues by persistent criticism of Senator Bob Packwood's (R-OR) behavior until his resignation; sponsor tax breaks for companies donating computers to schools; and promote higher drinking water standards.

Boxer, with some justification, has been called "The Last Liberal."[12] She was the only senator to get a perfect score from the liberal Americans for Democratic Action (ADA) in the 104th Congress and was ranked the most liberal senator by the *National Journal*. Boxer's self-described "fighting for California" mentality also results in a tendency to push equally hard for serious bills and those that stand no chance of passage, thereby irritating her political opponents but inspiring loyalty from supporters.[13]

Leading into the 1998 reelection campaign, Boxer appeared to have taken on a more moderate and senatorial style, which probably was not sufficiently recognized by opponents. As another sign of cooperation between California's senators, Feinstein offered her former seat on the powerful Senate Appropriations Committee (which had been lost in the 104th Congress) to Boxer when it reopened in 1997. Boxer combined her tenacity and hard-working attitude with negotiating skills to effectively gain funds for California projects. With a statewide constituency, Boxer also broadened her interests to include agricultural and high-tech concerns.[14]

THE 1998 PRIMARY

Campaign Opponents:
The Incredibly Shrinking Candidate Field

A large number of Republican candidates considered running against Boxer, but dropped out of consideration early on.[15] The rumored list included five Republican representatives: the late Sonny Bono, Tom Campbell, Christopher Cox, David Dreier, and Jerry Lewis. With the Republicans holding a majority in the House for the first time in a generation, a Senate run meant giving up real power and did not appear to be worth the risk for incumbent representatives.[16] Only Northern California Representative Frank Riggs, who would have faced a tough House reelection campaign, chose to run. Riggs suspended active campaigning part way through the primary season, citing a lack of funds and his late entry into the race.

The list of potential Republican candidates also included Huffington; Bill Jones, Secretary of State; wealthy business owner Noel Irwin Hentschel, who later ran unsuccessfully for lieutenant governor; actor and National Rifle Association leader Charlton Heston; and San Diego Mayor Susan Golding. Golding established an exploratory campaign committee, but quit in early January 1998 after making a "rational assessment" of her chances. Her campaign never gained momentum as Golding became heavily involved in promoting construction of a new sports stadium. Golding also was dissuaded by the early candidacy of Darrell Issa, the wealthy owner of a car alarm company and a fellow San Diegan. The prospect of raising enough funds to combat probable negative advertising by both Issa and Boxer simply was too daunting; Golding feared damaging her prospects for other offices when she is term-limited out of the mayor's office in 2000.[17]

Boxer's campaign staff appeared to have taken the threat of a Golding campaign very seriously. Golding appeared to be the candidate most able to recapture support from moderate Republican women voters, a key voting bloc, and would have been able to use Governor Wilson's campaign team. Boxer's campaign staff already had begun to compile information on Golding's issue positions and vote against a local gun control ordinance before Golding decided against running.[18]

The Fong-Issa Race

The Republican primary campaign thus ended up as a race between just two candidates: Darrell Issa and State Treasurer Matt Fong. Issa clearly had the early edge in terms of both organization and resources. Issa had become active in Republican politics in the early 1990s, serving on donor committees and chairing the volunteer committee for the 1996 Republican National Convention, held in San Diego. In addition, Issa had played a strong role in the successful initiative campaign for Proposition 209, which ended racial preference policies in California; Issa provided critical funds for signature gathering at a time when the initiative was floundering, and then served as co-chair of the campaign.[19]

Issa played on these strengths by announcing his candidacy in April 1997 and hiring five to six core staff members. By summer, the campaign had about ten full-time employees plus field offices around the state.[20] Issa decided to accept no political action committee (PAC) contributions and self-fund his campaign; he did receive about a half a million dollars in individual donations. To gain name recognition and identify differences between Issa's and Boxer's views, about $1.7 million was spent for radio advertisements from July until the end of the year. The ads ran mainly on conservative radio talk shows, Christian radio stations, and some country-western stations that were likely to have higher listener rates of "our type of voter": conservative, Republican, and mostly male.[21]

The Republican state convention in February 1998 was the high-water mark of the Issa campaign. Issa had established his conservative issue positions, was beginning to run television commercials, and had a set campaign strategy. Fong's campaign, in contrast, had a major turnover in key staff between 1997 and 1998 and was having difficulty in raising funds. Furthermore, Fong himself was viewed as a less dynamic candidate compared to the personable Issa.

The Issa campaign, however, began to unravel with a series of misjudgments and failed opportunities. For a first-time candidate, name recognition and image are absolutely critical. This is especially true in California, with its multiple television media markets and long, complicated ballot. The difficulty was compounded in the June 1998 primary with the implementation of an open primary system, allowing voters to select any candidate in a race, regardless of party affiliation.

The high-profile gubernatorial campaign easily overshadowed the Senate race. In internal polls, Issa's campaign found that he was often confused with wealthy airline executive Al Checchi. Checchi spent $30 million of his own money to saturate the television airways in an unsuccessful bid for the Democratic nomination for governor. His candidacy self-destructed in spectacular fashion in a sea of negative ads against one of his opponents and Checchi's own misleading claim of having marched with Dr. Martin Luther King.

At a time when Issa most needed to establish his own image, he unexpectedly cut about $3 million from his $15–16 million budget.[22] Issa's motivation appears to have been a combination of erroneously believing that the race was already won and concern about being linked with the free-spending Checchi.

With large sums of money already spent, the campaign had no choice but to give up reserved television airtime.[23] The campaign did not run ads during the period when absentee ballots were delivered and in many cases literally gave up prime spots directly to Fong's campaign.[24] Issa's campaign and political commentators have estimated that Fong, with only about $3 million raised for the entire primary, actually outspent Issa in the closing weeks of the campaign.

Issa also made several speaking gaffes, most notably referring to President Clinton as a "slut" for the Lewinsky sex scandal and saying that Clinton's remarks on greed in 1980s were an attempt at class warfare similar to that practiced by Hitler against the Jews.[25] The *Los Angeles Times* and *San Francisco Examiner,* in the final weeks of the campaign, ran stories critical of Issa's business practices. Issa's campaign quickly refuted the stories, but his staff believed that they filled a void in the minds of the voters in defining Issa's public image.[26]

The Issa campaign's most costly blunder, though, was a miscalculation about the type of voter support needed to win the primary election. With Issa running as a conservative Republican, the campaign deliberately decided against running television advertisements in the more liberal Bay Area, except for one early commercial. The campaign made this decision early on, under the rationale that Issa would pick up support elsewhere and that even the initial campaign budget needed to have some spending limits.[27] As discussed further below, Fong won the region virtually uncontested.

Matt Fong attempted to position himself as a conservative during the primary campaign. His television commercials used the slogan, "Conservative Republican. For Senate," and his campaign newsletter in the primary was called "The Conservative Candidate." Fong could take this approach and still attract support from moderates because of his relationship as the adopted son of March Fong Eu. The popular Eu, a Democrat, had led the effort to ban pay-toilets in women's restrooms while serving as an Assembly Member from the East Bay; served a number of terms as Secretary of State; and then served as United States Ambassador to Micronesia.[28] The fact that Matt Fong's political experience had been with administrative, not legislative positions, also worked to his advantage in the primary. Fong really did not have to commit to specific issue positions that might offend voters.

Boxer's campaign was practically nonexistent during the primary season. As the open primary attracted attention, the uncontested Republican nominee for governor was drawn into airing television commercials and participating in candidate debates. Boxer's campaign staff indicated that they were heavily pressured by members of the Democratic party leadership to do likewise, in order to minimize Democratic defections in the primary and demonstrate strength leading into the general election. Boxer's campaign decided to stand firm, both to conserve funds and to avoid revealing campaign strategies (along with potential weaknesses) to an opponent.[29]

Boxer herself seemed to go out of her way to avoid media attention, which hardly instilled confidence in her chances for reelection. As the Clinton sex scandal grew, she was placed in a no-win situation and did not immediately issue a statement condemning Clinton's actions. A long-time activist against sexual harassment by public officials, she normally would be expected to take a firm stand against President Clinton's behavior. Yet, Boxer had always been a strong Clinton supporter and was now related to the Clintons by marriage, with her daughter married to Hillary Clinton's brother.[30] The national media quickly dubbed Boxer the Democrat most likely to be affected by the scandal.

Primary Election Results

Fong narrowly won the Republican primary on June 2, 1998, capturing 45 percent of votes cast for Republicans compared to Issa's 40 percent. The regional results show that the race really had been Issa's to lose. Fong carried the Bay Area by a roughly 2.5 to 1 margin, but in the rest of the state Issa defeated Fong by approximately 67,000 votes. Issa also lost in the nearby Sacramento area. Issa, as expected, did best in his home region of San Diego and in other parts of southern California. Outside of the Bay Area, Issa lost by 10 or more percent in only five, rural counties.[31] These results indicate that a more competitive race in the Bay Area and more consistent advertising in the home stretch of the campaign could have won the nomination for Issa. The primary election results are shown in table 13.1.

Crossover voting by Democrats probably was not critical in the outcome of the election, but it did give Fong a higher victory margin and the appearance of momentum. *Los Angeles Times* exit polls showed that Fong received more votes than Issa among all party categories, but had much higher margins of victory among Democrats and independents. Fong had slightly smaller support from Democratic women as compared to the Democratic men.

Likewise, it is unlikely that Republican voters who crossed over to vote for Boxer impacted the outcome. Higher percentages of Republican women (11 percent) voted for Boxer as compared to Republican men (7 percent). Non-defecting Republican men favored Fong (43 percent to 37 percent) while Republican women were pretty evenly split between Fong and Issa (36 percent to 37 percent). Issa appeared more regularly with his wife in television commercials, including an "Outtakes" commercial that showed the Issas joking around. Issa's campaign also indicated that their own polls showed that some women voters simply found Issa more attractive than the balding Fong.[32]

The presence of Representative Frank Riggs' name on the ballot meant that he played a spoiler role. Riggs received 5 percent of the total vote and about 10.4 percent of the votes cast for Republicans. Riggs received more votes in one county than either Fong or Issa, defeated Issa in four additional counties, and Fong in one other. It is impossible to determine whether these votes would have switched in greater proportions to either Issa or Fong if Riggs had not been on the ballot. At most, the results show that voter preferences were fairly soft in the primary and could change significantly in the general election.

Even though Fong did not emphasize his ethnicity during the primary election campaign, he did significantly better among minority voters than did Issa. Only among Latino voters did Fong and Issa do equally well, each garnering

Table 13.1 Primary Election Results

Vote	Boxer	Fong	Issa	Riggs
Vote	2,574,264	1,292,662	1,142,567	295,886
Percent, Total	44	22	19.5	5
Percent, Party	92	45	40	10.4
Counties Won, Party	58	40	17	1
Sex (%)				
Male, 52	39	26	20	
Female, 48	48	19	18	
Party (%)				
Democrats, 48	73	10	5	
Republicans, 40	10	39	36	
Independents, 6	51	22	13	
Sex and Party (%)				
Democratic Men, 25	71	12	5	
Democratic Women, 26	71	9	6	
Republican Men, 25	7	43	37	
Republican Women, 19	11	36	37	
Race/Ethnicity (%)				
White, 69	35	26	24	
Black, 14	78	8	3	
Latino, 12	57	11	11	
Asian, 3	34	50	9	
Region (%)				
Los Angeles County (23)	699,624 (52%)	253,650 (19%)	221,555 (16%)	49,971 (4%)
Bay Area (10 counties) (25)	814,148 (55%)	316,237 (21%)	130,749 (9%)	78,114 (5%)
Rest of California (52)	1,060,492 (35%)	722,775 (24%)	790,263 (26%)	167,801 (5.5%)

SOURCES: California Secretary of State, *Statement of Vote, Primary Election,* June 2, 1998; *Los Angeles Times,* "Portrait of the Electorate," June 4, 1998.

11 percent of the Latino primary electorate. Among African Americans, Fong pulled 8 percent to Issa's 3 percent; among Asian American voters, the difference was 50 percent to 9 percent. Even though Asian American voters are a relatively small proportion of the electorate, they are becoming increasingly influential in western states.[33]

Boxer won only 44 percent of the vote in the primary, which was lower than what incumbents in other statewide offices received. Boxer carried Los Angeles County and the Bay Area outright, not all that unexpectedly because of Democratic edges in party registration. Boxer also received strong majorities among African American (78 percent) and Latino (57 percent) voters. Boxer did surprisingly well among Asian Americans, receiving about a third of their votes. Boxer also received about half of independents' vote. Given that in-dependents had greater incentive to vote in the competitive Republican race, this result is quite interesting.

Another positive sign for Boxer was the relatively high Democratic turnout in the primary, roughly 48 percent of all voters. As usual, the Republicans achieved a higher percentage of votes cast than their numbers would indicate, 40 percent of votes compared to 36 percent of registered voters. The numeri-cal disadvantage in party registration proved too difficult to overcome in this election, with the overall turnout running a rather average 42.5 percent of reg-istered voters. The Democratic party was obviously the more energized party. Union members seeking to defeat a ballot initiative restricting union political contributions sponsored a phone bank and get-out-the-vote efforts. The race for governor also may have sparked greater turnout among Democrats as com-pared to Republicans.[34]

Boxer most likely dodged a tougher opponent by Issa's defeat. Issa may have been the more conservative and inexperienced candidate, but he would have had a well-financed campaign that would have directly targeted Boxer's record early in the general election campaign season. A number of Issa's staffers had worked for Herschensohn in 1992 and remembered only too well how that race had turned in the closing weeks of the campaign. In fact, Issa's staff said, only partially in jest, that their unofficial mantra was "Don't underestimate Boxer."[35] A Boxer–Issa contest would have been expensive, long, and nasty.

By contrast, Fong's campaign ended the primary season essentially bankrupt. The Fong campaign needed to pay off debt from the primary, make a huge fundraising effort, and then develop an effective campaign strategy to fit the available resources. Thus, the Senate race did not become visible until the first televised debate in late August.

GENERAL ELECTION CAMPAIGN

Campaign Fundraising

The Fong campaign raised an estimated $11 million for the entire campaign, with $7 to $9 million coming in after the primary. Fong initially attracted fi-nancial and speaking support from a large number of prominent Republicans, including Speaker of the House Newt Gingrich, Governor Wilson, former Vice President Dan Quayle, New Jersey Governor Christine Todd Whitman, former vice presidential candidate Jack Kemp, and former Secretary of State George Shultz.[36] In spite of this show of support, Fong received little direct fi-nancial support from the national Republican party.[37] About a half million dol-lars had been given by mid-October, with another $800,000 given as an eleventh hour donation when it became apparent that Fong was losing. The Republican party traditionally has been reluctant to fund California candi-dates, assuming that fundraising is easier for candidates in such a populous and wealthy state, and preferring to target resources to less expensive races. Thus, the Fong campaign became a casualty of a classic Catch-22 situation: there was no need to provide large donations as long as he appeared to be within striking distance of a win; but if he appeared to be losing, it was his own fault and there was no sense in sending good money after bad. The lack of funding from traditional Republican party sources forced the Fong campaign to focus its fundraising appeals heavily on the Chinese-American community.[38]

The Boxer campaign suffered no such ambivalence from the national Democratic party; the campaign received the maximum legal limit of $3 million from the Democratic Senatorial Campaign Committee (DSCC), with some of the amount attributable to joint fundraising efforts with Boxer. Boxer also continued her pattern of working cooperatively with other statewide candidates. A joint committee was set up with gubernatorial candidate Gray Davis, which raised several million dollars from fundraising events hosted by President Clinton and the First Lady.[39] These events were so successful that funds beyond legal candidate limits were provided to Democratic get-out-the-vote efforts. The California Democratic party lent further support by running its own anti-Fong ad in October, which criticized Fong's positions on HMO reform.

Boxer attracted a large number of donations in her own right. She started 1998 with $1 million and had almost $4 million by the end of June from early presidential fundraisers and other contributions. Boxer benefited throughout the campaign from union PAC donations and the strong support of EMILY's List members. It was estimated that Boxer had received about $500,000 from EMILY's List members by mid-August and another fundraising letter was mailed to members in September.[40] By the end of the campaign, Boxer had received a record-breaking $1 million from EMILY's List members.[41] In campaign finance reports covering the period through November 23, 1998, Boxer had received 22 percent of individual contributions from out-of-state sources compared to 13 percent for Fong.[42]

Fong's fundraising ability would be quite respectable for most races in most states, but it was eclipsed by Boxer's totals. Boxer spent about $14 million, almost all of it in the general election campaign. Most importantly, Boxer was able to spend almost double the amount of the Fong campaign on television commercials. Even with this disparity, a well-strategized campaign might have led to a closer race and a backlash against Boxer. After all, the lavish spending in the primary race proved counter-productive for several wealthy candidates. Fong's aides, though, saw the fundraising difference as critical.[43]

The Clinton Scandal

The first part of the fall campaign season was dominated by media coverage of Clinton's sex scandal and Boxer's weak response. The campaign season kicked off with a August 26 debate at a Los Angeles television station, just days after Clinton's first apology for his behavior. Boxer was the more accomplished debater, but it was Fong's statement on the Clinton scandal that was the most memorable. Fong asserted, "This issue is not President Clinton's disgusting behavior. It is Barbara Boxer's actions. She has been unwilling to apply the same standard to the Democratic president as she did to Republicans. Barbara, your silence on this issue is deafening."[44] Boxer did criticize Clinton's actions, but failed to divert attention to other issues.

In spite of the perception that Boxer was in trouble, the scandal did not alter the Boxer campaign's core strategies. It did seem to impact Fong's approach and may have diverted attention away from the need to run a more issue-based campaign. The Fong campaign took a fairly reactive strategy to the Clinton scandal. Fong himself would comment on Boxer's hypocrisy and liberal views during stump speeches; he often tried to avoid bringing up the Clinton scandal and instead would respond to the inevitable questions on the subject. Fong's print advertisements included a subtle appeal to character issues, but his television commercials did not address the topic.

With the Fong campaign's hit-and-miss approach, Boxer's campaign staff saw the scandal not as a direct problem, but as a subject that prevented other campaign issues from receiving news coverage. Boxer campaigned continuously during the congressional recess in August, Labor Day weekend, and every weekend in September without any impact on the polls. Then, after the release of Clinton's taped grand jury testimony, the tone of press coverage changed. Boxer's campaign manager noted, "we had a flood of Monica, and all of a sudden the rain stopped and we got questions from reporters about issues."[45] Even if there was a backlash effect influencing Democratic voters, the most immediate impact on the Boxer-Fong race was to open up an opportunity for Boxer. Her support in the polls began increasing in the midst of her television campaign and before the House of Representatives' vote to launch an impeachment inquiry.[46]

Outreach to Ethnic and Racial Groups

Both campaigns made ongoing efforts to attract support from voters with different ethnic backgrounds. With California's increasing racial diversity, it is standard practice for candidates to do at least some advertising in foreign-language media. California now has a number of well-established bilingual newspapers for several different nationalities, several Spanish-language television stations, and international channels with programming from several Asian countries. Fong had the most extensive outreach program, with his first round of television ads having separate versions in English, Spanish, Mandarin Chinese, and Cantonese Chinese. Boxer's campaign did a Spanish-language version of only one commercial, one emphasizing gun control and labeling Fong "the gun lobby's favorite candidate."[47]

Fong's campaign made extraordinary efforts to reach the Asian American voters. In addition to television commercials and extensive campaigning by Fong's mother, about $100,000 was spent over the entire campaign season for ads in Chinese, Korean, Vietnamese, and Filipino newspapers. The advertisements contained subtle content differences, depending upon space limitations for languages that use characters and the type of group targeted.[48] For example,

one Chinese ad from early October differed from English materials in its or-
dering of issues. The text also included a section on personal character, translated approximately as follows:

> Fong is from a family that has political tradition. From the influence of
> his mother, March Fong Eu, Matt Fong understands the importance of
> integrity to a political figure. He is proud of his Chinese American back-
> ground and avoids shaming the community because of misbehaviors. Ms.
> Barbara Boxer's role model is President Clinton, who shames his family
> and his position. The record shows that Boxer wrote 143 bad checks
> when she was in Congress. How can we expect a person who is not able
> to balance her own checkbook to balance the budget for the nation?[49]

Fong's heavy emphasis on the Asian American community was rather surprising to the Boxer campaign, because Asian Americans were a small part of
the overall electorate and any likely Fong supporters probably were well aware
of his candidacy. Nevertheless, the Boxer campaign made a point of not conceding the Asian American vote. Boxer made a number of personal appearances
in Asian American communities and the campaign issued press releases and materials highlighting Boxer's accomplishments related to Asian Americans.[50] The
campaign also placed some ads in Asian American newspapers.[51]

Ironically, Fong's campaign efforts were partially offset by the overall coverage of the campaign by Asian American newspapers. These newspapers appear to have reported on both candidates' activities in depth. Boxer's campaign
noted an unprecedented level of interview requests from Asian-language papers and several requests for press passes to the Clinton fundraisers.[52]

Television Campaign Strategies

In contrast to his Chinese-language media campaign, Fong's television commercials took a much "softer" approach. Curiously, Fong's commercials were
more suitable for a cautious incumbent than a challenger seeking to portray
Boxer as being out of the mainstream. Fong's main advertising series began at
the end of September and mostly featured Fong speaking from behind a large,
polished wood desk with a Capitol-like building in the background. Each ad
closed with the slogan, "Matt Fong. A Good Man. A Great Senator." The commercials did not clearly define Fong in the eyes of the voters and, because
Boxer was never mentioned, failed to give voters a reason for selecting one
candidate over the other.[53]

The Boxer campaign, meanwhile, kept on course. Boxer's campaign manager, media consultant, and pollster had worked together since the 1992 campaign and essentially duplicated their previous strategy.[54] Benchmark polls
were done in July and the campaign decided to focus on specific issues rather
than either attacking Fong on his lack of legislative experience or covering
only Boxer's record. Fifteen to 20 commercials were filmed in July and August
and test-marketed with focus groups.

The ads ran virtually unchanged beginning around mid-September, except for an ad targeting Fong's environmental issues that could not be finalized until closer to air date. Boxer's campaign had to wait for Fong's responses to newspaper inquiries before being confident about his support of a low-level radioactive nuclear waste site and views on other environmental issues. Boxer's strategy all along had been to begin running ads late in the campaign when they could financially afford to "go on and stay on."[55]

The Boxer campaign prepared its television commercial strategy independently from gubernatorial candidate Davis's campaign, but their advertising dovetailed nicely together. Both campaigns emphasized similar issues, with the exception of Davis's anti-crime and pro-death penalty ads. The timing of both candidates' ads also was quite complementary. For example, Boxer's campaign would be running an abortion ad while Davis was promoting gun control and vice versa.[56]

The Boxer television campaign began innocuously with a pro-education and pro-family commercial, but then shifted into high gear with "compare and contrast" ads labeling Fong as an extremist on abortion, gun control, the environment, and HMO reform, while portraying Boxer as a moderate on those issues. Fong's campaign apparently thought that negative ads would be off-limits and cried foul.[57] One Republican political consultant went so far as to say that the Boxer ads "turned a mild-mannered Clark Kent into some sort of wacko anti-abortionist, water-polluting, nuclear-waste-dumping extremist."[58]

While the Boxer campaign may have exaggerated Fong's views, there were clear differences between the candidates on most issues, as listed in table 13.2, which Boxer exploited. Fong responded only to the abortion commercial. Fong appeared with his wife in a home-like setting to clarify his views: as an adoptee, he supported both adoption and a right to choose in the first trimester; supported parental consent for abortions by minors; and opposed late-term abortions.[59] This commercial showed Fong on the defensive when either ignoring the issue or drawing more attention to Boxer's views on late-term abortions would have been more productive. Trying to match Boxer on pro-choice views was an impossible task, given her 100 percent rating from the National Abortion Rights Action League (NARAL).

Support Shifts to Boxer

The Boxer camp began more continuous tracking of voter opinion around the third week of September. Boxer's polls showed the campaign turning roughly two weeks after the second ad began airing, as the ad campaign achieved saturation point.[60] Support then shifted rapidly. California opinion polls had tracked a seesaw race until the most widely circulated poll, the Field Poll, signaled an apparent shift to Fong in late September. These results seemed to mislead Fong strategists as his campaign issued a press release calling the Boxer campaign "a bust."[61] Other polls shortly thereafter indicated a tighter race, but then the *Los Angeles Times* published a poll on October 23 that showed a five-point Boxer lead.

Table 13.2 Issue Comparison: Barbara Boxer and Matt Fong

Issue	Boxer	Fong
Abortion	Extremely pro-choice; voted against absolute bans on late-term and partial-birth abortions.	Supported keeping abortion legal during first trimester of pregnancy; supports making adoption easier; supported parental consent.
Education	Long-time supporter of after-school programs; authored Computer Donation Incentive Act.	Supported vouchers for private schools.
Guns	For gun control; sponsored proposal to ban Saturday Night Specials.	Endorsed by gun rights groups. For increased punishment of criminals instead of further gun controls.
Environment	Environmentalist record, dating from first campaign for electoral office.	Alleged to support rollback of environmental laws.
Nuclear Waste	Opposed low-level nuclear waste facility in California unless proven safe.	Supported nuclear waste facility.
Military Spending	Service on House Armed Services Committee included focus on defense procurement problems; involved with efforts to minimize impacts from base closures in California.	Air Force Academy graduate; Lt. Colonel in Air Force Reserves. Supported increased spending and Star Wars defense system.
Taxes	Supported budget deals that resulted in a balanced budget.	Supported flat-tax proposal.
Campaign Finance	Supported McCain-Feingold proposal.	Supported lifting contribution limits.
HMO Reform	Sponsored bill to reform HMOs	Alleged in California Democratic Party ads to oppose reforms and support foreign interests.

SOURCES: Compiled from Boxer and Fong campaign packets, along with press coverage.

The race could have tightened again, especially with two of the largest newspapers in the state, the *Los Angeles Times* and the *San Francisco Chronicle* endorsing Fong. The endorsement by the traditionally liberal *Chronicle* could have been particularly damaging but was marginalized by an expose on October 25 by the *Chronicle*'s sister paper, the *San Francisco Examiner*.[62] It was revealed that Fong had made a $50,000 donation from his State Treasurer campaign account to the Traditional Values Coalition (TVC), a conservative Christian group that opposed homosexuality. The Reverend Lou Sheldon, the TVC's leader, declared himself a long-time friend of Fong's and said that the donation would be used to promote a proposed ballot initiative banning same-sex marriages. Around the same time, Fong solicited and received the endorsement of the Log Cabin Republicans, a gay rights group. The *Examiner* played up the apparent hypocrisy; Fong's own ambivalent statements supporting gay rights but being uncomfortable with same-sex marriages did not win him votes from either side.

The great irony is that the whole story was well-known months earlier. The Reverend Sheldon was rumored in political circles to be soliciting large donations in exchange for his group's support. Issa's campaign staff knew that the Fong campaign was playing up to conservative interests while pledging to take more moderate viewpoints in the fall. The Issa campaign even sent a press release to Christian radio stations during the primary season charging the hypocrisy of the Log Cabin Republican endorsement.[63]

Boxer's campaign also was well aware of the donation through its monitoring of campaign finance reports, but considered it a potential campaign finance violation. Fong was prohibited from using funds from the Treasurer's account for his Senate race and the Boxer campaign saw the donation as an indirect way of helping to fund TVC's slate mailer endorsing candidates. The story circulated among the press during the summer, but was not picked up.[64] The timing and spin on the eventual article could not have been more fortuitous for the Boxer campaign.

The final Field Poll came out on October 29, with the startling finding that Boxer had a commanding nine-point lead.[65] This poll seemed to catch everyone off guard and was met with some disbelief. Even Boxer's internal polls predicted a victory of only 6 to 7 percent (see figure 13.1).[66]

The Fong campaign responded by airing what became known as the "Mommy Ad." The commercial featured March Fong Eu, literally scolding Boxer for her negative advertising. The ad may have been directed to older voters, women, and moderates, but it was met with widespread ridicule, particularly when it was followed by a Fong attack piece with a faceless announcer slamming Boxer's liberal record.[67] Such tactics and apparent disarray in the Fong camp did nothing to stem the tide for a Boxer victory. It also likely cost him support among Asian Americans. Indeed, one political contact was told by an Asian American male friend that the ad "set the course of Asian American men back 20 years."[68]

Voter Turnout

A Boxer victory seemed well in hand as the election drew to a close, but there remained a concern about whether Democrats would really turn out to vote. Excerpts from a Boxer campaign letter made the turnout strategy quite clear:

> There are two things that matter in these last days of this election battle—getting a clear and strong message out to the voters about the issues that matter, and getting supporters to the polls. . . . We need to work equally hard to reach out to our base of support. . . . It's that simple. We need to get our message out so that people know what's at stake in this election.

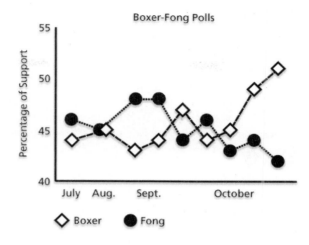

Boxer-Fong Polls

			Boxer	Fong
Mason Dixon	7/26–7/28	July	44	46
Field	8/18–8/24	Aug	45	45
LA Times	9/12–9/17	Sept	43	48
Field	9/27–10/5		44	48
PPI of CA	10/1–10/6	Oct	47	44
Mason Dixon	10/11–10/13		44	46
SF Examiner	10/16–10/18		45	43
LA Times	10/17–10/21		49	44
Field	10/21–10/27		51	42

FIGURE 13.1 Boxer-Fong Polls

In a state the size of California, the only way to do that is through television advertising. Mobilizing our supporters to get them to the polls is crucial. *We are organizing a massive get-out-the vote drive* to reach voters who might otherwise stay at home. So there we are—if more people come out and vote—we win. If they stay home, there's trouble.[69]

Here, too, circumstances favored the Boxer campaign. In addition to possible anti-Republican sentiment over the handling of the Clinton scandal, Democrats were energized by Davis's strong campaign for governor. Davis, leading by wide margins throughout the campaign, was able to donate funds to other candidates. Paradoxically, Democrats also were helped by yet another Governor Wilson–sponsored ballot measure. Just as union members rallied in the primary campaign to oppose restrictions on union political donations, teachers' unions came out in force to oppose Proposition 8, which would have set up new state inspections over public schools. In addition, an October survey by the nonpartisan Tomás Rivera Policy Institute found that Latino voters retained high negative ratings of Governor Wilson's performance and "wedge" politics and would vote in high percentages for Democratic candidates.[70]

The entire slate of Democratic candidates participated exuberantly at an election eve rally on the campus of the University of California, Los Angeles. In typical fashion, standing on one of her "Boxer boxes," the petite Boxer spoke from the podium and strayed from her stump speech to talk about her grandson's comment that when Boxer entered a room, people cheered "yeah!" In an ominous sign for Republican prospects, lieutenant governor nominee Cruz Bustamante led the crowd in a rap of "Get Out the Vote. Get Out the Vote."[71]

Election Results

The Democrats did even better than expected on November 3. They swept all the statewide offices except for two positions held by incumbent Republicans; increased their majority in the 80-seat Assembly from 43 to 48 positions; and increased their numbers in the Senate from 23 to 25 seats. Interestingly, the congressional races were more evenly divided; Republicans actually picked up one seat. The Democrats probably missed a golden opportunity to gain seats when several races turned out to be more competitive than anticipated.[72]

The increased influence of different racial groups was readily apparent in the election. The number of Latinos elected to political offices increased significantly, with Bustamante becoming the first Latino elected to statewide office since 1871. There appear to have been record turnout levels among Latino, black, and Asian American voters. However, there are discrepancies in the results between the Voter News Service and the *Los Angeles Times* exit polls because of differences in survey methodology. Both showed Hispanics with about 13 percent of the vote; the percentage of African American vote varied from 7 percent to 13 percent; and the Asian American vote from 4 percent to 8 percent.[73] The *Los Angeles Times* exit polls show a steady increase in Hispanic and African American turnout over the last three election cycles.

Boxer won reelection by a large 53 percent to 43 percent margin, or more than 800,000 votes. This excellent showing pales in comparison with Gray Davis's 20-point win in the governor's race, but it would be too simple to conclude that Boxer was just a beneficiary of Davis's landslide. The campaigns took upon a certain synergy that cannot be isolated. Boxer commented that Davis's "base of support is Southern California; mine is Northern California. My base is pro-choice women and environmentalists; his is teachers and unions. . . . When we got together it was like Katie-bar-the-door!"[74]

Boxer received strong majorities from African American and Latino voters, capturing about two-thirds of each, a result fairly consistent with other winning Democrats. Boxer even took about half of the Asian American vote. In terms of voting by gender, Boxer received the same proportion of the female vote as she did in 1992, about 57 percent, but increased her support among men to an almost even split with her opponent. Compared to the primary, Boxer increased her majority in Los Angeles County and the Bay Area, and won in other parts of Northern California. Boxer lost in the Central Valley and

the more conservative parts of Southern California, but by margins close to av-
erages received by other Democratic candidates. Boxer also narrowly won in
somewhat conservative San Bernardino County, where she had shrewdly established a field office.

The big dividing line was party registration. Eighty-six percent of
Democrats supported Boxer while 85 percent of Republicans supported Fong.
Boxer did have some support from moderate Republicans, capturing about
one-quarter of that bloc. Independents again split, but seemed to give a slight
edge to Boxer. The outcome really revolved around the continued high Democratic turnout, with Democrats having about a 49 percent to 39 percent edge
in votes cast; most of the final pre-election polls underestimated Democratic
turnout, making the results seem particularly dramatic. See tables 13.3 and 13.4
for a breakdown of voting results and exit polling information.

CONCLUSIONS

Racial Politics

The lessons to be learned from Boxer's reelection victory begin with the role
of racially- and ethnically-based politics. California is becoming a true multicultural state and candidates need to be sensitive to new ways of communicat-
ing with voters. At a minimum, candidates need to make outreach efforts and
place some advertisements in foreign-language and bilingual media. The Fong
campaign devoted far more attention to reaching these groups than did the
Boxer campaign, and he did pull in more Asian American and African American voters than had been typical for Republican candidates. However, an
equally important lesson that can be drawn from his campaign is that devoting
too much attention to a particular ethnic group can backfire if it means that
time and resources are diverted from more voter-rich sectors of the populace.
The Fong campaign clearly spent too much of its early effort in Asian American marketing, of little avail in the final election results. The fact remains that
party identification was the biggest predictor in this race and likely will be for
most future races.[75] Maximizing minority outreach efforts is fruitless without a
coherent campaign strategy that attracts both own-party and crossover support.

Gender Politics

Gender concerns also can provide opportunities for candidates to stumble. The
Fong campaign seemed to badly misjudge the relevance of gender, making the
mistake of using Fong's mother as a proxy for Fong himself. The Fong campaign also may have been attempting to appeal more to women by deciding to
respond to Boxer's abortion ad instead of seeking out other issues of concern
to voters. Unless a male candidate has a strong track record on women's issues,
obvious attempts to gain favor with women voters in the middle of a campaign
probably will do more to widen a gender gap than to close it.

Table 13.3 General Election Results

Vote	Boxer	Fong
Vote	4,410,056	3,575,078
Percent, Total	53	43
Counties Won	22	36
Sex (%)		
Male, 51	47	49
Female, 49	57	39
Party (%)		
Democrats, 48	86	12
Republicans, 39	13	85
Independents, 8	48	43
Sex and Party (%)		
Democratic Men, 23	84	15
Democratic Women, 28	88	10
Republican Men, 23	12	87
Republican Women, 18	14	82
Race/Ethnicity (%)		
White, 64	47	49
Black, 13	64	34
Latino, 13	69	24
Asian, 8	48	51
Region (%)		
Los Angeles County (24)	1,198,403 (61%)	704,782 (36%)
Bay Area (10 counties) (24)	1,286,597 (63%)	675,399 (33%)
Rest of California (52)	1,925,056 (45%)	2,194,897 (51%)

SOURCES: California Secretary of State, *Statement of Vote, General Election,* November 3, 1998; *Los Angeles Times,* "Portrait of the Electorate," November 5, 1998, S4.

In a broad sense, Boxer's competence as a candidate has been consistently underestimated, which must be attributed in part to gender. Even though the Boxer campaign was predictable, doing exactly what was expected with few adjustments from the successful 1992 campaign, its seriousness and competence were continually discounted. The Fong campaign, the national Republican party, and political pundits seemed quite surprised that the Boxer campaign would have a killer instinct. Scholars believe this form of subtle gender discrimination can be caused by "culturally ingrained expectations" that serve as a filter for interpreting the meaning of a candidate's actions.[76] In other words, male and female candidates can take the same actions, but they can be interpreted in radically different fashion.

Table 13.4 Comparisons Between the 1992 and 1998 Campaigns

Item	1992	1998
Primary system	Closed primary No crossover voting	Open ("blanket") primary Crossover voting
Primary competitiveness	Both primaries contested	Uncontested Democratic primary Contested Republican primary
Election cycle	Presidential election Both U.S. Senate positions	Gubernatorial election All statewide offices
Boxer's perceived vulnerabilities	House check-bouncing scandal Poor attendance record	Narrow victory margin in prior election. Liberal record within Republican-controlled Senate. Perceived hypocrisy on Clinton sex scandal.
Late revelations	Herschensohn had frequented adult newsstand that sold pornographic materials and had visited a strip club.	Fong had been endorsed by the Log Cabin (gay) Republicans and also contributed $50,000 to the Traditional Values Coalition.
Campaign spending	Boxer, $10.4 million Herschensohn, $7.9 million Most expensive Senate race in 1992.	Boxer, about $14 million Fong, about $11 million Estimated to be second most expensive Senate race.
Electoral margin	48% to 43%	53% to 43%

SOURCE: Compiled by authors.

Boxer and Feinstein were portrayed as television's "Cagney and Lacey" in the 1992 campaign, graduating to movie characters "Thelma and Louise" by 1998.[77] In this typecasting, Boxer always was portrayed as the more lightweight character of the two, ignoring her political savvy and tenacity. A slightly more accurate portrayal may be contained in Richard North Patterson's novel, *No Safe Place,* which has thinly disguised Feinstein and Boxer characters as secret enemies. In real life, Fong tried unsuccessfully to highlight Boxer's and Feinstein's differences, drawing accusations of sexism.[78]

When Boxer's strengths have been recognized, they have tended to be framed according to gender stereotypes, even in articles by female reporters. It is hard to imagine a male legislator being called a "Pekinese who latches onto a pant leg and won't let go. Her colleagues can't shake her loose, but they don't seem to mind her tugging either."[79] Even after Boxer's cooperation with other California Democrats in the 1998 election, Thomas Mann expressed amazement to a columnist at Boxer's and Feinstein's continued cooperation in swapping committee assignments. "Check to see if it's pure kindness. If so, it speaks volumes about the two. Maybe it's a gender thing. It fits the stereotype that women are better able to do these things than men."[80]

Campaign Strategies

Campaigning for political office in California is not for the faint-hearted. A successful candidate has to have guts to be patient, stake out a campaign strategy, and wait to run ads later in the campaign. This was the successful plan used by Davis in a competitive primary, Fong in his primary, and Boxer in the general election. Wealthy candidates who peaked early did not fare so well.

California campaigns may have seen the demise of purely negative advertising, but compare-and-contrast advertisements are here to stay. In this environment, the candidate who hesitates to define his or her candidacy is lost. Boxer's staff summed up the campaign by saying that Fong gave them a "huge opportunity" to "define the turf" and they just took it.[81]

The level of spending in the California election was astronomical. About $195 million was spent just on the ballot propositions for the November election. Boxer, Fong, and Issa together spent close to $40 million. One minor silver lining is that there may be some point of diminishing returns for spending on television commercials; money alone cannot overcome a candidate's lack of experience or campaign strategy.

Implications for the Future

The Democratic victories in 1998 in California do not necessarily mean that there will be an end to candidate-centered campaigns in the future. The current cohesion among prominent Democrats may dissolve as the new majority confronts complex policy issues. However, Republicans should take heed that California could effectively become a one-party state if voter turnout and party registration patterns stay the same. The success of the Davis-Boxer races may have set the stage for future races, especially if Latino voters continue to vote overwhelmingly Democratic. The Democrats look to be firmly in control of redistricting following the 2000 census, which could result in a Democratic majority in both California's congressional delegation and the U.S. House as a whole.

The Boxer race provides additional lessons for future elections. Boxer certainly was not an invincible candidate. Her campaign was well funded, but not particularly imaginative. Candidate recruitment needs to be considered early. Republicans already are making moves in that direction as Representative Christopher Cox announced in late 1998 that he was establishing an exploratory committee for a 2000 Senate bid. Finally, candidates for statewide offices across the country also would do well to emulate the Boxer strategy of cooperation with other candidates.

NOTES

1. Daniel J. Elazar, *American Federalism: A View from the States* (New York: Thomas Y. Crowell Company, 1966); Keith O. Boyum, Phillip L. Gianos, and Alan L. Saltzstein, eds., *California Government in National Perspective,* 3rd ed. (Dubuque, IA: Kendall/Hunt Publishing Company, 1998), especially chapters 2 and 3.

2. Sherry Jeffe, "California: The Not-So-Golden State Legislature," in *The Reform of State Legislatures and the Changing Character of Representation,* ed. Eugene W. Hickok, Jr. (Lanham, MD: Commonwealth Foundation/University Press of America, 1992), 101–112.

3. The Superintendent of Public Instruction, nominally a nonpartisan office, is included in this list.

4. For an excellent analysis of the changing California electorate and the differences between California's population and voting electorate, see Peter Schrag, *Paradise Lost: California's Experience, America's Future* (New York: The New Press, 1998).

5. For an analysis of the recent impact of naturalization rates on the size and partisanship of the Latino electorate, see Gary M. Segura, Dennis Falcon, and Harry Pachon, "Dynamics of Latino Partisanship in California: Immigration, Issue Salience, and Their Implications," *Harvard Journal of Hispanic Policy* 10 (1997): 62–80.

6. F. Chris Garcia and Rodolfo de la Garza, *The Chicano Political Experience* (North Scituate, MA: Duxbury, 1977); Rodney Hero, *Latinos and the U.S. Political System: Two Tiered Pluralism* (Philadelphia: Temple University Press, 1992).

7. Sue Tolleson Rinehart, "The California Senate Races: A Case Study in the Gendered Paradoxes of Politics," in *The Year of the Woman: Myths and Realities,* eds. Elizabeth Adell Cook, Sue Thomas, and Clyde Wilcox (Boulder, CO: Westview, 1994), 25–47.

8. Barbara Boxer with Nicole Boxer, *Strangers in the Senate: Politics and the New Revolution of Women in America* (Washington, DC: National Press Books, 1994), 123–145. Boxer has been married since age 20 to lawyer Stewart Boxer and has two children, Doug and Nicole.

9. EMILY's List is a donor network that pledges support to pro-choice, Democratic women candidates. Donations are bundled and forwarded to candidates.

10. Boxer, *Strangers in the Senate,* 81–82.

11. Ibid., 148–149.

12. Margy Rochlin, "The Last Liberal: Barbara Boxer's Toughest Campaign," *LA Weekly,* October 30–November 5, 1998, 20–23.

13. Philip D. Duncan, ed., *Politics in America 1994* (Washington, DC: Congressional Quarterly, 1993), 103–105; Philip D. Duncan and Christine C. Lawrence, ed., *Politics in America 1998* (Washington, DC: Congressional Quarterly, 1997), 86–87.

14. Faye Fiore, "In Senate, Boxer Still a Fighter but Her Style Softens," *Los Angeles Times,* May 21, 1998, A1.

15. William Claiborne, "California Senate Race Loses Sizzle; Novice's Deep Pockets, the Hot Economy Shrink GOP Field," *Washington Post,* May 25, 1998, A4. Steve Scott, "U.S. Senate," *California Journal,* May 1998.

16. Steve Scott, "Challenging Barbara Boxer," *California Journal,* August 1997, 26–30.

17. John Marelius, "Interview: Decision to Abandon Race was Rational Assessment," *San Diego Union-Tribune,* January 10, 1998, A1.

18. Rose Kapolczynski, Boxer Campaign Manager, interview by Marcia Godwin, November 23, 1998.

19. Matthew Cunningham, Issa Communications Director, interview by Marcia Godwin, December 1, 1998.

20. Ibid.

21. Ibid.

22. Mary Lynne Vellinga, "Ex-Aides: Issa Lost by Cutting Spending at End," *Sacramento Bee,* June 19, 1998, A1.

23. Among the items cut from the tentative budget were about $1 million in ads for Spanish-language television.

24. Cunningham, personal interview.

25. Tony Perry, "Millionaire Gets Lessons as Newcomer," *Los Angeles Times,* March 30, 1998, A3.

26. Eric Lichblau, "Accusations Abound as Race Turns Ugly," *Los Angeles Times,* May 27, 1998, A3; A. G. Block, "U.S. Senate," *California Journal,* July 1998, 13–15.

27. Cunningham, personal interview.

28. Tony Perry, "Blood Thicker Than Politics for Fongs," *Los Angeles Times,* October 21, 1998, A3.

29. Kapolczynski, personal interview.

30. Tony Perry, "Boxer Says She's Not Hypocritical About Clinton," *Los Angeles Times,* April 14, 1998, A3.

31. California Secretary of State, *Statement of Vote, Primary Election, June 2, 1998,* Sacramento, 1998. Available: http://www.ss.ca.gov.

32. Cunningham, personal interview.

33. Despite the recent elections of Gary Locke to the governorship in Washington state and David Wu from Oregon to Congress, nearly all of the scholarly analyses of Asian American political participation has focused on the local level. See, for example, Nicholas O. Alozie, "The Election of Asians to City Councils," *Social Science Quarterly* 73 (1992): 90–100; Leland T. Saito, "Asian Americans and Latinos in San Gabriel Valley, California: Ethnic Political Cooperation and Redistricting, 1990–92," in *Los Angeles: Struggles Toward Multiethnic Community,* eds. Edward T. Chang and Russell C. Leong (Seattle, WA: University of Washington Press, 1994).

34. Mark Z. Barabak, "Fierce Governor's Race Draws Voters to Polls," *Los Angeles Times,* June 3, 1998, A1.

35. Cunningham, personal interview.

36. John Howard, "Starting from Scratch, California Senate Hopeful Lines Up Funding," Associated Press, June 27, 1998. Dion Nissenbaum, "Fong Campaign Given Boost by Gingrich," *Riverside Press-Enterprise,* June 30, 1998.

37. Mark Z. Barabak, "Fong Backers Fear Loss of GOP Funds," *Los Angeles Times,* October 20, 1998.

38. In marked contrast to his advertising in English-language and Spanish-language media sources, nearly all of the Fong advertisements in the Chinese-language press and on Chinese language television shows included direct appeals for financial support. Translated by Ling Cao.

39. Boxer's campaign indicated that the Clinton fundraising events had been planned all along for late in the campaign season and had not been scheduled to coincide with the turn in public opinion on the Clinton sex scandal. Ticket sales were brisk for all of the Clinton events.

40. Tony Perry, "Boxer Warns of Offshore Oil Drilling," *Los Angeles Times,* August 25, 1998.

41. The Boxer campaign generated enormous enthusiasm among EMILY's List members. In a single day during the fall campaign, EMILY's List received a record-breaking $54,000 in checks made out to the Boxer campaign. By the end of the campaign,

nearly 11,000 checks had been forwarded to the Boxer campaign from EMILY's List members. See "Victory for EMILY's List, Democrats in 1998," *Notes From EMILY,* December 1998, 2.

42. FEC information available at http://www.tray.com/FECInfo.

43. Jenifer Warren, "Fong Fell Victim to Ad Strategy," *Los Angeles Times,* November 6, 1998.

44. Tony Perry and Amy Pyle, "Boxer, Fong Differences Spotlighted in Debate," *Los Angeles Times,* August 27, 1998, A1.

45. Tony Perry and Amy Pyle, "Boxer Vows She'll Press Ahead With Her Key Issues," *Los Angeles Times,* November 5, 1998, S5.

46. Mark Z. Barabak, "Boxer Takes the Lead in Senate Race with Fong," *Los Angeles Times,* October 23, 1998, A1.

47. Kapolczynski, personal interview.

48. David Chen, Fong's Asian Media Consultant, telephone interview by Ling Cao, November 16, 1998.

49. Fong newspaper advertisement, *International Daily,* October 3, 1998, A8, translated by Ling Cao.

50. Barbara Boxer for Senate, "Highlights of Senator Barbara Boxer's Record on Issues of Concern to the Asian Pacific American Community," July 1998.

51. Kapolczynski, personal interview.

52. Ibid.

53. A. G. Block, "U.S. Senate," *California Journal,* December 1998, 10–11.

54. According to Kapolczynski, Boxer's campaign manager, the pollster joined the campaign in the general election in 1992 while the other two staffers served throughout the 1992 campaign.

55. Kapolczynski, personal interview.

56. Ibid.

57. There is an increasing recognition among political scholars that there are important distinctions between contrast and attack ads. Purely negative ads have been found to be less effective than issue-based ads. See *Task Force on Campaign Reform, Campaign Reform: Insights and Evidence* (Princeton, NJ: Princeton University Press, 1998).

58. Ken Khachigian, cited by Warren, "Fong Fell Victim."

59. Jenifer Warren, "Boxer, Fong Square Off on Abortion," *Los Angeles Times,* October 16, 1998, A3.

60. Kapolczynski, personal interview.

61. Matt Fong for Senate, Press Release, "Field Poll Shows Matt Leading Boxer. Boxer's TV Campaign: a Bust," October 9, 1998.

62. Lance Williams, "Senate Candidate's Donation Undermines Moderate Image," *San Francisco Examiner,* October 25, 1998.

63. Cunningham, personal interview.

64. Kapolczynski, personal interview.

65. John Wildermuth, "Boxer Vaults to Big Lead," *San Francisco Chronicle,* October 29, 1998.

66. Kapolczynski, personal interview.

67. A. G. Block, "U.S. Senate," *California Journal,* December 1998, 10-11; Rob Morse, "Send Matt Fong to the Showers," *San Francisco Examiner,* October 29, 1998.

68. This person, not cited elsewhere in this chapter, asked to remain anonymous.

69. Friends of Barbara Boxer, Untitled Boxer campaign fundraising letter, October 1998; Tracy Seipel, "Boxer Drives for High Turnout," *San Jose Mercury News,* October 4, 1998.

70. Tomás Rivera Policy Institute, "California Survey Reveals What Latino Voters Really Think. Governor Wilson's Coattails Drag Down Other Republicans. Latino Voters Not Wooed by Political Parties," October 27, 1998.

71. Personal observation, Marcia Godwin, November 2, 1998.

72. Faye Fiore, "With Voting Over, Lesson for Candidates is Centrism," *Los Angeles Times,* November 5, 1998, S5.

73. Hector Tobar, "In Contests Big and Small, Latinos Take Historic Leap," *Los Angeles Times,* November 5, 1998, A1; Voter News Service exit polls, *CNN AllPolitics,* election night 1998.

74. Tony Perry and Amy Pyle, "Boxer Vows She'll Press Ahead With Her Key Issues," *Los Angeles Times,* November 5, 1998, S5.

75. This point was made in a Chinese-language article, which extensively quoted from Kent Wong, Director of the UCLA Labor Research Center. Wong argued that although it is natural for Chinese-Americans to support a Chinese-American candidate, issue positions and party affiliation are more important, and that on those grounds "Matt Fong cannot represent our community." See "Different Voices from Chinese American Community," *Daily World,* October 13, 1998, B3.

76. Shanto Iyengar, Nicholas A. Valentino, Stephen Ansolabehere, and Adam F. Simon, "Running as a Woman: Gender Stereotyping in Political Campaigns," in *Women, Media, and Politics,* ed. Pippa Norris (New York: Oxford University Press, 1997).

77. John Jacobs, "How Thelma and Louise Cooperate in the U.S. Senate," *Sacramento Bee,* November 24, 1998, B7.

78. Tony Perry and Amy Pyle, "Fong Contrasts Foe with Feinstein," *Los Angeles Times,* October 30, 1998, A3.

79. This quote is drawn from the article by Faye Fiore, "In Senate, Boxer Still a Fighter but Her Style Softens." Somewhat surprisingly, recent research shows that women journalists are somewhat more likely than men journalists to use gender stereotypes in their coverage of women candidates. See Kim Fridkin Kahn, *The Political Consequences of Being a Woman* (New York: Columbia University Press, 1996), 54.

80. Jacobs, "How Thelma and Louise."

81. Kapolczynski, personal interview.

14

★

Continuity and Change in the 1998 Congressional Elections

Sunil Ahuja
Robert Dewhirst

For the Republicans, 1998 began with a bang but ended with a whimper. For the Democrats, the news on election night was much better than pundits had anticipated. Even as the last votes were being tallied and memories of negative television commercials were fading quickly, partisans on each side of the 1998 congressional elections were found rushing to favored news outlets to claim victory. National figures appeared on network election analyses segments while candidates themselves were found more frequently on their local evening news shows airing before constituents.

The Democrats celebrated the election returns because they broke historic precedent; their party did not suffer losses in an off-year election, particularly one occurring in the sixth year of a presidency. In the Senate, the minority Democrats managed to retain their 45–55 margin, despite widespread talk that they would lose one or two seats. Over in the House, the news was even better for the Democrats. For the first time since 1934, a president's party (in this instance, the Democrats) gained seats in a midterm election. By most accounts, the Democrats were expected to lose between 10 and 15 seats, but instead picked up five. The subsequent 223–211 Republican majority would be the smallest House majority since the 221–213 they held in 1952.

The Republicans, although openly stunned by failing to score anticipated gains in each chamber, could nonetheless point to retaining majorities in both houses of Congress. While the Democrats were claiming to have surpassed even the most optimistic expectations, the Republicans countered by announcing plans to organize the incoming 106th Congress as the dominant party. Yet, the disappointing victory margins took their toll among the Republican faithful, as Speaker Newt Gingrich (R-GA) resigned both his position and place in the chamber amid intense debate among the party loyalists attempting to assign blame for their disappointing performance.

As the preceding 12 chapters have illustrated, there were numerous "roads to Congress" in 1998. Some candidates had no difficulty in winning, while others had to struggle. Before analyzing the "lessons learned" from these races, we discuss the overall voter characteristics in the 1998 election. We conclude with a look toward the 2000 election.

OVERALL VOTER CHARACTERISTICS

There was some continuity and some change in the 1998 election compared with previous elections. Undoubtedly, the biggest change, as noted above, was that the Democrats picked up seats in the House when they were expected to lose. Particular constituencies, such as blacks and Hispanics, increased their traditionally strong allegiances with the Democratic party, whereas the Republicans lost ground among their base, even from the wealthiest of voters. Turnout, despite being at the typically low level found in midterm elections, made a measurable difference in individual constituencies, and here again the Democrats outperformed the Republicans. There were, however, notable continuities. Incumbents, as usual, did exceptionally well and money was once again a potent force in the outcomes.

Of the incumbents seeking reelection to the House, 98 percent were victorious, a figure slightly higher than in 1996 but in general on par with the incumbents' performance in the postwar years. In the Senate, 93 percent of incumbents seeking reelection won, a number somewhat lower than in 1996 but still considerably higher than the average showings by incumbent senators during the postwar period. Among those who turned out, 48 percent voted for the Democratic candidate and 49 percent opted for the Republican nominee.

Exit polls show that men made up 49 percent of the electorate and women 51 percent. Men continued to favor the Republicans whereas women gave an edge to the Democrats. Among white men, support for Republican candidates dropped 5 percent from 1994, although this group still favored Republican over Democratic nominees by 57 percent to 39 percent. As one of the bright spots for Republicans on election night, white women did not dump Republican candidates (53 percent voted for Republicans and 44 percent for Democrats), something they have been doing increasingly in recent years. In terms of race, 88 percent of blacks voted for Democrats, up 3 percent from 1994, and nearly three-fifths of Hispanics did the same. Both blacks and Hispanics turned out at higher rates in this election compared to previous ones.[1]

Regarding age, Republicans did better than Democrats in the 60-plus category, although Democrats performed better in the 45–59 group. Among voters less than 45 years of age, both parties split even. In the income and education categories, Democrats continued to do better among lower income and less educated voters and Republicans maintained their superior performance among higher income and more educated people. But, as yet another misfortune for the Republicans, they lost significant ground (between 8 to 10 percent) compared with 1994 in one of their more reliable constituencies, those making more than $75,000 a year.[2]

Republican candidates performed best in the South, followed by the Midwest. Democrats did much better than the Republicans in the Northeast (54 percent voted for Democrats compared with 42 percent for Republicans), whereas both parties broke even in the West. Among the most crucial constituencies for each party, the Religious Right and union households played a strong role in this election. The labor vote has seen a resurgence in recent years, and in 1998 this group made up 22 percent of the voters, up from 14 percent in 1994. In those from union households, 61 percent voted for Democrats and only 35 percent for Republicans. In those from the Religious Right, which made up 13 percent of the electorate, 73 percent chose Republican candidates as opposed to 24 percent who voted Democratic. Finally, Catholics and Jews continued their solid support for Democrats, whereas Republicans maintained their strong hold on Protestants.[3]

The less than salutary turnout, expected in a midterm election, was supposed to help the Republicans. As stated in chapter 1, low turnout elections have tended to aid Republicans. And, as also alluded to earlier, in this election much would depend on which party was better able to energize its base. Despite the Republican party's best attempts to bring out the Religious Right voters, its most loyal base, by pouring millions of dollars in campaign commercials to highlight President Bill Clinton's unethical conduct with former White House intern Monica Lewinsky, the turnout among Christian conservatives actually dropped on election day. In 1994, this group made up 15 percent of the electorate; in 1998, it slipped to 13 percent. Many in the far right of the Republican party blamed their disappointedly low turnout on their candidates for not having "an agenda of major tax cuts and other issues important to this constituency."[4]

For the voters as a whole, Clinton's relationship with Lewinsky was not a major factor in their vote choice. As much as 60 percent of the electorate in a national exit poll said Clinton was not an issue in the voting calculus and that they were sending no message on impeachment. Indeed, the most important issue for voters in 1998 was education. Those who identified education as the top factor in their decision making voted Democratic by more than two to one. Also leading in the issues category was the state of the economy. As noted, this tends to help all incumbents, but this time it worked to the benefit of Democrats in particular. Among those who listed economy as the top issue, nearly two-thirds voted for Democratic candidates. Furthermore, of those who said they were financially better off compared to previous years, a significant majority pulled the levers for Democratic nominees.[5]

In the end, though, what seemed to have mattered most to voters is the extreme behavior by both parties. It was the liberal agenda in 1993 and 1994 that cost the Democrats in the 1994 election; it was the confrontational conservative crusade by House Republicans in 1998 that cost the Republicans in the 1998 election. As some have observed, "[r]ecent national elections have taught Democrats, and now Republicans, that voters are committed to moderation, and quick to punish the party they see as straying too far from the political middle."[6] Indeed, the most apt characterizations of the overall outcomes on election day seem to be support for the status quo and moderate change. Most voters did not want Clinton impeached, although they did want him reprimanded in some fashion for his admittedly improper behavior. Moderation was the name of the game in gubernatorial contests across the nation. From New York to Michigan and Texas to Florida, centrist governors, mostly Republican, won tremendous victories.[7] At the national level, then, most people were not mad and so they chose to stay the course. What of individual contests?

LESSONS LEARNED
FROM THE INDIVIDUAL RACES

At the individual level, continuity appears to have been more of the norm rather than change. Factors previously known to carry significant weight in congressional elections, such as the advantages of incumbency, the importance of local issues, and the power of money laid their usual claim in these contests. Low turnout and negative campaign commercials also worked their will as they have in the recent past.

No variable was more potent than the celebrated charm of incumbency. This, of course, should come as no surprise. It is a widely known fact that incumbents carry significant leverage into elections, and only exceptional challengers backed by lots of cash can unseat those in office. In the non-open seat races examined in this book, of the eight incumbents seeking reelection, seven won. The only incumbent to lose was former Senator Alfonse D'Amato (R-NY).

Incumbency exerts its influence in many different ways, as it did in 1998. Through casework and other means, incumbents are well recognized and well liked in their constituencies and, on account of the resulting good relationships with voters, they count on doing well on election day. The preceding chapters show incumbents precisely in this light. Particularly in the safe seats examined in this book, all four incumbents in both the House and the Senate were known for their hard work for their constituents. Throughout their careers, these incumbents have spent much of their time engaging in casework for the voters and fighting legislative battles to take home pork-barrel public works projects such as roads and bridges. As a result, these incumbents faced no noticeable opposition and their campaigns were relatively uneventful. Indeed, Representatives Christopher Smith (R-NJ) and Bill Clay (D-MO) as well as Senators Don Nickles (R-OK) and Barbara Mikulski (D-MD) were declared winners long before election day. Each won by at least 30 percent over his or her challenger.

Those incumbents holding contested seats had a somewhat rougher time at winning their reelection, as would be expected, although even in this category three out of four incumbents won. As junior members of the House, Representatives Loretta Sanchez (D–CA) and Jo Ann Emerson (D–MO) spent a great deal of their short tenure on establishing links with their constituents to expand and secure their electoral base. These two incumbents in particular had gone through bruising battles in their first election, and thus were understandably anxious to woo their constituents. So, for example, Sanchez made many trips back home to cater to her voters. Emerson, accused of being a "carpetbagger" in 1996, made a special effort to make appearances at key meetings and to speak to crucial communities in her district in order to fend off similar charges in 1998. These representatives knew the advantages of incumbency and conducted themselves accordingly.

As another continuity in congressional elections in 1998, campaigns were focused on local issues, and were largely won or lost based upon local concerns and candidates rather than national items. All politics was indeed local. In many of these campaigns, but particularly those for contested and open seats where issued were discussed, voter concerns were surrounding education, health care, Social Security, and minimum wage. While these might sound like national agenda items, the campaigns were fought with a distinctly local flavor. The candidates who won—such as Tammy Baldwin in Wisconsin's Second District, Baron Hill in Indiana's Ninth District, Charles Schumer in New York, and Barbara Boxer in California—were those who the voters felt would best address these issues on behalf of the local folks.

National issues, particularly the Clinton impeachment in 1998, were far from the front-burner items in these races. At the aggregate level, as mentioned above, nearly 60 percent of the voters in exit polls said they were sending no message on impeachment and did not consider it to be an important factor in their electoral choice. The Clinton impeachment issue appears to have been especially off the radar screen in safe seat races in 1998. Some challengers in contested races, such as Matt Fong in California's Senate contest, reluctantly brought it up, knowing that most voters were turned off by the entire matter. Open-seat races were also dominated by local concerns. Since Congress and the media were preoccupied with this issue the whole year, other national concerns received little attention.

Yet another variable that had its usual and expected impact on outcomes was the power of money. Along with the quality of the challenger, money has tended to be the most important variable shaping the results of congressional races. The money advantage has always favored incumbents. In 1998, safe incumbents raised far more money than their challengers did, and some even had significant amounts left over for the next election. Likewise, in contested races, Sanchez, Emerson, and Boxer outraised their challengers, whereas the playing field was somewhat more even in the New York Senate race. In that instance, however, Schumer, as an established member of the House, had cultivated a large base from which he received campaign contributions. In open-seat contests, the money advantage went to the more viable candidate.

Indeed, in open-seat races, the quality of the challenger, as measured by previous political experience, made a big difference. Baldwin and Hill had more experience than their challengers in the House contests. In the Senate open-seat races examined in this book, in Arkansas' race, Blanche Lambert Lincoln had served in the House and thus could draw on her network of connections. In the Ohio case, George Voinovich had most recently served as the state's governor, often thought to be best position from which to run for the U.S. Senate. Even in contested races, challenger quality was important. As the authors of chapter 12 point out, in New York's Senate contest, Schumer ranked higher than D'Amato on challenger quality measures and was therefore able to capitalize on that advantage in unseating the incumbent.

Furthermore, also in keeping with previous elections, many of these campaigns resorted to negative advertising. Once candidates "go negative," campaigns then become not so much about a discussion of issues as about the characteristics of candidates. Candidates most commonly tend to go negative toward the end of the campaign. In 1998, none appeared more negative than the Schumer-D'Amato race in New York. Both candidates spent the bulk of their campaign funds on attacking each other for having missed votes, for having cast improper votes, and for being generally lackluster on the job.

Aside from these continuities with previous congressional elections, the races in 1998 suggest certain departures from established norms. In responding to increasingly heterogeneous populations of states like California, New York, and New Jersey, campaigns in these areas enhanced their appeals to ethnic voters. More so than ever before, greater parts of campaign budgets were devoted toward targeting these constituencies. In California, for example, Boxer, Fong, and the Sanchez campaigns produced television ads and brochures in Chinese and Spanish languages. Candidates made appearances at key gatherings to make personal contacts. In New York and New Jersey, campaigns engaged in similar efforts. Such strategies, of course, were only fitting as these communities increase their presence at the polls.

Another factor in 1998 was the influx of "outside" money in House races, particularly in contested ones. In the last decade or so, Senate campaigns had been increasingly attracting funds from outside the states. Organizations on both the left and the right, through their political action committees (PACs), had been known for contributions to Senate candidates of their ideological leanings in other states. That trend now seems to be trickling down to the House districts. In 1998, some candidates in Wisconsin's Second District race were notable beneficiaries of labor or Religious Right money from the rest of the nation. Likewise, Sanchez and Robert Dornan in California's 46th District contest were both recipients of donations from outside groups that supported their candidacies. Indeed, the influence of outside money became a point of contention in these campaigns. To the extent that House races attract national attention and the candidates in those contests are ideologically charged (as they were in both of these races), this trend will only grow in the future.

Apart from these continuities and changes in the election, two other elements are worth mentioning. While turnout was nationally lower in 1998 than other midterm congressional elections, in some individual contests candidates depended on maximizing voter turnout. Indeed, in some campaigns, strategies reflected the national arguments that the outcome would hinge on whichever side was better able to energize its base. Thus, the Baldwin campaign in Wisconsin's Second District made a particular effort to invigorate the younger voters, many of whom were amenable to Baldwin's socially liberal views. Likewise, the Boxer campaign in California made a special appeal to black and Hispanic voters. Turnout efforts were an important strategy in both of these camps and the more successful candidate in that endeavor won the race.

In open seat contests, another issue that carried weight was the influence of the departing incumbent on the party's nominee to succeed the member. Some retiring members have been much more active than others in electing their successors. In two of the four open seat races studied in this book, the departing member played a measurable role. Former Representatives Lee Hamilton and Scott Klug raised money for, endorsed, and made important campaign appearances with their party's nominee. Hamilton played a particularly visible role in that regard. Over on the Senate side, the retiring Dale Bumpers as well as John Glenn stayed almost completely out of the process. Glenn refused involvement, arguing that he had returned to being an astronaut. In cases where retiring members involve themselves, the advantages of incumbency can be carried over to at least the first election of the successor.

These lessons indicate that, compared to previous elections, there was a good deal of continuity in the 1998 election. Most incumbents prevailed, contests were determined by local factors, money was critical, campaigns went negative, and the like. Therefore, in many of the races covered in this book, there were noteworthy similarities. The biggest factor differentiating the strategies of individual campaigns was whether the candidate running was an incumbent or a challenger. Incumbents made heavy use of the advantages available to them, whereas challengers struggled to play catch-up, largely unsuccessfully. In the races for the Senate, though, challengers were not as handicapped as in the contests for the House, but even there, most failed.

Our intention has been to examine candidates and campaigns at the individual level and learn how people win or lose congressional elections. We have shown how candidates made a variety of decisions in campaigns. We have observed how they made appearances, gave speeches, sought endorsements, produced ads, articulated issues, raised money, and decided a host of other elements with reference to their campaigns. We have seen how each candidate plotted strategies to win, although for some that task was easier than for others. This approach and these races supplement our understanding of contemporary congressional elections and show a previously unseen side of elections.

LOOKING TOWARD 2000

What do these races tell us about congressional elections in 2000? For the Republicans, the 1998 returns seemed to ignite a power shift from the party's

Capitol Hill delegation to its governors. The growing sentiment among Republican insiders appeared to be that the "can do" governors had the enviable track record of pragmatically administering their states while the congressional Republicans were viewed as being too eager for confrontation. Not surprisingly, George W. Bush, the Texas governor, soon became the popular favorite to win the party's presidential nomination in 2000.

On the other side, the 1998 election results seemed to energize the Democrats. Their early consensus seemed to be evolving toward developing a "center to left" coalition for the next two years. With the close partisan division in the House shrinking still further, Minority Leader Richard Gephardt withdrew his presidential aspirations in favor of working toward winning control of the House in 2000. This left Vice President Al Gore as the clear favorite to win the party's presidential nod over Bill Bradley, a former Senator from New Jersey. Bradley's fate hinged on his ability to raise early campaign donations and to put together solid organizations to run in the initial 2000 contests of the Iowa caucuses and the New Hampshire primary.

NOTES

1. "Exit Poll: Around the Nation," *Washington Post,* November 5, 1998.
2. Ibid.
3. Ibid.
4. Thomas B. Edsall and Claudia Deane, "A Good Day's Work for the Democrats," *Washington Post National Weekly Edition,* November 9, 1998, 13.
5. Ibid.
6. Terry M. Neal and Richard Morin, "A Rush Back Toward the Center," *Washington Post National Weekly Edition,* November 9, 1998, 15.
7. Dan Balz and David S. Broder, "For the GOP, a Painful, Difficult Road Ahead," *Washington Post National Weekly Edition,* November 9, 1998, 14.

Index